WILLIAM BYRD O.

1674-1744

WILLIAM BYRD
OF WESTOVER
1674-1744

PIERRE MARAMBAUD

UNIVERSITY OF NICE

UNIVERSITY PRESS OF VIRGINIA

Charlottesville

ENDPAPERS: REPRODUCED FROM *The Fry & Jefferson
Map of Virginia & Maryland* (1752). COURTESY OF
THE TRACY W. MCGREGOR LIBRARY, AT ALDERMAN LI-
BRARY, UNIVERSITY OF VIRGINIA.

Contents

Preface   vii

Introduction   Colonial Virginia, 1650–1750   1

PART ONE   BYRD'S LIFE AND PERSONALITY

Chapter I   Early Life in England and Virginia (1674–1704)   15
Chapter II   The Planter at Westover (1705–1715)   25
Chapter III   In England Again (1715–1726)   34
Chapter IV   Back in Virginia (1726–1744)   47
Chapter V   Byrd's Personality   58

PART TWO   MAN OF LETTERS

Introduction   73
Chapter VI   Virtuoso   76
Chapter VII   Cavalier   92
Chapter VIII   Diarist   106
Chapter IX   Chronicler   117
Chapter X   Amateur   130

PART THREE   PAINTER OF COLONIAL VIRGINIA

Introduction   141
Chapter XI   The Plantation World   144
Chapter XII   Colonial Society   182
Chapter XIII   Public Life   205
Chapter XIV   The Frontier   228
Chapter XV   Legend and Reality   256

CONCLUSION

Appendix   Byrd's Family   279
Bibliography   280
I   William Byrd's Works   280
II   William Byrd's Correspondence   282
III   Books and Articles on William Byrd   287
Index   291

Preface

THIS study of the life and times of William Byrd II cannot be anything but tentative, because scholars in recent years have continued to turn up new sources for historical studies of colonial Virginia. In particular, the invaluable microfilm program of the Virginia Colonial Records Project, still under way, will bring new publications and will promote a better understanding of the social history of early eighteenth-century Virginia. There has been no full-length study of William Byrd II since Professor Richmond C. Beatty's biography in 1932. In the meantime, three diaries by Byrd have been published, and many of his manuscript letterbooks have been gathered and made available to scholars, especially by the Virginia Historical Society in Richmond and by the Research Department of Colonial Williamsburg. Thus the time may be felt to have come for a new survey of the only notable writer in Southern colonial America.

This work is not primarily a biography but an attempt at an all-round study of Byrd and his times. Following a brief biographical part intended mainly to emphasize the essential traits of Byrd's personality, Part II aims at an assessment of the man of letters in his various activities, some of which have been discovered only in the last three decades. But the most important section, Part III, treats the picture of colonial Virginia in the early eighteenth century that emerges from Byrd's works. A comparison with other contemporary sources confirms the outstanding value of his testimony. The legends which in later centuries often distorted the picture of colonial Virginia made it seem advisable to introduce the work with a rapid survey of colonial life, which, it is hoped, will enable the ordinary reader to follow the rest of the study.

Quotations from materials written in the seventeenth and eighteenth centuries (from manuscript sources and published editions) have been modernized in regard to spelling and capitalization, and punctuation has been regularized.

References to Byrd's diaries are usually to dates of entries, as these may be of some importance, but in case of repeated facts they are to pages for the sake of conciseness. I wish to thank Louis B. Wright and Marion Tinling for permission to quote from their editions of *The*

Secret Diary of William Byrd of Westover, 1709–1712 (Richmond, 1941) and *The London Diary (1717–1721) and Other Writings of William Byrd of Virginia* (New York, 1958) and Mrs. Tinling and the heirs of Maude H. Woodfin for permission to quote from *Another Secret Diary of William Byrd of Westover, 1739–1741* (Richmond, 1942).

For *The History of the Dividing Line, The Secret History, A Journey to the Land of Eden,* and *A Progress to the Mines,* references are to Louis B. Wright's edition of *The Prose Works of William Byrd of Westover: Narratives of a Colonial Virginian* (Cambridge, Mass., 1966), although the important editions of Thomas H. Wynne (1866), John S. Bassett (1901), and William K. Boyd (1929) have been consulted extensively. For permission to quote from Wright's edition of the *Prose Works* I am grateful to Professor Wright and to The Belknap Press of Harvard University Press.

For want of an authoritative edition of Byrd's correspondence, references to his letters have been made to the best published text; but whenever possible, dates, names of correspondents, and texts of letters have been collated with available manuscripts. The most acute difficulty appeared with the "Letters of the Byrd Family," published by the *Virginia Magazine of History and Biography* in 1927–29; for these, references are given in the footnotes to the printed text, however poor, but the reader should also consult the Bibliography, where the safer texts are listed.

Any study of Byrd and early eighteenth-century Virginia must make extensive use of the work of such predecessors as Philip A. Bruce, Thomas J. Wertenbaker, Jay B. Hubbell, Louis B. Wright, and many others. My debt to them is great. The completion of this work was made possible by a Fulbright-Hays grant and by the help of many American libraries between Richmond and Boston, whose welcome was marked by unfailing kindness and patience. Among these the Virginia Historical Society and its staff stand highest in my gratitude for generous hospitality in their research room at Battle Abbey in Richmond and for permission to use their numerous manuscripts on colonial Virginia. My thanks are more particularly due to Mr. William M. E. Rachal, Mr. Howson Cole, Mr. Waverly Winfree, and Mr. James Fleming of the Virginia Historical Society; Mr. W. J. Van Schreeven, former State Archivist at the Virginia State Library and his assistant, Mr. J. W. Dudley; Mr. George H. Reese, then of the Research Department of Colonial Williamsburg; and all my friends at the University of Richmond.

My research was supervised by Professor Bernard Poli, of the Sorbonne, who gave me the most kindly and valuable advice following the dreary reading of successive drafts.

Since this study was completed in September 1968, chapters VII–IX were published in slightly different form in the *Virginia Magazine of History and Biography*, LXXVIII (April 1970), 144–83.

P. M.

August 26, 1970
Richmond, Virginia

Colonial Virginia
1650-1750

Colonial Virginia
1650-1750

W HEN *Gone with the Wind* was made into a motion picture in
1940, Margaret Mitchell was annoyed "at the profusion of
white columns on the Georgia plantation homes, put there by Holly-
wood as a concession to traditional notions about the South, despite
the explicit statement in the book that Tara was a rambling old farm-
house."[1] For many well-read people, the South conjures up discordant
notions derived from *Uncle Tom's Cabin, Gone with the Wind*, or
the distorted pictures of degraded people given by William Faulkner
or Erskine Caldwell. The South has now been for more than a century
the most controversial region of the United States, the subject of a
double legend which is fairly well epitomized in Miss Mitchell's novel.
The Old South stands out as a land of romance and charm, as it was
sketched in such idealized pictures as Thomas Nelson Page's *In Ole
Virginia* (1887); and the later South, after the Civil War, appears essentially as a land of violence, where a gulf of incomprehension and
hatred has opened between Northern and Southern minds, or between
poor whites and former slaves.

The first legend shows colonial Virginia with the idyllic aspect of
beautiful mansions filled with fine furniture imported from England.
There refined cavaliers and ladies lived in splendor, whiling their time
away with riding or pleasant conversation, with dancing and flirta-
tion, surrounded by multitudes of servants and slaves. This popular but
fanciful picture, still confirmed, as Louis B. Wright has remarked, "by
the very perfection of the restoration of colonial Williamsburg,"[2]
faithfully portrays some aspects of the lives of wealthy planters, late
in the colonial era, but it should be set aside resolutely when dealing
with earlier periods such as the one in which William Byrd of Westover lived.

The kind of society that prevailed in Virginia was early determined
by the main product in the country. Tobacco could be grown and
transported easily along the waterways to be shipped to England and
processed there. Roads—what few there were—remained in poor re-

---

[1] Virginius Dabney, *Below the Potomac* (New York, 1942), p. 16.
[2] *The Cultural Life of the American Colonies* (New York, 1957), p. 5.

pair; so the bays and rivers favored the development of plantations in the Chesapeake region, particularly up the various rivers: the James, Appomattox, York, Rappahannock, and Potomac. One of the major conclusions of Arthur P. Middleton, in his exhaustive study, *Tobacco Coast: A Maritime History of Chesapeake Bay in the Colonial Era*,[3] is that the presence of Chesapeake Bay was "the principal factor in the development of Virginia and Maryland." The network of navigable streams leading into the Bay, along with the fertility of the soil, rendered possible the adoption of tobacco as the staple crop, and these two factors accounted for the rapid increase of the Chesapeake colonists in wealth and in number. This same network of navigable streams obviated the necessity for towns as commercial centers.[4] Thus tobacco came to impose a one-crop system which created the prosperity of Virginia and shaped its social life. It was soon discovered that tobacco exhausted the soil in about seven years, so that planters had to possess great tracts of land and cultivate them by turns. The poor man on a small farm soon exhausted his fields and had to push on farther west, into the frontier region. This need for land, as much as the status of gentleman conferred by the possession of a large estate, explains the particular intensity of the land hunger that appeared among the colonists and the formation of a society of planters scattered over a wide area along the rivers. There were few towns, and those were small ones. The social group was the plantation. In the words of Professor Wright, "conditions of life in the colony prevented the growth of towns and placed a monopoly of trade in the hands of great planters."[5] Society was early divided into three main groups: servants and slaves, yeomen, and the great planters. The majority were plain farmers. Every newcomer could claim fifty acres per head; with a large family, he could have a few hundred acres and become a landowner. Indentured servants who had served their time generally settled on their own farms to grow tobacco. "In the seventeenth century," Thomas J. Wertenbaker said, "not one planter in fifty could be classed as a man of wealth, and even so late as 1704 the number of well-to-do was very

[3] Newport News, Va., 1953.
[4] The fact had been observed as early as 1688 by John Clayton in his letters to the Royal Society (*The Reverend John Clayton, A Parson with a Scientific Mind*, ed. Edmund Berkeley and Dorothy S. Berkeley [Charlottesville, Va., 1965], p. 53). The remark was repeated in the 1697 report to the Board of Trade by Henry Hartwell, James Blair, and Edward Chilton (*The Present State of Virginia, and the College*, ed. Hunter D. Farish [Charlottesville, Va., 1964], pp. 11–14), and by Hugh Jones in 1724 (*The Present State of Virginia*, ed. Richard L. Morton [Chapel Hill, N.C., 1956], p. 73).
[5] *The First Gentlemen of Virginia* (San Marino, Calif., 1940), p. 47.

narrowly limited."[6] Only one in fifteen then owned more than a thousand acres; most had no servant and ran their farm as a family business.

After the Restoration, tobacco prices slumped from six pence to a penny a pound because of increased production and the enforcement of the Navigation Acts, which gave English merchants a monopoly on the tobacco trade. The small farmer found it very difficult to make a living, while the great planter, with extensive lands, many white servants and black slaves to cultivate his estate, and an agent in London or Bristol to look after the sale of his crop, could still live in plenty.

Even in the era of small planters, social and political leadership had been vested in a few families, generally well-educated and belonging to the middle or upper middle class. But the plantation in fact required and developed an aristocratic oligarchy. The growth of slavery in the last decades of the seventeenth century only increased the chasm between small farmer and rich planter. The latter even served as agent or middleman for his less-favored neighbors, for he had his own wharf along the river where the goods could be shipped off to England; he bought commodities abroad for them and for himself and made a profit by trade as well as by farming.

Thus the great planters, in spite of their small number, gradually acquired an enormous influence, both economic and social. Whether they descended from gentleman, merchant, tradesman, or early adventurer, they all belonged to the ruling class and developed the same ideas about family and society. They tried to become landed proprietors as similar as possible to the country gentry of England. They were proud of their achievement and their power. "There are no lords, but each is sovereign on his own plantation," said a French Huguenot visitor at the end of the seventeenth century.[7] Robert Carter, the richest planter in Tidewater Virginia, who died in 1732 leaving 300,000 acres of land, 1,000 negroes, and 10,000 pounds in money, was known by the sobriquet of "King" Carter.[8] Proud they certainly were, and some of them may have been narrow-minded and tyranni-

---

[6] *The Planters of Colonial Virginia* (Princeton, 1958), p. 157. According to John Spencer Bassett, "the average well-to-do Virginian of the period owned as much as three thousand acres of land, while there were in every community a few people who owned much more" (Bassett, ed., *The Writings of Colonel William Byrd of Westover* [New York, 1901], p. x; hereafter cited as Bassett). But the rent-roll of Virginia for 1704–5 shows that in Henrico County, where William Byrd I had most of his lands, only six or seven planters out of 260 owned 3,000 acres or more. (For the rent-roll, see below, p. 181, n. 132.)

[7] [Durand of Dauphiné], *A Huguenot Exile in Virginia*, tr. and ed. Gilbert Chinard (New York, 1934), p. 110. This was in 1686/87.

[8] *Virginia Magazine of History and Biography*, XXXII (1924), 19.

cal, but most were conscious of their social responsibilities and the obligations that their power imposed. Their model was the English gentleman of the time, or rather the ideal picture of him to be found in Peacham's *Compleat Gentleman*, Castiglione's *Book of the Courtier*, or Allestree's *The Whole Duty of Man*, which were in the libraries of most planters of consequence. They developed a love of luxury which evoked the magnificence of Renaissance gentlemen. They ordered furniture, tapestries, jewelry, silver plate, and even portraits and expensive clothes from their London agents. They believed in the gentlemanly accomplishments described in courtesy books: "The cardinal virtues that the gentleman was still expected to believe in were the same that had won the praise of Renaissance writers: fortitude, prudence, temperance, justice, liberality and courtesy."[9] All planters prided themselves particularly upon their hospitality, which was noted by most observers. They extended a welcome to all strangers traveling in the colony, to any visitor who broke the monotony of daily routine in isolated plantations. If he offered pay, they felt offended at such gross ignorance of local customs.

The Virginia aristocracy insisted upon etiquette and courteous manners in social relations. They were sociable people, and many plantation festivities helped their children to acquire the polish proper to gentlemen's offspring. This formality, together with the relative scarcity of women, tended to develop in the men a chivalrous attitude toward the fair sex. Dancing was the most popular of all social entertainments, and was sometimes carried to what many felt to be excess.

Other favorite pastimes of the Virginia gentry were hunting, horse racing, cockfighting, and card playing. Robert Beverley, Byrd's brother-in-law, described another sport common at the beginning of the eighteenth century: "They have another sort of hunting, which is very diverting, and that they call vermin hunting; it is performed afoot, with small dogs in the night, by the light of the moon or stars. Thus in summertime they find abundance of raccoons, opossums, and foxes in the cornfields, and about their plantations; but at other times they must go into the woods for them."[10] Almost everybody owned a horse, to cope with the distances between plantations; most planters took pride in their horsemanship. Horse racing was very popular, but it was regarded as "a sport for gentlemen only," although anyone could be a spectator and betting was heavy.[11] Gambling was also prev-

[9] Wright, *First Gentlemen*, p. 91.
[10] *The History and Present State of Virginia* (1705), ed. Louis B. Wright (Chapel Hill, N.C., 1947), p. 309.
[11] "History of York County in the Seventeenth Century," *Tyler's Quarterly Historical and Genealogical Magazine*, I (1919-20), 264.

alent throughout the colonial period, and in 1686–87 the same French Huguenot mentioned above, traveling through the country with Virginia gentlemen, remarked that his companions spent the night gambling for high stakes.[12] There was also some heavy drinking, but a gentleman was expected to carry his liquor well.

Thus came to prevail a self-imposed code which went with the status of gentleman, the planter's pride even though it was often freshly acquired. This code did not consist merely of externals, and these men did not reach their high position without a great amount of hard work. As Professor Wertenbaker observed, they had to perform "the hundred and one tasks required in the conduct of the plantation: the raising of stock, the planting and tending of tobacco, the laying out of orchards, the building of fences, the purchasing of goods from the English importers, the care of the sick, the superintendence of plantation manufacture."[13] They kept a close personal watch on all the details of farm management and had no time to be idle fops, although they made a place in their lives for the entertainments of the gentry. They never thought of shirking their duties, particularly the one they placed first—service to the community and the state. As much as their economic power, their sense of social responsibility appears in the various aspects of everyday life—in education and in religion as well as in military and political affairs.

One of their first concerns was to provide for the education of their children. But the great distances between the scattered plantations made education an individual enterprise: "Economic conditions, rather than conscious plan or Machiavellian design, gave the families of wealth a monopoly, to all practical intents, of educational opportunity."[14] Schools were too often inaccessible; yet the planters realized that their children must have sufficient education to enable them to manage their estates in the future. So they tried to hire a tutor, two or three families often sharing the expense; sometimes they established a kind of plantation school where the children of less-prosperous neighbors could be taught at the same time. Many of the tutors were Scots, sometimes with Scottish degrees, but in many cases they were merely indentured servants with sufficient education to teach the rudiments. Occasionally the children of the poorer farmers were taught to read by the parson, if there was a church near by. More often these children received scraps of instruction from their parents, if they were

[12] Durand of Dauphiné, *Huguenot Exile*, p. 148.
[13] *The First Americans, 1607–1690* (New York, 1927), pp. 259–60.
[14] Wright, *First Gentlemen*, p. 97. On education in the Southern colonies, see Edgar W. Knight, ed., *A Documentary History of Education in the South before 1860* (Chapel Hill, N.C., 1949), I.

literate. The richest planters used to send their children to England to
live with relatives who could give them a less rustic upbringing. But
this might prove hazardous: besides the danger of the long sea voyage
and the mortality from smallpox or any other illness, there was "the
possibility that an English education would unfit them for life in the
colony, as sometimes happened."[15] After the creation of the College
of William and Mary in 1693, it became unnecessary for children to
go abroad, although the practice did not stop in some families. Not
until the second half of the eighteenth century did native tutors educated in the young colonial universities begin to be preferred over
those likely to transmit to their charges a Scottish or even an English
accent. Although some parents began to think that English education
was inappropriate for Virginia youths, most continued to believe in
the traditional value of a classical education on the same lines as that
available in England. Planters' sons were expected to acquire sufficient
knowledge to understand lawbooks when they became justices of the
peace or members of the Council. The great planters felt morally
bound to improve or at least maintain their own education: "The cultivation of their intellects saved the planters of the upper class from
dull provinciality."[16] Most of them had libraries which, however
small, helped them in the various tasks of the management of their
plantation and of the colony. These books, ranging from works of
piety to treatises on medicine or law, along with an encyclopedia and
a few classical authors, were often borrowed by neighbors and
friends.[17]

But in spite of its utilitarian trend, the education of the planters had
aims beyond the purely practical. It was intended to give them a sense
of leadership, and it also had a religious purpose, despite the contrast,
too often exaggerated, between New England and the South. It was
felt that learning played an important part in the furtherance of godliness and that every child should be able at least to read the Bible, how-

15 Wright, *Cultural Life*, p. 112. In the earlier decades of colonial history, smallpox often proved fatal for young men of promise who had gone to England for
an education. Fear of such occurrences and the desire to provide a safer education close to home hastened the establishment of colleges in America. See John
Duffy, *Epidemics in Colonial America* (Baton Rouge, La., 1953). See also Byrd's
letter to his nephew Frankie Otway, Feb. 16, 1740, *VMHB*, XXXVII (1929),
p. 33. Speaking of his son, Byrd writes: "So many of our youngsters have died
lately of the smallpox there [in England] that his mother would be in agonies to
send him very soon." Hugh Jones in 1724 also mentioned this danger (*Present
State*, p. 82).

16 Wright, *First Gentlemen*, p. 186.

17 See *ibid.*, 117–54, and George K. Smart, "Private Libraries in Colonial Virginia," *American Literature*, X (1938), 24–52.

ever poor his parents might be. One of the main arguments advanced for the creation of the College of William and Mary was "the want of able and faithful ministers."[18] In religion as well as in education, the great planters felt it their duty to act as leaders. Even though their piety was perhaps not so remarkable as that displayed in New England, they considered religion an essential feature of a well-ordered state. They were the staunchest colonial defenders of the Established Church, which in Virginia was always stronger than all other denominations together. There was no bishop in the colony, but the Bishop of London, who had the supervision of the colonial Church, appointed a commissary to represent him. The greater planters who served as churchwardens and vestrymen (generally selected from the best families in the district) exercised a strong influence:

As the first gentlemen in the county, apart from the prestige they derived from being the principal guardians of public morals, they were looked up to as the models of all that was most polished and cultured in their respective parishes. It was one of the happiest features of that early society that each community possessed in its vestry a body of men prompted as well by every instinct of birth, education and fortune, as by every dictate of their official duty, to set the people at large a good example in their personal deportment and in their general conduct.[19]

It was their duty not only to guard public morality but to see that church attendance and Sabbath observance (the latter required by laws) were obeyed. They even read the prayers themselves when there was no minister in the parish.[20] In Virginia, nearly as much as in the Northern colonies, religion had a pervasive influence every day of the week. Yet it was not so conspicuous, and clergymen coming from England were sometimes shocked by the informality of the churches, where Low Church ritual generally prevailed. Besides, the plantations were so distant that some people rode twenty or thirty miles to attend the services. This caused many customs to be modified: weddings and funerals were often held in homes, and many planters buried their dead in plantation graveyards instead of the churchyard.[21]

[18] William W. Hening, ed., *The Statutes at Large, Being a Collection of All the Laws of Virginia* (New York, 1809–23), II, 25 (March 1660/61).

[19] Philip A. Bruce, *The Institutional History of Virginia in the Seventeenth Century* (New York, 1910), I, 63–64.

[20] At one time there were 22 ministers to serve 50 parishes. See Samuel C. McCulloch, "James Blair's Plan of 1699 to Reform the Clergy of Virginia," *William and Mary Quarterly*, 3d ser., IV (1947), 73, and William Stevens Perry, ed., *Historical Collections Relating to the American Colonial Church* (Hartford, Conn., 1870–78), I, 11.

[21] See Jones, *Present State*, p. 97; see also George M. Brydon, *Virginia's Mother Church* (Richmond, 1947).

The leading planters controlled military affairs, since they commanded the militia in their respective counties. It was their task to ensure the protection of their region against Indian attacks. Of course, the dangers of Indian warfare decreased as years went on and the colony became more densely populated. During the Indian raids of 1676, several servants were killed on the plantation of William Byrd's father, who decided to send his family to England until the trouble was over. The Indian forays, though rarer, continued far into the eighteenth century and justified the continuation of militia musters. Moreover, the colonels of the militia, as a Swiss traveler observed at the beginning of the century, were "used for police as well as military duty."[22] Thus the defense of the colony and the enforcement of the law were among the main concerns of the upper class, who in this respect gave much personal attention to the good order of their community.

Such service to the state resulted in the gentry's political leadership; most of the important offices went to the great planters. They served their counties as revenue officers, sheriffs, or justices of the peace. They were elected to the House of Burgesses, and the most influential among them were chosen as members of the Council of State. Even offices with little or no material reward were practically monopolized by the upper class, merely for the honor of service, or simply from a sense of duty to the community.

The only elections in the colony were those to the House of Burgesses. In the eighteenth century the suffrage bore a close resemblance to that of the mother country.[23] But in spite of fairly democratic conditions, the electors almost invariably returned to office members of the ruling families, who came to look upon these functions as privileges linked with social position, birth, and wealth.

The members of the Council were appointed by the king on the recommendation of the governor. They formed the upper house of the legislative body and also served as a supreme court. One of the most remarkable characteristics of the Council was its independence of the governor. Because of its stability, it remained the chief ruling force in the colony while the royal representatives came and went. Its members consistently upheld the interests of the planters even against those of the Crown, showing the kind of spirit that was later to lead to the Revolution. They often came into conflict with the governor or the Board of Trade in London, which they considered ignorant of real

22 "Report of the Journey of Francis Louis Michel from Berne, Switzerland, to Virginia, October 2, 1701–December 1, 1702," tr. and ed. William J. Hinke, *VMHB*, XXIV (1916), 26.
23 Bruce, *Institutional History*, II, 630.

colonial conditions because it was too far away. The governor's social influence was sometimes greater than his political power, for he was looked upon as a member of the English aristocracy, at once the representative of the king, of the Court, and of fashionable London.

As the colony grew in the eighteenth century, the plantations of the Tidewater area developed a more settled society, and Williamsburg became a real colonial capital with its own social season, when the planters and their families gathered for convivial entertainment. Large plantations became more numerous in the Tidewater area, while the back country was being peopled by smaller farmers, very often as tenants of the greater planters. Many people who had failed to make a living in Virginia left for North Carolina: the good land in Virginia was taken up, and land was much cheaper in North Carolina; besides, it was almost impossible to sue someone there who had run away from his debts in the Old Dominion.[24]

In the first half of the eighteenth century the great planters of Virginia reached the height of their power. The qualities that made them are excellently summed up by Professor Wright:

They were determined, forceful men, creating in the wilderness a society that one day would make a great nation. Often they worked under tremendous handicaps, handicaps that agrarian society still suffers: low prices, overproduction, high freights, a wasteful economy. But they succeeded in establishing themselves as independent, fearless citizens of a commonwealth that prized its heritage of the common law, the traditions and rights of free Englishmen. With all their ambition to acquire land and wealth (amounting at times to inordinate greed) they never made wealth an exclusive end in itself. Property they accumulated to establish their families that they might take their proper place as leaders in society. . . . With all their shortcomings, the gentlemen-planters of the early eighteenth century created a society that could produce Washington, Jefferson, Marshall, and other statesmen who shaped a new nation.[25]

Among the founders of that society, Byrd was one of the greatest, one might almost say the ideal embodiment of them all.

[24] *The Prose Works of William Byrd of Westover, Narratives of a Colonial Virginian*, ed. Louis B. Wright (Cambridge, Mass., 1966), p. 186; hereafter cited as *Prose Works*.
[25] Louis B. Wright, *Cultural Life*, 1957, p. 10.

PART ONE

Byrd's Life and Personality

I knew him well when in England,
and he was reckoned a very polite,
ingenious man.

Peter Collinson to John Bartram, n.d.

CHAPTER I

Early Life in England and Virginia
1674-1704

WILLIAM BYRD I (1652–1704), the son of a London goldsmith, was a maternal grandson of Thomas Stegge, a sea captain who had long been a trader in the Southern colonies, having lands of his own in Virginia. The captain's son, Thomas Stegge, Jr., inherited his American estate and settled in Henrico County, where he became a man of influence. Shortly before his death in 1670, as he had no heir, he persuaded his nephew William Byrd I to come to Virginia. The young man inherited both his uncle's fortune and his social position when he was only eighteen. In 1673 he married a young widow of the same age as himself, Mary Filmer,[1] the daughter of a Cavalier gentleman, Warham Horsemanden, who was soon to return to England. The first child of the marriage was William Byrd II, born on March 28, 1674; later came three daughters, Susan, Mary, and Ursula, and another son, who died in infancy.

The estate of eighteen hundred acres that William Byrd I had inherited near the falls of the James was then an outpost on the frontier and remained within the range of Indian raids until the end of the century. In 1676, after a number of Indian attacks upon the plantations, Nathaniel Bacon led the militia in reprisals against them, without any commission from the governor. Captain William Byrd, a few of whose servants had been murdered, accompanied Bacon at the head of part of the militia after sending his family to England. But the young planter managed to steer his way out of that troubled period without any damage to his estate or to himself. He was neither among the signers of a resolution to follow Bacon in August 1676 nor among the people excepted from pardon by Governor Sir William Berkeley in his proclamation of February 10, 1676/77.[2]

---

[1] Her first husband was the third son of Sir Robert Filmer, the author of *Patriarcha*. See an abstract of the will of Samuel Filmer in *VMHB*, XV (1907–8), 181. On the Filmer family in Virginia, see *ibid.*, LXVIII (1960), 408–28.

[2] Public Record Office, London, Aug. 4, 1676, CO 1/37, ff. 130–31, and Feb. 10, 1676/77, CO 5/1371, ff. 276–86 (all P.R.O. citations are to microfilm). Byrd naturally would write a date between Dec. 31 and March 25 in the Old Style; that is, according to the Julian Calendar, in which the new year began on March 25. Except in the case of the diaries, which are always dated in the New Style,

The proximity of Indian tribes, although a danger at times, was soon turned to good account by the young planter. He expanded the trade with them that his uncle had begun, and he soon became the leading Indian trader in Virginia. Near his plantation, not far from the present site of Richmond, began the Trading Path, the trail which his caravans of about fifteen men with a hundred packhorses followed, sometimes for more than four hundred miles, reaching as far as the lands of the Catawbas and Cherokees in what is now South Carolina.[3] There his traders bartered cloth and blankets, pots and pans, hatchets and guns, rum and all manner of spirits, for bear and deer skins, beaver and otter pelts.

With his neighbors he also exchanged many imported articles for tobacco. He imported white indentured servants, to be sold into service for a term of years, and black slaves from Africa or the West Indies. Later, when private owners were allowed to use their ships in the slave trade, at the end of the century, he became the chief owner of a slave ship which was captured by a French privateer off the coast of West Africa.[4]

As his fortune increased, William Byrd I's influence in public life progressed very quickly. As early as 1676 he was a captain in the militia of Henrico County, and less than four years later he was a colonel. At the same time he was escheator of Henrico County, and he had already been a member of the House of Burgesses. In 1680 he was appointed to the Council by Governor Culpeper, and he was to become president of the Council in the last year of his life.

During a visit in England in 1687, he was appointed Auditor of the Public Accounts of Virginia and receiver general of the colony, not without what John S. Bassett calls "considerable manoeuvering" in order to get "an office which he valued chiefly for its salary."[5] Of all the public posts that he held, there is no doubt that this is the only one that brought him money. He had to receive and report on all the sums collected in the colony for the Crown, chiefly from quit-

---

I have indicated such interim dates according to the convention, by giving both years.

[3] "Letter of William Byrd I to Lane and Perry, May 10, 1686," *VMHB*, XXV (1917), 51–52.

[4] Louis B. Wright, "William Byrd I and the Slave Trade," *Huntington Library Quarterly*, VIII (1945), 379–87. This article contains two papers written by young William Byrd II, then agent for Virginia in London, "Mr. Byrd's Petition to the King Concerning the Ship *William and Jane* (1700)," and his "Reply to the Reasons Offered by the French Senegal Company for Condemning the English Ship *William and Jane* Which They Took upon the Coasts of Portudal."

[5] P. xxiv.

rents (two shillings a year for a hundred acres, or the equivalent in tobacco) and a tax on all the tobacco exported from Virginia (two shillings a hogshead,[6] or the equivalent in tobacco). These sums indeed were usually paid in tobacco, which the receiver general sold at the end of each year at a fairly low price to the members of the Council, who thus made a profit out of it, a practice common to English officials of the time. When William Byrd the elder died in 1704, he was one of the richest men in Virginia and one of the most influential, both socially and politically. Since 1690 he had been living in a well-furnished wooden mansion which he had built on his new estate of Westover in Charles City County, a place nearer the center of political life in the Old Dominion and safer from Indian attacks than his home farther up the James.[7]

When William Byrd II was seven, he was sent to England again in order to get a good education under the care of his maternal uncle, Daniel Horsemanden. His sisters were also educated in England, where Susan eventually married and lived out her life. William went to Felsted Grammar School in Essex, under Christopher Glasscock, a famous teacher of the time. There Oliver Cromwell had once sent his sons. The boy certainly received an excellent classical instruction, with a thorough grounding in Latin and Greek, and probably Hebrew. In 1685, in a letter to the headmaster, William Byrd the elder expressed his satisfaction at his son's progress.[8] But it was not his intention to make a bookworm of him. When the boy was sixteen, he was dispatched to Holland "to imbibe some of the fine business sense of the Dutch."[9] Yet he soon expressed his desire to return to England, where his father then instructed him to report to his agents, the firm of Perry and Lane, to complete his training in business, "wherein I hope," he said, "you will endeavor to acquaint yourself that you may be no stranger to it when necessity will require you to attend to it."[10] This was in July 1690. Less than two years later Byrd's education took another turn: in April 1692 he entered the Middle Temple, and he was called to the bar in April 1695.

In the world of the Inns of Court, the young man was certainly as much attracted by the brilliant social life of wits and writers as by the

[6] A hogshead equaled 500 to 600 pounds of tobacco (see Hening's *Statutes at Large*, II, 466; Hartwell, Blair, and Chilton, *Present State*, p. 59; Middleton, *Tobacco Coast*, p. 101).

[7] See Byrd I to Perry and Lane, Aug. 8, 1690, *VMHB*, XXVI (1918), 390–91.

[8] Letter of March 31, 1685, *Virginia Historical Register*, II (April 1849), 80.

[9] Bassett, p. xliii.

[10] Letter of July 25, 1690, *VMHB*, XXVI (1918), 131.

reading of lawbooks. Among his contemporaries at the Middle Temple were William Congreve and Nicholas Rowe, although they were his seniors by a year or two.[11] There was also John Oldmixon, the author of *The British Empire in America* (1708), who in the preface to the 1741 edition of his book asserted that for the section on Virginia he had been greatly indebted to Colonel Byrd, "whom the author knew when he was of the Temple." Byrd probably knew Thomas Southerne, who was a former student at the Temple, and from a letter written about ten years later we know that he came to be on intimate terms with William Wycherley. He was a regular theater-goer anyway, for his letters of subsequent years show that he was very familiar with the characters of Restoration plays as well as with actors and actresses.[12] His taste for the drama persisted for the rest of his life, and his own library contained several hundred volumes of Elizabethan and contemporary English plays, and a number of French plays.

One of his fellow students at the Middle Temple we know from a letter that Byrd wrote more than forty years later: Benjamin Lynde, of Salem, Massachusetts, who became Chief Justice in that colony in 1728. Byrd's letter gives the reader a hint of their gay student days; he wishes he could go to Salem:

I want to see what alteration forty years have wrought in you since we used to intrigue together in the Temple. But matrimony has atoned sufficiently for such backslidings, and now I suppose you have so little fellow feeling left for the naughy jades that you can order them a good whipping without any relenting. But though I should be mistaken, I hope your conscience, with the aid of three score and ten, has gained a complete victory over your constitution, which is almost the case of, Sir, your, etc.[13]

Among the friendships that Byrd formed at that time, one stands out particularly. Sir Robert Southwell, whom he probably knew through some of his father's business acquaintances, took a fatherly interest in him and introduced him to the polite circles of London.[14] It was through Sir Robert, who for several years had been president

---

[11] Richmond Croom Beatty, *William Byrd of Westover* (New York, 1932; hereafter cited as Beatty), p. 44.

[12] William Byrd, *Accounts as Solicitor General of the Colonies and Receiver of the Tobacco Tax, 1688–1704; Letters Writ to Facetia by Veramour* (privately printed, Baltimore, 1913), pp. 20, 31.

[13] Letter of Feb. 20, 1735/36, *VMHB*, IX (Jan. 1902), 244.

[14] Copies of four letters from Byrd to Southwell, written in July and August 1701, are among the William Byrd Papers (1701–1745), Virginia Historical Society, Richmond, and also in the Alderman Library, University of Virginia, Charlottesville.

of the Royal Society, that Byrd was elected a member of that body on April 29, 1696, when he was only twenty-two. Sir Robert also introduced him to Charles Boyle, Richard Bentley's young adversary in the Phalaris controversy; Boyle, later Earl of Orrery, was to remain one of Byrd's lifelong friends. Thus was Byrd brought into contact with men of learning and science and with some of the noblemen who were to be his patrons as well as theirs. Long after his final return to Virginia he maintained a correspondence with many of them, and he could even show off their portraits in his picture gallery at Westover.

In 1696 Byrd was back in Virginia and soon entered upon a political career which his father's position certainly made easier. In September of that year he should have represented Henrico County in the House of Burgesses. But at that time he had taken advantage of an opportunity to return to England as the representative of the Virginia Assembly, on whose behalf he presented an address to the Board of Trade in June 1697.[15] At the end of the same year, he represented the governor, Sir Edmund Andros, in a controversy with Commissary James Blair about the new College of William and Mary. A meeting was called by the Bishop of London at Lambeth Palace to hear his representative in Virginia and the governor's lawyer. Byrd was unfortunate in his adversary, for Blair was a formidable opponent who had already exerted great efforts to raise money for the college.[16]

The governor was accused by Blair of hindering the progress of the clergy in the colony and obstructing the interests of the new college. Among other things, Blair claimed that Andros had refused a gift of bricks for one of the buildings and encouraged people to refuse to pay their share. Byrd maintained that the governor had always acted in favor of the College. He accused the commissary of misstatement and exaggeration in order to obtain the dismissal of the governor and have him replaced by "his righteous patron Mr. Nicholson," then acting governor of Maryland; although Byrd doubted very much whether Nicholson in time would fare any better than Andros with that overbearing man, Commissary Blair. Byrd did his

[15] *VMHB*, III (1896), 425; W. Noel Sainsbury, *Abstracts* (MS. vols. in Virginia State Library transcribed in 1873 from papers concerning Virginia in the Public Record Office, London), 1691–1697, p. 309 (letter of the Council of Virginia, April 24, 1697, received June 21, read Aug. 23).

[16] For Blair's hostility to Andros, see Michael G. Kammen, "Virginia at the Close of the Seventeenth Century," *VMHB*, LXXIV (1966), 145–50. For Blair's efforts to raise money for the College, see Beatty, pp. 22–23; *Prose Works*, p. 220; and Edmund Berkeley, Jr., "Three Philanthropic Pirates," *VMHB*, LXXIV (1966), 433–44.

best, but it was not likely that the heads of the Church would be more impressed by a young lawyer than by their own representative.[17] This then was a failure for Byrd.

In spite of this failure, the Council appointed Byrd agent for Virginia in London in October 1698, and his next important action came when a difference arose between the Assembly and the new governor, Francis Nicholson, over the question of sending aid to New York for its war against the Five Nations. In December 1701 the Crown, through the governor, requested Virginia to raise nine hundred pounds and send a company of soldiers. Governor Nicholson dryly gave the order in the king's name, but the Virginians refused. This was one of the first controversies between the colonies and the English government.

On behalf of the majority of the councillors and burgesses, Byrd presented a petition to the king. They complained that appeals from the New York colonists were becoming too frequent and were due mainly to their inability to live at peace with the Indians; that Virginia was as much exposed as New York and needed her money and soldiers; and finally, that conscription would lower in several ways the Virginia revenue paid to the Crown and would weaken the colony, which would then be an easy prey to the Spanish enemy.[18] But the governor and the Board of Trade objected to the sending of a petition through anyone but the governor, the new queen refused to grant Byrd an audience, and the Council was formally rebuked by the English government for its irregular proceeding. In England, both the Privy Council and the Board of Trade took a cold view of the efforts of the Virginians, while they were highly in sympathy with the governor. The Virginia Council replied submissively that they had not been aware of the irregularity of their proceeding and would henceforth discontinue it. This was the end of Byrd's agency in

---

[17] For Byrd's part in the Andros-Blair controversy, see Louis B. Wright, "William Byrd's Defense of Sir Edmund Andros," *WMQ*, 3d ser., II (1945), 47–62. See also Byrd's certificate of admission to Lincoln's Inn, London, dated Oct. 22, 1697 (photocopy and translation among Byrd Manuscripts, V.H.S.); and a memorandum that on Nov. 2, 1697, William Byrd "was admitted in the room of the late William Smith, Esq., pursuant to the ruling made at the Council held there the 28th of October" (translation of the Latin document, copy in Va. State Lib.).

[18] Sainsbury, *Abstracts*, 1628–1715, pp. 329–32 (Byrd's petition to the Queen, March 26, 1702; Address of the Council of Burgesses of Virginia to the King, n.d., received March 30, read March 31; Order of Council presented by Byrd to the Board of Trade, March 26, 1702). *Journals of the House of Burgesses of Virginia*, ed. H. R. McIlwaine (Richmond, 1905–15), III, 313–16 (Sept. 27, 1701).

London.[19] About the same time he applied for the office of secretary of Virginia, but despite a favorable recommendation from the Board of Trade he failed to obtain the appointment, which was granted to the former incumbent's assistant.

The quarrel between Governor Nicholson and the Virginia planters, however, was not closed; it went on intermittently until the governor made an enemy of Commissary Blair, who joined the planters to obtain his dismissal in 1705.[20] Before the end of his agency, Byrd had protested to the Board of Trade against Nicholson's attempt to discourage the production of flax and cotton for fear the demand for English textiles would be reduced. When, shortly after, the price of tobacco went up, the planters lost their interest in cotton, but they did not forget Nicholson's insistence on English interests against Virginian liberties. Byrd's brother-in-law, Robert Beverley, in his *History and Present State of Virginia*, accused Governor Nicholson of "desiring a charitable law that the planters shall go naked" and of wanting to hang Virginians "with Magna Charta about their necks."[21] In fact, the planters battled Nicholson on all issues except perhaps the essential one—the intention of the Board of Trade and the governor to insist that the planters who held thousands of acres should pay quitrents in full, a heavy and hitherto unenforced expense for them.[22]

Besides these general grievances which were common to all planters, Byrd and his father had personal grudges against the governor. In wartime Byrd the elder had advanced money to the colonial government, expecting to be repaid out of the quitrents; but Nicholson declared that he would get his money only as the duty on tobacco was collected. To crown all, the governor was trying to divide the offices of auditor and receiver general, both held by William Byrd I. Nicholson was unsuccessful for a time but finally carried out his scheme after the elder Byrd's death. In spite of many disappointments, this was a fruitful period for William Byrd the younger. His service as agent in London taught him much about the world on the fringes of the government and the Court. He learned how colonial matters were dealt with by the Board of Trade and the Privy Council and how

[19] See Louis B. Wright, "William Byrd's Opposition to Governor Francis Nicholson," *Journal of Southern History*, XI (1945), 68–79.

[20] "The Fight to Depose Governor Francis Nicholson: James Blair's Affidavit of June 7, 1704," ed. Samuel C. McCulloch, *ibid.*, XII (1946), 403–22.

[21] Pp. 104–7.

[22] See W. Stitt Robinson, Jr., *Mother Earth: Land Grants in Virginia, 1607–1699* (Richmond, 1957), pp. 59–65; and John Locke, "Some of the Chief Grievances of the Present Constitution of Virginia, with an Essay towards the Remedies Thereof," ed. Michael G. Kammen, *VMHB*, LXXIV (1966), 156–57.

their opinions might be influenced. Such experience was to prove valuable later on in his career as a councillor in Virginia.

But during these years in England, Byrd was not exclusively concerned with political matters—far from it. He moved in the fashionable circles of society and probably went to Tunbridge Wells in the summer of 1700, as was then the custom. In that elegant resort he tried his hand at the kind of verse written by those whom Sir Richard Steele called the "water poets":

> Drusilla warms us with her fire
>> Which her too icy breast denies:
> At every smile, some swains expire,
> At every frown some hero dies.[23]

These products of courtly wit, conceived in the leisure of such spas as Bath, Epsom, Tunbridge Wells, or Scarborough, were intended to lavish extravagant but earnest praise upon women of fashion:

> Slight is the subject, but not so the praise,

in that world where Jove, as Alexander Pope said,

> Weighs the men's wits against the lady's hair.

"Inamorato L'Oiseaux," the self-portrait that Byrd wrote later, shows him preeminently as an admirer of the fair sex.[24] In the summer of 1703 he sent some letters to a lady whom he called "Facetia," actually Lady Elizabeth Cromwell, then 29 years old. She was no beauty but was very lively and witty, which made the name Byrd chose for her particularly appropriate: "She has wit enough to be Minerva, or pride enough to be Juno, and yet I warrant she had rather be addressed by the name of Venus."[25] She seems to have been very popular among the aristocratic circles of London. She was the only daughter and heiress of Vere Essex, fourth Earl of Ardglass and Baron Cromwell, and after her father's death in 1687 she had styled herself Baroness Cromwell, although she could not really inherit the title. Even so, she was "an heiress of two thousand pounds a year," in the words of Narcissus Luttrell the chronicler.[26] Byrd seems to have been strongly attracted by the aristocratic charm of the lady, if we

---

[23] *Another Secret Diary of William Byrd of Westover, 1739–1741, with Letters and Literary Exercises, 1696–1726,* ed. Maude H. Woodfin, tr. Marion Tinling (Richmond, 1942), p. 248. Cf. Pope's *Rape of the Lock,* Canto V, 67–70.

[24] *Another Secret Diary,* p. 276.

[25] *Ibid.,* p. 285.

[26] *A Brief Historical Relation of State Affairs, 1678–1714* (Oxford, 1857), Oct. 7, 1703.

are to believe the first letter he wrote her after she had started on a journey to Ireland:

The instant your coach drove away, Madam, my heart felt as if it had been torn up by the very roots, and the rest of my body as if severed limb from limb. I could not have shed a tear, if I might have gained the universe. My grief was too fierce to admit of so vulgar a demonstration. My soul was perfectly put out of tune, my senses were all stunned, and my spirits fluttered about my heart in the last confusion. Could I at that time have considered that the only pleasure I had in the world was leaving me, I had hung upon your coach and had been torn in pieces sooner than suffered myself to be taken from you. May you be diverted while in Ireland, but may you find nothing there to please you.[27]

Byrd's hope was not to be fulfilled, for the young lady did find someone there to please her—Byrd's own friend Edward Southwell, Sir Robert's son, then Secretary of State in Ireland.[28] She never answered the letters of Byrd, who must have been among her suitors for some time before her departure. "Is there nothing in nature, Madam, can prevail upon you to break this cruel silence?" He went on writing, however, relating the current gossip of the town through fictitiously named characters whom she must have recognized easily. He also gave her a lively picture of Oxford, where he went to witness "the Act," the formal maintaining of theses by candidates for degrees —an occasion for questionable jokes played by undergraduates upon their elders.[29] After he had acted the neglected lover for some time, Byrd neither died of grief nor killed himself when at the beginning of autumn the lady married Southwell. He wrote to his friend: "I firmly believe your joys will outlive the common term of conjugal happiness, because the nymph you have married has variety enough to satisfy the inconstancy of any man living. She comprehends all the agreeable qualities of her sex and consequently will give you neither provocation nor excuse to go abroad for change."[30] To "Facetia," when she accompanied her husband to Ireland, he sent a pleasant, witty letter, paying her elaborate but more restrained compliments:

I hope, Madam, this will have the good luck to find your ladyship and your fellow traveler safe by a warm fire amongst the wonders of the Peak. I easily imagine how much you are to contribute to the recovery of Qui-

[27] *Accounts, Letters*, p. 2 (June 12, 1703).
[28] See copies of four letters from Byrd to Edward Southwell, dated between June 26, 1703 and Feb. 19, 1703/4, Byrd Papers (1701–1745), V.H.S., and Alderman Lib., U. Va.
[29] *Accounts*, p. 11 (July 20, 1703).
[30] *Another Secret Diary*, p. 191.

etissa[31] by your comfortable presence. That is a remedy so pleasant that if one could secure a large dose of it, 'twould make a misfortune change its name into a happiness. 'Tis ten thousand pities you should go and throw away that virtue upon Ireland, a country so disagreeable that even toads and spiders disdain to live in it. Though I must be so just as to allow it one thing to boast of beyond the greatest advantages of England, which is the honor of having produced a person so extraordinary as your ladyship. For that good reason I could forgive that kingdom anything but the injury of taking you from us.[32]

"Facetia" was to die of consumption in 1709, only a few years after her marriage. But in this one-sided love affair, Byrd at least managed to lose no friendship, and this bears out what he said of himself: "Whenever Inamorato lost a mistress, he got a friend by way of equivalent."[33] Yet it is hard to forbear thinking that, in this case as in many others later on, his heart was less engaged than his reason.

[31] "Facetia's" aunt.
[32] *Another Secret Diary*, pp. 200–201.
[33] *Ibid.*, p. 279. Lady Betty Cromwell's portrait was one of those which adorned Westover (see Mrs. Mary Willing Byrd's will, *VMHB*, VI [April 1899], 346).

CHAPTER II

The Planter at Westover
1705-1715

WHEN his father died on December 4, 1704—of the gout, the doctor said—Byrd was still in London. Sailing as soon as possible after receiving news of the event, he landed in Virginia in August 1705. His father's will made him sole heir of a large estate totaling more than 26,000 acres. His mother had died in 1699; he had hardly known her, except in early childhood and during his short stay in Virginia in 1698. His sisters were left only minor legacies. One of them, Ursula, who married Robert Beverley, the future historian of Virginia, had died in October 1698 at less than seventeen, after giving birth to a son. Susan had married John Brayne in England and settled there; two of her children were sent over to Virginia to live at Westover a few months before her death in 1710.[1] Byrd's third sister, Mary, later married James Duke, sheriff of James City County.[2]

Byrd took possession of the estate as soon as he arrived in Virginia. He had already taken steps to secure the political offices his father had held. In April 1705 he had been confirmed by the queen in the offices of auditor and receiver general. But before he could take them over, the two posts were divided, and in October he was left with only the latter. There had been previous endeavors to separate the two functions upon pretense of incompatibility. The Board of Trade had asked for a written opinion from the Council, which answered that the salary was too small for two persons. Byrd prepared complete statistics of his father's accounts, showing that the yearly income averaged one hundred pounds, less than the 7½ per cent of the quitrents that the law allowed him. But before he could send these figures, the Board of Trade concluded that it was safer not to concentrate the two functions in the hands of one man, in order to avoid all tempta-

---

[1] *Executive Journals of the Council of Colonial Virginia*, ed. H. R. McIlwaine and Wilmer L. Hall, (Richmond, 1925-45), III, 27 (Aug. 16, 1705); *VMHB*, XXXV (July 1927), 236; *Secret Diary*, June 28 and Dec. 11, 1710.

[2] He always mentioned her as "my sister Duke" (see *Secret Diary*, Feb. 6, 1709), and once wrote: "I sent my cousin Brayne [his niece Susan Brayne] to visit her aunt Duke" (Byrd, *The London Diary [1717-1721] and Other Writings*, ed. Louis B. Wright and Marion Tinling [New York, 1958], April 6, 1721).

tion to defraud the Crown. Byrd remained receiver general at a salary of 3 per cent, raised to 5 per cent in 1710.[3]

He also applied for his father's seat on the Council through the new Virginia agent in London, Nathaniel Blakiston. But the Board of Trade answered that "though their Lordships had a good opinion of Mr. Byrd as a fit person to serve Her Majesty in that place, yet Messrs. Smith and Lewis having actually been in the Council and only left out by mistake, their Lordships thought themselves obliged to reinstate them before they recommended Mr. Byrd." Byrd had to wait until 1708, when a new vacancy occurred and he was appointed on the recommendation of several influential people, among them Micajah Perry, the wealthy London merchant and future Lord-Mayor, agent of the Byrd family in England. Byrd was sworn in on September 12, 1709, and remained a councillor until his death in 1744.[4]

At thirty-one, just back from London and the Court, with one of the greatest fortunes in Virginia, Byrd was among the most eligible young men in the colony. Susceptible to the ladies as he was, it would have been very surprising if he had remained a bachelor for long. Besides, the household at Westover needed feminine management. Byrd believed in marrying within one's own social circle, into families at least equally favored by fortune. A few months after his return, he courted "Fidelia," the beautiful Lucy Parke, but not without first securing her father's approval and ascertaining what portion she was to receive.[5]

She was the youngest daughter of Colonel Daniel Parke, a rakish and violent gentleman who was often reproved from the pulpit for adultery by Commissary Blair.[6] About 1697 this wild gentleman left his wife and daughters in Virginia to go to England, where he became one of Marlborough's aides-de-camp. As such, he brought to the queen the news of the victory at Blenheim and was rewarded with the governorship of the Leeward Islands. He was about to leave Lon-

---

[3] See *Executive Journals of Council*, III, 29 (Sept. 4, 1705); *Secret Diary*, April 17, 1710.

[4] Sainsbury, *Abstracts*, 1705–1707, p. 376 (Byrd's application on Dec. 17, 1705) and p. 377; *Secret Diary*, June 16 and Sept. 12, 1709.

[5] *Another Secret Diary*, pp. 214–21. A letter from "Veramour" to "Fidelia," dated Feb. 4, 1705/6, was published in George W. P. Custis, *Recollections and Private Memoirs of Washington*, ed. Benson J. Lossing (New York, 1860), pp. 16–17n., but was erroneously attributed to Byrd's brother-in-law John Custis.

[6] Parke had his revenge when he forcibly expelled the commissary's wife from a pew in the Jamestown church to which he felt some right–although it was only reserved to his father-in-law by a former marriage (L. G. Tyler, *Williamsburg, the Old Colonial Capital* [Richmond, 1907], p. 125).

don for his new post when Byrd wrote to him, asking permission to pay his addresses to Lucy: "If you can entertain a favorable opinion of my person, I don't question but my fortune may be sufficient to make her happy, especially after it has been assisted by your generosity."[7] Colonel Parke did promise to assist with a thousand pounds, but unfortunately the sum was forgotten and remained among his many debts when he died in 1710.

During the period of his courtship, Byrd, as "Veramour," wrote a few letters to his "dearest Fidelia" in the usual style of his love letters: "What would some lovers give for this lucky occasion of beginning a billet-doux! The moment I begin to write, I am entertained with the cooing of two amorous turtles. . . . I cannot forbear envying these innocent lovers for the blessing they enjoy of being always together; while I, poor I, must lament the want of my dear, dear turtle for many days." Yet there is a touch of unexpected humor at times: "Nothing but a lover's magnifying fancy can conceive the horrible distress I was in from what you told me on Saturday night. No tender-hearted widow was ever in so much pain at the loss of a first husband or, which is still worse, at the disappointment of a second, as I was at that unexpected story."[8] Byrd's marriage to Lucy took place on May 4, 1706. Colonel Parke was absent, but they were married "not only with his consent, but at his earnest desire,"[9] which made their disappointment all the greater when the colonel's will was produced after his death.

Parke's eldest daughter, Frances, and her husband, John Custis, both appear frequently in Byrd's diary. Both daughters had inherited their father's violent temper, and John Custis's epitaph, which he wrote himself, reveals that his bachelor days were the only peaceful time of his life.[10] Byrd's own married life was far from calm, and his household was often in an uproar because of his quarrels with his spoiled and temperamental wife. On one of those occasions Byrd observed that "she was in the wrong," adding with smug satisfaction: "For my part I kept my temper very well."[11] But these quarrels, however violent, never lasted long, and they were soon reconciled. *The Secret Diary* shows the sincerity of their mutual affection. Lucy

[7] *Another Secret Diary*, p. 221 (to Don Altiero) and var. p. 223.

[8] *Ibid.*, pp. 218, 216.

[9] "Byrd Title Book," *VMHB*, XLVII (1942), 238.

[10] Custis, *Recollections*, pp. 16–17. The widow of the Custises' son Daniel Parke Custis (born on Oct. 15, 1710; see *Secret Diary*) married George Washington, who thus became the adoptive father of the Custises' grandson.

[11] *Secret Diary*, July 9, 1710.

gave him four children, only two of whom survived infancy—two daughters, Evelyn, born in 1707, and Wilhelmina, born in 1715. A son, Parke, died on June 3, 1710, when only nine months old.

In the same year, the grandfather for whom the infant was named was killed in a riot in Antigua. His authoritarian administrative policies in the Leeward Islands had made him unpopular from the start.[12] A good part of his fortune went to a bastard daughter. To Frances Custis, his eldest daughter, he left his Virginia estates, part of which were to be sold in order to meet his debts, and to Mrs. Byrd he bequeathed a thousand pounds. Byrd felt that his wife had been "fobbed off" with an insignificant part of her father's property.[13] He had already begun to buy several tracts of land of from two to four hundred acres here and there, not far from his plantations near the falls of the James. But now his land hunger, added to his pride which made him unwilling to see the Parke estate pass out of the family, led him to take over the lands that were to be sold and to assume his father-in-law's debts in return. This proved a bad bargain, for the debts ran to a larger sum than had first been calculated. Years later, Byrd wrote to his brother-in-law John Custis that he had already paid out a thousand pounds more than he had expected. As a result of this error of business judgment, he found his later life saddled with debts to his London agent, Micajah Perry, who had also been Parke's agent and creditor. Perry had helped Byrd obtain appointment as a Virginia councillor, and Byrd considered him a trusted friend. But it seems that the merchant, in the schedule he sent of Parke's debts in England, left out a mortgage of more than two thousand pounds on an estate which he said was worth four thousand. Richmond C. Beatty inclines to think that this was a deliberate fraud on the part of the Perrys, although there is no definite proof.[14] Whatever the case, Parke's debts were so numerous and varied that it was a long time before Byrd could know exactly the extent of the obligations he had assumed. Thus a burden which was already heavy at the start became even heavier than he had expected. In his letter to Custis in July 1723, he complained that Perry charged to his account several debts that had turned up after Parke's death and which, according to their agreement, "did not belong to him to pay."[15]

[12] On Parke's career, see *VMHB*, XX (1912), 372–76, and George French, *The History of Col. Parke's Administration* (London, 1717).

[13] "Byrd Title Book," *VMHB*, XLVII (1942), 238.

[14] *Secret Diary*, Feb. 2, 1712; Byrd to John Custis, July 29, 1723, *VMHB*, XXXVI (1928), 38; *Beatty*, p. 75.

[15] *VMHB*, XXXV (1927), 377–78, and XXXVI (1928), 37 (letter of July 29, 1723).

Some time before his father-in-law died, Byrd, who all his life was ambitious of dignities and high offices, had tried to buy the governorship of Virginia. A few months before, in September 1709, he had already written to England "to make interest for the government of Maryland,"[16] without any result despite several recommendations. Since the year 1704, when Lord George Hamilton, Earl of Orkney, had been appointed Governor of Virginia for life, he had remained in England and several lieutenant governors had ruled the colony in his place. On March 31, 1710, Byrd was apprised of a new failure:

Mr. Bland . . . brought me several letters from England, and among the rest two from Colonel Blakiston who had endeavored to procure the government of Virginia for me at the price of a thousand pounds of my Lady Orkney, and that my Lord agreed, but the Duke of Marlborough declared that no one but soldiers should have the government of a plantation, so I was disappointed. God's will be done.[17]

In July 1710, the appointment that Byrd had sought was given to Colonel Alexander Spotswood, a soldier who had been wounded at Blenheim. The first years of Spotswood's administration (those covered by Byrd's *Secret Diary*) were marked by unbroken harmony in public affairs. There was no discord between the Council and the lieutenant governor, who were all busy trying to cope with troubles caused by the Tuscarora Indians in North Carolina. In the entry of his diary for October 7, 1711, Byrd noted: "I received a letter from the governor by express, by which I learned that sixty people had been killed by the Indians at Neuse and about as many at Pamlico in North Carolina, and that he would meet me at Major Harrison's." Baron Christopher de Graffenried, a Swiss who organized and financed the settlement of some of his countrymen in North Carolina, and John Lawson, surveyor general of the same colony, had been captured by the Tuscaroras. They eventually released the baron, but they burned Lawson at the stake "because he had been so foolish as to threaten the Indian that had taken him."[18] Spotswood took Indian hostages, and for their exchange specified that the Indians "should deliver two children of the great men of each town . . . to be educated at our college."[19] He also began mustering an army for the

[16] *Secret Diary*, Sept. 19, 1709.
[17] *Ibid.*, March 31, 1710.
[18] *Ibid.*, Oct. 8 and 19, 1711.
[19] Alexander Spotswood, *The Official Letters of Alexander Spotswood*, ed. R. A. Brock (Richmond, 1882–85), I, 121–22; *Secret Diary*, pp. 425 and 516 ff. See also Thomas H. Wynne, ed., *History of the Dividing Line and Other Notes, from the Papers of William Byrd of Westover in Virginia, Esquire* (Richmond, 1866), II, 192–95.

defense of Virginia. North Carolina twice called on Virginia for assistance but seemed to expect their allies to do all the work, so that the governor and the Council of Virginia were soon disgusted with the North Carolinians, whom they believed, moreover, to have been responsible for allowing the situation to become so critical. The Virginians finally let their neighbors do the fighting south of their common border, and eventually arranged a peace between the Carolinians and the Tuscaroras when the latter had been vanquished and their fort pulled down. During these years of Indian troubles, the Virginia Council approved Spotswood's "frugal management and singular diligence in putting the country in a posture of defense." In the autumn of 1713, when peace was definitely concluded with the Indians, Byrd was one of the men chosen by the Council to draw up an address to Governor Spotswood praising his diplomacy and wisdom.[20]

But when there were no longer any external concerns, the governor turned his attention to what were in his opinion the two essential defects of colonial administration: the excessive power of the Council, which was imperceptibly usurping the authority of the Crown, and the lack of efficiency in the collection of the quitrent revenue. In the latter endeavor he came into conflict with Byrd, who as receiver general did none of the collecting himself but had the work done by the sheriffs through their deputies. Spotswood cast no reflections on Byrd's honesty but felt that these taxes passed through too many hands and consequently were greatly reduced before they reached the coffers of the Crown. The sheriffs were gentlemen, the governor admitted, but their deputies were only those who paid most for the office.[21] In 1713 Byrd had already proposed a new plan for collecting the quitrents through four deputy receivers to be appointed for that purpose and to be responsible to the receiver general.[22] The governor received the suggestion coldly, simply because it was not of his own contrivance, said Byrd. But, more probably, the representative of the Crown did not wish to see new offices created while some posts became mere sinecures. On the other hand, Byrd preferred that the local taxes should be spent in the colony for the pay of colonial officers.

In July 1714 Spotswood asked Byrd and Philip Ludwell, Jr., the auditor, to propose a better scheme. A family quarrel may have pro-

[20] *Legislative Journals of the Council of Colonial Virginia,* ed. H. R. McIlwaine (Richmond, 1918–1919), I, 516 (Nov. 14, 1711); I, 558 (Nov. 7, 1713).

[21] *Official Letters,* II, 86 (Jan. 27, 1714/15).

[22] See Byrd's defense, submitted to the Board of Trade Sept. 27, 1716, V.H.S. (cf. Sainsbury, *Abstracts,* 1715–1720, p. 563).

vided grounds for a more personal animosity between the governor and the two councillors who proceeded to join forces against him. Ludwell, an in-law of Byrd's, had inherited the property of Governor Berkeley, whose widow had married his father. Spotswood claimed that part of the estate belonged to the Governor of Virginia, for it had originally been given to Berkeley in his official capacity.[23]

In response to the governor's request, Byrd merely repeated his earlier suggestion, which the governor ignored altogether. In November 1714 Spotswood made a proposal of his own, using the existing system instead of creating special collectors. The sheriffs were to collect the rents at places appointed by their county courts, and not to travel as before; they were to receive a 5 per cent commission instead of 10 per cent; and they were to settle directly with the receiver general at Williamsburg. Planters who chose to pay the receiver general in person were to receive a discount of 8 per cent. Finally Spotswood proposed to sell the quitrent tobacco to the highest bidder instead of by private sale.

In reply, Byrd objected that sheriffs were changed too often to be good collectors and that reducing their commission from 10 to 5 per cent would not make them any better. Granting a discount amounted to giving away the king's money, which they had no right to do. The new system would increase the expenses of the receiver general. As for the method of selling the quitrent tobacco, he thought it would not work because the buyers would agree among themselves to avoid bidding against each other.[24]

When Spotswood finally called for a vote on his own plan, the Council passed it despite Byrd's and Ludwell's opposition. The new scheme proved far more effective than the old, and a year later the governor could declare that "one third of the Crown lands in this colony has this year yielded a greater revenue than the whole did formerly."[25]

Thus in their half-private feud with the governor, the two proud councillors were not followed by their colleagues and were defeated. But when Spotswood set out to maintain the prerogative of the king's representative against the growing power of the Council, he brought this body down upon himself almost unanimously. The Council was

[23] See Louis R. Caywood, "Green Spring Plantation," *VMHB*, LXV (1957), 67–83; Charles E. Hatch, Jr., "The Affair near James Island, or the Battle of Green Spring, July 6, 1781," *ibid.*, LIII (1945), 172–96.

[24] See *Executive Journals of Council*, III, 389–91 (Dec. 8, 1714), and Spotswood, *Official Letters*, Dec. 1, 1714, and Jan. 27, 1714/15, II, 80–87.

[25] Spotswood to the Lords of Treasury, July 15, 1715, *Official Letters*, II, 117. On the whole contention about quitrents, see *ibid.*, pp. 80–117.

composed of the leading planters, the representatives of an oligarchy jealous of its rights, and most of them were allied by marriage. In this contest Byrd was to take a prominent part because of his legal training, which was better than that of most other councillors.

The General Court, the highest in the colony, was composed of the governor and the Council or part of it. Prior to 1710, the five or six months' interval between two meetings of the General Court hindered the speedy execution of justice. In 1710 the right of habeas corpus was extended to Virginia, and it was decreed that two courts of oyer and terminer be held annually in December and June, while the General Court sat in April and October.[26] Shortly after, Spotswood got a law passed specifying that the privilege of the Council to sit on the General Court did not restrict the power of the Crown's representative to set up courts of oyer and terminer including persons who were not councillors;[27] this was particularly advisable when the interests of councillors were involved, since six of the twelve members were of one family.[28] As John S. Bassett remarked, "there was much truth in Spotswood's assertion, but there was a weakness in his position, due to the fact that his proposition would give the appointment of the judges to the governor." In December 1712 Spotswood brought in the Speaker of the House of Burgesses and two leading members of the Assembly to form with some of the councillors the court that was to try a man for his life.[29] But the councillors objected and refused to serve. The governor dropped the matter in Virginia but referred it to the Board of Trade, which pronounced in his favor in June 1716 after long reflection. This decision and the events that followed were to revive the dispute during Byrd's next stay in England.

Toward the end of 1713 Byrd asked for leave of absence for some time, "having some private affairs of his own to transact in England

[26] See Lyon G. Tyler, "Writ of Habeas Corpus," *WMCQ*, 1st ser., III (1895), 151–53; *Secret Diary*, June 5, 1710.

[27] Hening, *Statutes at Large*, III, 489; Spotswood to the Lords of Trade, April 5, 1717, *Official Letters*, II, 224.

[28] Spotswood to the Lords of Trade, Sept. 27, 1718, II, 304; compare Gov. Drysdale to the Lords of Trade, June 29, 1726, P.R.O., CO 5/1320, ff. 41–42, Va. Colonial Records Project microfilm: "The gentlemen of the best estates here are so nearly linked by blood or by intermarriages that I cannot judge it advisable to put the power of judicature in the General Court too much into one family."

[29] Bassett, pp. lxviii–lxix; W. C. Ford, *The Controversy between Lieutenant Governor Spotswood and His Council and the House of Burgesses on the Appointment of Judges on Commissions of Oyer and Terminer* (Brooklyn, 1891), p. 9.

the nature of which require his private attendance."[30] Indeed, his difficulties with the settlement of Colonel Parke's debts may have been the original reason for the trip, but there is no doubt that when he sailed he intended to use the opportunity to carry on the fight against Spotswood from a more favorable place, near the central power in London. Fresh personal grievances against the governor arose when Spotswood, late in 1714, managed to get a law passed creating a company to monopolize the Indian trade.[31] Byrd probably hoped, with the help of his English friends, to have Spotswood recalled, and perhaps—if luck would have it—to get the government of Virginia for himself.[32] So in March or April 1715 he departed for England, leaving his family at Westover. He did not expect to stay even as long as a year in Europe, but in fact circumstances delayed his return to Virginia for five years.

[30] Sainsbury, *Abstracts*, 1706–1714, p. 444 (Jan. 25, 1714).
[31] "Act for the Better Regulation of the Indian Trade, Virginia, 1714," ed. W. Neil Franklin, *VMHB*, LXXII (1964), 141–51.
[32] *London Diary*, April 20, 1719.

CHAPTER III

In England Again
1715-1726

DURING the next five years, Byrd was very busy in England, straightening out the involved affairs of his late father-in-law and working for the Virginia Council against Lieutenant Governor Spotswood. When he realized that he was to stay longer than he had expected, he sent for his wife, who came over in the summer of 1716, leaving in Virginia their two daughters, Evelyn, then nine years old, and Wilhelmina, a baby born in the fall after Byrd's departure. But before the year was out Mrs. Byrd died of smallpox, on November 21, 1716, after a very short and sudden illness. Byrd wrote to his brother-in-law John Custis: "No stranger ever met with more respect in a strange country than she had done here from many persons of distinction, who all pronounced her an honor to Virginia. Alas! How proud was I of her, and how severely am I punished for it! But I can dwell no longer on so afflicting a subject, much less can I think of anything else."[1]

And yet, less than two months after his wife's death Byrd was writing his first letter as a suitor to a twenty-four-year-old young lady whom he called "Sabina":

Where a woman is agreeable as well as beautiful; that is, when besides an enchanting form she knows how to entertain you with her humor, when she can soften you with an obliging look, and charm you with a graceful behavior, when her air, her mien, her manner conspire to please and delight you, surely to love such a woman is just, not only by the allowance of reason, but from the impossibility of avoiding it.[2]

Miss Mary Smith was the younger daughter of a rich and proud commissioner of excise whom Byrd named "Vigilante." Byrd lived across the street and could see the lady from his window. The affair was conducted in the style of French romances, with a secret correspondence in invisible ink, because of "Vigilante," "the old dragon that guards the Golden Fruit." When in July 1717 the "deciphering elixir" failed to work, "Sabina" expressed her "great surprise and disappointment." But a few days later she damped Byrd's enthusiasm:

---

[1] Dec. 13, 1716, in Custis, *Recollections*, p. 33.
[2] *Another Secret Diary*, p. 300.

"Sure you think me a very odd nymph, when you imagine I would carry on a secret correspondence with any gentleman. That would look as if I intended to dispose of my own person, whereas I am determined to be carried to market by my father."[3] Periodically she urged him to stop writing, or she sent his letters back, though she was never so cruel as to discourage her suitor completely. Indeed she even went so far as to suggest how he could forward his suit, and gave him a lesson in military tactics:

I desire you if I have any interest in your heart, not to pursue your address in this distant manner: but if you must attack me, let it be in the forms. A woman is no more to be taken than a town by random shot at a distance, but the trenches must be opened, and all the approaches must be regular, and rather than abide the last extremity, 'tis possible the garrison may capitulate, especially if terms be offered that are honorable. 'Tis a sad case when a swain is so intolerably dull, that his mistress must prescribe her own method of being taken; however, supposing this blindness to proceed from pure passion, I will befriend it so far as to tell you that my brother is entirely in my interest: and if you can get into his good graces, he may negotiate this important affair betwixt us to both our satisfactions. I expect you'll make the most of this hint, for when a mistress gives her lover advice, she never forgives him if he don't follow it. Adieu.[4]

Byrd did make the most of the hint and lost no time in getting acquainted with Lord and Lady Dunkellen, "Sabina's" elder sister and brother-in-law. Within a month he wrote to "Sabina's" father a "state of his circumstances." He explained that he owned about 43,000 acres and 220 slaves in Virginia, as well as "a prodigious quantity of stock of every kind," and that he could count on a yearly income of fifteen to eighteen hundred pounds; he did not care what fortune John Smith would give his daughter; he engaged to live in England and to settle his whole estate upon Mary Smith, except for a dowry of four thousand pounds in favor of his two daughters.[5] But "Vigilante" was convinced that an estate out of England was "little better than an estate in the moon" and that this was a "chimerical match" for his daughter. As for "Sabina," she seems to have been under the thumb of her father, and she expressed her resolution to be obedient, desiring her suitor "never to write at all."[6] Despite "Sabina's" decision, Byrd did not give way to despair until on March 31 he received a messenger from her and confessed in his diary: "Then came Mr. Orlebar with a message from Miss Smith that I should not trouble her any more

---

[3] *Ibid.*, pp. 299, 301, 307.
[4] Jan. 23, 1718, *ibid.*, pp. 315–16.
[5] *London Diary*, Feb. 18, 1718; *Another Secret Diary*, pp. 321–24.
[6] *Another Secret Diary*, pp. 318, 329–30 (March 11, 1718).

with my letters or addresses, and returned my letter that I wrote last to her. I was very much concerned but said little to him, but when he had gone I cried exceedingly." A few days later, he made an unsuccessful attempt to borrow ten thousand pounds from Perry to settle upon Miss Smith; he had not really expected to succeed, and could not blame the merchant for refusing. He was kept informed by the Dunkellens, who encouraged him to hope against hope, but within a month he learned that a rival's proposal had been accepted. He then wrote "Sabina" a spiteful and ungallant letter, of the kind "he could an if he would": "I have the proper arguments in my strongbox to persuade any man of justice and common sense not to marry a gentlewoman that has proceeded so far with another gentleman." She was lucky that he could never abase himself to such an act. The rival, Sir Edward Des Bouverie, called upon Byrd on May 8, probably with the intention of challenging him to a duel, as there was some talk of it a few days later.[7] Byrd's version runs thus: "He told me he had received a letter from me, which I denied. But I told him the whole story of my affair with Miss Smith, which he allowed to be wrong in her, and yet told me he would proceed, to which I said much good may it do him."[8] Byrd was convinced that "Sabina" had resolved "to sacrifice both her character and inclination to her interest," and felt (so he said) "much obliged to Mrs. Smith for being so charitable" to him "as to cure entirely the wounds of her eyes by the imprudence of her behavior."[9] "Sabina" was married at the beginning of July 1718, but she died three years later.

Byrd had been sorely smitten. He had even gone so far as to renounce all his light-of-loves and had resolved to keep himself for his dear Miss Smith, though such heroism did not last a month. Yet he had really taken the whole affair very much to heart. Cured he may have been, but he still recorded dreaming of "Sabina."

He had his daughters sent over to England about that time: Evelyn in September 1717 and Wilhelmina in April 1719.[10] But he placed them with friends or relatives for their education and went on living the varied social life of a man of fashion, calling on friends, going to masquerade balls or to the theater, playing cards, or visiting light

[7] *London Diary*, April 7–8, 1718; *Another Secret Diary*, p. 349 (Byrd to Sabina, April 28, 1718); *London Diary*, May 16, 1718.

[8] *London Diary*, May 8, 1718. About the letter mentioned here, which was probably written by Lord Dunkellen, and in which Miss Smith was called "bitch and jilt," see *Another Secret Diary*, p. 357 (to Chevalier de Booby, May 10, 1718) and *London Diary*, May 7, 1718.

[9] *Another Secret Diary*, pp. 358–59.

[10] Byrd to John Custis, Oct. 19, 1717, Emmet Collection, New York Public Library; *London Diary*, April 17, 1719.

women. He had not given up his search for an heiress. In March 1719 he turned his attention to a certain widow Pierson whom he had met a few months earlier at the Spanish ambassador's. She refused him because of his two daughters and "persisted in her objection against being a mother-in-law [that is, a stepmother]." He proposed again several times but finally had to admit his failure. This, however, does not seem to have affected him so much as the loss of Miss Smith. Immediately after the rejection of his last proposal to the widow Pierson, he went and consoled himself with a light woman of his acquaintance.[11] In August 1719 he spent a month in the fashionable watering place of Tunbridge Wells. When he returned, he was kept busy winding up his affairs in England, for the political situation in the Old Dominion had made it necessary for him to sail back to the colony.

When Byrd had arrived in London in the spring of 1715, he had been received with consideration. The Lords of Trade soon called upon him and another Virginian to give information about the Indian war in South Carolina. Both declared that in their opinion the English Indian traders were entirely responsible for these troubles, because they often took provisions from Indians and only paid "what they thought fit," or "debauched the Indians' wives and daughters."[12]

Shortly after, in August, he presented a memorial to the Board of Trade on behalf of the Virginia Assembly, asking that the quitrents should be held for the use of the colony and not put in the English Treasury, as was contemplated by the new king, George I. Byrd explained that the tobacco tax of two shillings a hogshead yielded about three thousand pounds a year,[13] and the quitrents from twelve to fifteen hundred pounds. Since the expenses of the Virginia government were approximately thirty-five hundred pounds, the latter duty was a necessary complement to the tobacco tax, and the surplus was needed for such emergencies as Indian attacks or foreign invasions. Spotswood's opinion did not really differ from Byrd's, but he wanted the Board of Trade to accede to his own request, not to that of the colonial Assembly or its agent: he alone, as the king's representative,

[11] *London Diary*, April 15, July 7, 1719.

[12] Sainsbury, *Abstracts*, 1715–1720, p. 453 (July 26, 1715); compare *Prose Works*, p. 311.

[13] The tobacco tax of two shillings per hogshead had been established in 1680 at the instigation of Governor Culpeper after Bacon's Rebellion (Hening, *Statutes at Large*, II, 466–69). At no other time before the American Revolution did the Crown persuade a colonial assembly to grant a permanent and independent source of revenue (see Jack P. Greene, *The Quest of Power: The Lower Houses of Assembly in the Southern Royal Colonies, 1689–1776* [Chapel Hill, N.C., 1963], p. 127).

was the proper channel to transmit grievances to the king's government in London.[14] The Board's decision satisfied both sides: the surplus was to be left in the colony, but that fact should not induce the Assembly to make "extravagant expenditures."

This success greatly encouraged Byrd, who now endeavored to obtain in England the repeal of the two Virginia laws that Spotswood had got passed in 1714, one for the payment of debts in tobacco and the other for the creation of a company to be given a monopoly of the Indian trade. In regard to the latter law, Spotswood based his argument on the abuses committed by indiscriminate traders; Byrd, who was about to leave Virginia when the law was passed and had not been asked to take stock in the company, did his utmost against it and was greatly helped by the English hatred of monopoly. Both laws were finally repealed in July 1717.[15]

Meanwhile in Virginia, Spotswood had come to an open quarrel with Philip Ludwell, the auditor. The latter refused to submit his books to the governor, who suspended him pending decision in England and wrote to the Board of Trade charging both Ludwell and Byrd with obstructing the execution of his quitrent policy. In London, William Blathwayt, auditor general of the Plantations and Secretary at War, understood that Spotswood was led by the desire "to have the management of the revenue in his own or his creature's hands."[16] He anticipated the governor's charges and removed Ludwell from office before the case came up before the Board of Trade. In March 1716 Byrd had already sold his office of receiver general for five hundred pounds to one of his fellow councillors, James Roscowe, to avoid being placed any longer under the governor's supervision; he would thus be in a better position to oppose him. Besides, under existing circumstances, the post had become difficult for Byrd to manage by deputy while he was in England.

Byrd wrote a defense against Spotswood's charges, taking up each technical point. One answer on a more general charge is interesting, as it shows Byrd's belief that he was defending both the colony and the Crown against the tyranny of the governor: "We never opposed any of his regulations that appeared to be for the honor or interest of

---

[14] Sainsbury, *Abstracts*, 1715–1720, p. 456 (Aug. 11, 1715), p. 478 (Oct. 24, 1715). Compare Spotswood, *Official Letters*, II, 132 (Oct. 24, 1715).

[15] Sainsbury, *Abstracts*, 1715–1720, pp. 540–49 (discussion before the Board of Trade, July 10, 1716), p. 616 (advice of the Board of Trade to repeal the two acts, June 29, 1717), and p. 630 (order of the King in Council, July 31, 1717). It is interesting to note in this connection that in 1682 Byrd's father had tried to secure for himself the same kind of monopoly of the Indian trade that his son was fighting against in 1715 (Bassett, p. xxii).

[16] Sainsbury, *Abstracts*, 1715–1720, p. 560.

the Crown, and if they appeared otherwise, or seemed to be formed upon particular pique, our opposition was very reasonable, even though it was against a gentleman who thinks all contradiction insolent."[17] When the defense was submitted to the Board of Trade, however, neither Byrd nor Ludwell was any longer in office, and the matter was dropped. But the whole affair illustrates the feelings that prevailed at the time between Byrd and the governor. Byrd's own opinion is clearly expressed in a letter written to his brother-in-law Custis in October 1716: the receiver general "must either be a slave to his [Spotswood's] humour, must fawn upon him, jump over a stick whenever he was bid, or else he must have so much trouble loaded on him as to make his place uneasy. In short, such a man must be either the governor's dog or his ass; neither of which stations suit in the least with my constitution."[18]

Meanwhile the Board of Trade had decided that the governor had the right to appoint special oyer and terminer courts unless there was a colonial law to the contrary. As there was none, the decision roused the whole Council against Spotswood, though hitherto they had been mostly favorable to him. When the governor appointed a special court consisting of five councillors and four noncouncillors, only one of the former was willing to sit. A majority of the Council—eight of them—signed a petition against the decision and sent it to the Board of Trade.[19] Byrd later expressed his pleasure in a letter to Ludwell: "I am glad to find that the Council is fairly engaged with the Lieutenant Governor. They have a good cause, and I hope I shall be able to procure justice to be done them."[20] Although Byrd himself had once proposed the creation of a supreme court differentiated from the Council, in order to avoid having judges who knew no law and to

[17] "The Answer of William Byrd to the Observations of Alexander Spotswood, Esq., upon His Mismanagement of the Revenues of Virginia" (1716), pp. 8–9, point 10, Lee-Ludwell Papers, V.H.S. See also, in the same collection of papers, "The Answer of William Byrd II to the Governor's Demand for Explanation" (1716): Byrd expresses his opinion that a detailed enumeration of "the inconveniencies" the Council apprehends from the measures taken by the governor, "instead of peace in the government, and a good understanding between Your Honor and the Council (which we have been desirous to preserve) would drive things to a greater rupture and perhaps might be represented as a misbehavior to our governor." The text of Spotswood's charges appears in *Official Letters*, II, 176–87.

[18] Oct. 2, 1716, in Custis, *Recollections*, p. 29.

[19] These were Robert Carter, James Blair, Philip Ludwell, John Smith, John Lewis, William Bassett, Nathaniel Harrison, and Edmund Berkeley (P.R.O., CO 5/1318, ff. 239–43). If Byrd had been present in Virginia, he would have made the number of opponents nine out of twelve.

[20] Byrd to Ludwell, Sept. 24, 1717, Lee-Ludwell Papers, V.H.S.

be able to pay out of the quitrents more salaries that would be spent in Virginia, he was quite ready to help his colleagues against Spotswood, his pet aversion.

But Spotswood once again objected to "private agents" having free access to the Lords of Trade, who now refused to receive any more addresses through Byrd, although he might still be heard as one of the Council. In order to have more weight, Byrd wrote to Ludwell suggesting that the Assembly should have its own agent in London, since Blakiston, appointed by the Council, was under Spotswood's influence. Byrd was duly elected to this office in April 1718, and when the governor vetoed the bill that appointed him, the Burgesses decided to pay Byrd's salary themselves.[21] From then on Byrd was very active, first before the Board of Trade and then in an appeal to the Crown. He had already pointed out "the very fatal inconvenience that may follow upon the putting it into the sole power of a governor to try any person by what judges he may think most proper."[22] What had been acceptable if the judges really held their posts for a long time could not be allowed if the governor was to be able to change them as he pleased. In fact, as Professor Beatty remarked, "the struggle was one between colonial self-government and imperial control. . . . Here, in germ, were the principles of the Revolution of 1776."[23] Although the Assembly might have favored Spotswood's special courts, upon which they could serve, the majority of the Burgesses were hostile to him because they felt that he restricted the power of the colony to govern itself. Their opposition was based on two widely different considerations: on the Indian question and on the belief that the governor's schemes for the protection of the frontier would lead to higher public expenses without their being consulted. When Spotswood called for an election, hoping to induce the newly elected Burgesses to accept an Indian law without the objectionable features of the 1714 law, he was defeated for the same reasons.[24]

In London, the attorney-general expressed the opinion that legally

[21] Byrd to Ludwell, Oct. 28, 1717, "Some Colonial Letters," *VMHB*, III (1896), 353; Spotswood to the Board of Trade, June 24, 1718, *Official Letters*, II, 278.

[22] This was written not as agent for the Burgesses in 1718 as stated by W. P. Palmer (*Calendar of Virginia State Papers*, ed. Palmer [Richmond, Va., 1875], I, 190–91), but as a councillor, a few months earlier. See Byrd to the Lords of Plantations, n.d., received in London on Oct. 10, 1717, read before the Board on Nov. 13, 1717, P.R.O., CO 5/1318, ff. 124–27, Virginia Colonial Records Project microfilm, V.H.S.

[23] Beatty, p. 95.

[24] See the "Advice to Freeholders," first printed by Jack P. Greene in "The Opposition to Lieutenant-Governor Alexander Spotswood, 1718," *VMHB*, LXX (1962), 39–41.

the governor did have the power of calling special courts, though he advised that it be used only on extraordinary occasions.[25] Then the Board of Trade declared that the opposition did "not come from the people of the colony, but from those persons who would engross the privilege of being sole judges in all criminal causes";[26] the Crown rejected Byrd's appeal. In the meantime Spotswood had forced the Council to admit his right to appoint judges; he had announced that he would name councillors only, provided they acknowledged that they sat by virtue of the governor's appointment and not because they were councillors.[27] Having thus overcome all opposition in the colony, he wrote on July 1, 1718 to his superior Lord Orkney, the nonresident governor, proposing to have the "most turbulent" members of the Council removed from their posts. Byrd was among these, and Spotswood alleged that his long absence from the colony disqualified him for such an office.[28] Lord Orkney proposed an investigation, and things dragged on for some time. In December, Byrd wrote a letter to the Board of Trade saying that no members of the Virginia Council should be removed on Governor Spotswood's accusations until they had presented their cases; but a week later he noted in his diary: "The Council of Trade took my letter very ill."[29] In February 1719, Spotswood again wrote to urge the dismissal of "that implacable gentleman Byrd" from the Council.[30] The Board immediately recommended that the king appoint Mr. Cole Digges in Byrd's place. Then really fearing for his Council seat, Byrd realized that the only remedial step was to humble his pride. He called on all his most influential friends for help, and on March 2 he went "to Colonel Blakiston's and proposed to go to Virginia to make peace between the governor and the Council upon the governor's own plan." Two days later, he added, "I went to Colonel Blakiston's and with him to my Lord Orkney's, who received me very coldly, and we had a sort of a scold; however at last he heard my proposal about peace between his deputy and the Council."[31]

[25] See Sainsbury, *Abstracts*, 1715–1720, p. 678, for the petition of Byrd to the King, Feb. 2, 1717/18, "that the judges of the General Court may be appointed justices of the said Court of Oyer and Terminer except in cases of an extraordinary nature."

[26] *Ibid.*, p. 691 (March 3, 1717/18).

[27] *Executive Journals of Council*, III, 470 (May 14, 1718); see also p. 494 (Dec. 9, 1718).

[28] Spotswood to the Board of Trade, Sept. 27, 1718, *Official Letters*, II, 304.

[29] *London Diary*, Dec. 4 and 11, 1718. Compare Sainsbury, *Abstracts*, 1715–1720, p. 741 (letter of Dec. 4, received Dec. 5, read Dec. 10).

[30] Sainsbury, *Abstracts*, 1715–1720, p. 752.

[31] *London Diary*, March 2, March 4, 1719.

So on March 24, the unexpected mediator sent to the Board of Trade a copy of his plan, which was read on April 8 and seconded by Lord Orkney. The Board recommended Digges to succeed a deceased councillor, thus giving Byrd a respite, but they also suggested that Peter Beverley be given Byrd's place. Byrd immediately begged his patron the Duke of Argyle to speak for him. He himself saw James Craggs, one of the Secretaries of State, "who promised to get me leave to stay in England and keep my Council place."[32] But he was not to get off so lightly. When on June 25 the question came up before the Privy Council, the matter was referred to a committee which on October 28, "upon consideration of [Byrd's] long services . . . and that he hath engaged to return with the first shipping to Virginia," agreed "humbly to recommend him to His Majesty's favor for his continuance in the said Council."[33]

Byrd left London on November 24, 1719, and went aboard ship at Dover on December 9, after securing the protection of a letter to Spotswood from the Duke of Argyle.[34]

After a two months' voyage, Byrd reached Williamsburg on February 8, 1720, and proceeded to Westover five days later. In the meantime he had sent a letter to Spotswood, along with other letters he had brought from England, but the governor's answer, he said, "put an end to all my hopes of peace."[35] So he deemed it wiser not to return to town before the arrival of the king's order to restore him to the Council. He did not go to the Capitol until April 25; four days later, rather unexpectedly came the reconciliation between the governor and his adversaries. Byrd wrote his own version of it to Sir John Percival, one of his English friends, with a few embellishments:

Now this country is made much more agreeable than it was by the entire reconciliation we have lately brought about betwixt the governor and the Council. All the people's grievances are redressed now, neither are any of those hardships to be repeated which I used to complain of. I have had so great a share in this happy revolution that should I do nothing else while I tarry here, I should think I made a very prosperous voyage, and had some claim to the reward that is promised to peacemakers. 'Tis really a wonderful change in a very little time, amongst a most divided people, to see peace and friendship revive, and all former animosities forgot, as if they had all tasted the waters of forgetfulness. But before the governor and I could be

[32] P.R.O., CO 5/1318, f. 557; *London Diary*, April 16, April 20, 1719.

[33] *Calendar of Virginia State Papers*, I, 195. In his diary, Byrd had merely noted on Sept. 13: "I resolved this day to go to Virginia to take care of my affairs."

[35] *London Diary*, Feb. 9, 1720.

[34] "To Duke Dulchetti," *Another Secret Diary*, pp. 368–71.

friends, 'twas necessary to let out all the sharp humors in a conversation so full of reproaches that 'twas more likely to end in an immediate war than an approaching peace; yet it took quite another turn, and we were perfect good friends for days afterwards, and extended our reconciliation over the whole country. Never was there a more general rejoicing than at this pacification, and indeed not without reason, for the heat of both parties was run so high that all friendship and conversation was quite lost, and it must soon have ended in a general confusion.[36]

This reconciliation did not prevent further differences between Byrd and the governor, but these were not serious and later, when Spotswood had retired to the life of a Virginia planter, they became good neighbors and tolerable friends. The result of the long struggle between governor and Council was in fact a stalemate. The Council no longer had enough influence in London to have a governor removed, but neither had the governor been able to obtain Byrd's removal from the Council. In order to govern Virginia he had to reach an accord with the plantation gentry. Spotswood and the Council had only succeeded in neutralizing each other until the Burgesses would eclipse both governor and Council and assume the leading role in Virginia politics.

This, however, had been a narrow escape for Byrd, and he must have felt very glad to have emerged unscathed. Although no party could really boast of a victory, the dignity of the Council was unabated, and they felt that they had fought for the rights of the colonists. As John S. Bassett put it: "Instead of throwing the councillors, who through abilities and position were the natural leaders of the community, into an inane espousal of the rights of the Crown, it developed in them a strong colony sense. They felt that they were Virginians first of all."[37] Years later, in the perspective of history, it might be said that the spirit of the American Revolution was looming on the political horizon.

During the following months Byrd was busy reordering his plantations. In 1717 he had sent over to Virginia his nephew John Brayne, the orphaned son of his sister Susan, "to make himself acquainted with my affairs," but on his return in 1720 he found "several things extremely amiss," and many matters in which Brayne "had been to blame"; a separation soon followed.[38] At this time he also made some

---

[36] Byrd to Percival, June 22, 1720, *Another Secret Diary*, p. 370n.

[37] P. liii.

[38] In a letter to Charles, Earl of Orrery, dated March 6, 1719/20, Byrd wrote: "I find my affairs in so much disorder here that I fear I must abide by them till next spring, when I shall have the pleasure of returning to the joys of London" ("Letters upon Various Occasions to and from John Earl of Orrery, His

improvements at Westover. After learning that the plague had appeared in Europe, he devoted part of his leisure, during the winter of 1720–21, to writing a treatise on the plague which was published in England in 1721.[39] Meanwhile, in December 1720, the Burgesses had chosen Byrd again as their agent "in an affair relating to a treaty with the five nations of Indians," with a salary of four hundred pounds. Spotswood again objected to any interposition between himself and the English government, but proposed to agree on condition "that the instructions to be given . . . be signed by the governor, and that the solicitor enter into bond to the governor not to meddle in Great Britain with any other affair of this government."[40] Byrd would not consent to have his hands bound in any way, and the Burgesses rejected the amendment of the governor, who had to give way.

So Byrd was back in England early in the fall of 1721 as Virginia agent. We do not know whether he had anything to do with Spotswood's removal in 1722. If he still hoped to succeed his old adversary, his hopes were dashed once more with the appointment of Hugh Drysdale.[41]

Once again Byrd was bent on his quest for an heiress in the fashionable circles of London. In the fall of 1722 he was forty-eight and becoming a little old-fashioned, though still reasonably eligible. He paid court to a young widow of twenty-nine whom he called "Charmante."[42] She was Lady Elizabeth Lee, a granddaughter of Charles II and his mistress Lady Castlemaine, Duchess of Cleveland; and she was later to marry the poet Edward Young. Such at least is Maud Woodfin's identification of "Charmante," a most plausible one although there are still some puzzling facts in the whole affair.[43] "In the begin-

---

Family and His Friends," I, pt. 1, 6, Houghton Library, Harvard University, Cambridge, Mass.). Byrd to John Custis, Oct. 19, 1717, Emmet Collection, New York Public Library; *London Diary*, Feb. 14, 1720.

[39] See *London Diary*, pp. 496–509 (Feb. 14–March 22, 1721), and *Another Secret Diary*, pp. 411 ff.

[40] *Journals of Burgesses*, V, 300 (Dec. 14, 1720); 308 (Dec. 20, 1720); compare Spotswood's address to the Burgesses in *Legislative Journals of Council*, II, 657 (Dec. 19, 1720) and *London Diary*, Dec. 20, 1720.

[41] Leonidas Dodson, *Alexander Spotswood, Governor of Colonial Virginia, 1710–1722* (Philadelphia, 1932), pp. 226–76. About the date of Byrd's arrival in England, we only know that the *Journal of the Commissioners for Trade and Plantations* (London, 1925), IV, 328, alludes to him as "late arrived from Virginia" on Nov. 10, 1721.

[42] *VMHB*, XXXV (1927), 383–88. These letters from Byrd to "Charmante," dated between Oct. 23 and Nov. 9, 1722, are the last he wrote to her, although another is included in his Commonplace Book, V.H.S., pp. 85–92.

[43] *Another Secret Diary*, pp. xxxii–xxxiv.

ning," said Byrd, "she gave the writer . . . the plainest marks of her favor." But soon she discouraged his suit because—he thought—of "private scandal she had received about him," perhaps through his rival. He complained that she had chosen to do so in a public place. In spite of the courteous tone of his last letter to her, he resented what he looked upon as undeserved rudeness and later described her as "a lady who had more charms than honor, more wit than discretion."[44]

About three months later he proposed to another lady who appears in his correspondence as "Minionet."[45] For some time they had been exchanging character sketches, "pictures" as he called them. He had sent her his own character sketch as "Inamorato L'Oiseaux," but it does not seem to have convinced her to "smile upon his passion."

Beside his own love affairs, Byrd was greatly concerned in 1723 about the courtship of his elder daughter by an English nobleman. Evelyn was then sixteen and was to be presented at Court before her return to Virginia. Family tradition would have it that her suitor was the Earl of Peterborough, but the third earl, who was a fashionable and witty old gentleman of sixty-four, some time later married the famous singer Anastasia Robinson. The suitor may have been the third earl's grandson Charles Mordaunt, who inherited the title in 1735,[46] or more probably some younger brother in the family. Byrd at one time feared that his daughter would elope with her lover, "Erranti"; he wrote a letter to each of them, commanding her "never more to meet, speak or write to that gentleman" and warning him that if Evelyn married against her father's wishes he would cut her off with "a splendid shilling."[47]

Though Byrd strongly disapproved of an elopement for his daughter and thought himself obliged to point out to her the rocks upon which she would certainly shipwreck all her happiness in this world,[48] he felt no such scruple in his own case. In May 1724 he married Maria Taylor, a twenty-five-year-old heiress, waiting, however, more

[44] Constance C. Harrison, "Colonel William Byrd of Westover, Virginia," *Century Magazine*, XLII (1891), 171 (copy of the letter in Byrd's Commonplace Book, V.H.S., p. 91).

[45] *Another Secret Diary*, pp. 371–80. "Minionet" may have been Molly Jeffreys (*ibid.*, p. 272n).

[46] See Collins's Peerage. Charles Mordaunt was married in 1720 and his wife lived until 1726. Nevertheless, this thesis was adopted by Marion Harland in her novel *His Great Self* (Philadelphia, 1861), in which she made use of many Byrd family traditions.

[47] "To Amasia" and "To Erranti," July 20, 1723, *Another Secret Diary*, pp. 381–85. Byrd alluded to John Philips's burlesque poem published in 1705.

[48] *Another Secret Diary*, p. 383.

than two weeks to disclose the fact to his new mother-in-law, "Medusa," for he anticipated some trouble with her.[49] Nine months later, Byrd found himself a father again. He was still in debt to Perry. His income was smaller and his expenses were greater than when he lived in Virginia, especially with a new family. It became necessary to go back to the colony, although he hoped to return to England free of debt in a few years.[50]

[49] "To Medusa," May 26, 1724, *Another Secret Diary*, p. 386.
[50] He kept until 1729 the chambers in Lincoln's Inn which he had bought from Sir George Cooke in July 1719 (*London Diary*, pp. 289–91, and Byrd to Mr. Spencer, May 28, 1729, "Letters from Old Trunks," *VMHB*, XLVI [1938], 243–44).

CHAPTER IV

Back in Virginia
1726-1744

D URING the months that followed Byrd's arrival in Virginia in
the early spring of 1726, he was very busy straightening out his
affairs in the colony and striving to increase the yield of his plantations. Overseers were far less efficient when the master was three
thousand miles away, and their accounts called for minute inspection.
He had not been able to depend upon his own nephew, John Brayne,
to see that the work was done; how could he depend upon mere
strangers, indifferent servants? Life in London had been expensive
too, and his debt was still great. His family was growing again. They
had left Anne, a baby hardly a year old, the Earl of Orrery's god-
daughter, in England with Maria's sister; she would only join her
parents at Westover in 1730, after her aunt's marriage.[1] But three
other children were born in the years 1727 to 1729, Maria, William,
and Jane. There were also the two daughters of Byrd's first marriage,
Evelyn and Wilhelmina, who had returned from England with them.
Fortunately Maria was a far better housewife than Lucy and thoroughly adapted herself to her new life in Virginia.

Byrd resumed his seat on the Council on April 28, 1726, but he was
still on the lookout for the honor and profit of a higher office. After
the death of Lieutenant Governor Hugh Drysdale, he wrote to Lord
Orrery, to the Duke of Argyle, and to Lord Islay, his most influential
friends in England, in order to secure their help in getting an appointment which would solve his financial difficulties quickly.[2]

Once more Byrd's hope was frustrated. In 1727, however, he was
appointed one of the three Virginia commissioners to settle a long
dispute over the boundary line with North Carolina. The first Carolina charter, in 1663, had specified that the colony should be limited
northward by the thirty-sixth degree of latitude, whereas the second,
in 1665, had fixed the line about thirty miles farther north (36° 30′).

[1] Byrd to Charles, Earl of Orrery, June 18, 1730 (Letters upon Various Occasions, I, pt. 1, pp. 168–69). Maria Taylor's sister married Francis Otway,
who became a colonel in the English army; many of Byrd's later letters are
addressed to him.

[2] Byrd to Lord Orrery, Feb. 2, 1726/27, The Orrery Papers, ed. Countess of
Cork and Orrery (London, 1903), I, 52.

The disputed strip of land was inhabited by settlers holding property grants either from Virginia or from Carolina, and some shady characters made the most of the uncertainty of the jurisdiction. A previous commission had failed to solve the matter because of ill will and obstruction on the part of the North Carolina representatives. This time, in case the joint commission was unable to come to an agreement, the King had empowered the three Virginians to finish the survey alone. The work was first delayed by the death of one of Byrd's colleagues, which necessitated a new appointment. Finally the commissioners received their instructions on February 13, 1728, and the line was run in the spring and fall of the same year. The party, composed of seven commissioners, four surveyors, forty laborers, and a chaplain, met at Currituck Inlet, on the coast, on March 5.[3] After a short dispute about the starting point, on which the Virginians magnanimously conceded, they proceeded westward. The surveyors and some of the laborers had to cross the hitherto unexplored Dismal Swamp.[4] One of Byrd's colleagues, William Dandridge, was ill; the other, Colonel Richard Fitzwilliam, who appears as "Firebrand" in *The Secret History*, always sided with the Carolinians whenever a difference arose between the commissioners or the surveyors of the two colonies. At the beginning of April, after six weeks in the wilderness, in spite of various difficulties, they had carried the line as far west as the Meherrin River, 73 miles from their starting point. There they decided to suspend their work until the fall, for snakes were becoming dangerous. In the interval, because of some disagreements he had had with Fitzwilliam, Byrd desired to be excused from the next journey unless it was clearly understood that he alone would be in command of the Virginian party, and he carried his point.[5] The expedition was resumed on September 20, and they reached the fertile valley of the Roanoke. But on October 5, the Carolina commissioners told Byrd that they did not intend to go any farther since they were already well beyond the settled country; he answered that the Virginians would go on by themselves. That night there was a discussion between Byrd and his two colleagues, which ended in a quarrel between Dandridge and Fitzwilliam. Byrd

---

[3] *Prose Works*, pp. 168–69, 176, 335. The second Carolina charter appears as an appendix to the *History of the Dividing Line, ibid.,* pp. 322–23. One of the Carolina commissioners was also a surveyor.

[4] See the brief description in a letter to Lord Orrery, dated May 27, 1728 (*Orrery Papers*, I, 79–81), in which some details anticipate Byrd's *History of the Dividing Line.*

[5] Compare *Prose Works*, pp. 88–91, and Byrd to Governor Gooch, Sept. 1, 1728, "Letters from Old Trunks," *VMHB,* XLVI (1938), 242–43.

("Steady," as he calls himself in *The Secret History*) at one time feared that it would end in a duel, but he managed to reconcile them.[6] After the departure of Fitzwilliam and the Carolinians, Byrd's party went some 75 miles farther on, to the Appalachian foothills, where they stopped because of the advanced season, having surveyed a total distance of 241 miles. This was one of the most adventurous expeditions in Virginia since the cavalcade of the Knights of the Golden Horseshoe led by Governor Spotswood over the Blue Ridge Mountains in 1716.[7]

These explorations had convinced Byrd that the fertile valleys they had seen in frontier lands would soon be settled. Their value would then increase greatly. When the North Carolina government paid its commissioners by granting them some of the tracts that had been surveyed, Byrd made an arrangement with one of them who wanted ready money. For two hundred pounds, a little more than his own salary for the expedition, he bought twenty thousand acres at the confluence of the Dan and the Irvine rivers.[8] Later, in 1743, he added six thousand acres to that estate, which he named the Land of Eden, with a double meaning since Governor Eden was then serving in North Carolina. When he had first seen the place, during the survey of the dividing line, Byrd had already noted its beauty: "This prospect was so beautiful that we were perpetually climbing up to a neighboring eminence, that we might enjoy it in more perfection." He had admired it again as they journeyed back. It was, he said, "exceedingly rich," "as fertile as the lands were said to be about Babylon," and he concluded that "a colony of one thousand families might, with the help of moderate industry, pass their time very happily there."[9] He hoped to settle the place with Swiss immigrants, whom he deemed the best colonists he could find. As early as January 1729, Byrd had purchased a plantation on Meherrin River, "that might serve as a convenient stage or halfway house" to the distant territory he owned on Roanoke River.[10] As another stopping place between Westover and the Land of Eden, between 1730 and 1738 he acquired more than five thousand acres where the Staunton and the Dan rivers join to form the Roanoke.[11] These were favorable

---

[6] *Prose Works*, pp. 104–7.

[7] See the Journal of John Fontaine, in *Memoirs of a Huguenot Family*, ed. Ann Maury (New York, 1853), pp. 245 ff., esp. pp. 283–90.

[8] *Prose Works*, pp. 289–91 and 413.

[9] *Ibid.*, pp. 250, 289–90.

[10] More exactly it is the Dan, which was for Byrd "the south branch of the Roanoke," the Staunton being the north branch.

[11] Bluestone Castle. See *Prose Works*, pp. 384–85.

tracts: between the Land of Eden and the sea, along the Dan and Roanoke rivers, there were no falls to interrupt the navigation of small craft, "except the great ones, thirty miles below Moniseep Ford"; "and I have been informed," he added, "that even at those great falls, the blowing up a few rocks would open a passage at least for canoes, which certainly would be an unspeakable convenience to the inhabitants of all that beautiful part of the country."[12]

In 1732 Byrd, who knew nothing about the mining business, decided to find out whether it would be worth his while to venture into this industry on his lands. So in September of that year he set out for Colonel Spotswood's home at Germanna, along the Rappahannock. Byrd described the former Lieutenant Governor, with whom he was now on friendly terms, as "the first in North America who had erected a regular furnace."[13] On his way, Byrd stopped at Mr. Charles Chiswell's; that gentleman, who after heavy losses was just beginning to make money with the mines at Fredericksville, gave him much valuable advice on the subject. A good mine had to be near a navigable waterway and required one hundred and twenty slaves. In time, after a total expenditure of twelve thousand pounds, the owner could expect a yearly profit of about thirty-two hundred pounds. The magnitude of the enterprise must have cooled Byrd's interest. After visiting the mines and the furnace, he also registered Chiswell's opinion that it was useless to equip a forge in the colony, for "the Parliament of England would soon forbid us that improvement, lest after that we should go farther and manufacture our bars into all sorts of ironware." Then Byrd rode on to Spotswood's place at Germanna, where he stayed for six days and learned more about iron. Spotswood confirmed the information he had already received and told him how "his long absence in England, and the wretched management of Mr. Graeme, whom he had entrusted with his affairs, had put him back very much." Such an enterprise required the constant presence of the owner. The particulars Byrd gathered during his journey determined him to stay out of the mine business, which

[12] *Ibid.*, p. 255. On Byrd's acquisitions of land, see "Byrd Title Book," *VMHB*, XLVII (1939)–L (1942).

[13] *Prose Works*, p. 357. In fact, blast furnaces and forges had been in operation in New England as early as mid-seventeenth century. The Indian massacre of 1622 terminated production at the first full-scale ironworks in Virginia, located at Falling Creek, a few miles south of the falls of the James (see Charles E. Hatch, Jr., and Thurlow G. Gregory, "The First American Blast-Furnace, 1619–1622," *VMHB*, LXX [1962], 259–96). For Germanna, which was first settled in 1714 by twelve Protestant families to provide artisans for Spotswood's ironworks, see John W. Wayland, *Germanna, Outpost of Adventure* (Harrisonburg, Va., 1956); *Prose Works*, p. 355.

he found too risky. He was not "mine mad," like some people in Virginia.[14]

A year later, Byrd set out with his friend Major William Mayo to make a survey of the lands they possessed along the Dividing Line. On the way, he visited his property at the fork of the Roanoke:

My land there in all extends ten miles upon the river; and three charming islands, namely, Sappony, Occaneechee, and Totero, run along the whole length of it. The lowest of these islands is three miles long, the next four, and the uppermost three, divided from each other by only a narrow strait. The soil is rich in all of them, the timber large, and a kind of pea, very grateful to cattle and horses, holds green all the winter.[15]

When they had reached the Land of Eden, they spent a little more than three days surveying the property, which extended over about fifteen miles along the Dan, with a breadth varying from one to three miles. One evening they encamped "in a charming peninsula" near a small river: "It contained about forty acres of very rich land, gradually descending to the creek, and is a delightful situation for the manor house." In his mind's eye he could already see the future settlement. Of another place he said: "I could not quit this pleasant situation without regret, but often faced about to take a parting look at it as far as I could see, and so indeed did all the rest of the company." And he concluded: "Happy will be the people destined for so wholesome a situation, where they may live to fullness of days and, which is much better still, with much content and gaiety of heart."[16] It is in such passages that the reader can feel what a willful distortion of truth it is to present Byrd, as some have done in modern terms, as "a great real estate promoter." Despite all his London years, his life was deeply rooted in Virginia; he had the countryman's reverence for earth and nature, and the colonist's sense of a quest for a new paradise.

In 1735 Byrd was appointed one of the three Crown representatives to determine the bounds of the Northern Neck, between the Rappahannock and Potomac rivers, in northern Virginia. These territories were all claimed by Lord Fairfax, who soon appointed a rival commission with himself at the head of it. The two parties accused each other of unfairness. In London, the attorney general sided with Lord Fairfax, and the two surveying bodies completed their work independently in the fall of 1736. Byrd sent a report to England in 1737. These lands, he stated, had been granted "much in the dark" by

[14] *Prose Works*, pp. 346–54, 358, 388, 408.
[15] *Ibid.*, pp. 384–88.
[16] *Ibid.*, pp. 394, 399.

Charles II even before his Restoration; later on, other settlers had moved into the disputed tracts, and the claims of Lord Fairfax amounted to the incredible total of more than five million acres.[17] When both sides had submitted their reports, the king decided in favor of Fairfax.

In the meantime, Byrd had decided to rebuild Westover, which was probably undertaken in 1730 or 1731.[18] The old wooden structure had been replaced by a brick building in the Georgian style. But this construction must have been expensive, and Byrd's debt on account of the Parke estate was still troublesome. The interest was high, and he was hard pressed by Perry for the payment of the principal. Besides, Perry gave him less for his tobacco than other merchants did. Byrd had tried again to enlist the help of his friend Sir Charles Wager, the First Lord of the Admiralty: "I wish I could persuade you to take a little upon my account by speaking a good word for me to your friend Sir Robert" Walpole.[19] But Wager could not or would not procure for him the governorship that would have allowed him to get out of Perry's clutches. At the beginning of 1736, he even contemplated selling Westover to discharge his debts. In July, however, he was more hopeful: "My affairs are now a little mended with Alderman Perry. I am selling off land and negroes to stay the stomach of that hungry magistrate. I had much rather incommode myself a little than continue in the gripe of that usurer. I have already lessened my debt near a thousand pounds, and hope to wipe off the whole score in a short time."[20] A few months later, in April and May 1737, he advertised in the *Virginia Gazette* for the sale of lots in Richmond, the new town whose founding he had suggested four years before, during his journey to the Land of Eden.[21] These lots were parts of Byrd's former plantations on the north bank of

[17] Byrd's report was published in Bassett, pp. 401–10.

[18] Beatty says "by 1736"; but in 1735 Byrd had a plat made of the grounds and main buildings of Westover, which in 1736 he was trying to sell. As Bassett observed, "he would hardly have done this before he built" (p. lxxxi). Besides, in a letter to Mr. Spencer (May 28, 1729) Byrd announced: "In a year or two I intend to set about building a very good house" ("Letters from Old Trunks," *VMHB*, XLVI [1938], 244).

[19] Byrd to Sir Charles Wager, July 2, 1736, *VMHB*. IX (1901), 125.

[20] Byrd to Mrs. Pitt, of Bermuda, Jan. 6, 1735/36, *ibid.*, IX (1902), 238; to Mr. Beckford, Dec. 6, 1735, *ibid.*, 234–35; to Captain Parke, Feb. 3, 1735/36, *ibid.*, 246; to Wager, July 2, 1736, *ibid.*, IX (1901), 124.

[21] *Prose Works*, p. 388. The original map of Richmond, drawn by Byrd in or before 1737 and with his signature on it, is in the Virginia State Library. The first lots were sold to John Coles in June 1737.

the James near the falls; some sales were still being mentioned in the diary for 1739–41.

About the same time, Byrd solicited Admiral Wager's help again to get an appointment to an office much less pretentious than a governorship, that of surveyor of customs, "which, if granted, would disentangle me from all my difficulties and make me perfectly easy." "The place . . . is worth five hundred pounds a year and not unpleasant in the execution. If, therefore, by your credit with Sir Robert Walpole you would be pleased to get it for an old friend, it would make him happy in his declining years."[22] But again Wager could or would do nothing.

During the same period, Byrd endeavored to induce German Swiss to come to Virginia and settle on the Land of Eden. The hope of finding Swiss settlers had long been in his mind, and about 1735 he wrote to a Mr. Ochs, who was to bring to the colony a boatload of his countrymen: "I had much rather have to do with the honest industrious Switzers than the mixed people that come from Pennsylvania, especially when they are to be conducted by so prudent a person as yourself."[23] But the "honest industrious Switzers" did not come, and Byrd had to abandon his scheme momentarily. When his title to the Land of Eden, which had been questioned,[24] was finally recognized in 1736, he tried again. He made a contract with a Swiss agent, Samuel Jenner of Bern, to sell land on the Roanoke. In 1737 that agent published a tract, *Neu-gefundenes Eden* describing the fertility and healthfulness of that land.[25] This publicity seems to have borne fruit, since in July 1737 Byrd wrote hopefully to the Earl of

[22] Byrd to Wager, May 4, 1737, *VMHB*, XXXVI (1928), 358–59. He also asked Peter Collinson for his support (Byrd to Collinson, July 5, 1737, Byrd Letterbook, 1736–1737, pp. 35–37, V.H.S.).

[23] *VMHB*, IX (1902), 228. Compare A. B. Faust, "Swiss Emigration to the American Colonies in the Eighteenth Century," *American Historical Review*, XXII (1916), 21–44. In April 1737 Byrd was still corresponding with Mr. Ochs to settle one hundred families on his land at Roanoke (Byrd to Ochs, April 30, 1737, Byrd Letterbook, 1736–1737, pp. 12–13, V.H.S.). Johann Rudolph Ochs in 1711 wrote a 100-page tract intended to attract settlers to Carolina, based on John Lawson's *New Voyage to Carolina*, ed. F. L. Harriss (3d ed., Richmond, 1960).

[24] *VMHB*, IX (1901), 116–18 (a letter of May 23, 1735 apparently written to some important person in North Carolina), and IX (1902), 232–34 (to Gov. Johnston of North Carolina, Dec. 2, 1735).

[25] *William Byrd's Natural History of Virginia, or the Newly Discovered Eden*, ed. and trans. from a German version by R. C. Beatty and W. J. Mulloy (Richmond, 1940). Jenner had used notes provided by Byrd but had made far greater use of Lawson's *New Voyage* (see P. G. Adams, "The Real Author of

Egmont: "I expect a colony of three hundred Swiss in October next."[26] In the following year, two hundred and fifty German Swiss embarked for Virginia to settle Byrd's Carolinian lands, for the price of three pounds per hundred acres. But after a four months' voyage the ship was wrecked on the American coast, and only a handful of survivors reached the shore: "Some few of these unhappy wretches are gone upon my land to make a beginning," Byrd wrote to a friend; but they had lost most of their possessions.[27]

After this failure there was nothing else to do but solicit Scotch-Irish to come upon his property, though he personally did not much like those tough people who swarmed over the country and continually pushed on in search of more and better land; they would not be stable settlers, but if they paid their three pounds . . . He wrote to his friend John Bartram the botanist, who lived in Philadelphia, stressing the advantages of the Roanoke lands. But Quakers were unwilling to leave Pennsylvania and settle among those Virginians who "look perhaps more on a man's outside than his inside."[28] He tried a Mr. Campbell at Norfolk, who directed Scottish settlers to Carolina:

It is a pity your Argyle clan makes their first trip to Cape Fear, where both the climate and soil are worse than Roanoke. . . . Besides, in Carolina there is nothing but paper money, and that depending on a fund so precarious that the value is perpetually sinking. At Roanoke there is a healthy climate, a fruitful soil, with great plenty of fish and fowl, and that will be a great ease to newcomers.[29]

In September 1740 he wrote: "I expect the arrival of two hundred Highlanders with their Lairds, to whom I believe I shall sell a considerable tract of land upon Roanoke, which will enable me to balance all accounts both with the worthy magistrate and all the world besides."[30] But once more his hope was frustrated.

Yet he never lost heart, and continued to pay Perry several hundred pounds each year; but in 1740, he still owed a thousand pounds

William Byrd's *Natural History of Virginia*," *American Literature*, XXVIII [1956], 211–20.)

[26] Letter of July 2, 1737, Byrd Letterbook, 1736–1737, p. 33, V.H.S.

[27] Byrd to John Bartram, March 23, 1738/39, *WMCQ*, 2d ser., VI (1926), 313–14; see also Lloyd H. Williams, "The Tragic Shipwreck of the Protestant Switzers," *WMQ*, 3d ser., IX (1952), 539–42.

[28] *WMCQ*, 2d ser., VI (1926), 310.

[29] Byrd to Mr. Campbell, Nov. 3, 1739, *VMHB*, XXXVI (1928), 359.

[30] Byrd to Mr. Christopher Smith, Sept. 1740, Byrd Letterbook, 1739–1740, p. 33, V.H.S.

and was trying to borrow money to discharge his debt. Despite a bad tobacco crop in 1738,[31] his diary for 1739–41 expresses no concern: Byrd probably felt that at last he was reaching the end of his financial cares. His land hunger was so great that in those years he acquired about four times as much land as he already possessed. In 1735 he had obtained from the Virginia Assembly a grant of 105,000 acres on the south branch of the Roanoke, between the Dan and the North Carolina line, just below the confluence of the Hico and the Dan, about twenty-five miles east of the Land of Eden. This had been granted free of taxes for two years, on condition that he would settle "one family at least upon every one thousand acres." When he failed to do so because of the shipwreck of Jenner's Swiss colonists, he had to pay the ordinary taxes, which amounted to five hundred and twenty-five pounds. But he could not bring himself to give up such good lands, and he paid up the taxes by 1740, though they were not formally patented until April 1742.[32]

The international situation was deteriorating, as Byrd's entry in his diary for August 29, 1739 shows: "Tom Short brought word from town that we should have a war and that it was proclaimed in England." In fact, Admiral Edward Vernon was on his way to take the Spanish stronghold of Porto Bello on the Panama isthmus, but war was not actually declared till October. Byrd, like most Virginia planters, had a poor opinion of a ministry that was willing to be led by the pusillanimous directors of the South Sea Company, and that had "endured all the late insolences of the Spaniards so tamely"; Byrd's views on the subject are expressed quite clearly in his conversation with Spotswood related in *A Progress to the Mines*.[33] Like most English colonists, he resented the so-called "right of search" exercised by "guarda costas": under pretense of repressing illegal smuggling, they confiscated ships and cargoes on the flimsiest pretexts. He was alarmed at the damage caused to English trade and would have liked to see the Spaniards driven from North America, particularly from Florida. One the other hand, Spain saw her colonial commerce greatly reduced by the smuggling, which profited both British vessels and the population of Jamaica at the expense of the Spanish revenues. The day after he had heard the news of the War of

---

[31] Byrd to Sir Charles Wager, May 26, 1740, *VMHB*, XXXVII (1929), 103–4; Byrd to Mr. Lamport, Aug. 23, 1738, *ibid.*, IX (1901), 127.

[32] *Calendar of Virginia State Papers*, I, 223 (June 11, 1735); Byrd to Mr. Leaberger, Nov. 12, 1740, and Byrd to Mr. Tschiffeley, Nov. 15, 1740, Byrd Letterbook, 1740–1741, pp. 10–11, V.H.S.; *Executive Journals of Council*, V, 38 (Dec. 10, 1740), and "Byrd Title Book," *VMHB*, L (1942), 177–78.

[33] *Prose Works*, p. 364.

Jenkins' Ear, Byrd wrote to Walpole his opinion as to the policy to be pursued:

By reading over the history of England, I find we never make war at a less expense or with greater advantage than when we stand upon our own legs and trust altogether to our wooden walls. . . . A great superiority at sea will secure us from invasion and at the same time enable us to insult the enemy's coasts and intercept their fleets. . . . It is . . . the interest of Great Britain to decide all her disputes upon her own element, and even let the people on the continent fight their own battles.[34]

Yet Byrd soon forgot his own sound premises and, in a letter to the First Lord of the Admiralty, sketched a grand scheme for expelling the Spaniards from the New World.[35]

When the Cartagena expedition began, Governor William Gooch left the colony to serve as colonel and quartermaster general of the Virginia forces. Commissary James Blair, as the oldest member of the Council, replaced him as acting governor from October 1740 to July 1741. But Blair was then eighty-five years old, and almost completely deaf. "The country," wrote Byrd, "is a little dissatisfied with being governed by an ecclesiastic, and the rather because of his great age and infirmities." Blair could not sit on the Supreme Court: "This I am forced to perform in his stead, being next oars, while he now and then nods in the chair."[36] Byrd's pride may have been tinged with envy, though there is no evidence that he ever tried to hinder the commissary from becoming acting governor in Gooch's absence.

When Byrd finally succeeded to the presidency of the Council after Blair's death in 1743, it was little more than an honor: the function had often been his already. He had almost given up all hope of getting it officially. Anyway, he was now one of the most respected and influential members of the colony, and he lived peacefully at Westover, among his family. He had lost his eldest daughter Evelyn in 1737, but Wilhelmina had been married for a few years; and in 1742 his family had been twice allied to that of the proudest planter in Virginia, "King" Carter: Anne had become the second wife of Charles Carter, King Carter's third son, and Maria had married Charles's younger brother Landon.[37] Byrd had discharged all his debts and owned some 179,000 acres when he died on August 26,

---

[34] Byrd to Walpole, Aug. 20, 1739, *VMHB*, XXXVI (1928), 357–58. See also Basil Williams, *The Whig Supremacy, 1714–1760* (Oxford, 1939; rev. ed., 1962), pp. 207–9.

[35] Byrd to Sir Charles Wager, May 26, 1740, *VMHB*, XXXVII (1929), 103.

[36] Byrd to Francis Otway, Feb. 10, 1740/41, *ibid.*, XXXVII (1929), 30.

[37] See Appendix, p. 279 below, and Bassett, pp. 444 ff. (a few errors are corrected by Miss Woodfin in *Another Secret Diary*, p. 31).

1744. He was buried at Westover near his daughter Evelyn. On his monument in his garden was carved an epitaph which, after summing up his life, concluded:

> To all this were added a great elegance of taste and life,
> The well-bred gentleman and polite companion,
> The splendid economist and prudent father of a family,
> With the constant enemy of all exorbitant power,
> And hearty friend to the liberties of his country.

CHAPTER V

Byrd's Personality

"THE well-bred gentleman and polite companion": These words from Byrd's epitaph form a perfect epitome of what he tried to be all his life. As one of those "first gentlemen of Virginia" described by Professor Wright, he "thought of himself as the colonial equivalent of such noblemen as his friend the Earl of Orrery."[1] Although his father was of middle-class origin, he really belonged to the gentry. No reader of his should ever forget the influence of his education in England and his long stay in the mother country. Of the first fifty-two years of his life he spent more than thirty in Europe. During his years in England he moved in aristocratic circles. In a way he was never a complete colonial, but a Virginian in London and a Londoner in Virginia. After living for so long in the fashionable society on the fringes of the Court, he never lost touch with his London friends. Much of his time in Virginia was devoted to his correspondence with them.

One of the most outstanding traits of his character is his pride, which he noted in his fairly sincere self-portrait of "Inamorato L'Oiseaux": "His person was agreeable enough, though he had a certain cast of pride in his look, which clouded some of the grace of it."[2] This impression is borne out by the portraits that were painted of him, particularly that by Sir Godfrey Kneller in 1704.

By nature a kindly man and one who had, he said, "almost as many friends as he had acquaintance,"[3] Byrd nevertheless was conscious of his superiority and was never an equalitarian. A letter sent in 1729 to one of his business correspondents in England shows his aristocratic disdain for tradesmen of a certain kind:

You will herewith receive the invoice for my family, and [I] beg you will please to employ your interest with the tradesmen not to send all the refuse of their shops to Virginia. Desire them to keep them for the customers that never pay them. 'Tis hard we must take all the worst of their people and the worst of their goods too. But now shopkeepers have left off their

---

[1] *First Gentlemen*, p. 329.
[2] *Another Secret Diary*, p. 279 (1722 [?]; see p. 45).
[3] *Ibid.*

bands, their frugality, and their spouses must be maintained in splendor, 'tis very fit the sweat of our brows should help to support them in it. Luxury is bad enough amongst [peo]ple of quality, but when it gets among that order of men that [stand] behind counters, they must turn cheats and pickpockets to [get] it, and the Lord have mercy on those who are obliged to trust [to their] honesty.[4]

When Byrd criticized the social class from which his own father had come, it was mainly for their occasional failure to remember their station in life. But he felt the same contempt for people of importance when they demeaned themselves. In *A Progress to the Mines* he told the story of a planter's daughter who had married her uncle's overseer:

Had she run away with a gentleman or a pretty fellow, there might have been some excuse for her, though he were of inferior fortune; but to stoop to a dirty plebeian without any kind of merit is the lowest prostitution. I found the family justly enraged at it, and though I had more good nature than to join in her condemnation, yet I could devise no excuse for so senseless a prank as this young gentlewoman had played.[5]

Byrd was a proud man, and when he was awarded "the best pew in the church" on December 18, 1710, he could not forbear noting it in his diary; he was as mightily pleased as was Pepys upon receiving for the first time a letter addressed to "Samuel Pepys, *Esq.*" But he was so conscious of his superiority that he rarely felt the need to assert it. He knew how to keep his distance. He could share with cheerful optimism the hardships of the other members of the expedition on the Dividing Line; yet he always preserved the dignity befitting a leader. When a coarse jest was aimed at the chaplain he did not laugh. "I left the company in good time, taking as little pleasure in their low wit as in their low liquor, which was rum punch."[6] He could recount with a sense of amusement the weakness of some of his companions for Indian squaws or for country wenches,[7] but he could not, as one of their leaders, succumb to temptation and show before his men the partiality for women which his diary reveals abundantly.

He was no snob, however. While he always tried to abide by the code of the gentleman, he found it natural that common people should not, and observed them with a smile of kindly toleration. It was only to be expected that they should be ruled by their passions, by their senses. He was not above them himself, but he could keep himself in hand when among his inferiors. "His memory is in nothing so punctual

[4] To . . . , June 27, 1729, Byrd Letterbook, 1729, pp. 11–12, V.H.S.
[5] *Prose Works*, pp. 342–43.
[6] *Ibid.*, pp. 80–81.
[7] *Ibid.*, pp. 222, 224.

as in performing of promises. He thinks himself as firmly bound by his word as by his hand and seal, and would be as much ashamed to be put in mind of one as to be sued for the other," he said of himself.[8] But he was too sensible to trust to a gentleman's word in a court of justice, though he felt that a gentleman's word should be his bond. When, during the expedition on the Dividing Line, one of his fellow commissioners insisted that "a gentleman should be believed on his bare word without evidence and a poor man condemned without trial," Byrd did not accept this current opinion which, he dryly remarked, "agreed not at all with my notions of justice."[9]

Byrd's hospitality was typically Virginian: generous and free. He entertained his friends and neighbors, or chance visitors, with the same conviviality, even though he sometimes found it a burden because it encroached upon the time he used to devote to his reading. In 1710 he decided to be more chary of inviting people on Sundays after church so that his servants should not have too much work on the Lord's Day and might go to church. But this resolution was soon broken, and a month or two later he noted: "After church I invited abundance of gentlemen home where we had a good dinner."[10] Indeed it was almost impossible for a Virginia planter of some importance to avoid this.

Byrd, who consistently believed in the ideal gentleman described in so many courtesy books and based on Aristotle's doctrine of the golden mean, tried to observe the principles of temperance and moderation in all things. "Inamorato," he said, "is a great friend to temperance, because 'tis the security of all other virtues." He sometimes happened to drink too much in convivial company, particularly when he went to Williamsburg. The day when he was sworn a member of the Virginia Council, he admitted that he "drank too much French wine" at the President's. But on the whole such occasions were not very frequent: "He abhors all excesses of strong drink because it wholly removes those guards that can defend a man from doing and suffering harm."[11] He had a partiality for milk, which he judged to be good for the health, and once recommended a milk diet to his friend Major Nathaniel Harrison.[12] For a time he made a rule to eat of only one dish at each meal and carefully noted in his diary the rare

---

[8] *Another Secret Diary*, p. 280.

[9] *Prose Works*, p. 71. See the anecdote told by Wright in *First Gentlemen*, pp. 42–43, n. 7.

[10] *Secret Diary*, July 9, July 23, Aug. 20, Sept. 24, 1710; see also Oct. 1 and 15, 1710.

[11] *Another Secret Diary*, p. 280; *Secret Diary*, Sept. 12, 1709.

[12] *Secret Diary*, March 11 and 13, 1712.

occasions when he transgressed it. In those days of feasting and drinking excesses, he may be considered to have been fairly temperate.
All his life he was careful of his health. He took regular exercise, and
besides sports and games of various kinds, among which walking,
riding, and hunting were uppermost, he recorded almost every day
that he had "danced his dance." This appears in all his diaries between 1709 and 1741, and was certainly some sort of rhythmical
exercise.

The gentleman's regard for moderation also appears in Byrd's attitude to religion. "His religion," he wrote in his self-portrait, "is
more in substance than in form, and he is more forward to practice
virtue than profess it. . . . Of all cheats in the world he has least charity
for the holy cheat, that makes religion bawd for his interest and serve
the Devil in the livery of godliness."[13] He hated the violent excesses
of Puritanism and there was not the least touch of mysticism in him,
but he was sincerely religious nonetheless. Like most Virginia planters, he was an Anglican and believed that the Established Church was
essential to a civilized and polished society. He was a regular churchgoer, said his prayers devoutly even when out in the open,[14] and read
many books of divinity, of which he had about one hundred and fifty
in his library. Sermons were not always of sustained interest, but he
expressed sincere regret when he happened to sleep at church: "We
rode to Jamestown Church, where Mr. Commissary preached. When
church was done I gave ten shillings to the poor. Nothing could
hinder me from sleeping at church, though I took a great deal of
pains against it." When there was no service, he replaced it with
some edifying book: "We prepared to go to church, but the parson
did not come, notwithstanding good weather, so I read a sermon in
Dr. Tillotson at home." Archbishop John Tillotson, whom he may
have heard preach in London, was one of his favorite authors, whose
works, he said, affected him very much and even made him shed tears
of repentance.[15]

Religion was really linked with every important act of his life.
He entered every detail of his devotions, day after day, morning and
evening, though he sometimes had to confess: "I neglected to say my
prayers, for which God forgive me."[16] When his first boy, Parke,
was born on September 6, 1709, he entered these words in his diary:
"I returned God humble thanks for so great a blessing and recommended my young son to His divine protection." And when the child

---

[13] *Another Secret Diary*, p. 280.
[14] *Secret Diary*, May 4, 1709.
[15] *Ibid.*, April 24, April 3, 1709; May 7, 1710.
[16] *Ibid.*, pp. 30, 32, 45, 48, 52, 58, and so on.

died nine months later, Byrd's resignation was expressed with the same simple words, borrowed from Job and the prayer for the dead: "God gives and God takes away; blessed be the name of God. . . . My wife was much afflicted but I submitted to His judgment better, notwithstanding I was very sensible of my loss, but God's will be done."[17] He faced his business misfortunes in the same spirit; when a merchant ship that carried some of his goods was wrecked in a storm, he wrote: "My loss was very great in this ship where I had seven hogsheads of skins and sixty hogsheads of heavy tobacco. The Lord gives and the Lord has taken away, blessed be the name of the Lord." But we cannot help feeling that on such occasions his natural cheerfulness is involved as much as religious submission to the will of God, for he added: "However I ate a good supper of mutton and asparagus. Then we went to dance away sorrow. I had good health, good thoughts and good humor, notwithstanding my misfortune, thanks be to God Almighty."[18]

When the Dividing Line expedition set out, Byrd found it seemly that a chaplain should accompany the party. In his two relations of the journey, he sometimes allowed himself a mild joke about the parson, but he never made light of religion. When Sunday came, even in the wilderness, he dressed and attended the service, as was his duty since he was one of the leaders and was expected to set a good example. On November 3, 1728, they decided "to move a Sabbath Day's journey of three or four miles," after the chaplain had "put on his casuistical face and offered to take the sin upon himself"; the clear result was that they lost two days afterwards. Perhaps God intended it as a lesson to all of them. "Nevertheless," Byrd concluded, "by making this reflection, I would not be thought so rigid an observer of the Sabbath as to allow of no work at all to be done or journeys to be taken upon it. . . . On the contrary, I am for doing all acts of necessity, charity and self-preservation upon a Sunday as well as other days of the week."[19]

In 1709, at the age of thirty-five, Byrd wrote his religious creed, which he amended a few months later. It has been preserved to this day on the first leaf of the notebook containing his diary for that period.[20] There is indeed in his creed what Professor Wright called

[17] *Ibid.*, June 3, 1710. See John Evelyn on the death of his son Richard (*Diary*, Jan. 27, 1657/58).

[18] *Secret Diary*, May 6, 1709. See also July 10, 1709.

[19] *Prose Works*, pp. 65, 123, 284. See also *Secret Diary*, July 3, 1709: "I wrote a letter to England, notwithstanding it was Sunday."

[20] *Secret Diary*, May 30, 1709; Feb. 13, 1710. The text of the creed was published by Wright, *ibid.*, p. xxviii.

"a leaning towards the rationalism that characterized eighteenth-century intellectuals."[21] "I believe that God made Man . . . and inspired him with a reasonable soul to distinguish between good and evil; that the law of nature taught him to follow the good and avoid the evil because the good tends manifestly to his happiness and preservation, but the evil to his misery and destruction." Yet to call such rationalism "deistic"[22] is certainly going too far. Byrd, like many of his contemporaries, believed that "there can be nothing in Christian religion which contradicts the clear and evident principles of natural reason."[23] Deists believed that natural religion alone was sufficient, without need for any Christian revelation. Byrd on the contrary, following such divines as Dr. Samuel Clarke and Archbishop Tillotson, expressed his belief in the Fall of Man, in Christ's mission to redeem Man, and in a future Resurrection when every man shall be given his due. This is not deism, but the Christian rationalism of the Cambridge Platonists and the Latitudinarians.[24] When in December 1710 an epidemic killed some of his slaves, Byrd regarded this as a visitation of God for his own sins: "These poor people suffer for my sins; God forgive me all my offenses and restore them to their health if it be consistent with His Holy will."[25]

Byrd's sincere piety at times inclined him to severity in the discipline of his household, particularly in the early years at Westover, and he was quite conscious of the fact. "He sometimes allows too little to the frailty of mankind," he said of himself; "this makes him a little too severe upon faults which it would not be unjust to forgive. However he would not have transgressors punished to procure them pain, but reformation. It proceeds from his hatred of the fault, and not of the offender."[26] He occasionally lost his temper but soon regretted speaking too crossly to some of his servants.[27] He had to punish his slaves now and again, but he disliked whipping them, and the culprit often got off with a threat. When his first wife caused one of the slave girls to be burned with a hot iron, he was very angry and quarreled with her.[28] On the whole, Byrd was a kindly master by the standards of his time.

[21] Wright, *First Gentlemen*, p. 346.
[22] Wright, *Secret Diary*, p. xxi.
[23] Edward Synge, *A Gentleman's Religion* (London, 1710), p. 74.
[24] See in Byrd's Commonplace Book, pp. 98–99, an analysis of William Wollaston's *Religion of Nature Delineated* (1722), upholding the same theories as Samuel Clarke.
[25] *Secret Diary*, Dec. 29, 1710.
[26] *Another Secret Diary*, p. 281.
[27] E.g., *Secret Diary*, May 13, 1709, or *Another Secret Diary*, Dec. 24, 1739.
[28] *Secret Diary*, July 15, 1710.

Although Byrd was highly interested in all aspects of contemporary learning, there ran through his character a vein of credulity or superstition which might seem to contradict his rationalism. This virtuoso who liked to correct vulgar errors about the flora and fauna of his country believed that red-haired girls were inclined to lewdness and that no spiders could live in Ireland.[29] His attitude toward dreams is particularly significant. They were always noted down, and frequently interpreted. Sometimes they were fairly simple. "The Indian woman died this evening, according to a dream I had last night about her." "About eight nights ago I dreamed that several of my Negroes lay sick on the floor and one Indian among the rest, and now it came exactly to pass." But others required ingenious interpretations: "It is remarkable that Mrs. Burwell dreamed this night that she saw a person that with money scales weighed time and declared that there was no more than eighteen pennies worth of time to come, which seems to be a dream with some significance either concerning the world or a sick person." This Byrd was unable to guess, but the true explanation came a few days later: "Mr. Harrison . . . died about four o'clock this morning, which completed the eighteenth day of his sickness according to Mrs. Burwell's dream exactly." Once he thought that his dream announced his wife's death; another time he dreamed that he saw a flaming star in the air and concluded: "I fear this portends some judgment to this country or at least to myself."[30] Another similar vision was still more ominous:

Some night this month I dreamed that I saw a flaming sword in the sky and called some company to see it, but before they could come it was disappeared; and about a week after my wife and I were walking and we discovered in the clouds a shining cloud exactly in the shape of a dart and seemed to be over my plantation, but it soon disappeared likewise. Both these appearances seemed to foretell some misfortune to me which afterwards came to pass in the death of several of my Negroes after a very unusual manner.[31]

That "very unusual manner" seemed to give decisive proof of the supernatural character of the visions. After all, such things were of frequent occurrence in the Bible. And fortunately all bad dreams did not prove true: a sincere prayer might avert the misfortune. Sometimes a dream might even be a good omen, though one should be chary of feeling too hopeful! "This morning I dreamed that my

---

[29] *Prose Works*, pp. 348, 194; *Another Secret Diary*, p. 201.

[30] *Secret Diary*, April 8, 1709; July 21, March 31, and April 10, 1710; July 15, 1709; June 21, 1710.

[31] *Ibid.*, Dec. 31, 1710.

sloop was arrived from Barbados. God send it may prove true, as sometimes dreams have been true!"[32]

On board the ship that brought him back to Virginia in December 1719, he was wakened by a dream that his daughter Evelyn, who was still in London, had died of the smallpox, like her mother three years before; he felt melancholy all day. A week later the fact seemed to be confirmed: I "dreamed that my daughter appeared to me with one hand only, from whence I judged that one of my daughters is dead, and because it was the left hand that was left, I concluded that the youngest daughter is alive and the other dead, as I dreamed before." It was a long time before he could be undeceived, as news from England was so much slower in coming than his dreams. A few months before, during his courtship of Miss Smith, he had ventured to consult "a conjuror called Old Abram," but in spite of his biblical name the man's happy predictions did not come true.[33]

Superstition, however, is far less prominent than rationalism in Byrd's character, when he is compared with many of his contemporaries.[34] He was among those intellectuals of the early eighteenth century whose great problem was to reconcile reason and science with religion. This they could only do by playing down miracles and stressing the reasonable nature of Christian ethics. Byrd's uneasy interest in dreams, in the fantastic and the unexplained, is in some way a token of the sincerity of his religious belief.[35]

Another of his characteristics stands out most clearly in his diaries, because like Pepys he wrote only for himself: his susceptibility to women. "Never did the sun shine upon a swain who had more combustible matter in his constitution than the unfortunate Inamorato," he confessed in his self-portrait. "The struggle between . . . the King and the Parliament in England was never half so violent as the Civil War between this hero's principles and his inclinations." It must be admitted that it was too often a lost fight, though "his principles have been sometimes happily supported by the misadventures of his love." Byrd thought that "he lived more by the lively movement of his passions than by the cold and unromantic dictates of reason,"[36] but

[32] *Ibid.*, Jan. 5, 1710.

[33] *London Diary*, Dec. 29, 1719; Jan. 7, 1720; Feb. 10, April 4, May 1, 1718.

[34] See Addison on witchcraft (*The Spectator*, [London: Everyman's Library, 1950], no. 117). In 1681, in *Sadducismus Triumphatus*, Joseph Glanvill, one of the prominent members of the Royal Society, still considered that disbelief in witchcraft was a form of materialism. In England, the laws on witchcraft were not abolished until 1736.

[35] See the Bishop of Worcester's opinion quoted in *Secret Diary*, March 31, 1710.

[36] *Another Secret Diary*, pp. 276–77.

this requires some qualification, for his attitude to women varied according to their social status and to a certain code to which he adhered.

In the fashionable circles of London or of Virginia, "he often frequented the company of women, not so much to improve his mind as to polish his behavior. There is something in female conversation that softens the roughness, tames the wildness, and refines the indecency too common among the men. He laid it down as a maxim that without the ladies, a scholar is a pedant, a philosopher a cynic, all morality is morose, and all behavior either too formal or too licentious."[37] This indeed was a commonplace thought, which Otway had versified in *Venice Preserved*:

> O woman! lovely woman! nature made thee
> To temper man; we had been brutes without you.

His diary testifies this liking for the company of women of all ages, and many of his letters were addressed to female correspondents. Those he courted in the London society of the time he always addressed in the artificial style of French romance. He paid them the kind of elaborate compliments which were then considered the mark of a passionate and romantic lover, a cavalier falling in love at first sight with some bewitching beauty. And yet, whenever "Veramour" (as he called himself in these letters) felt the sting of passion, whether for "Facetia" or "Sabina," for "Charmante" or "Minionet," his attachment was controlled carefully enough. It did not last long after he had been rejected, and he soon started on another quest. He was conscious of what he called this "wavering in his resolutions" and had his own explanation for it: "In some frolics no state appeared so happy to him as matrimony; the convenience, the tenderness, the society of that condition made him resolve upon his own ruin, and set up for a wife. He fancied it too sullen, too splenetic to continue single, and too liable to the inconveniences that attend accidental and promiscuous gallantry." So for the sake of convenience "he would work himself violently in love with some nymph of good sense. . . . And when he was in love no man ever made so disengaging a figure. . . . He would look like a fool, and talk like a philosopher, when both his eyes and his tongue should have sparkled with wit and waggery. He would sigh as ruefully as if he sat over a dead friend and not a live mistress. No wonder this awkward conduct was without success." If he could not master his combustible heart, at least he managed to

[37] *Ibid.*, p. 281.

control the fire. When he worked himself violently in love with some beauty, she was always of a good family, and unattached: "He never interloped with another's wife or mistress, but dealt altogether where the trade was open and free for all adventurers."[38]

This rule, however, he obser.ed only in his dealings with women of his own circle, as *The London Diary* shows at least on one occasion. Byrd had won the favors of one whom he believed to be a gentle-woman. "I wrote a letter to Mrs. C–r–t–n–y to excuse my not meeting her because she was a married woman," he noted two days later. But he must soon have been undeceived about her quality, and his remorse vanished accordingly, for he met her again a few days later "and gave her a guinea," which evidently placed their relationship on quite a different footing.[39]

In *The Secret Diary*, Byrd's weakness for women does not appear too often. Once at Williamsburg he kissed a Mrs. Chiswell after a game "till she was angry," he said, "and my wife also was uneasy about it and cried as soon as the company was gone. I neglected to say my prayers, which I should not have done, because I ought to beg pardon for the lust I had for another man's wife." He sometimes stole a kiss from an inn servant or a Negro girl,[40] but he did not indulge in such amorous excesses as marked the period of *The London Diary*. While the forty-three-year-old widower pursued his courtship of Miss Smith, he often picked up some light women in the street, in St. James's Park, or in some bagnio of the town. For a time he kept a mistress, whom he finally dismissed for infidelity. He was not, however, without some pangs of conscience, and periodically tried to give up wenching. On one such occasion, his young cousin Daniel Horsemanden, a frequent companion in his gallant expeditions, walked home with him lest he should pick up a whore. And once he confessed: "Endeavoured to pick up a woman, but could not, thank God." Alas, when he could not trust God to help him, his good resolutions did not last long, and he had to content himself with asking the Lord to forgive him. In 1720, when he traveled back to Virginia, he took along with him a young maidservant who soon became his mistress. At the end of the same year, he "resolved to forbear Annie by God's grace" and fortified his decision by reading *The Whole Duty of Man*, which he said edified him very much. But this New Year's resolution failed again, and he was unable to give up Annie completely. Even after his second marriage, in his old age, he was often

---

[38] *Ibid.*, pp. 277–78, 280.
[39] *London Diary*, Jan. 28 to Feb. 8, 1719.
[40] *Secret Diary*, Nov. 2, 1709; April 21, 1710; Oct. 21, 1711.

tempted by the pretty face of some young maidservant in his own household and was very sorry to say that he had "played the fool with Sally" or with Marjorie.[41]

This man who was so fond of conversation in society, particularly in the company of women, also loved retirement, which, he said, is necessary to man at times, "that while he is acquainted with the world he may not be a stranger to himself." For this reason, he added, "he commonly reserved the morning to himself and bestowed the rest upon his business and his friends."[42] This leisure he usually devoted to reading, in order both to brush up his knowledge of the classics and to keep abreast of the times. In his conversation he liked to evoke memories of the writers, painters, and scientists he had known in London. During his "progress to the mines" in 1732, he enjoyed telling his companions an anecdote about *The Beggar's Opera*, which had been played in London only four years before; although he had not seen it, he owned the book and could make use of the gossip he had heard through his English friends.[43] Byrd's reading certainly aimed higher than mere social success of this kind, but it was not unpleasant all the same to be regarded as one familiar with the literary circles of the metropolis.

He collected not only books but also pictures and prints, and achieved a reputation as a connoisseur among his Virginian friends.[44] In London, he had taken drawing lessons in 1717–18 from Eleazar Albin, a teacher of water-color drawing.[45] In 1704, he had had his portrait painted by Sir Godfrey Kneller. It was probably in Kneller's studio that he became acquainted with Charles Bridges, a minor artist in the spirit of the Lely-Kneller tradition who soon after Byrd's remarriage in 1724 made a portrait of the second Mrs. Byrd.[46] When in the spring of 1735 Bridges came over to Virginia with an introduction to Lieutenant Governor William Gooch, Byrd was one of the first influential men who gave the painter occasion to "show the coun-

41 *London Diary*, June 16, Dec. 13, June 11, 1718; Dec. 25–31, 1720; *Another Secret Diary*, pp. 70, 93, 166, 168, etc.

42 *Another Secret Diary*, p. 281. In his Commonplace Book, p. 24, Byrd noted: "The nearest way to know other people well is to get intimately acquainted with ourselves."

43 *Prose Works*, pp. 345–46.

44 John Custis to Byrd, April 10, 1723, Custis Letter-Book 1717–1741, Library of Congress.

45 *London Diary*, Dec. 13 and 20, 1717; Jan. 6, 14, 17, 21, 28, 31, Feb. 4, 11, 14, March 4, 1718.

46 See Henry W. Foote, "Charles Bridges, 'Sergeant Painter of Virginia,' 1735–1740," *VMHB*, LX (1952), 3–55.

try his art." And in December 1735, Byrd recommended Bridges to Colonel Spotswood in the following words:

The person who has the honor to wait upon you with this letter is a man of a good family, but either from the frowns of Fortune or his own mismanagement, is obliged to seek his bread a little of the latest in a strange land. His name is Bridges, and his profession painting, and if you have any employment for him in that way he will be proud of obeying your command. He has drawn my children, and several others in this neighborhood; and though he has not the masterly hand of a Lely or a Kneller, yet had he lived so long ago as when places were given to the most deserving, he might have pretended to be the Sergeant Painter of Virginia.[47]

Another of Byrd's artistic friends was William Dering, who opened a dancing school in Williamsburg in 1737, but was also a musician and a painter. In 1740 and 1741 he often visited Byrd at Westover, entertaining his host by playing the French horn, while the planter would show him the collection of prints that he had bought in England years before.[48] Thus the master of Westover appears to have been one of the first patrons of the arts in Virginia, in an age when cultural matters were only just beginning to awaken some interest among the colonists.

Perhaps because of his very contradictions or incongruities, Byrd appears as a most human character, far more attractive than most New England diarists. He did not probe so deep into his own soul, but the portrait of his personality that emerges from his writings is in the end more true to life, with its light and shade, than the dull and flat images of more virtuous men. He was both proud of his position and conscious of his foibles. He admitted his tendency to laziness but could work hard in the management of his estate. Despite his instinctive egoism he never neglected his public duties. This pleasure-loving man, so prone to little vanities and to the weaknesses of the flesh, sincerely tried to amend himself, with the help of religion, ethics, or merely social conventions, though his will was not always equal to the situation. "Passionate and sorely sensible of injuries," he was not spiteful however: "If the sun go down upon his wrath, it will be sure to rise upon his reconciliation. An injury never

[47] *Ibid.*, IX (1902), 236–37. Colonel Spotswood must have followed Byrd's advice and commissioned Bridges to paint his portrait (see Foote, "Charles Bridges," p. 31).

[48] J. Hall Pleasant, "William Dering, a Mid-Eighteenth Century Williamsburg Portrait-Painter," *VMHB*, LX (1952), 56–63; *Another Secret Diary*, March 1 and July 31, 1741 (see also *London Diary*, March 7, April 12, Oct. 10, 1718, July 1, 1719).

festers or rankles upon his mind, but wastes itself in the first sally of indignation." This indeed is borne out by the numerous quarrels with his first wife, which rarely outlived the day and never endangered their marriage. It is no exaggeration to say, as he does, that "good nature was the constantest of his virtues," and that "he had as many friends as he had acquaintance."[49] His diary shows his constant desire to help his friends and neighbors, and his benevolence to "his people" on the plantations. "His good nature," he added, "is so universal as to extend to all brute creatures,"[50] and it is a fact that in winter when it snowed he "ordered drums of wheat to be thrown to the poor birds."[51]

A man of action who at times would have liked to pass for a man of letters, a man of the world who enjoyed the pleasures of life but unostentatiously followed the practices of his religion without experiencing the pangs of conscience of New England Puritans, Byrd reveals almost as fascinating a personality as Pepys. He gains much by a deeper acquaintance, and the discovery of his diaries has made it easier to approach his true self, to find the man under the uniform of the colonel, the dignity of the councillor, and the elegance of the writer. "Hardly anybody liked him that did not know him, and nobody hated him that did," he said of himself.[52] And without any regular practice of introspection, he knew himself well and judged himself honestly, like many brother diarists.

49 *Another Secret Diary*, p. 279.

50 *Ibid.*, p. 282.

51 *Ibid.*, Jan. 3, 1741. For the expression of his pity for animals, see also *Prose Works*, p. 299.

52 *Another Secret Diary*, p. 279.

PART TWO

The Man of Letters

An Indian scribble.

Byrd to Peter Collinson, July 18, 1736, about a letter of his own which Collinson had shown to Sir Charles Wager

Introduction

IN THE middle of the seventeenth century, John Selden commented in his *Table Talk*:

'Tis ridiculous for a Lord to print verses; 'tis well enough to make them to please himself, but to make them public is foolish. If a man in a private chamber twirls his bandstring or plays with a rush to please himself 'tis well enough, but if he should go into Fleet Street and set upon a stall and twirl his bandstring or play with a rush, then all the boys in the street would laugh at him.

Many of Byrd's contemporaries among the upper class still agreed with Selden's opinion. "If Byrd himself had an ambition to be a man of letters," said Professor Wright, "it was the well-bred and somewhat casual ambition affected by a gentleman."[1] Besides, a man of Byrd's varied and absorbing interests could not deliberately devote himself to a literary career. He never seriously attempted publication. When he carefully rewrote *The History of the Dividing Line*, it was evidently with some intention to publish it one day, but he was never quite satisfied with his work, and it remained unpublished till a century later, in 1841. From the rough journal he had kept in the woods, he had first prepared a narrative, *The Secret History of the Line*, which under fictitious names described the persons of the surveying expedition and the incidents that had befallen them. As many gentlemen had done before him, Byrd wrote chiefly for the entertainment of some of his English friends, among whom it circulated for a time. Peter Collinson, a London merchant who was also a naturalist and a member of the Royal Society, heard of it and begged the privilege of seeing a copy. But in his answer Byrd expressed his reluctance to show something that was not licked into shape like a bear cub: "I own it goes against me to deny you such a trifle, but I have one infirmity, never to venture anything unfinished out of my hands." He offered to send him the rough journal and added:

This is only the skeleton and groundwork of what I intend, which may some time or other come to be filled up with vessels and flesh, and have a

---

[1] *First Gentlemen*, p. 336.

decent skin drawn over all, to keep things tight in their places and prevent their looking frightful. I have the materials ready and want only leisure to put them together. I must only desire you not to suffer this journal to go out of your hands nor a copy of it, unless Sir Charles Wager should have a fancy to see it.[2]

Unfortunately, Byrd never did finish anything to his own satisfaction. He was too much of a perfectionist, as Professor Wright observed. But it should be added that he was then too busy trying to extinguish his debts. To another friend he wrote in 1737:

I am obliged to you for the compliments you are pleased to make to my poor performances. It is a sign you never saw them, that you judge so favorably. . . . It will sound like a joke when [I] tell you that I have not time to finish that work. But it is ve[ry sure] I have not, for I am always engaged in some project for improving our infant colony. The present scheme is to found a city at the falls of James River, and plant a colony of Switzers on my land upon Roanoke.[3]

Yet in the same year he told Collinson that he expected to finish the *History* during the following winter and asked his friends to make arrangements for some cuts to illustrate the description of some of the wild animals in Virginia.[4] So he did intend to have the book printed one day, and he must have had the same intention when he wrote out *A Journey to the Land of Eden* and *A Progress to the Mines*. He also copied out in the North Carolina notebooks[5] a number of letters addressed to various persons under fictitious names, and some character sketches drawn in the manner of the seventeenth century. Some of the letters he kept for personal, sentimental reasons, but many of these pieces were literary exercises written for the sake of the composition. They were reserved for private circulation among friends, if not for publication. In his diary, he sometimes noted reading old letters at Westover or reading aloud to the company some of his own writings. The only piece published in his lifetime was the anonymous pamphlet *A Discourse Concerning the Plague*.

With his aristocratic indifference to publication, his proud reluctance to print something that was not finished to his taste, and his numerous other occupations which came before writing, Byrd must be considered essentially an amateur. He appears one even in his sense of humor, which is partly the result of his detachment. It would be ungentlemanly to become impassioned over his own writings, or for

[2] Byrd to Collinson, July 18, 1736, *VMHB*, XXXVI (1928), 355.

[3] Byrd to Mark Catesby, July 1737, Byrd Letterbook 1736–1737, p. 31, V.H.S.

[4] Byrd to Collinson, July 5, 1737, *ibid.*, p. 35.

[5] Published by Maude Woodfin in *Another Secret Diary*.

that matter to take anything too seriously, even religion. Only look at those passionate Puritans of New England who were professedly such godly men . . . though some of them sold their poisonous contraband rum up and down the coast! Byrd's humor generally comes from his indulgent awareness of a discrepancy, a disparity between the ideal and the real, between what men profess and what they practise.

He probably kept his diary during the greater part of his life, though only portions of it have come down to us. Except for his letters and character sketches, everything he wrote was in journal form. It was most natural to him and allowed him the greatest freedom in the expression of his own ideas and personality. His writings are not devoid of variety: they show him by turns as a virtuoso and as a cavalier, but always the diarist predominates—a man of wide experience, keen insight, and urbane wit, portraying his own life as well as the colonial society of his time.

CHAPTER VI

Virtuoso

B YRD was only twenty-two when he was elected to the Royal Society on April 29, 1696, probably through the influence of Sir Robert Southwell, who was then president. In the next year, the young man was elected to the Council of the Society; another new member was Isaac Newton. Byrd was reelected to the Council in 1700 and 1702.

Byrd was proud of his membership, which certainly was of much consequence in his later intellectual pursuits; he always liked to look upon himself as a man of science, constantly investigating botanical or medicinal subjects. He contributed only one paper to the *Transactions* of the Society, in the year after his election. It was a short description of an albino Negro: "An Account of a Negro Boy that is Dappled in Several Places of his Body with White Spots."[1] But he showed a never-failing interest in the activities of the Society. He received and kept in his library all the published volumes of its *Philosophical Transactions* from 1669 to 1719,[2] and three years before his death he wrote to Sir Hans Sloane, then President of the Royal Society, to complain that his name had been left out of the published list of members: "I take it a little unkindly, Sir, that my name is left out of the yearly list of the Royal Society, of which I have the honor to be one of its ancientest members. I suppose my long absence has made your secretaries rank me in the number of the dead, but pray let them know I am alive and by the help of ginseng hope to survive some years longer."[3]

When the news of his father's death hurried him back to Virginia, Byrd wrote from Westover to Sir Hans, who was then Secretary of

---

[1] *Philosophical Transactions of the Royal Society*, XIX (Dec. 1697), 781, reprinted in *WMQ*, 3d ser. VI (1949), 285–86. On Nov. 13, 1710, Byrd mentioned in his diary that he had seen another "white Negro" from Nigeria. On the whole subject, see Maude Woodfin, "William Byrd and the Royal Society," *VMHB*, XL (1932), 23–34, 111–23.

[2] See Bassett, p. 416.

[3] Byrd to Sloane, April 10, 1741, "Letters of William Byrd II and Sir Hans Sloane Relative to Plants and Minerals in Virginia," *WMCQ*, 2d ser., I (1921), 200. On ginseng, the medicinal root, see below, pp. 84–85.

the Society, to explain that his numerous occupations had not permitted him to make any observations on the country. He went on to regret the absence of real scientists in Virginia; there were not even real doctors: "They are generally discarded surgeons of ships who know nothing above the very common remedies." But the country was not so unhealthy as some ignorant writers pretended, and if cases of ague were so common, they were mostly due to the fact that Virginians ate too much fruit. As for abrupt changes of temperature which caused so many colds, he had tried to adapt his body to them by going for a plunge in the river twice a week all through the previous winter. With his letter he sent a small box containing rattlesnake root, a remedy used by the Indians and by English traders against the bite of snakes; it also contained samples of "hypoquecuana," or ipecac, and of another root used for "dry gripes and wind colic," on which he wanted expert opinion. And he concluded:

When I have more time, I hope to be able to do more service. In the meantime do me the justice to believe that nobody has better inclinations to promote natural knowledge than myself, and if you will direct me after what manner I may be most serviceable to the society and to the commonwealth of learning, I will readily obey you. If you have anything curious there I should be obliged to you if you will please to favor me with a knowledge of it.[4]

Thus Byrd's curiosity appears to have been as strong as his zeal.

He wrote again to Sir Hans two years later, saying that he had tried to grow "hippecoacanna" in his own garden, but without success. He sent along some pokeberries, which might be used as a dye if the right way of preparing it could be found: "Therefore, I beg of you to tell me the best way to fix dyes, of which we are very ignorant."[5] He deplored the gaps in his own scientific education which prevented him from being as useful as he desired: "I wish I were acquainted with the ways of trying the virtues of plants, of which we have here a surprising variety, but our ignorance makes them of no use to us. . . . I have strong inclinations to promote natural history, and to do service to the Society: I wish I were qualified to do it with effect, but my best endeavors you may always depend upon." He added samples of a poisonous weed, and of another which killed worms better than any he knew. He recounted how he had used rattlesnake root as a cure for diarrhea, taken like a tonic, in a little canary. But he had to confess that he owed this illness to his wintry

[4] Byrd to Sloane, April 20, 1706, *ibid.*, p. 189.

[5] *Phytolacca americana*, or Virginia poke, is now grown all over Europe and serves to color wine.

plunges in the river and had thought it wiser to discontinue them.[6]

Another letter in June 1710 explained how difficult it had been to ship Sir Hans thirty pounds of "hippecoacanna" the year before. He had found some trouble in getting it in such quantity, and the customs duties were high. Could not Sir Hans manage to get it custom free? Byrd, however, contemplated sending greater supplies of this medicine to London for a profit, if his correspondent thought there was a market for it. And he added once more: "I wish you would please to give yourself the trouble to let me know how the Royal Society thrives, and to assure them that I shall always be ready to do them what service I can in this country. . . . I beg of you to send me your account of Jamaica, and if there be any other good voyage published since I left England, or any other curious piece, to send it me and pay yourself out of the profits of the cargo."[7]

In 1712 Byrd dissected a muskrat which one of his overseers had brought him, "and got out the musk which is in two glands not far from the anus"; and on another occasion he went with Mark Catesby, the naturalist, into the neighboring swamp to see the nest of a hummingbird "with one young and one egg in it."[8]

Byrd's diary shows that when he was back in England after 1715, his interest in the Society never flagged. He dined at Pontack's with the other members before going to Crane Court, where they held their meetings.[9] Sir Isaac Newton was then president; he had been reelected every year since 1703 and was to hold the post until his death in 1727, when Sir Hans Sloane succeeded him. On November 20, 1718, Byrd was proud to propose his friend Sir Wilfred Lawson to be a member. To his great satisfaction, Lawson was duly elected on December 11 and received into the Society about a month later. Byrd attended the meetings very regularly, though he was sometimes disappointed in them. "We had nothing but trifles," he noted on February 5, 1719. But on March 5 he was greatly interested by "several curious things in anatomy," and on April 2 they had "several letters about the ball of fire that was seen in the sky on the nineteenth of last month." In the summer of 1719, when he interrupted his stay at Tunbridge Wells and came back to London for a few days to arrange his newly furnished chambers, he found some time to go "to

6 Byrd to Sloane, Sept. 10, 1708, *WMCQ*, 2d ser., I, 190.

7 Byrd to Sloane, June 10, 1710, *ibid.*, pp. 193–94.

8 Secret Diary, Feb. 27, May 24, 1712. Catesby was the author of *The Natural History of Carolina, Florida and the Bahama Island*s (1731); he resided from 1712 to 1719 with his brother-in-law, Dr. William Cocke, Secretary of Virginia.

9 *London Diary*, Jan. 9, Oct. 30, 1718.

Crane Court to see the great snake twenty-four feet long and twenty inches round from the East Indies."[10]

During the long periods he spent in England, Byrd was acquainted with the London virtuosi, and when he lived in Virginia he corresponded with many of them. Some were the most distinguished scientists of the time; others were just gentlemen who dabbled in science —ever since Charles II's reign it had been fashionable for gentlemen to play at being scientists of some kind. Besides Sir Robert Southwell and his friend Sir Hans Sloane, Byrd met at Crane Court many of the greatest scientific minds of the time. Byrd's great friend Charles Boyle, later third Earl of Orrery, had been known in his college days as the youthful defender of the Ancients in a famous controversy with Dr. Bentley on the authenticity of the Phalaris letters; his father was the great physicist and chemist Robert Boyle, one of the founders of the Royal Society just after the Restoration, whose *Physical Experiments* and other works were in Byrd's library. Sir John Percival, later the first Lord Egmont, was then known for little else than for being Sir Robert Southwell's nephew.[11] But the great Sir Isaac Newton presided over the meetings of the Society during much of Byrd's stay in England, and his works were also in the library at Westover. Another acquaintance of Byrd's was Sir Samuel Garth, the popular physician, who was the model for Byrd's portrait of "Dr. Glysterio," "an eminent physician at the coffee-house, a poet at the college, a sloven at Court, a beau in the country, and a madman everywhere." This "notorious skimmer of the sciences" had gained a large practice "by being much a better poet than a physician."[12] His mock-heroic poem *The Dispensary*, describing a battle between physicians and apothecaries, was well known; Byrd himself, in the entry of his diary for April 3, 1711, noted that he "read in *The Dispensary* to the ladies till night." Another leading physician in London was Dr. John Radcliffe, who patronized the waters of Tunbridge Wells against those of Bath.[13] Diet was Dr. George Cheyne's particular hobby, and Byrd followed some of his precepts on the subject while he wrote his *Secret Diary*.[14] Both Radcliffe's *Dispensary* and Cheyne's *Essay of*

[10] *Ibid.*, July 28, 1719.

[11] In 1732 he was one of the group that founded Georgia under the leadership of James Oglethorpe.

[12] *Another Secret Diary*, pp. 209–11.

[13] See a character sketch of Dr. Radcliffe in Byrd's Commonplace Book, pp. 61–62.

[14] In his Commonplace Book, Byrd entered "some rules for preserving health," and among them is the one he followed at the time of his *Secret Diary* (1709

Health and Long Life had their place in the Westover library, together with about one hundred and fifty other medical books, ancient and modern, from Hippocrates' *Aphorismi* to Harvey's and Sydenham's works.

Byrd was always greatly interested in natural history, and his last version of *The History of the Dividing Line* contains many descriptions of the wild animals that were then to be encountered in Virginia. These descriptions are concerned not only with the animals' outward appearance but also with their habits, their attitude to man or to other living creatures, and their possible usefulness to mankind. This he certainly looked upon as one of the most instructive parts of his work.

Byrd's interest in the natural world was essentially utilitarian, a characteristic which is emphasized by a comparison of his book with his brother-in-law's. Robert Beverley, who lacked Byrd's embryonic training in scientific matters and was quite conscious of this shortcoming,[15] evinced the same eager curiosity, but his deep love of nature roused him at times to real flights of poetry which are absent from Byrd's pages. One of the best examples is Beverley's description of a Virginia garden:

All things thrive in it most surprisingly. You can't walk by a bed of flowers but besides the entertainment of their beauty your eyes will be saluted with the charming colors of the hummingbird, which revels among the flowers and licks off the dew and honey from their tender leaves on which it only feeds. Its size is not half so large as an English wren, and its color is a glorious shining mixture of scarlet, green, and gold. . . . Upon these flowers [honeysuckle] I have seen ten or a dozen of these beautiful creatures together, which sported about me so familiarly that with their little wings they often fanned my face.[16]

Byrd, on the other hand, was no Thoreau, and his descriptions, though more precise and complete, are more sober. One of the rivers in the path of the surveying expedition was particularly difficult to cross because of beavers:

Those industrious animals had dammed up the water so high that we had much ado to get over. 'Tis hardly credible how much work of this kind they will do in the space of one night. They bite young saplings into proper lengths with their foreteeth, which are exceedingly strong and sharp, and afterwards drag them to the place where they intend to stop the water.

---

onwards): "Eat of no more than one thing at one time, and let your drink be only water, or at best but wine and water" (p. 46).

[15] Beverley deplored his "want of skill in the works of nature," *History*, p. 10.

[16] *Ibid.*, pp. 298–99.

Then they know how to join timber and earth together with so much skill that their work is able to resist the most violent flood that can happen. In this they are qualified to instruct their betters, it being certain their dams will stand firm when the strongest that are made by men will be carried down the stream.[17]

After explaining how to catch "these sagacious animals," Byrd left the subject, for he did not want such digressions to be too long. But on the way back, six weeks later, he observed: "The beavers had dammed up the water much higher than we found it at our going up, so that we were obliged to lay a bridge over a part that was shallower than the rest, to facilitate our passage."[18] And he went on to tell how the beavers make their houses with several entrances, and do their work in gangs in the dead of night. He exploded the story of their biting off their testicles when they are pursued, a story taken on trust by Pliny, and he explained that their strong smell comes from a pair of glands placed near the testicles. Finally he commented on the poor taste of their flesh and on the quality of their beautiful fur, warm but light and soft.

This is but one example of the thorough descriptions that Byrd inserted in the journal of the expedition. He enlarged upon wild turkeys, their weight, heavy flight, and fast running, and the use the Indians made of their spurs to sharpen arrows.[19] Bears seemed to be one of his favorite subjects; details about them are scattered in various passages, because the hunters of the party often killed one to provide their fellow travelers with meat, each time giving the writer an opportunity to add a few touches to his picture of the animal. Elsewhere Byrd told of panthers and wildcats, elks and buffaloes, cranes and wild pigeons, raccoons and squirrels, and Carolinian alligators, all of which he described as carefully as possible.

As another sample of such specific portraits, here is the opossum:

In the evening one of the men knocked down an opossum, which is a harmless little beast that will seldom go out of your way, and if you take hold of it will only grin and hardly ever bite. The flesh was well tasted and tender, approaching nearest to pig, which it also resembled in bigness.[20] The color of its fur was a goose gray, with a swine's snout, and a tail like a rat, but at least a foot long. By twisting this tail about the arm of a tree, it

[17] *Prose Works*, pp. 233–34.

[18] *Ibid.*, p. 304.

[19] *Ibid.*, p. 226.

[20] See William Strachey's definition in the short dictionary of the Indian language that he appended to *The Historie of Travell into Virginia Britania, 1612* (ed. Louis B. Wright and Virginia Freund [London, 1953], p. 175): "**Aposoum:** a beast in bigness of a pig and in taste alike."

will hang with all its weight and swing to anything it wants to take hold of. It has five claws on the forefeet of equal length, but the hinder feet have only four claws and a sort of thumb standing off at a proper distance. Their feet, being thus formed, qualify them for climbing up trees to catch little birds, which they are very fond of. But the greatest particularity of this creature, and which distinguishes it from most others that we are acquainted with, is the false belly of the female, into which her young retreat in time of danger. She can draw the slit, which is the inlet into this pouch, so close that you must look narrowly to find it, especially if she happen to be a virgin. Within the false belly may be seen seven or eight teats, on which the young ones grow from their first formation till they are big enough to fall off like ripe fruit from a tree. This is so odd a method of generation that I should not have believed it without the testimony of mine own eyes. . . . I could hardly persuade myself to publish a thing so contrary to the course that nature takes in the production of other animals, unless it were a matter commonly believed in all countries where that creature is produced and has been often observed by persons of undoubted credit and understanding.[21]

Plants engaged Byrd's attention as much as animals. He was particularly interested in botany in so far as he might discover some colonial plants which could serve as substitutes for others more common in Europe. Thus olive trees could not stand Virginia winters, but they could be replaced by sesames, which yield sweet and wholesome oil: "This would grow very kindly here and has already been planted with good success in North Carolina by way of experiment."[22] Very good ale could be made from Indian corn. A brief description of the sugar tree in *The Secret History* is expanded in the later version.[23] As for textiles, both hemp and flax could be grown in the colony, but the former, however good, was not profitable, because labor and freight made it too expensive.[24] Another plant, an evergreen with pale yellow flowers, which he called silk grass, had leaves that the Indians twisted into a very strong thread: "As this species of silk grass is much stronger than hemp, I make no doubt but sailcloth and cordage might be made of it with considerable improvement."[25] Byrd was always on

---

[21] *Prose Works*, pp. 276–77. See Robert Beverley, p. 154, and John Lawson, *New Voyage*, p. 127, for other similar, though shorter, descriptions of the opossum.

[22] *Prose Works*, p. 291.

[23] *Ibid.*, pp. 104, 235–36. See also Byrd's letter to an unknown correspondent, June 25, 1729, Byrd Letterbook 1729, p. 29, V.H.S. (published under wrong name and date in *VMHB*, XXXVI [1928], 117).

[24] *Prose Works*, pp. 349, 363.

[25] *Ibid.*, p. 300. Various fiber-bearing grasses seem to have been designated by

the lookout for such plants as might be turned to advantage by the colonists.

Botany and medicine are closely allied. Besides sending plants to Sir Hans Sloane for study by the greatest botanists of England and collecting seeds for the Bishop of London, Byrd gathered herbs for remedies. Even in England there was a belief in the efficacy of American herbs and a faith in strange Indian or Negro recipes. In 1729 a Negro slave was freed by the Virginia Council as a reward for his revelation of medical secrets.[26] Byrd shared this interest in native remedies, which still lingers in some backward areas even today. He often experimented with those that Indian traders had learned from the natives. In *The History of the Dividing Line* he described some colonial plants and their uses, particularly their medicinal virtues. There was the rattlesnake root mentioned in the letters to Sir Hans Sloane: "The root is in shape not unlike the rattle of that serpent and is a strong antidote against the bite of it. It is very bitter and where it meets with any poison works by violent sweats, but where it meets with none has no sensible operation but that of putting the spirits into a great hurry and so of promoting perspiration." Rattlesnakes disliked this plant so much that they could be handled safely by someone who had smeared his hands with its juice: "Thus much I can say on my own experience: that once in July, when these snakes are in their greatest vigor, I besmeared a dog's nose with the powder of this root and made him trample on a large snake several times, which, however, was so far from biting him that it perfectly sickened at the dog's approach and turned its head from him with the utmost aversion."[27] Years later, when John Tennent, a Williamsburg doctor, published an *Essay on the Pleurisy* which William Parks the printer advertised in his *Virginia Gazette*,[28] Byrd spread the news among his English friends of the Royal Society that the rattlesnake root had been found to cure pleurisy and gout; and when the Virginia doctor

---

the name of silk grass from Strachey to Byrd. For early attempts by settlers to start a textile industry, see Charles E. Hatch, "Mulberry Trees and Silk Worms: Sericulture in Early Virginia," *VMHB*, LXV (1957), 3–61.

[26] *Secret Diary*, Oct. 14, 1710; *VMHB*, XXXIV (1926), 103–4. On colonial medicine, see Wyndham B. Blanton, *Medicine in Virginia in the Seventeenth Century* (Richmond, 1930), and *Medicine in Virginia in the Eighteenth Century* (Richmond, 1931).

[27] *Prose Works*, pp. 226–27. Byrd gives an example of the root's efficacy in *Secret Diary*, Sept. 23, 1712. On the scientific identification of the plant, see a 1687 letter of John Clayton to Dr. Nehemiah Grew, *Clayton*, pp. 28, 31.

[28] In the *Virginia Gazette*, Oct. 1–8, 1736, Parks published a letter of John Tennent who claimed to have cured all but one of thirty-three patients.

decided to go to London, Byrd gave him a letter of introduction to Sir Hans Sloane.[29]

Another interesting plant was that "ipocoacanna" which he had sent to Sir Hans and "which in this part of the world is called Indian Physic." A minute description of ipecac follows:

This has several stalks growing up from the same root about a foot high, bearing a leaf resembling that of a strawberry. It is not so strong as that from Brazil but has the same happy effects if taken in somewhat a larger dose. It is an excellent vomit and generally cures intermitting fevers and bloody fluxes at once or twice taking. There is abundance of it in the upper part of the country, where it delights most in a stony soil intermixed with black mold.[30]

About the Peruvian bark, the bark of the cinchona tree, Byrd had little to say, for "this popish medicine" had long been known in Europe under the name of Jesuits' bark. He only remarked in a letter that its taste was as bitter as its virtue was great: we "know not whether we should curse the Jesuits for filling our mouth with so bad a taste, or bless them for discovering so good a medicine."[31] In his diary he often mentioned "taking the bark" against fevers.

As early as December 1710, Byrd was among the first in America to speak of ginseng, which was in high esteem in China.[32] In *The History of the Dividing Line* he mentioned that during the expedition he used to chew a root of ginseng while he walked along, to prevent fatigue; and after explaining in what parts of the world it can be found, he sang its virtues, which were those of a panacea:

It gives an uncommon warmth and vigor to the blood and frisks the spirits beyond any other cordial. It cheers the heart even of a man that has a bad wife, and makes him look down with great composure on the crosses of the world. It promotes insensible perspiration, dissolves all phlegmatic and viscous humors, that are apt to obstruct the narrow channels of the nerves. It helps the memory, and would quicken even Helvetian dullness. 'Tis

[29] Byrd to Mark Catesby, July 1737; to Lord Egmont, July 2, 1737; to Peter Collinson, July 5, 1737, Byrd Letterbook, 1736–1737, pp. 31, 33, 36, V.H.S.; Byrd to Sloane, May 31, 1737, *WMCQ*, 2d ser., I (1921), 195.

[30] *Prose Works*, p. 229. The "ipecuana" of the *Secret Diary*, Aug. 6, 1711, is certainly the same plant. In 1672, Byrd's son-in-law Charles Carter was still trying to find a market for it in England: "We have also a species of the Ipeacuacana growing wild in our woods which when cultivated is equally strong and efficatious as that used in Britain" (letter to Peter Wylche, April 10, 1762, quoted by Robert L. Hilldrup, "A Campaign to Promote the Prosperity of Colonial Virginia," *VMHB*, LXVII [1959], 418).

[31] *Prose Works*, p. 340; Byrd to Mrs. Otway, Oct. 2, 1735, *VMHB*, IX (1901), 123–24.

[32] *Secret Diary*, Dec. 23, 1710.

friendly to the lungs much more than scolding itself. It comforts the stomach and strengthens the bowels, preventing all colics and fluxes. In one word, it will make a man live a great while, and very well while he does live. And what is more, it will even make old age amiable, by rendering it lively, cheerful and good-humored.[33]

When he visited Colonel Spotswood in 1732, he was delighted to find about twenty roots of "this king of plants," and "carried home his treasure with as much joy as if every root had been a graft of the Tree of Life." In 1735, as his brother-in-law Major Francis Otway had been ill for some time, he asked rhetorically: "Does anything affect your head, your stomach, or your liver, or does your blood circulate too sluggishly? Do your spirits run low or flutter about your heart? If you have any of these complaints pray try what ginseng, that plant of life, can do for you." There is nothing very scientific here, and it reads rather like the worst type of patent medicine advertisement. Byrd was hardly more sober when he confided to the President of the Royal Society his conviction that "ever since the Tree of Life has been so strongly guarded the Earth has never produced any vegetable so friendly to men as ginseng." He praised "the cordial quality of the ginseng": "What I recommend it for is to cheer the animal spirits and feed the flame of life."[34] He was carried away by his enthusiasm; but after all, medicine was still full of fads and fancies when Byrd had long been dead.

Despite such exaggerations, which were not uncommon, Byrd was held to be a good amateur doctor, and neighbors often sent to him for advice and drugs: "In the evening," he wrote on February 13, 1709, "I took a walk and met Dick Cocke's servant who in the absence of the doctor sent to me for two or three purgatives. I sent him some blackroot sufficient for three doses but refused to send him any laudanum because I think it is bad for the gripes." Once when he had a long bout of malaria, he kept a fairly good clinical record of his symptoms and treatment.[35] In the latter he did not always agree with the doctor, but his illness did not affect his sense of humor:

In the afternoon [he noted on August 8, 1711], I continued very easy till about four o'clock, and then I had a little shiver which was presently suc-

---

[33] *Prose Works*, p. 292.

[34] *Ibid.*, p. 361; Byrd to Major Otway, Oct. 6, 1735, *VMHB*, IX (1901), 121; Byrd to Sir Hans Sloane, Aug. 20, 1738, April 10, 1741, *WMCQ*, 2d ser., I (1921), 197, 199. Having once sent ginseng to Sir Robert Walpole, Byrd felt almost offended that Walpole gave it all to Sir Hans Sloane: "An Emperor of China might have thought it worth his acceptance" (Byrd to Peter Collinson, July 5, 1737, Byrd Letterbook, 1736–1737, p. 36, V.H.S.).

[35] *Secret Diary*, Aug. 5–19, 1711.

ceeded with a moderate fever. About five o'clock came the doctor who expected to find me very ill. However he pronounced me worse than I thought myself and began to recommend the bark to me, which I refused to take because I thought I should get well without it. In the evening my sister Custis came because she heard I was dangerously ill, and when she came the doctor and the three women made such a hubbub and noise that I retired upstairs and told the doctor the bark was a fit remedy for him to prescribe because it made people deaf. I slept about half the night, thank God Almighty.

In fact Byrd probably knew more about medicine than many doctors of his time in Virginia, and even in England. But he had read so much in ancient authors as well as in the works of contemporary scientists that he often accepted their views without much discrimination. He accounted "a ridiculous superstition" the refusal to kill a tarantula for fear the people who had been bitten by it might never recover completely; but he believed in the power of music to cure the bite of that villainous insect.[36] Not so very long before, Elias Ashmole, one of the best-known representatives of what Douglas Bush has called "this often murky penumbra of science," hung three spiders above his head and was very pleased to find that they had driven his ague away.[37] Such credulity was still far from uncommon at the time even among people who passed for adepts in science. In its early years, the Royal Society itself had been most seriously interested in the tarantula and in the popular belief attached to it. A certain ailment, which began with a red spot resembling the sting of an insect and developed into something similar to St. Vitus's dance, was believed to be due to the bite of the tarantula; and the cure was said to be ensured when the diseased person danced to the accompaniment of a certain kind of music. The question was brought to the attention of the Society by Dr. Martin Lister late in 1671. Inquiries seem to have followed, particularly in Italy where the disease and its wonderful cure were most frequently reported, for a few months later the *Philosophical Transactions* for May 20, 1672, contained an extract from a letter by Dr. Thomas Cornelio, "a Neapolitan Philosopher and Physician," who gave the results of his investigations: he mentioned one sufferer who believed himself to have been bitten by a tarantula but died in great pain in spite of the musical remedy. The Italian correspondent of the Royal Society concluded that the whole thing was "a fable" which had grown out of "vulgar prejudice." These numbers of the *Philosophical Transac-*

---

36 *Prose Works*, pp. 297–98.
37 Ashmole, *Diary*, April 11, 1681, ed. R. T. Gunther (Oxford, 1927), p. 116.

tions were in Byrd's library and certainly gave him part of his information on the tarantula.[38] Nevertheless, he was still inclined to believe in "the wonderful effects of music" to expel "this whimsical disorder." Indeed many virtuosi were, as Samuel Butler said in his satirical poem "The Elephant in the Moon," men

> who greedily pursue
> Things wonderful, instead of true;

they were collectors of scientific curiosities more often than real students of nature, and sometimes their curiosity was greater than their science.

In *A Discourse Concerning the Plague*, Byrd was led to set almost on the same plane details taken from the Bible, from Homer, and from modern observation. Even a virtuoso and a scientist could hardly forbear stating first what the Bible had to say on his subject. It would have been dangerous for science to neglect the religious view in any such matter. Besides, most of the original members of the Royal Society had been Puritans, and a Puritan tinge remained for a long time a characteristic of the Society. After briefly and somewhat perfunctorily fulfilling his duty in four pages, however, Byrd went on: "Having thus far acted the part of a divine and a Christian, I will now beg leave to put on the different characters of a physician and a naturalist. I will endeavor, out of the most celebrated authors, to describe this destructive disease, its most frequent causes and symptoms, and after all, conclude with some proper preservatives, both public and private, against it."[39]

He had actually read a large number of books on the subject by the greatest physicians of the time; these works were in his own library at Westover. He repeated Dr. Jerome Cardan's observation that the plague appears in various forms, gave a definition of the most common variety in Europe from Dr. Thomas Willis, and enumerated its symptoms from Dr. Thomas Sydenham. This does not mean that he accepted all the arguments of these learned authors: "Dr. Sydenham is very circumstantial and exact in describing the plague, with its progress, symptoms and cure; but says hardly anything of the ways of preventing this great evil."[40] Dr. Willis, on the other hand, mentioned various methods to prevent it, but "he seems somewhat superstitious in the belief of the extraordinary power of amulets; not

---

[38] *Philosophical Transactions*, VI (Nov. 20, 1671), 3002. *Ibid.*, VII, (May 20, 1672), 4066–67. For the existence of these volumes in Byrd's library, see Bassett, p. 416.

[39] *Another Secret Diary*, p. 421.

[40] *Ibid.*, p. 433.

from the animating hopes they fill the patient withal, but from the effluvia and natural force of the ingredients themselves"; and Byrd was amused rather than convinced by the reasoning of the physician. With such a mortal disease, he warned the reader, almost all hope lies in prevention rather than cure. If the patient's constitution is not strong enough, medicine can do very little for him. Besides, the plague assumes various forms at different times and in different places. If we know so little about it, he added, it is because "very few physicians will venture their precious persons very near those that are sick," and thus "it is hardly possible they should ever be acquainted with the distemper enough to do any great service."[41]

The end of Byrd's pamphlet is devoted to the best methods of prevention. Lists of general and individual rules are headed by religious measures against contagion. The government should appoint a general fast, "to humble ourselves and deprecate the vengeance of an offended God." As for individuals, "the first and surest preservative of all will be a most humble and sincere repentance of our sins, and an unfeigned amendment of life, that God may be thereby moved not to pour out the terrors of His fury upon us, nor involve us in the general calamity." Among the other "prudent measures" recommended by Byrd, some are of particular interest. He advised a purgative, an infusion of tobacco in strong wine, with which to anoint the lower part of the abdomen, and a cordial two or three times a day: "a moderate glass of canary or palm wine, in which Virginian snake-root has been infused so long as to make it agreeably bitter." Both the virtuoso interested in medicine and the Virginia planter in him agreed on the virtues of tobacco to escape the mortal effects of the plague: "Instead of all other amulets, and preferably to them all, we shall find a singular virtue against the plague in fresh, strong, and quick-scented tobacco. The sprightly effluvia sent forth from this vegetable, after it is rightly cured, are by nature particularly adapted to encounter and dissipate the pestilential taint, beyond all the antidotes that have been yet discovered." Like many other poisons tobacco could be very good when correctly used. After listing a few instances of remedies made from tobacco, Byrd enlarged on the fact that the American colonies where that plant grows in large quantities had never been visited with the plague and that in the Great Plague of 1665 the houses of London tobacco merchants escaped the infection. Furthermore, although in the century preceding that fateful year this calamity had struck England about once every twenty years, there had been no recurrence of it for fifty-four years. The only cause that

41 *Ibid.*, p. 435.

could reasonably be ascribed to the fact, in Byrd's opinion, was the great increase in the consumption of tobacco. The scientists of Crane Court had calculated what part of the smoke that covers London must come from tobacco: "This it is that in probability purges our air, and corrects those noisome damps, that might otherwise beget contagious diseases amongst us."[42] Great Britain and Holland, the two countries in Europe that used tobacco most, had both been longest free from the plague. So at a time when the reappearance of the plague in Marseilles was a cause of fear in all Europe, the best hope of salvation from the contagion lay in the consumption of more and more Virginian tobacco in England.

We should wear it about our clothes and about our coaches. We should hang bundles of it round our beds and in the apartments wherein we most converse. If we have an aversion to smoking, it would be very prudent to burn some leaves of tobacco in our dining rooms, lest we swallow the infection with our meat. It will also be very useful to take snuff plentifully made of the pure leaf, to secure the passages to our brain. Nor must those only be guarded, but the pass to our stomachs should be also safely defended, by chewing this great antipoison very frequently.[43]

Byrd's remedies must have seemed really drastic to his readers.

This was indeed trying to kill two birds with one stone. As much as a medical brochure, the pamphlet was written as a kind of propaganda to increase the sales of Virginia tobacco, "that bewitching vegetable," as he called it at the beginning of *The History of the Dividing Line*.[44] But the author, who described himself conventionally as "a lover of mankind," sincerely believed in the curative powers of tobacco, although with a touch of wishful thinking. Whatever its scientific validity may be, the booklet on the plague was no worse than many others which were published in the same period. From his membership of the Royal Society and his long acquaintance with the virtuosi of the time, Byrd had acquired, or at least developed, a taste for careful observation, the basis of contemporary science.

[42] *Ibid.*, pp. 436, 437, 438, 439, 441–42.

[43] *Ibid.*, p. 442. For the early belief in the curative powers of tobacco, see Sarah A. Dickson, *Panacea or Precious Bane: Tobacco in Sixteenth Century Literature* (New York, 1954). On the other hand, Byrd's son-in-law Charles Carter, in a 1761 letter setting forth the necessity for Virginia to break away from its unhealthy economic dependence upon tobacco, explained that it was harmful to the health: "Indeed, if the common consumers were sensible of the great proportion of poisonous quality contained in this narcotic plant, they would be induced to lay it aside, to preserve their healths and save their money" (*VMHB*, LXVII [1959], 412–13).

[44] *Prose Works*, p. 158.

Even considering the great influence of the scientific movement during the second half of the seventeenth century, it is clear that Byrd was particularly affected by it. He accepted the general theory of the Royal Society about the problem of knowledge: he wanted to shake off the yoke of authority; he believed in the deceitfulness of the senses and in the necessity of careful experimenting. "Experience [is] the best philosopher in the world," he wrote to Peter Collinson in 1736.[45] But he was not always a good judge of conflicting testimonies and was sometimes carried away by his personal convictions. In natural science, a sphere which had become respectable, and even a dominant interest for many virtuosi, Byrd's work only turned to details. His was the humble work of a modest auxiliary of modern science and an amateur; no great work assuredly, but very typical of a period and of the influence exerted by the Royal Society on its ordinary members.

Nor was Byrd any exception in the American colonies: scores of almost or wholly forgotten men—teachers, preachers, physicians, or simply amateur lovers of "philosophical pursuits"—were stimulated by the urges of the European enlightenment and the sense of a special American destiny. The wide scientific curiosity of the virtuosi of that "learned and inquisitive age" led Thomas Sprat's "perfect philosophers" to have as many correspondents overseas as they could find.[46] About twenty-five colonial Americans were fellows of the Royal Society. The son of the first governor of Massachusetts, John Winthrop, Jr., himself governor of Connecticut, was among the first, as early as 1663. Among Byrd's acquaintances was Peter Collinson, a London merchant who, being a member of the Society, procured specimens from the New World for English virtuosi through business relations.[47] Another was John Bartram, once his guest at Westover, a Philadelphia naturalist who was later appointed botanist to the king and sent all sorts of American plants to the royal gardens; Linnaeus himself, in his great modesty, called Bartram the greatest contemporary botanist.[48] A typical American virtuoso was Lieutenant Governor Cadwallader Colden of New York, who was also a cor-

[45] Byrd to Collinson, July 18, 1736, *VMHB*, XXXVI (1928), 354.

[46] See Raymond P. Stearns, "Colonial Fellows of the Royal Society of London, 1661–1788," *WMQ*, 3d ser., III (1946), 208–68, and Brooke Hindle, *The Pursuit of Science in Revolutionary America, 1735–1789* (Chapel Hill, N. C., 1956), chs. II and III.

[47] See Earl G. Swem, "Brothers of the Spade: Correspondence of Peter Collinson and John Custis of Williamsburg, Va., 1734–1746," *Proceedings of the American Antiquarian Society*, LXVIII (1948). Colonial Williamsburg has copies of letters of Peter Collinson to John Custis and of Bartram to Collinson (originals in Bartram Papers, Pennsylvania Historical Society).

[48] See Ernest Earnest, *John and William Bartram* (Philadelphia, 1940).

respondent of Linnaeus and of the leading members of the Royal Society, and who wrote on yellow fever and the "throat disease" (diphtheria), besides his better-known *History of the Five Indian Nations*.[49] The same spirit of curiosity, intent on accurate observation of animals and plants, later led Benjamin Franklin to create the American Philosophical Society in 1743, with the same end in view, "the promotion of useful knowledge." This was the American transposition of the Royal Society and of its spirit, collecting data on useful plants, animals, and minerals and encouraging useful inventions. The modest work of Byrd and the activity of Bartram and others may be said to have paved the way for those who, beyond the mere curiosity of the early virtuosi, achieved genuine scientific thought— for Franklin, the first American scientist, and his successors.

[49] See Alice M. Keys, *Cadwallader Colden* (New York, 1906).

CHAPTER VII

Cavalier

IN ALL the known portions of his diary, Byrd often mentioned
that he "wrote English," by which he meant literary exercises of
the kind that were published in 1942 by Miss Woodfin in *Another
Secret Diary*. Such literary entertainment was then common in the
society of London or at the fashionable spas of England.

Besides the specimens contained in the manuscript notebooks at
the University of North Carolina, Miss Woodfin identified as Byrd's
some *vers de société* attributed to a "Mr. Burrard," in *Tunbrigalia, or
Tunbridge Miscellanies for the Year 1719*. Previous volumes of *The
Tunbridge Miscellany* had already appeared in 1712, 1713, and 1714,
and others were to come out in later years. As was stated by the
title of the first volume, it consisted "of poems written at Tunbridge
Wells this summer, by several hands." These poems, after circulating
among the fashionable society of the watering place during the season, finally found their way into print despite their poor quality.
The personal character of these madrigals and epigrams was their
main interest in the eyes of the idle set that had abandoned town and
court for a few weeks. Byrd appears as "the complete product of his
environment, the sophisticated gentleman and man-about-town of
Augustan society, mirroring its interest and outlook and literary
fashions."[1] His poems are neither better nor worse than most. They
merely follow the literary fashion of those circles and do not deserve
more than one quotation by way of example:

On Mrs. Lethulier
See how triumphantly her beauty blooms,
Commanding sacrifice by hecatombe!
Next view the happy pledge of youthful years,
Which in such conscious modesty appears.
The rosy blushes peep, and then retire,
Then come again, and tender love inspire.
Who, when she dances, can her movement see
But's yielding heart beats time by sympathy?
Beauty to her is not derived from chance,
But right convey'd by just inheritance.[2]

[1] Willie T. Weathers, "William Byrd: Satirist," *WMQ*, 3d ser., IV (1947), 28.
[2] *Another Secret Diary*, p. 408.

In 1704, Byrd wrote a ribald parody of a short poem by Anne Finch, later Lady Winchelsea: her verses "Upon a Sigh" were burlesqued by those "Upon a Fart," and he flattered himself that the latter "cured that lady of her itch to poetry."[3] But all this is of little or no literary value, except perhaps "A Song," which was used by Colley Cibber at the end of his play *The Careless Husband*:

> Sabina with an Angel's face
>   By Love ordain'd for joy
> Seems of the siren's cruel race,
>   To charm and then destroy.
> With all the arts of look and dress
>   She fans the fatal fire:
> Through Pride, mistaken oft for Grace,
>   She bids the swain expire.
> The god of Love, enrag'd to see
>   The nymph defy his flame,
> Pronounced this merciless decree
>   Against the haughty dame:
> Let Age with double speed o'ertake her;
>   Let Love the room of Pride supply;
> And when the fellows all forsake her,
>   Let her gnaw the sheets and die.[4]

With this exception, Byrd's scanty production has all the artificiality of the fashionable versifying which was published year after year, in so many miscellanies of the early eighteenth century.

---

[3] *Ibid.*, p. 244.

[4] *Ibid.*, pp. 202–3. The identification was made by Carl Dolmetsch of the College of William and Mary. The play was produced late in 1704 and printed in 1705. The song could not have been composed or even copied out in 1718 after the affair with Mary Smith, placed as it is in the North Carolina notebook among writings which all date back to 1703–1706 (e.g., letters to "Facetia," *Another Secret Diary*, pp. 197 and 200; the portraits of Sir Robert Southwell [d. 1702], p. 206, and of Sir John Huband [d. 1710], p. 208; letters to "Fidelia," written at the end of 1705 or the beginning of 1706, pp. 214–220). Judging from its place in the notebook, the song was most certainly entered in 1704, or 1705 at the latest, whether composed by Byrd and used by Cibber, or written by Cibber and copied out by Byrd. But if it had only been a copy of a poem by Cibber or any other, it would probably have been entered in a commonplace book rather than in the notebook. The Commonplace Book (V.H.S.) of a later period contains various writings, essentially quotations, summaries of books read, reflections on Byrd's reading, copies of letters (rare apart from "Charmante's"); whereas the notebook, it seems, only contains Byrd's own compositions. So the song may well have been composed by Byrd in or before 1704 and used by Cibber with the last line softened. The name of "Sabina" for Mary Smith would then be a mere coincidence, or more probably it was chosen after the end of the affair, when Byrd was copying out their correspondence in the notebook.

Much of the prose Byrd wrote during his London years is of a similar type, though of different value: a kind of fashionable "prose de société" written for the entertainment of his friends. Character sketches enjoyed great popularity all through the seventeenth century and well into the eighteenth, with their epigrammatic and humorous description of the foibles of man, and less often of his virtues. Abstract portraits like Joseph Hall's or Nicholas Breton's might denounce man's weaknesses and hypocrisies; or sophisticated descriptions like Sir Thomas Overbury's might ridicule a social group. John Earle, in amusing and kindly satire, preferred to analyze and understand the idiosyncrasies of his contemporaries. The Westover library contained the well-known volumes of characters sketched by Theophrastus and La Bruyère,[5] which Byrd must have known early. In any case, portraits were most common even in letters and essays: Addison and Steele in their *Spectator* often tried their hand at the genre, and almost anyone with pretensions to wit practised it as a pastime. Most of these characters depicted individuals rather than types, under the influence of French example. To sketch well-known figures in society, or to sketch oneself, had become a fashionable occupation after the Restoration, in imitation of the salons of Paris. These compositions circulated only in manuscript among people of quality for whom a particular delight lay in the identification of the originals.

Byrd seems to have had a particular liking for this kind of exercise. He attempted it at the turn of the century, and in 1722 he exchanged "pictures" with "Minionet." In one of his letters to her he explained why satire should be easier than panegyric, which he felt required more genius: "Satire is much the easier work of the understanding, because Nature is always at hand to assist us, when we attempt to sink the character of our neighbor below our own; but to bestow beauties upon others that may eclipse ourselves is so much against the grain as to be exceedingly difficult."[6]

Yet he himself wrote panegyrics of his patrons: "Duke Dulchetti," on the Duke of Argyle, is of indifferent value because of its partisan tendency; the duke was not always as favorably judged as in Byrd's sketch, where the writer touches with a gentle hand upon the foibles of the great nobleman. But "Cavaliero Sapiente," a portrait of Sir Robert Southwell, in which Byrd expresses his grateful admiration for the man who had superintended his education in England and sponsored him for membership in the Royal Society, shows great

[5] See Bassett, pp. 422, 434.
[6] *Another Secret Diary*, p. 374-75.

sincerity of feeling; its style exemplifies the taste for antithesis, most eagerly sought by character writers:

He had alone the secret of giving pleasure to others, at the very moment he felt pain himself. While he was young, he was wise enough to instruct the old, and when he came to be old, he was agreeable enough to please the young. All that had the honor of his conversation confessed that he had a peculiar talent of mixing delight with information. Religion appeared in all her charms when he was practising it; he had zeal without bitterness, devotion without hypocrisy, and charity without ostentation. His principles were so firmly riveted that he was able to converse in a corrupt court above thirty years without any prejudice to his integrity. During that whole time, he signalized his fidelity to his Prince without forfeiting his duty to his country.[7]

And Byrd, remembering his own youth, added: "He knew how to infuse his own bright qualities into all that had the happiness of his tuition. . . . He was so great a master of persuasion that he could charm people into their duty, without the harsh methods of discipline and severity."

Byrd also wrote panegyrics about ladies of his acquaintance who had died young and were somewhat idealized in his memory. Such was the case with "Melantha," Lady Mary Calverly Sherard: "Perfection like lightning only dazzles the world for a moment and then shuts in above the clouds"; or again with "Indamira": "Thus good, thus engaging was Indamira, and was so happy as to die in the noon of her beauty and her virtue. Very unlike other flowers, she withered not upon her stalk, but was transplanted in full bloom into Paradise."[8]

Although Byrd could talk the language of preciosity and pay elaborate compliments of that kind, satire was more congenial to him. As in his panegyrics, he used fictitious names of Italian appearance for his characters, names which betray the contemporary influence of Italian opera in England. Addison noted "the gradual progress which it has made upon the English stage"; he did so with mixed feelings, and deplored a certain want of common sense in the audience, while he admired the famous singer, Signior Nicolini, who was "capable of giving a dignity to the forced thoughts, cold conceits and unnatural expressions of an Italian opera."[9] Byrd, who was always careful to follow the fashion, had seen Nicolini play and was an habitué of the Duke's Theater in Lincoln's Inn Field, where the first opera in English was presented during the time when he wrote his *London*

---

[7] *Ibid.*, p. 207.
[8] *Ibid.*, pp. 228–29, 297–98.
[9] *The Spectator*, no. 18 and no. 13; see also no. 29.

Diary.[10] But for him these Italian names were no abstractions; they were individuals, not types, and their names, when they did not evoke some literary model, suggested the main psychological trait of the original. "Count Sufficiento" "has an infinite fondness for his own person without having any rival but his mother. . . . He really has wit; but it is overcharged with so much ill nature that it all sours into railing and slander." He is "constantly ready to sacrifice a good friend to an ill jest. . . . He has no good nature for others because he lavishes his whole fund of kindness upon that bleak phantom, himself." His self-complacency is as characteristic of him as untidiness is of "Cavaliero Slovena," who wears dirty linen "till it drop from his back, out of a complaisance to those familiar little creatures that inhabit his person. He has so sensible a negligence in his dress that those who have the happiness to be near him may not only see, but even smell that he is a philosopher." Of a very proud but plain lady, "Altana," Byrd said: "Nobody can pretend to commend the brightness of her eyes without giving a very dark account of his own"; and yet, he added, "her wit has force enough to make a man discredit the faithful testimony of his eyes, and sets off the disadvantages of her person, as much as a great fortune does other harmless faces." The irony of the first remark, the satirical edge of the last hit, do not preclude kindliness and humor. There is never any really malicious sting in Byrd's "pictures," only a kind of smiling pleasantry. His good nature always comes uppermost, and he finds some quality worthy of praise in each character. Thus "Rampana" "is not apt to think much, and yet speaks better without thinking than other ladies do with it. . . . She loves the conversation of those that have sense, but does not renounce the company of those that have none; because she has the charity to improve them when they are with her, and the pleasure of laughing at them when they are gone."[11] "Cavaliero Bonini," a man of honor, endowed with the noblest qualities, is so full of benignity and softness that it gives him "too strong a disposition to the fair sex"; he is not

so narrow-hearted as to love but one. . . . But he manages this foible with so much dexterity and precaution that each nymph thinks herself in possession of his whole heart. No woman after she has given up the ghost can keep a secret more faithfully than he conceals his intrigues, so that though it is possible he may have made some ladies suffer in their virtue, yet he never made them suffer in their reputation. From whence we may con-

[10] See *Another Secret Diary*, pp. 265, 454; *London Diary*, pp. 67, 70, 75, 76, 90, 97, and so on.
[11] *Another Secret Diary*, pp. 204–5, 206, 211, 194.

clude that he takes care of their safety in this world, but leaves it to them to provide for their security in the next.[12]

Somewhat longer than these characters is "The Female Creed," a satire on women's credulity and superstition which Byrd must have written about 1725, shortly before his final return to Virginia.[13] This pamphlet of twenty-five pages enlarges upon the belief in spirits and fairies, witches and fortunetellers, dreams and visions, and lucky numbers, such superstitions being considered particularly typical of women. Byrd's raillery, however, is not to be taken too seriously: as we have seen, he was himself quite willing to consult an astrologer or to read some meaning into his own dreams. "The Female Creed" certainly adds nothing to Byrd's fame; it is mostly a pretext for a string of short anecdotes, some of them fairly coarse. Sometimes an occasion arose for a satiric hint at contemporary political corruption:

That great oracle of equity, Count Bribantio, had a vast partiality for five, provided it had three significant cyphers after it. Insomuch that whenever his eyes happened to be dazzled with this charming number, especially when it could be made guineas, his Whig integrity all forsook him in an instant. Under so powerful a temptation he could not forbear prostituting the King's conscience of which he was the unworthy keeper, and quite forgot that he was the Guardian of the Widow and the fatherless.[14]

Like the caricatures of local tyrants in the novels of Fielding and Smollett, Byrd's portraits often had their models in real life.

The symbolic techniques of coffee-casting, a thriving branch of fortune-telling, provided further opportunities for political satire: "If an ass or an owl chance to be there, the happy caster will have a fair hit to be an alderman, but if the beast's ears appear longer, or the bird's countenance graver than ordinary, there are hopes he may come to be a judge." Again, "if a ravening wolf be in the cup, the man may rise in the Navy and grow to be a captain of a man-of-war, or if he be a land officer, and good for nothing else, he may live to be a Governor in His Majesty's Plantations."[15] Governors had been for years Byrd's pet aversion, all the more as his efforts to become one himself had proved fruitless. But all statesmen were much the same: a man's fate can be read in his hand or from a mole on his skin, and "a mole under the ingenious Jack Sheppard's left ear portended he would come at

[12] *Ibid.*, p. 209.

[13] *Ibid.*, pp. 447–75.

[14] *Ibid.*, pp. 468–69.

[15] *Ibid.*, p. 453. For Byrd's low opinion of captains of the Royal Navy, founded on their commercial activities, see his letter to Lord Orrery dated March 16, 1719/20, in *Orrery Papers*, I, 31–32.

last where most Ministers of State deserve to come, to the gallows."[16]

Such quotations might suggest a more serious purpose than is really the case. Most often the pamphlet is just pleasant satire with names easily deciphered by a reader belonging to Byrd's coterie; like "Altana" they might have appeared already in his "pictures." A good instance is "the unfortunate Dripabunda, who when she fancied she saw the ghost of her deceased husband, died away for fear the good man was come to life again," in spite of the inconsolable grief that her name suggests.[17] All this is nothing but the fashionable entertainment of a gentleman with some pretensions to wit in Queen Anne's times; it will give some idea of the kind of humor to be found in Byrd's writings.

The still unpublished Commonplace Book purchased by the Virginia Historical Society in December 1964 contains, among other notes and remarks, maxims or moral reflections in the manner of La Rochefoucauld, either inspired by or translated from Byrd's readings. He jotted down *sententiae* on friendship or on envy, such as the following: "Envious persons are doubly miserable, when ill happens to themselves and when good happens to other people"; "Envy follows a man in prosperity as close as the shadow does a body in sunshine"; "Invidious persons are gnawed by envy as much altogether as iron is with rust." Sometimes the entries are closer to paragraph length. Thus on brevity: "A man of wit may sometimes abound in words, but a man of sense never, because he knows how to proportion his expression to his subject. Most things may be comprehended in very few words, without abusing the patience and offering violence to the ears of the audience. A long discourse rather tires than instructs, and loses all that force and spirit with which a natural . . . brevity abounds." Or again on divine retribution: "God is pleased to punish some notorious sinners here, lest we should distrust his Providence in this world: but he does not punish all, lest we should disallow his judgement in the next."[18] In the Commonplace Book there are also many observations or anecdotes even coarser than those in "The Female Creed."

Byrd's love letters, with their ornate style and polished wit, their forced metaphors and artificial badinage, belong to that type of literature written by and for the fashionable circles of the metropolis. Sincerity is not the main quality of these formal, affected letters. They

[16] *Another Secret Diary*, pp. 454–55.

[17] *Ibid.*, p. 449.

[18] Commonplace Book, pp. 32, 12, 25, 28, V.H.S. The Commonplace Book was found by Mrs. Edmund H. Tucker among family papers of her son-in-law, Mr. Tazewell Ellett III. See *Richmond News Leader*, Dec. 18, 1964.

are a conventional, fashionable pastime more than the expression of any passionate feelings. When "Sabina" returned some of his letters unopened, Byrd marked them with an asterisk in the notebook where he copied them out; and he underlined the sentences with which he was best pleased, with the thoughtful intention of saving them for later letters. One of these passages is so bombastic and melodramatic as to be quite ridiculous:

> But if to my unspeakable misfortune you should disdain my offer, yet at least you will have this advantage by the audience you give me, that you will from thenceforth rid yourself of an offensive lover, and the earth soon after of the most miserable wretch that breathes upon it. I will fly with eagle's wings to that country where war is hottest, and where death may be courted on the surest terms. There, except destruction be as coy as you are, I shall not fail to put a glorious end both to a slighted passion and a detested life. When you hear that I am dead, bestow at least one sigh upon me, and own that it was you I loved, and not your fortune. You may depend upon it that the last breath I draw shall be a prayer for your happiness. And then let me conjure you, my dearest Sabina, not to be surprised if by a faithful friend I send you a present when I am dead, which you were so unkind as to refuse when I was living, that is, a faithful heart, embalmed and wrapped up in the two first letters which you did me the honor to write to me.[19]

Byrd seems to have been thoroughly pleased with this full-flavored blend of French romance and Jacobean drama.

One letter among others, in which he protests his "sincere and unaffected" passion, is but a patchwork of the purple passages in several earlier letters rejected by his fair lady:

> No husband with tender ears can ever be more punished by the outrageous eloquence of his consort than I have been lately by my dear Sabina's silence. I have longed for her answers with an impatience beyond that with which one in a burning fever longs for drink. Imagine, for God's sake, the restlessness, the torment that such a wretch endures, and then tell me if with all your good nature you can give it the man that adores you. Write therefore, I conjure you by all the charms of your dear person. . . . All I can do, all I can say betrays my inclination, and all my looks are love. . . . What has my charmer then to fear, or what imaginable reason can she have who is compassionate to all other creatures, thus to torture the man that devotes himself to serve her? . . . The charms of her body are beyond everything but the superior charms of her mind. Who can discern the piety she shows to her father without adoring her? She confines herself from all those pleasures that befit her age and condition, for the better pleasure of obliging him. She is content to spend her blooming youth in

[19] *Another Secret Diary*, p. 314 (Byrd underscored the entire passage).

obscurity, to make his age and infirmities more supportable to him. She chooses to stew in a close room to divert him rather than rove about in the wide world to entertain herself. She sweetens all his peevishness with good humor, and softens his frowns with her smiles. His years and want of health are to her an excuse in full for all his unaccountable humors. There is a most obliging cheerfulness in all her behavior to him, that adds a grace and a loveliness to the most charming of all duties. O my dear enchantress, who can perceive this divine quality in you without concluding very naturally that a tender daughter never fails to make a tender wife, especially when he reflects that this is but one of the legion of virtues you possess?[20]

Sincere Byrd may have been, but unaffected he could never be in this kind of letter. When reflecting on his own conduct, he was quite conscious how awkward and even ridiculous he became when he wanted to express his love: "Instead of that life and gaiety, that freedom and pushing confidence which hits the ladies, he would look as dismal as if he appeared before his judge, and not his mistress." He was unable "to leave off the style of romance" even when he tried, and could do no more than call her Miss Smith instead of "Sabina."[21] He could not express himself in any but that artificial style, stilted, pompous, bombastic.[22]

And yet, whenever Byrd wrote to some feminine correspondent without any intention of courting her, he avoided that bad taste and developed a free, easy, humorous style which is a world away from the preceding examples. To one of his kinswomen whom he called "Lucretia" he wrote in the perfect tone of cavalier badinage:

I protest your very follies are so agreeable that it needs a world of distinction and a great deal of cynic philosophy to discover them to be follies. You have the art of making those little imperfections so charming that it is impossible to find fault with them; they are in you what discord is in music and serve only to make you more enchanting. . . . For God's sake, Madam, do not grow too wise therefore, nor too perfect, for fear of being less agreeable. . . . Let me . . . conjure you, dear cousin, till the dreadful age of thirty-one (when you know a woman's game is up), to mix nine grams of folly with one of wisdom, if you have a mind to do remarkable execution. That is the just proportion which Ovid and all the doctors in the deep science of Love allow to a woman that would be irresistible. More than this would make you a coquette, and less a prude, both which characters are detestable.[23]

[20] *Ibid.*, pp. 327–28; compare pp. 305, 306, 308, 309.

[21] *Ibid.*, pp. 278, 316.

[22] Byrd's letters to "Charmante" in 1722 are in the same vein: see, for instance, the first lines of the letter of Oct. 23, 1722, and the long account of a dream in the letter of Oct. 26, *VMHB*, XXXV (1927), 383–86.

[23] *Another Secret Diary*, pp. 283–84.

A relation of a journey in which he was "packed in a stagecoach for six long days together with the most disengaging company in the universe" gives him an opportunity to draw humorous portraits of his fellow travelers.[24] There was a country parson who had never been out of his own parish "since he left the University, which was the year after the Restoration." He had some learning but could not air his knowledge without pedantry: "He attacked the poor women according to the rules of logic, and endeavored by a syllogism to confute the coachman that the monosyllable 'gee' was improper to anything but a cart horse." He knew nothing of the world and thought that "Virginia was an island without Ganges in the East Indies and that it was peopled first by a colony sent thither by William Rufus." It was fortunate that he was always smoking strong tobacco, because it defended his neighbors from worse smells about his person. "To add to his other perfections he was a stiff virulent Jacobite, and maintained that kings had a divine right to put a curb into the mouths of their subjects and ride them as hard as they pleased"; the king "had full power to dispose of their estates, their liberties and their persons as he in his infallible wisdom should thing fit." In the next town, however, he was denounced by a Quakeress for speaking against the government and was taken into custody. This kind of portrait in dialogue and actions anticipates those Fielding or Smollett were to draw when their heroes were let loose on the road.

In the same coach there was also "a certain female of that sort ycleped a prude." She was, Byrd said, "a virgin of thirty-three or thereabouts with a face that would not tempt one five hundred leagues from land. Her features were all stiffened with a long habit of squeamish airs which she had given herself for fourteen years together. She had no part of her free and easy but her tongue, which I own moved with a surprising facility. . . . Most of her eloquence was leveled at the disorders of her own sex; the license women took, she said, was intolerable in a Christian country." But her neighbors were to learn later that "this saint of untainted virtue, this unsullied, unpolluted nymph had a child by her uncle's coachman, and made this journey on purpose to meet him at one of the inns by the way." There is indeed in this page what Willie T. Weathers termed "a Hogarthian quality" which "is reproduced time and again in *The Secret History of the Line*."[25]

Another letter is a portrait of "Incendia," a gentlewoman who, after she had been deserted by her husband, came to live at Westover as a

24 *Ibid.*, pp. 286–90.
25 "William Byrd, Satirist," p. 32.

companion for Byrd's wife. Unfortunately, Byrd was soon confirmed in his opinion that "it is dangerous to admit a woman into your house who had lived very uneasily with her own spouse, for she will not fail to infect any other wife she converses with, with her own humors and infirmities." She was the cause of "very unpleasant controversies" between Byrd and his wife, because she "also preached up a very dangerous doctrine, that in case a husband does not allow his wife money enough, she may pick his pocket or plunder his scrutoire to do herself justice, of which she is to be her own judge."[26]

What might be called Byrd's cavalier writings, mostly composed during the years he spent in England, partake of the spirit of the times, though rather on the conservative side. They evince the detachment and the taste for satire which still prevailed at the turn of the century. Under the thin veneer of elegance and classic form sometimes appear the outspokenness and cynicism, even the coarseness, of the Restoration, although Byrd, considering early-eighteenth-century manners, felt that "his conversation was easy . . . and inoffensive, never bordering either upon profaneness or indecency."[27] Sentiment was then beginning to color wit into humor, according to Thackeray's famous definition of humor as wit and love. But there must be no unbecoming seriousness, no vehement passion. To be impassioned would not befit the dignity of a gentleman. He may be romantic, but conventionally so, without offending against the proprieties, against the refined delicacy of speech of French romance. Outside the sphere of formal gallantry in which Byrd was so stiff, he can be most entertaining in his amused appreciation of human weaknesses. When he gave rein to his humor and to his own personality, in his diverting portrayal of life we get a glimpse of the truly gifted artist he might have been if he had devoted himself exclusively to literature.

These were letters that Byrd entered in the North Carolina notebook with some idea that they were worth recording. Others written to relatives or friends, whether in England or more rarely in Virginia, are in fact no less interesting; and the same can be said of a few business letters. To Colonel Martin Bladen, Commissioner of Trade and Plantations, he wrote an account of the Dividing Line expedition, dwelling on the hardships they surmounted "living great part of the time in the wild woods; in the lower part of the work, plunging through mire and nastiness; and in the upper part of it, climbing over mountains and precipices and scuffling through thickets almost im-

---

[26] *Another Secret Diary*, pp. 291–92.
[27] "Inamorato L'Oiseaux," *ibid.*, p. 279.

penetrable." He "humbly hoped" that they deserved four hundred pounds and that Bladen would help him to obtain that sum for the members of the expedition. At the same time he proposed a scheme "greatly for the public service as well as for the advantage of the persons who are concerned therein": "the opening a canal between the rivers of Virginia and Carolina."[28] To a London merchant he observed apropos of a poor tobacco crop: "The mysteries of trade are as great as those in religion, or else three or four crops, to the people of common understanding, should afford some hopes of keeping the market at least where it was, and not let it sink to nothing. What comes home this shipping will be moderate in quantity. . . . If the scarcity of a commodity will not raise the value of it, I will depend no more on old musty maxims." How different from the dry, matter-of-fact business letters of his father! To the same merchant he gave a joking hint: "Mrs. Byrd wishes you married, God forgive her, because she fancies you would be able to manage female commissions better."[29] When he wrote to Colonel Spotswood at Germanna to announce his own appointment as one of the commissioners to settle the bounds of Lord Fairfax's estate in the Northern Neck, he added pleasantly: "I suspect the Council has done me this honor with the wicked design of wearing the oldest out first, and making a vacancy near the chair. Yet this may happen to be best, because so much exercise and change of air may probably renew my age, and enable me to hold out with the most vigorous of them, except your old friend the Commissary." Of Sir John Randolph in Williamsburg he inquired how a doctor friend of theirs came off in an amateur performance of *The Busybody*: "With many a clap I suppose, though I fancy he would have acted more to life in the comedy called *The Sham Doctor*. But not a word of this for fear in case of sickness he might poison [me]."[30]

Yet Byrd's most entertaining letters are always those he sends to his female correspondents. His sister-in-law, Mrs. Otway, had an "aversion to writing,"[31] and he chaffed her about it:

I have looked out as sharp, all this year, for an epistle from my dear sister, as a broken gamester does for a dinner, or [a] St. Sebastian privateer for a prize, but alas to no manner of purpose; our ships have dropped in one

[28] Byrd to Bladen, June 1729, *VMHB*, XXXVI (1928), 113–16.

[29] Byrd to Mr. Christopher Smith, Aug. 23, 1735, and March 20, 1736/37, *ibid.*, IX (1901), 118; XXXVI (1928), 213.

[30] Byrd to Spotswood, Dec. 22, 1735, *ibid.*, IX (1902), 236; to Randolph, Jan. 21, 1735/36, *ibid.*, 241.

[31] Byrd to Major Otway (fragment, no date), *ibid.*, IX (1901), 130.

after another in spite of the Spaniards, though in my opinion they left the most valuable part of their cargo behind when they came without your dispatches.[32]

But when letters came he was lavish with pleasantly irrelevant comparisons: "All the dudgeon I had conceived for my dear sister's silence vanished at the sight of two of her letters, just as a lover's despair does when Sacharissa vouchsafes to smile, or just as Spousy's tears dry as soon as she has gained her point of tender-hearted Miky."[33]

"Cousin Taylor," a relative of his second wife, was one of his favorite correspondents, for she wrote long letters full of London society gossip. When they had not heard from her for a long time, he exclaimed in mock melancholy: "Well, I perceive my dear cousin Taylor begins to treat me for all the world as she does injuries, that is to forget me. 'Tis so long since I heard from her that, unless I read her former letters as often as I do the Psalms, I should have forgot her hand."[34] But he readily pardoned her as soon as she wrote:

I certainly forget your neglect the moment you are so good as to remember me again. One smile makes amends for many frowns; as your good Catholics say, Paradise will pay us abundantly for all we suffer in Purgatory. All the penance I can find in my heart to enjoin you for your silence last year (if it be reasonable to punish one of the voluble sex for silence) is to say a great deal to me the next.[35]

When she wrote to his wife but not to him, he protested in mock vexation:

I always rejoice to hear of my dear cousin Taylor's health and happiness, let the news come from what hand it will, though nobody, in my opinion, tells it half so agreeably as herself. But alas! my envious stars have grudged me that satisfaction this year, which, if I may own the truth, has mortified me to the quick. 'Tis true Mrs. Byrd had been favored with a letter, and I sympathized as much as I could in the pleasure it gave her. But after all sympathy is very flat, and at best only a joy at the first rebound. I love to have the ball tossed directly to me, and catch it before it reaches the ground.[36]

[32] Byrd to Mrs. Otway, Sept. 20, 1740, *ibid.,* XXXVII (1929), 106–7.

[33] Byrd to Mrs. Otway, Oct. 2, 1735, *ibid.,* IX (1901), 121–22.

[34] Mrs. Taylor to Byrd, Jan. 8, 1742, *ibid.,* XXXVII (1929), 110–18; Byrd "to Cousin Taylor," July 28, 1728, *ibid.,* XXXVI (1928), 43. "Cousin Taylor" may have been the "Lucretia" of *Another Secret Diary,* mentioned above, p. 100.

[35] Byrd "to Cousin Taylor," March 20, 1736/37, Byrd Letterbook, 1736–1737 V.H.S., pp. 10–12.

[36] Byrd "to Cousin Taylor," July 2, 1736, *VMHB,* XXXVI (1928), 217–18.

Byrd's correspondence, save for pure business letters, was part of his effort to maintain as close a bond as possible with the fashionable society of London; if they were to keep up a correspondence, he must send them interesting letters, with exotic or humorous details, so that the ships might still bring those puffs of English air. But this kind of writing was also a way of "exercising his English" and furbishing up the skill he had acquired during his London years. It reminded him of the polished circles he had long frequented, and set him apart from many would-be colonial squires on their outlying plantations, however large and flourishing.

His letter writing is no outstanding achievement, but it does evoke the elegant conversation of contemporary wits. It has none of Swift's vigor, and it often lacks Addison's ease. It is less natural than the *Tatler*, which he liked to read, for his own public is restricted to the upper class, his lifelong model, responsible for some of his forced, conventional wit, and for his occasional coarseness too.[37] But in spite of all strictures, his letters give an attractive picture of a Virginia planter in London or an English gentleman exiled on a colonial plantation. They are certainly not the most truly Virginian of his works; yet perhaps they shed a stronger light on the various sides of his personality; and they show how he came to acquire the pleasant style that no other writer was able to achieve in Southern colonial literature.

[37] For examples of this coarseness in Byrd's correspondence, it is generally necessary to go to the manuscripts, since the letters published in magazines were often bowdlerized. See Byrd to Mrs. Otway, June 1729 (on the penalty for fornication), Byrd Letterbook, 1729, and Byrd to Cousin Taylor, March 20, 1736/37, Byrd Letterbook, 1736–1737 V.H.S., pp. 10–12. See also in Byrd's letter to Mrs. Taylor, Oct. 10, 1735, the anecdote printed by Bassett (p. 395) but left out in *VMHB*, IX (1902), 229, as "a story which might have passed in the days of Fielding or Smollett, but not suited for modern pages."

CHAPTER VIII

Diarist

BYRD'S diaries were not published until recently. According to family traditions, he never failed to keep a detailed journal in shorthand when absent from home.[1] In fact, as we now know, he kept it at Westover as well as when he was away, and it is fairly probable that he did so throughout most of his adult life, but that a great part of it has been lost.

Three portions have come to light in our century. The earliest known diary, covering the period from February 1709 to September 1712, was purchased from the estate of R. A. Brock in 1922 by Henry Huntington as part of a collection of Virginia manuscripts. It lay in the Huntington Library, San Marino, California, until it was discovered in 1939. Deciphered by Mrs. Marion Tinling (who was also to transcribe the other shorthand diaries) and edited by Louis B. Wright, it was published in 1941 as *The Secret Diary of William Byrd of Westover.*

Another part of Byrd's diary, from August 1739 to August 1741, was published in the next year. First identified in 1925 by the librarian of the University of North Carolina, it fills a large part of two notebooks in Byrd's handwriting which belong to that university. Miss Woodfin heard about them in 1936 when she was gathering material for a biography, and she finally edited and published these manuscripts as *Another Secret Diary of William Byrd of Westover* in 1942.[2]

A third portion, the second chronologically, dating from December 1717 to May 1721, had been since 1876 in the Virginia Historical Society in Richmond. It remained unnoticed until news of the discovery of the other portions caused it to be brought to light. It was not published immediately, however; Byrd's relation of his sexual excesses during that period of his life partly explain the hesitancy of the Virginia Historical Society; and there are those who believe that Byrd's reputation has suffered rather than gained by the publication of *The London Diary.* But in addition to his life in England until

---

[1] Marion Harland, *His Great Self,* p. 17. In her girlhood in the middle of the nineteenth century, the author of the novel had been a friend of the owners of Westover (descendants of the Harrisons of Berkeley).

[2] *Another Secret Diary,* p. vii.

December 1719, this diary does cover more than a year after his
return to the colony, and there is no denying the fact that, besides
permitting a truer apprehension of some sides of his character, it pro-
vides useful information about the sincerity of his reconciliation with
Spotswood. It was finally edited and published by Professor Wright
in 1958.

When the existence of these diaries became common knowledge,
Byrd was hailed as "an American Pepys."[3] Like his famous English
counterpart, he had written a day-by-day account of his life that he
had really intended to keep secret. In England the first book on
shorthand, or "characterie" as it was then called, had been published
in 1588 by Timothy Bright: *Characterie, or The Art of Short, Swift,
and Secret Writing by Character.* In this title the word *secret* was not
the least important. In following years, Protestant travelers to countries where the Inquisition was powerful used to carry Bibles in
shorthand. There was then no palpable distinction between shorthand and cipher. Such modes of writing had two great advantages:
a busy man was glad to be able to write more swiftly; but since the
system was little known, he could also count on comparative secrecy,
which sometimes was of no mean interest to him. Pepys's shorthand
had been based on that of Thomas Shelton, who had explained his
method in his *Short Writing* in 1626 and later perfected it in his
Tachygraphy in 1638. Byrd used a different system of writing
adapted from that of William Mason, the most famous stenographer
of London in the later decades of the seventeenth century.[4] In 1672
Mason published *A Pen Pluckt from an Eagle's Wings*, which after several reprints appeared in a revised version in 1701, *La Plume
Volante, or the Art of Shorthand Improved.* This, the author said
in his preface, had been "composed after forty years' practice and improvement of the said art, by the observation of other methods and
the intense study of it." Mason used to teach his system to lawyers,
parliamentarians, and other people, and his last revision was the one
employed by Byrd, with small modifications. It omits most vowels,
and a dot can have more than half a dozen different meanings. As
Byrd, unlike Pepys, wrote even proper names in shorthand, these
had to be identified from a skeleton of consonants, a sometimes impossible task. This was really a secret writing at the time, particularly
in Virginia, four thousand miles from Mason's school.

Mason's book does not seem to have been in the Westover library,

[3] Louis B. Wright and Marion Tinling, "William Byrd of Westover, an
American Pepys," *South Atlantic Quarterly*, XXXIX (1940), 259–74.
[4] The discovery was made independently by Mrs. Tinling and Edward J.
Vogel (*Another Secret Diary*, p. iv–v).

which suggests that Byrd was already familiar with his system when he came back from England in 1705. He may have started writing his diary some time after the turn of the century, in 1702 or 1703, as an exercise in shorthand, and then gone on partly out of habit, and partly because he found some personal interest in it. But why should a man keep a diary if he expects it to remain secret?

A person of romantic disposition may write a journal intended for others; and as a result it may show a tendency to exaggeration, whether in self-idealization or in the proud and defiant exposition of personal shortcomings. The writer tends to paint himself as he would like to be seen, not as he is. But this is a particular kind of diary, of little interest to the reader as far as reality is concerned, unless he can see through the false portrait. It is more like an auto-biographical novel than a diary. Such is not the case with Byrd or Pepys or most of the diarists of their time.

More interesting is the man whose aim is sincere self-analysis, who wants to follow the old precept "know thyself," generally through a desire for moral progress. Addison once recommended to every one of his readers "the keeping a Journal of their lives for one week, and setting down punctually their whole series of employments during that space of time. This kind of self-examination would give them a true state of themselves, and incline them to consider seriously what they are about."[5] The diarist's stimulus may also be mere narcissism, a yearning to contemplate one's own life almost from the outside, as one might look at a stranger's, but with greater curiosity and more intimate knowledge. Or finally the diary may be regarded as a means for locating past events at their proper date and in their true perspective, another memory more faithful than the human one because time cannot efface written words so easily.

In many places Byrd's diary is certainly nearer the last type, though the preceding motives cannot be set aside entirely. The need for secrecy results from the intimate nature of some of the writer's revelations. He recorded what could be told to no one but himself. Professor Wright remarked that "by some quirk of character a few individuals feel impelled to write down even their meannesses; perhaps it is an instinct for purgation through the confessional."[6] Byrd, like Pepys, really felt the urge to say everything, as a Catholic may do in confession, and in fact many of the secret diaries which have eventually come to light were written by Protestants, who

[5] *The Spectator*, no. 317, March 4, 1712.
[6] *Secret Diary*, p. viii.

lacked the emotional outlet that confession affords. This accentuated self-consciousness was expressed in many Puritan diaries of the seventeenth century, both in Great Britain and in New England, whereas in Catholic France the more formal autobiographies were more common. Though Byrd was no Puritan, he was deeply religious, and this instinct for purgation may partly explain the existence of his diary, along with the universal and timeless autobiographical impulse, the irresistible need to talk of oneself to oneself.

Byrd freely admitted his moral failings to himself, particularly in *The London Diary*, which records the period after the death of his first wife when he launched into the cheapest pleasures of the flesh that the town could provide. He certainly had more to confess at that time than when he lived at Westover, or even when he let himself slide into gambling habits during his visits to Williamsburg. But the other portions of the diary also contain intimate revelations which he could not have intended for any reader but himself, not even the closest friend or relative.

The conviction that his diary would always remain secret led him to record with uninhibited sincerity all sorts of particulars about his daily routine and his main preoccupations: his food and work, his illnesses and remedies, the books he read and the people he met, the pleasures and sorrows he experienced, a complete catalog of his sexual life, and of prayers said or forgotten. We can expect the sincerity of such diaries to be greater than that of most autobiographies or personal letters, which are always intended to be read by others, even if only by a restricted circle. A man may deceive himself or intentionally close his eyes to certain facts, but when he is honestly looking for truth, such writings may be considered the nearest possible approach to complete sincerity, because they reveal his innermost self.

Byrd's diary is intimate but not introspective. It is very different from the many Puritan autobiographies or diaries written in New England during the colonial era. Samuel Sewall's *Diary*, for instance, gives a picture of contemporary life and an intimate record of his social and business activity, but its main concern is his spiritual life, which engrossed his thoughts. Jonathan Edwards's *Diary* is first and foremost an intense, and sometimes morbid, quest for personal holiness and moral perfection among "sinners in the hands of an angry God." John Woolman's *Journal*, no less sincere but less morbid, is the spiritual autobiography of a Quaker who, in his endeavor to be "faithful to the light," came close to being a mystic. The constant self-examination of each of these writers, as he passed through temptation, doubt, struggle, ecstasy, humility, or pride, was but another pilgrim's progress to the Land of Beulah and the Celestial City. Except for Sewall, these diarists had little or nothing to say about this world, about everyday life, about social facts, customs, behavior, or dress.

Not so with Byrd. His religion was no mere lip-devotion, but like Pepys he was a sensualist to the core. In him as in Pepys there was much more of human frailty than in those overanxious Puritan diarists of New England, or in John Evelyn, self-restrained and serious. Byrd did not exaggerate his weaknesses; neither did he idealize himself. A well-balanced individual, he just stated facts plainly, and he did not seem to feel any real shame, although he expressed sincere regret at his failings: "Then went home in the chair and kissed the maid till I committed uncleanness, for which God forgive me"; "Then walked home, but took a woman into a coach and committed uncleanness. Then I went home and prayed to God to forgive me."[7] He knew that perfection does not belong to this world; it was not within his reach; but on the whole he was not too much perturbed, apparently, about God's forgiveness.

Like Pepys again, Byrd expressed his concern for trivialities and domestic problems of the simplest kind. Here is his record of an ordinary day at Westover in 1710:

I rose at six o'clock and read the Psalms and some Greek in Cassius. I said my prayers and ate milk for breakfast. My maid Anaka was better, thank God. The Captain's bitch killed a lamb yesterday, for which we put her into a house with a ram that beat her violently to break her of that bad custom. We played at billiards. It rained with a northeast wind. I ate roast beef for dinner. In the afternoon we played at cards and were very merry. The pool lasted so long that we played till eleven o'clock at night. I neglected to say my prayers, but had good health, good thoughts, and good humor, thanks be to God Almighty.[8]

Vanity, lust, or ambition were faithfully and objectively recorded. "I had a great deal of wit this day, more than ordinary," Byrd noted on October 29, 1710. The diary also reveals more engaging qualities, which give greater dignity and charm to his personality. Here is the portrait of a man emerging entry after entry, no saint assuredly, but a man in whom good and bad were blended.

Both Byrd and Pepys always did their best to keep up appearances and to hide their weaknesses behind a veil of dignity and respectability which fell when at night they were alone with pen and notebook. Outwardly they show a stern sense of propriety. Between the grave

---

7 *London Diary*, March 2, May 1, 1718.
8 *Secret Diary*, Feb. 23, 1710.

and dignified figure of Councillor Byrd as he appeared to his contemporaries and the man so frankly revealed in his diary, there is the same kind of difference as between Mr. Pepys, the respectable, hardworking civil servant, and the author of the famous nightly confessions. Humanity then appears without disguise, as we can never see it except perhaps in ourselves. With both diarists, instinctive egoism did not preclude public zeal. The spirit and the flesh sometimes clashed in an unexpected manner: "In the afternoon I took a flourish with my wife, and then read a sermon in Tillotson."[9] Thus is man shown in all his changeableness or even his contradictions.

Besides their significance as a work of self-expression and a picture of eternal humanity, Byrd's diaries are of particular value as historical documents. Like Pepys's volumes again, they are all the more trustworthy as they were not intended to be published. And they are all the more useful as they represent the only Southern diaries of the early eighteenth century to have been written by a man of importance. After the record of Renaissance exploration and early settlement found in the famous narrative of Captain John Smith, or the less known description of Virginia by the first Secretary of the colony, William Strachey, in *The Historie of Travell into Virginia Britania*, there is very little direct information about that part of America. The misrepresentations of Oldmixon's account of the colony in his manuscript for *The British Empire in America*, published in 1708, led Robert Beverley, Byrd's brother-in-law, to write his own *History and Present State of Virginia* in 1705. A similar work was published in 1724 by the Reverend Hugh Jones with the same intention. And in 1727 appeared another study of *The Present State of Virginia and the College*[10] in which Commissary Blair had a hand. But such pictures were not unaffected by Virginia prejudices; Hugh Jones himself insisted that "if New England be called a receptacle of dissenters and an Amsterdam of religion, Pennsylvania the nursery of Quakers, Maryland the retirement of Catholics, North Carolina the refuge of runaways, and South Carolina the delight of buccaneers and pirates, Virginia may be justly esteemed the happy retreat of true Britons and true churchmen."[11] These authors felt it their duty to stand up for Virginia and were themselves tainted with partiality. If we except Byrd's, the first Southern diaries of any real interest are those of Landon Carter, Byrd's son-in-law, and of Philip Vickers Fithian, a graduate of Princeton who in 1773 went to northern Vir-

[9] *Ibid.*, Sept. 10, 1710.
[10] Hartwell, Blair, and Chilton, *Present State*.
[11] *Present State*, p. 83.

ginia as a tutor for the children of Robert Carter, one of "King" Carter's grandsons.[12] But these, as well as George Washington's own diaries,[13] give a picture of a later generation.

Thus Byrd's diary stands out as the only extensive one from the South during the early eighteenth century, and almost during the whole colonial period—the only counterpart of the fairly numerous New England journals. This gives it considerable importance for the study of American history. Written by a prominent figure in the colony, it brings as much information about political affairs as about everyday life on a plantation. Though with long interruptions, it covers thirty years of the history of Virginia. That period saw the formation of a society which was to give leaders to the new nation half a century later. The publication of Byrd's diaries has helped to correct some vulgar errors about colonial life and has greatly increased our knowledge of those formative years—as much perhaps as all the collections of public records concerning Virginia. Through Byrd's pages we reach a better understanding of the Virginia ruling class. We can realize the true proportion of activity and leisure in the lives of the great planters, or the very indifferent comfort of their houses despite relative luxury. We are more conscious of their paternal attitude toward servants and of their difficulties with people who were too often incompetent and ill-trained. We discover the barriers raised by class consciousness in the smallest details of everyday life, not only between master and servant, but also between white indentured servant and black slave. We are given a clear picture of manners and customs, and of economic and political conditions, from the supreme importance of the sovereign weed tobacco to the sessions of the Council or the duties of a militia commander.

These diaries, widely separated in time as they are, bear evidence of a natural evolution both in the colony and in Byrd's personal life. At the beginning, Indian raids still threatened Tidewater plantations; by the forties, the frontier had already been pushed back to the foot of the Appalachians, and Indians had almost completely disappeared from the coastal plain. The first portion of the diary shows the married man in his late thirties, with a quick-tempered young wife who knew little about household management; in those strenuous years the planter was trying hard to improve and extend his properties, per-

[12] *The Diary of Colonel Landon Carter of Sabine Hall, 1752–1778*, ed. Jack P. Greene (Charlottesville, Va., 1965); Philip V. Fithian, *Journal and Letters of Philip Vickers Fithian, 1773–1774*, ed. Hunter D. Farish (Williamsburg, Va., 1943); see also Louis Morton, *Robert Carter of Nomini Hall: A Virginia Tobacco Planter of the Eighteenth Century* (Williamsburg, Va., 1941).

[13] *Diaries, 1748–1799*, ed. John C. Fitzpatrick (Boston, 1925).

sonally supervising the work of his overseers. In the second portion (or at least the part of it that was written in Virginia), the widower in his middle forties looked after much of the domestic husbandry, with the help of a few white servants that he had brought back from Britain with him; between two voyages to England, he reorganized his plantations, which had lacked the owner's supervision for too many years; but his interest was still turned toward London, where he hoped to return in the near future. The last portion pictures the Colonel in his late sixties, surrounded by a family again, in a quiet household. He no longer intended to leave Virginia, and managed his properties from Westover. He traveled less often to his scattered plantations but still went on frequent visits to Williamsburg. He was richer and could afford more leisure in his old age, although he was still active and his diary never became retrospective.

Another evolution, however, can be observed in the entries themselves, which became shorter and shorter as the years passed. They cover about fifteen lines each in *The Secret Diary*, though they sometimes reach twenty. They average twelve lines in *The London Diary* and only seven or eight in the last one. Samples of ordinary days chosen from each of the diaries in the same month of the year will give a fair and easy illustration of the change.

On August 12, 1710, Byrd wrote,

I rose at five o'clock and read a chapter in Hebrew and some Greek in Lucian. I said my prayers and ate boiled milk for breakfast. I danced my dance. I had a quarrel with my wife about her servants who did little work. I wrote a long and smart letter to Mr. Perry, wherein I found several faults with his management of the tobacco I sent him and with mistakes he had committed in my affairs. My sloop brought some tobacco from Appomattox. Mr. Bland came over[14] and dined with us on his way to Williamsburg. I ate roast shoat for dinner. In the afternoon Mr. Bland went away and I wrote more letters. I put some tobacco into the sloop for Captain Harvey. It rained and hindered our walk; however we walked a little in the garden. I neglected to say my prayers, but had good health, good thoughts, and good humor, thank God Almighty.

Ten years later, on August 2, 1720, he wrote:

I rose about five o'clock and read a chapter in Hebrew and some Greek in Lucian. I said my prayers and had milk for breakfast. The weather was cold and cloudy, the wind west. I danced my dance. Sam G–r–d–n's mare broke into my pasture, of which I sent him word and let him know I would shoot her if she came there again. I wrote some English till dinner and then

[14] Richard Bland was Byrd's neighbor and lived at Jordan's Point, facing Westover on the south bank of the James.

ate some fish again. After dinner I put several things in order and then wrote two letters to Williamsburg till the evening and then took a walk about the plantation. At night I talked with my people and particularly with Tom who had taken a vomit because he had an ague. His vomit had worked very well and he was better, thank God. I said my prayers and retired, but committed uncleanness, for which God forgive me.

And here is the entry for August 13, 1740, after twenty more years had passed: "I rose about five, read Hebrew and Greek. I prayed and had tea. I danced. The weather was very hot and clear, the wind southwest. I read Latin and played piquet and billiards and read Latin till dinner when I ate roast pigeon. After dinner we played piquet again and I read Latin till the evening when we walked to visit the sick. I talked with my people and prayed."

The last example is more concise by far. This is not to be entirely attributed to the lesser activity of the old man, since it appears even in Byrd's way of reporting the same facts. It is no wonder then that the first diary, more detailed and set for a longer period in the Westover surroundings, should be the most interesting in the eyes of the modern reader. It therefore seems that if other portions of Byrd's diary were to be discovered now they would add little to what is already known of him. Professor Wright finds that "the entries are often dull, tedious and repetitive."[15] This cannot be denied when Byrd's diary is compared to Pepys's. The latter is more gossipy, a desirable quality in this kind of writing. Pepys wrote an average of thirty lines to describe the events of each day. The shorter its entries, the more repetitive a diary appears, particularly if it is used to record trivial facts; this is a characteristic of Byrd's *Another Secret Diary*. We never feel that Pepys is too lengthy, and we sometimes wish Byrd had given a more detailed account of his life at Westover. Had his aim been to reconcile everyday life and spiritual life, Byrd might have been more detailed in his entries. But he was not an introspective man, and his even temper and moderate sensitivity helped prevent those feelings of uncertainty and restlessness that made men probe into their souls. This aspect of Byrd's character is reflected in his very style, with its small number of adjectives, words which are essential for description of places, events, and feelings.

Another reason for Byrd's occasional tediousness may be found, of course, in the greater monotony of daily life on the plantation, as compared with the variety of London life. This is why *The London Diary*, more than the other two, calls up memories of Pepys and invites comparison with him. There we can see Byrd strolling in St.

---

[15] *Secret Diary*, p. xxv.

James's Park with the fashionable crowd, or going to Will's Coffee-
house to talk with friends, paying visits to ladies, attending confer-
ences in connection with the political affairs of Virginia, putting in an
appearance at Court and kissing the King's hand, going to plays, con-
certs, masquerades, and assemblies at the Spanish ambassador's, dining
at Pontack's with the members of the Royal Society before a meeting
at Crane Court, visiting friends at their country places, and going to
Tunbridge Wells in summer when the fashionable world deserted the
town. Inevitably the parts of this diary written in Virginia pall upon
the reader and seem weaker by comparison, except perhaps for Byrd's
visits to Williamsburg, when he meets friends and attends sessions of
the Council. Byrd's diary, though as frank as Pepys's, is inferior in
wealth of details and in variety. Where Byrd's entry runs thus: "Mr.
Custis told me several things concerning managing the overseers
which I resolved to remember,"[16] Pepys would probably have gone
on to explain what these "several things" were. Perhaps Byrd felt this
advice was too complex to be condensed in the few lines of an entry;
or that he could remember it easily, so that it was not worth writing
down. In any case it shows that Byrd did not give a thought to the
feelings of a prospective reader. In this respect his diary may be
judged superior to Evelyn's. The latter, partly because it was not in
secret writing, is less confidential. Its entries, irregular in length, were
not always written day by day. Byrd left us a continuous flow of entries of fairly even length describing what he did or saw each day. In
the whole course of his three extant diaries, he interrupted his record
of events only twice: on the last two days of 1709 and during a
month's illness in the fall of 1740.[17]

These documents are really the daily chronicle of an age, jotted
down on the spur of the moment, without giving a second thought to
turns of expression. While disclosing the interesting personality of a
versatile man, they also bring to life a complete panorama of eighteenth-century Virginia and are for the student of the period an unequaled mine of information. Details, allusions, remarks, and passing
judgments weave an ample and close backdrop; they lay out a varie-
gated, lifelike mosaic which restores the atmosphere of colonial Virginia with the utmost truthfulness. Yet these diaries may easily be
disappointing on a literary plane: Byrd can but suffer from a compari-

---

16 *Ibid.,* Feb. 13, 1712.

17 *Another Secret Diary,* p. 104. In case of a short illness of two or three days,
Byrd would catch up again after he had recovered (for an example, see *Secret
Diary,* June 5, 1712). There are no entries for April 7, 1712, and March 21, 1740.
Two other interruptions, Jan. 6–Feb. 13, 1721, and Sept. 8–Dec. 5, 1739, are due
to leaves missing in the manuscripts.

son with Pepys in this respect, as a good Elizabethan dramatist must from a comparison with Shakespeare. There is only one Pepys as there is one Shakespeare; which is no reflection on others, but rather an acknowledgment of superhuman size, as high above the rest, to repeat Dryden's apt quotation of Virgil, "Quantum lenta solent inter viburna cupressi."

CHAPTER IX

Chronicler

B YRD transcribed three portions of his diary from the original shorthand and put them into shape, though still in the journal form. Some of his friends read the manuscripts and pressed him to have them published. Yet this was not done until 1841, nearly a century after his death.[1] These portions were, in chronological order, *The History of the Dividing Line, A Progress to the Mines,* and *A Journey to the Land of Eden,* describing journeys made respectively in 1728, 1732, and 1733. All three journals are largely impersonal, particularly when compared with the secret diaries. In those days, no one (and a gentleman less than any other, perhaps) could contemplate the publication of their most private thoughts and intimate feelings; these had to be expurgated before such writings could be presented to the public.

The last two parts are merely records of overseeing trips. In *A Progress to the Mines,* in which Byrd reached the highest degree of detachment and objectivity possible to him, he reconciled the need "to oversee his overseers" with the desire to get precise information on mines and furnaces in Virginia. He carefully recorded everything that he learned about the extraction and melting of iron ore. Incidentally he mentioned a new method of preparing a different variety of tobacco, cheaper and less subject to fire, though not so fragrant. He was not averse to enjoying a bit of scandal concerning his hosts or neighbors,[2] and he sometimes drew a brief sketch of a picturesque character. Such was Monsieur Marij, whom he met at Thomas Randolph's:

He had been a Romish priest, but found reasons, either spiritual or temporal, to quit that gay religion. The fault of this new convert is that he looks for as much respect from his Protestant flock as is paid to the Popish

[1] *The Westover Manuscripts: Containing the History of the Dividing Line Betwixt Virginia and North Carolina; A Journey to the Land of Eden, A.D. 1733; and A Progress to the Mines. Written from 1728 to 1736, and Now First Published,* ed. Edmund Ruffin (Petersburg, Va., 1841). The Westover Manuscripts, reedited in 1866 by Thomas Wynne, were bought by the Virginia Historical Society in 1962.

[2] *Prose Works,* p. 377, 367. On Germanna, see page 50, note 13.

clergy, which our ill-bred Huguenots don't understand. Madam Marij had so much curiosity as to want to come too; but another horse was wanting, and she believed it would have too vulgar an air to ride behind her husband. This woman was of the true Exchange breed, full of discourse but void of discretion, and married a parson with the idle hopes he might some time or other come to be His Grace of Canterbury. The gray mare is the better horse in that family, and the poor man submits to her wild vagaries for peace's sake. She has just enough of the fine lady to run in debt and be of no signification in her household.[3]

Another entertaining portrait is that of Mrs. Spotswood's sister. Near a shady lane and a marble fountain, there was "a covered bench, where Miss Theky often sat and bewailed her virginity." The next day was her birthday:

Upon which I made her my compliments and wished she might live twice as long a married woman as she had lived a maid. I did not presume to pry into the secret of her age, nor was she forward to disclose it, for this humble reason, lest I should think her wisdom fell short of her years. She contrived to make this day of her birth a day of mourning, for, having nothing better at present to set her affections upon, she had a dog that was a great favorite. It happened that very morning the poor cur had done something very uncleanly upon the colonel's bed, for which he was condemned to die. However, upon her entreaty, she got him a reprieve, but was so concerned that so much severity should be intended on her birthday that she was not to be comforted; and . . . she protested she would board out her dog at a neighbor's house, where she hoped he would be more kindly treated.[4]

Yet in the evening Miss Theky was "good-natured enough to forget the jeopardy of her dog." Such anecdotes were intended to relieve the instructive part of Byrd's narration, the aim of all literature still being "to teach and delight," as in Sir Philip Sidney's time; "to serve and please at the same time," as Defoe repeated in other words to the same purpose.

Byrd's narrative is always cheerful, and his humorous turn often appears in jocular remarks, mostly about the relations between men and women. He admired the wild prospect of a river, "full of rocks over which the stream tumbled with a murmur loud enough to drown the notes of a scolding wife." At Colonel Spotswood's, he said, "our conversation with the ladies, like whip sillabub, was very pretty but had nothing in it." A noisy stream was compared to a nagging wife,

---

[3] *Ibid.*, p. 344. The Reverend James Marij, or Marye, rector of the parish of St. James' Northam in Goochland County, had married Letitia Maria Ann Staige.

[4] *Ibid.*, pp. 358–59.

the insipid conversation of some women to a tasteless drink, and man was the philosophical victim of his helpmate. One evening the colonel and his guest reluctantly interrupted an absorbing discussion to obey a summons of the ladies to supper and to bed: "So very pliable a thing is frail man when women have the bending of him." Byrd's good-humored jests sometimes recall memories of "The Female Creed," but with a lesser degree of coarseness. This kind of light, universal satire is not very original, whether it is aimed at women or doctors. Colonel Martin had an elder brother in Ireland, "a physician, who threatens him with an estate some time or other; though possibly it might come to him sooner if the succession depended on the death of one of his patients."[5] There is no real sting in it, and here again the conventional butts of comedy help to make the narrative more readable.

Just as readable, but just as serious under the pleasant tone, is the journal of the expedition to the valley of the Roanoke in 1733, to survey the Land of Eden which Byrd had visited five years before and bought shortly after. Portraits are naturally in smaller number, since it was a journey not in the settled part of the colony but in the wilderness of the back country. There they met the "tall, meagre figure" of Colonel Drury Stith's enthusiastic miner, Byrd's henpecked "first minister" at the Bluestone Castle plantation, or the old Indian to whom the writer gave a bottle of rum, "with which he made himself very happy and all the family very miserable by the horrible noise he made all night."[6] And among the members of the small expedition was an authoritative little man, Major James Mumford, who on the first night "made the first discovery of an impatient and peevish temper, equally unfit for both a traveler and a husband." But when a few days later the woodsmen of the party discovered the fresh track of a great body of Northern Indians, "the little Major, whose tongue had never lain still, was taken speechless for sixteen hours." Byrd was quick to seize the note of comedy in characters and events. When they returned to Bluestone Castle, the wife of the henpecked overseer received them, he said, "with a grim sort of a welcome, which I did not expect, since I brought her husband back in good health—though perhaps that might be the reason." The weather could give him an opportunity for a waggish comparison: "The heavens loured a little upon us in the morning, but, like a damsel ruffled by too bold an address, it soon cleared up again." Even a misadventure could suggest a pleasant name for some unknown stream, "which we called Jesuit's Creek, because it misled us."[7] Sometimes Byrd hit upon a concise sentence

[5] *Ibid.*, pp. 341, 359, 363, 375.
[6] *Ibid.*, pp. 383, 407–8, 382.
[7] *Ibid.*, pp. 383, 393, 407, 388, 402.

which sums up the situation in a nutshell: when an unmerciful rain put out their fire, he observed: "We preferred a dry fast to a wet feast."[8] When all is said, the *Journey to the Land of Eden* is a serious work, designed mostly as propaganda in order to attract settlers, but it is never solemn or dull.

Byrd's best literary achievement, however, is undoubtedly *The History of the Dividing Line*, which he worked at, on and off, for about ten years. As usual, he had kept his diary during the whole survey of the line, and upon his return to Westover in the fall of 1728, he sent to the Board of Trade a thirty-two-page report on the difficulties that the expedition had surmounted. The document was accompanied by a letter emphasizing the hardships endured by the men.[9] This was certainly intended to ensure adequate payment for the Virginia surveying party, and it was successful, since the Board assigned one thousand pounds from the Virginia quitrents to meet all expenses.[10]

In the following years Byrd expanded his rough diary into *The Secret History of the Line*, which remained unpublished until the 1929 edition of William K. Boyd. The manuscript circulated among Byrd's London friends, for whose entertainment it seems to have been written. The names of the participants were disguised under such illuminating pseudonyms as "Firebrand," "Merryman," "Plausible," "Puzzlecause," or "Shoebrush"; the surveyors for Virginia were "Orion" and "Astrolabe," and Byrd himself was "Steady." The narrative was quite frank about the difficulties and quarrels between members of the expedition. Byrd received many compliments about the style and the entertaining qualities of his work and was urged to publish it.[11] But in 1737 he told Peter Collinson that he was writing a new version of his *History*, which he hoped to finish during the following winter.[12] The new narrative was twice as long as *The Secret History*, and its 250 pages gave an entirely different account of the expedition, intended for a much wider public, although as we have seen he never really attempted publication.

---

[8] *Ibid.*, 391.

[9] P.R.O., photocopy in the V.H.S. The text was printed in a different version in *The Colonial Records of North Carolina*, ed. William L. Saunders (Raleigh, N.C., 1886), II, 750–98.

[10] For the sharing out of the sum, see *Prose Works*, p. 336.

[11] For a good example of the care with which Byrd had already revised this first version, see five pages of the manuscript reproduced by Maude H. Woodfin in her article on "The Missing Pages of William Byrd's Secret History of the Line," *WMQ*, 3d ser., II, (1945), 66–70.

[12] In the final version, there are allusions to events that happened as late as 1736 (cf. *Prose Works*, p. 281).

In the final version, both because of its different reading public and of its more literary aim, Byrd omitted many details of *The Secret History* and added a greater number of new ones. First, he suppressed personal details which probably remained from the rough diary kept in the woods: for instance, he left out the fact that his fellow travelers hid from Byrd the false news of the death of his son until the glad tidings came that the boy had in fact recovered from a serious illness. In the first relation, he spoke his mind quite freely about the members of the surveying party, since he wrote only for his most intimate acquaintances. But when he considered publication, his pride in his country induced him to show off Virginia as the most civilized of the American colonies, and he decided to tone down to the utmost the disputes with Fitzwilliam or with the Carolinian commissioners. The quarrel in which Byrd barely prevented Fitzwilliam from hitting Dandridge with the leg of the table and finally managed to reconcile his two colleagues was passed over in silence in *The History of the Dividing Line*: "In the afternoon, Mr. Fitzwilliam, one of the commissioners for Virginia, acquainted his colleagues it was his opinion that by His Majesty's order they could not proceed farther on the line but in conjunction with the Commissioners of Carolina; for which reason he intended to retire the next morning with those gentlemen." And the disagreement is passed off with a slightly malicious jest: "They stuck by us as long as our good liquor lasted, and were so kind to us as to drink our good journey to the mountains in the last bottle we had left."[13]

Five short speeches delivered to the men to keep up their spirits were cut out or just briefly mentioned. One of them, in a rather high-flown style, was made just before the crossing of the Dismal Swamp, beginning: "Gentlemen, we are at last arrived at this dreadful place which till now has been thought impassable. . . ." It was reduced to the following sentence: "After reposing about an hour, the commissioners recommended vigor and constancy to their fellow travelers, by whom they were answered with three cheerful huzzas, in token of obedience."[14] The letters exchanged by the two commissions before their first meeting were also suppressed as immaterial to the ordinary reader.[15] Thus did Byrd lighten and improve his narrative while also rendering it less personal.

The Secret History of the Line had given a frank account of the violence that had been displayed toward women on half a dozen oc-

---

[13] *Prose Works*, pp. 142–45, 106–7, 237.

[14] *Ibid.*, pp. 63, 190.

[15] See William K. Boyd, ed., *William Byrd's Histories of the Dividing Line betwixt Virginia and North Carolina*, 2d ed. (New York, 1967), pp. 21–29.

casions by members of the expedition, particularly by Virginians; the commissioners then had failed to enforce discipline.[16] But such unfavorable facts were quite unseasonable in the version intended for the general reader in England. So most of these passages were omitted, and the only example that remained of such outrages was treated rather lightly: "A damsel who assisted in the kitchen had certainly suffered what the nuns call martyrdom, had she not capitulated a little too soon. This outrage would have called for some severe discipline, had she not bashfully withdrawn herself early in the morning, and so carried off the evidence."[17]

These cuts and omissions, whether made for literary reasons or out of patriotic feelings, were amply compensated by the numerous additions Byrd made to his former narrative. Besides an abundance of details about the flora and fauna of Southern Virginia or about Indians and Indian life, which were to furnish the instructive side of the book, he added many remarks that created what Professor Beatty called "the most singular divergence between the two works."[18] Whereas *The Secret History* had contained only one disparaging comment on North Carolinians, Byrd took them as his butt in the later version. Certainly, as Professor Beatty suggested, he knew that "the readiest way in which to exalt his own colony was by disparaging every other." Yet this does not detract from his sincerity, and his criticism had a firm basis in truth. He presented the people of "Lubberland" as "intolerably lazy" fellows who "loiter away their lives," "in a climate where no clergyman can breathe." "They do not know Sunday from any other day, any more than Robinson Crusoe did. . . . But they keep so many Sabbaths every week that their disregard of the Seventh Day has no manner of cruelty in it, either to servants or cattle."[19] In fact, Byrd's poor opinion of his southern neighbors was shared by most Virginians. Similar sentiments had been expressed in print by Hugh Jones in 1724, and Governor Spotswood in 1711, less than a year after his arrival in the colony, observed: "The country of North Carolina has long been the common sanctuary of all our runaway servants and of all others that fly from the due execution of the laws in this and Her Majesty's other Plantations." It was the expression of an ingrained desire to maintain law and order in a longer-settled colony, as well as of a sort of class consciousness dividing the landowner, however small his property, from the destitute adventurer—the sense of

16 *Ibid.*, p. xxvi. For examples, see *Prose Works*, p. 59 and p. 73.
17 *Prose Works*, p. 224.
18 Beatty, p. 143.
19 *Prose Works*, pp. 192, 204, 194 and 195.

superiority that hard-earned possession feels toward failure, whether from misfortune or laziness or inability. As was observed by a critic, "*The Dividing Line* justifies its name metaphorically as well as literally, for in this journal crops up repeatedly the scorn of the prosperous and efficient Virginia landowner for the poor white trash of North Carolina."[20]

Byrd's partiality, however, was not directed only against North Carolinians. Again like most Virginians, he often gave vent to his contempt for New Englanders and for Quakers. This originated in a keen sense of ridicule rather than in downright hostility. He acknowledged the positive qualities of the former, though he said they might "be ridiculed for some pharisaical particularities in their worship and behavior"; but their merchants were over-mercenary despite their professed godliness: they drove hard bargains with the North Carolinians, carrying off their tobacco without paying any duty on it, and selling them such bad rum that it was commonly called "kill-devil."[21] A Quaker like William Penn himself was hardly better, if we were to believe a piece of London gossip that Byrd reported about him:

This ingenious person had not been bred a Quaker but, in his earlier days, had been a man of pleasure about the town. He had a beautiful form and very taking address, which made him successful with the ladies, and particularly with a mistress of the Duke of Monmouth. By this gentlewoman he had a daughter, who had beauty enough to raise her to be a duchess and continued to be a toast full thirty years. But this amour had like to have brought our fine gentleman in danger of a duel, had he not discreetly sheltered himself under this peaceable persuasion.[22]

A man who thus ignored the code of honor forfeited by his pusillanimity all right to the name of gentleman.

By these hits at the other colonies Byrd's *History of the Dividing Line* appears partly as a work of propaganda in favor of Virginia. But that kind of regional prejudice was only a particular form of his tendency to vent his personal opinions, whether on the degree of strictness of the Sabbath, or the error committed by the first English

[20] Spotswood to the Earl of Rochester, July 30, 1711, in *Official Letters*, I, 108. For Hugh Jones's opinion, see above, p. 111. Lucy L. Hazard, *The Frontier in American Literature* (New York, 1927), p. 58.

[21] *Prose Works*, pp. 162, 176, 205. Cf. a passage about "your saints from New England" in a letter of Feb. 20, 1735/36 to Byrd's old friend Benjamin Lynde, Chief Justice of Massachusetts, *VMHB*, IX (1902), 243-44. See also the beginning of Byrd's letter to Lord Egmont, July 12, 1736, *American Historical Review*, I (1896), 88.

[22] *Prose Works*, p. 167.

adventurers in not marrying Indian girls, or the necessity of making a survey of the Appalachians before the French thought of taking "that natural fortification."[23]

Byrd's essential aim, however, was literary, and in order to make his book more readable, he added character sketches or anecdotes in which his sense of humor always reveals itself. Near the starting point of the line, he met

a marooner that modestly called himself a hermit, though he forfeited that name by suffering a wanton female to cohabit with him. . . . As for raiment, he depended mostly upon his length of beard and she upon her length of hair, part of which she brought decently forward and the rest dangled behind quite down to her rump, like one of Herodotus' East Indian pygmies. Thus did these wretches live in a dirty state of nature, and were mere Adamites, innocence only excepted.[24]

The next day the group encamped in the pasture of a small planter whose wife "in the days of her youth, it seems, had been a laundress in the Temple, and talked over her adventures in that station with as much pleasure as an old soldier talks over his battles and distempers and, I believe, with as many additions to the truth."[25] While the surveying party were in the settled part of the country, people flocked about them, "to behold such rarities as they fancied us to be," Byrd amusedly observed.

The men left their beloved chimney corners, the good women their spinning wheels, and some, of more curiosity than ordinary, rose out of their sick beds to come and stare at us. They looked upon us as a troop of knights-errant, who were running this great risk of our lives, as they imagined, for the public weal; and some of the gravest of them questioned much whether we were not all criminals condemned to this dirty work for offenses against the state.[26]

In such passages the mischievous twinkle in Byrd's eye reminds one of the novelists of the next age, Fielding and Smollett.

Byrd liked to tell a story, and he felt compelled to digress for a good one. A Mr. Wilson, who lived on the edges of the Dismal Swamp, recounted how a man once ventured into it and lost his way, but managed to steer himself out in an unexpected manner: he took a fat louse out of his collar and exposed it to the daylight on a piece of paper. "The poor insect, having no eyelids, turned himself about till

[23] *Ibid.,* pp. 284, 160–61, 221, and 271–72.
[24] *Ibid.,* pp. 179–80.
[25] *Ibid.,* p. 180.
[26] *Ibid.,* pp. 182–83.

he found the darkest part of the heavens, and so made the best of his way toward the north." The members of the party who had to cross the Swamp kept cheerful in spite of the difficulties they encountered, "and merrily told a young fellow in the company, who looked very plump and wholesome, that he must expect to go first to pot if matters should come to extremity." The jest made him thoughtful, and he became very industrious, "that so there might be less occasion to carbonade him for the good of his fellow travelers." But when the provisions were almost exhausted, "now it was that the fresh-colored young man began to tremble every joint of him, having dreamed the night before that the Indians were about to barbecue him over live coals."[27]

It is hard to say how far Byrd put into practice the theory that he set forth in a letter to his cousin Mrs. Taylor in 1735: "Like French historians, where we do not meet with pretty incidents, we must even make them, and lard a little truth with a great deal of fiction."[28] But two versions of an incident that occurred on one of the first nights they spent in the open show how he improved his narrative. About midnight, one of the Carolinian commissioners ventured a visit to the Virginian camp where his colleagues slept under the open sky: "And his curiosity was so very clamorous that he waked me, for which I wished his nose as flat as any of his porcivorous countrymen."[29] It is interesting to see what this passing remark became in the final narrative—a short sketch in which a touch of lyricism turns to comedy:

Our landlord had a tolerable good house and clean furniture, and yet we could not be tempted to lodge in it. We chose rather to lie in the open fields, for fear of growing too tender. A clear sky, spangled with stars, was our canopy, which, being the last thing we saw before we fell asleep, gave us magnificent dreams. The truth of it is, we took so much pleasure in that natural kind of lodging that I think at the foot of the account mankind are great losers by the luxury of feather beds and warm apartments. The curiosity of beholding so new and withal so sweet a method of encamping brought one of the senators of North Carolina to make us a midnight visit. But he was so very clamorous in his commendations of it that the sentinel, not seeing his quality either through his habit or his behavior, had like to have treated him roughly. After excusing the unseasonableness of his visit and letting us know he was a Parliament man, he swore he was so taken with our lodging that he would set fire to his house as soon as he got home, and teach his wife and children to lie, like us, in the open field.[30]

---

[27] *Ibid.*, pp. 190–91, 197–98.
[28] Letter of Oct. 10, 1735, *VMHB*, IX (1902), 229 (or Bassett, p. 395).
[29] *Prose Works*, p. 61.
[30] *Ibid.*, p. 187.

At its best, Byrd's humor recalls Addison's. It is bathed in a light of indulgent irony and sets up as a model the elegance of mind and manners that should belong to the gentleman. But it often keeps something of the coarseness of Restoration wit, particularly where women are concerned. Describing the women at an Indian town, he remarked that their charms "might have had their full effect upon men who had been so long deprived of female conversation but that the whole winter's soil was so crusted on the skins of those dark angels that it required a very strong appetite to approach them." Yet after a night there, he added, "Our chaplain observed with concern that the ruffles of some of our fellow travelers were a little discolored with pochoon, wherewith the good man had been told those ladies used to improve their invisible charms."[31] As in his other works, Byrd liked a jest about the gentle sex. On the subject of Edenton in North Carolina, he mentioned the havoc parakeets make in orchards and added a brief description of those birds: "They are very beautiful but, like some other pretty creatures, are apt to be loud and mischievous." Byrd knew that women can be the bane of their poor partners' lives. Near Edenton again, people dug wolf pits "so deep and perpendicular that when a wolf is once tempted into them he can no more scramble out again than a husband who has taken the leap can scramble out of matrimony." But man, being reasonable, should humor his helpmate's fancies and understand the workings of her mind. There was a shrub in Virginia whose leaves had a fresh, agreeable smell, Byrd said, adding casually: "I am persuaded the ladies would be apt to fancy a tea made of them, provided they were told how far it came and at the same time were obliged to buy it very dear."[32] In a story set in the wilderness and concerned only with men, such remarks bespeak the importance of women in Byrd's life. Had he rewritten his *London Diary* as he did *The History of the Dividing Line*, it might have been something not far in spirit from James Boswell's *London Journal*, with the same zest for love affairs and the same sense of humor, though probably more concerned with facts and less with feelings and sentiments. This is indeed what distinguishes Byrd most from

[31] *Ibid.*, pp. 218–22. Pochoon or puccoon, the Virginia poke (cf. page 77, note 5), which bears berries staining a purplish red. Strachey had already mentioned this in his *Historie of Travell* (p. 71), and explained: "Pocones is a small root that groweth in the mountains, which being dried and beat into powder turned red, and this they use for swellings, aches, anointing their joints, painting their heads and garments with it, for which they account it very precious and of much worth" (p. 122).

[32] *Prose Works*, pp. 206, 253.

such men as Pepys or Boswell: he does not show the same degree of imagination and sensibility.

Byrd sometimes inadvertently repeated himself. Such is the case for the remark that intermarriage would have been the only way to convert Indians, or the comparison between the flesh of the bear and that of the dog.[33] The same considerations on scalping were offered twice, as were the definition of rockahominy and the way to catch beavers.[34] In spite of this occasional carelessness, the style in *The History of the Dividing Line* is easy and graceful. Like most of his contemporaries, Byrd liked a good image or comparison, particularly when it had a humorous effect: "The trees that grew near it looked very reverend with the long moss that hung dangling from their branches." The babbling of a brook aroused his verve: "We luckily came upon a crystal stream which, like some lovers of conversation, discovered everything committed to its faithless bosom." Near an overhanging rock "that strikes the eye with agreeable horror" (one of the first shivers of early Romanticism, like Thomas Gray's in the Alps), there was "a very talkative echo that, like a fluent helpmeet, will return her goodman seven words for one, and after all be sure to have the last."[35]

Byrd's comparisons were often based on classical allusions, of the kind that comes naturally to such a man of learning as he was. All the members of the surveying party were eager for the honor of crossing the Dismal Swamp: "Hercules would have soon sold the glory of cleansing the Augean stables, which was pretty near the same sort of work." A foul smell came from the place: "Not even a turkey buzzard will venture to fly over it, no more than the Italian vultures will over the filthy Lake Avernus."[36] As they were going round the swamp, they tried to locate the surveyors who were crossing it: "We ordered guns to be fired and a drum to be beaten, but received no answer, unless it was from that prating nymph, Echo, who, like a loquacious wife, will always have the last word and sometimes return three for one."[37] Once they came to a place named Crane Creek because of "great armies of cranes, which wage a more cruel war at this day with the frogs and the fish than they used to do with the pygmies

[33] *Ibid.*, pp. 160–61, 221, 245, 262.

[34] *Ibid.*, pp. 249 and 280, 259 and 313, 234 and 304.

[35] *Ibid.*, pp. 172, 254, 317.

[36] *Ibid.*, pp. 188, 194.

[37] *Ibid.*, p. 195. The first version of the comparison, in *The Secret History*, was far briefer, and coarser too: "We had no answer but from that prating slut, Echo" (*Prose Works*, p. 66).

in the days of Homer."[38] It is clear from these examples that Byrd's classical allusions are never dull or pedantic. Besides the fact that they always come naturally, they were often given a humorous coloring that calls to mind the vogue of the mock-heroic poem or the use Fielding was soon to make of classical mythology and mock-heroic battles in the novel to enliven and adorn the narrative.

A comparison of Byrd's *History* with Beverley's or Jones's works would readily reveal the gulf that lies between them. First of all, it would emphasize what the *History* is *not*: it is not a treatise, though it may contain just as much information on colonial Virginia. Byrd may go back to Captain Smith or to William Strachey for some detail, he may use the same materials as Beverley or Jones, but he always weaves them in with the informal manner of the diarist. There is just that touch of elaboration which belongs to the essay of the "tatler" style of Steele or Addison, derived from Abraham Cowley and Sir William Temple, whose prose works were all in Byrd's library. Teaching was not his primary aim; it would hardly be fitting for a gentleman; he wanted to entertain his reader, and managed to instruct him all along, unobtrusively.

Thus Byrd reached far higher than Hugh Jones, who had no style,[39] or than Robert Beverley, who aimed at a plain one, without circumlocution or adornment, except on the rare occasions when he got carried away by his enthusiasm. Beverley rejected all affectation: "I am an Indian," he informed the reader in the 1705 preface to his book, "and don't pretend to be exact in my language. But I hope the plainness of my dress will give him the kinder impressions of my honesty, which is what I pretend to. Truth desires only to be understood, and never affects the reputation of being finely equipped."[40] Simplicity and plainness were almost an obsession with him, in his style as in his private life. Not so with Byrd who, without resorting to the farfetched comparisons which marred some of his cavalier writings, aimed at an easy and elegant style, with a tinge of humor. And in this respect his achievement was unequaled in all the literature of colonial America.

Long before the publication of Byrd's writings, Washington Irv-

38 *Prose Works*, p. 309.

39 "I have industriously avoided the ornamental dress of rhetorical flourishes, esteeming them unfit for the naked truth of historical relations, and improper for the purpose of general propositions" (*Present State*, p. 48).

40 *History*, p. 9. "Indian" was then a usual term for colonists born in America. Cf. *Huguenot Exile*, pp. 137–38, or a letter of Byrd to Peter Collinson in 1736, calling one of his own letters "an Indian scribble" (*VMHB*, XXXVI [1928], 354).

ing's friend James Kirke Paulding, a Northern writer more deeply
interested in the South than most others, visited Virginia in 1816 and
read the manuscript of *The History of the Dividing Line.* "The style
of this work," he wrote, "is, I think, the finest specimen of that grave,
stately and quaint mode of writing fashionable about a century ago,
that I have met with anywhere."[41] The precision of the terms may be
questioned; elegant might be nearer the mark than "grave" and "stately," and the quaintness Paulding found there may reflect his own
affinities as much as Byrd's characteristics. But it is true that by its
style *The History of the Dividing Line,* more than anything written
in New England in the same period, recalls Addison and his contemporaries. Two years after the publication of Byrd's volume, William
Gilmore Simms, that romantic and passionate witness of the Old
South, wrote a favorable but equitable appraisal of the book and of
Byrd's style:

> The style of the narrator is very simple, but very happy. His mind is not
> only clear and manly, but it is lively and ingenious. He is no dry relator of
> his experience, gives us no tedious details, appreciates at a glance, and with
> the true traveler's instinct, the things and topics of interest, and passes, with
> light and easy pen, over those which, however necessary to the narrative,
> are yet so likely, in ordinary hands, to fatigue, and not inform, the reader.
> A frank, direct business tone, mingled happily with a playful temper, im-
> proves and freshens every page of this diary, for it is nothing more; and
> without aiming at effect, or indulging in sentimentality, the writer yet con-
> trives to invest his unimposing subject with a charm that beguiles the read-
> er onward with confidence in his companion which increases at every
> step.[42]

The History of the Dividing Line is both more literary and more
entertaining than any other of Byrd's works. We may know his times,
his country, and himself better through his letters and his newly discovered diaries, but his strongest claim to literary fame still rests on
his account of the expedition along the North Carolina border.

[41] *Letters from the South* (New York, 1817), I, 29.
[42] *Magnolia,* new ser., II (April 1843), 259–60.

CHAPTER X

Amateur

THE preceding chapters have made it clear, we hope, that Byrd cannot really have any claim to the appellation of man of letters, so secondary was this occupation in his own eyes. Many reasons combined to prevent him from being more than an amateur.

The middle-class origin of his family proved to be the first of those hindrances. His father, like many other great Virginia planters, belonged to a trading family distinguished for its industry and shrewdness; he took advantage of every opportunity to increase his wealth and improve his social status, although his financial interests always outweighed his social ambition. That hard-working man was bent on making a fortune first of all, and his son was no less land hungry, no less a businessman. From the time when he inherited the family plantations, their management remained his primary concern. Even when he contemplated living the rest of his life in England, he never lost sight of his colonial interests.

Byrd's education, despite its thorough classical grounding,[1] actually helped contribute to his interest in business. By his father's order he had finished his education at a merchant's and studied law in the Temple. Commerce and law always held a privileged place in his mind from then on, almost as much as in his father's. He never forgot that he was to run a Virginia plantation one day. As early as 1724 Hugh Jones observed that planters were "generally diverted by business or inclination from profound study and prying into the depth of things, being ripe for management of their affairs before they have laid so good a foundation of learning." In Byrd's case, it was business, not inclination, that diverted him from study. His learning was anything but superficial; he was not, like so many of his colleagues, more inclined to "read men by business and conversation than to dive into books";[2] he acquired much more than the useful, practical knowledge that was necessary to manage a large plantation; but he was too much

---

[1] His familiarity with the classical languages was far greater than was usual at the time. He once related that he had provoked his wife to acid remarks by conversing in Latin with a parson when in company (*Secret Diary*, Nov. 11, 1709).

[2] *Present State*, p. 80.

a realist, too practical-minded to devote all his time, or a great part of it, to purely speculative literature.

In his reading, he showed no particular bent for any one kind of literature, and he was too eclectic in this respect to come under one exclusive influence. He read in many different languages, both ancient and modern, and in many directions: poetry and medicine, divinity and the novel, morals and geometry; he was interested in all forms of arts and science. Professor Wright has observed that "Byrd's books represent a collector's library rather than the accumulation of constantly used works." On the other hand, Wright has also postulated that surely "pioneers did not go to the expense and trouble of gathering books merely for show,"[3] and although Byrd may not have read all of his thirty-six hundred books, he collected them for use, even though sometimes a book might be only a provision for some indefinite future need. His attitude was like that of one early colonist, who resolved, he said, "to mind my business here, and next after my pen, to have some good book always in store, being in solitude the best and choicest company."[4] Byrd, too, living on the outposts of civilization, felt that books, apart from mere practical use, were "the best and choicest company," far more than they were incentives to deep thinking. The influence of his diversified reading appears in his style, in his capacity for a well-turned sentence, rather than in his ideas, which show little originality and were familiar to most cultivated men of his times. His reading, like the presence of some company, was a form of leisure; it was to be tasted, not drunk deep; it should never become too much of an uphill task.

Byrd's early life as a man-about-town, mixing with the aristocracy and the fashionable society, emphasized this tendency, for he admired these people and was inclined to adopt the kinds of literature they favored—madrigals, short poems, character sketches, correspondence. Such literature was never time-consuming. It was essentially marked by its aristocratic elegance and sophisticated artificiality; it showed a decided bent for lighthearted wit and dignified conversation. For these self-styled amateurs, publication was always considered of minor importance.

Nor did Byrd's later life as a planter and councillor in Virginia modify his attitude to literature. Above all he remained a gentleman of the Plantations overseas, both an aristocrat and a businessman. He did not have much time to indulge in his occasional inclinations or pretensions to literary achievements. His financial difficulties were

[3] *First Gentlemen*, pp. 119, 123.
[4] John Pory, in *Narratives of Early Virginia, 1606–1625,* ed. Lyon G. Tyler (New York, 1907), p. 286.

a further hindrance, after his unfortunate decision to assume his father-in-law's debts. They delayed for a long time the final draft of *The History of the Dividing Line*. Besides, there had long been no book printer in Virginia, and while Byrd lived in the colony any publication in England would have met with many obstacles because of the distance; he was not interested enough to surmount them. Even after the establishment of a printing-house in Williamsburg in 1730, there was little incentive to literary work in the colony. Furthermore, Byrd's *History* was not written for Virginians: it aimed at giving some idea of the colony to the English public, and perhaps attracting some of them as settlers. For Byrd, writing could only be a hobby for his leisure hours, and he always viewed it as such. Both his diary and his correspondence reflect this attitude.

The influence of the Royal Society itself, which all his life remained a constant and powerful one, did little to alter his view of the matter. He might have been interested in the more general and speculative aspects of scientific knowledge; but he probably felt out of his depth there, and in his studies the utilitarian tendencies of the Society appeared in the shape of a particular curiosity about the natural world of his native country. He never lost sight of Virginia and the interests of Virginia planters. The main value of Byrd's observations lies in his scrupulous application of the methods recommended by the Royal Society in description or analysis, particularly in the realm of natural science. These he applied to a study of the flora and fauna of his country. He was bent on finding concrete uses for the scientific knowledge he gathered, whether in colonial medicine or in the discovery of substitutes for products that could not be found or grown in the climes of Virginia. "The truth of it is," he wrote to Sir Hans Sloane in 1737, "our woods abound with so many useful plants that, would you do as much good after you are dead as you do while you are alive, you must improve the scheme of Dr. Radcliffe, and bequeath in your will an exhibition for one or more plantary physicians, whose travels should be confined to this part of the world only, where nature seems to be more in her youth, and to come later and fresher out of her Creator's hand."[5] And in case any colonial plant should prove successful against some frequent and dangerous illness, for instance against "that British plague the small-pox," it might perhaps become of great financial interest for Virginia . . . and for himself.[6] Although ginseng and the rattlesnake root did not come up to his expectations, he never lost faith in them; when

[5] Byrd to Sloane, May 31, 1737, *WMCQ*, 2d ser., I (1921), 196.
[6] Byrd to Sloane, Aug. 20, 1738, *ibid.*, p. 198; see also pp. 199–200.

the reports of the Royal Society were negative or indifferently good, he preferred to believe that those "noble plants" had lost all their virtue during the ocean voyage.

His family, his education, and his whole life tended to make him more gentleman-planter than writer and prevented him from taking anything but a passing interest in his own writings. The only literary occupations that he could carry through were, most naturally, his correspondence and his diary, for they both took little time and could be considered useful occupations for the planter. Byrd's original diary partakes of the nature of the register or minute book more than of anything else, and it must have been occasionally useful in his business affairs. As for his rewritten journal, it shows quite decidedly the bias of an active propaganda in favor of Virginia, a country in need of more settlers, whom Byrd would have been quite ready to welcome on his own lands. He always seems to be on the lookout for people who might be attracted by his engaging description of the colony and of the possibilities it could afford them. This, of course, is not intended as a reflection on Byrd's sincerity when he praised his country. But in a way, "utility first" might be his motto in his writings. Otherwise they were kept for his leisure hours, and must be looked upon as a mere pastime. Personal and public affairs, those of his own plantations and of Virginia, always came first.

Despite the diversity of his reading, his thought remained fairly simple—one might almost say sketchy. It shows no real complexity, no searching self-analysis, no metaphysical anxiety, no deep philosophy or wild imagination, but only precise observation, exact description, and clear narrative. He was a steady, well-balanced man, mentally and emotionally. His extensive reading did not really make his thought deeper or exert any great influence on it. His reading, however, often betrays a real obsession: the fear of becoming countrified, of losing touch with London and the mother country. Byrd still felt himself a true Englishman at heart, though living overseas, as did even those colonists who had not spent so many years as Byrd had in England. The enlightened society Byrd had consorted with for so long was still a model that he badly missed, for it had no equal in Virginia. He tried to keep in touch by various means. He found a concrete link in his letters to English friends, in his continued relations with the Royal Society, in the attention he gave to current events and present interests, or in the buying of books. He thus kept up with the latest intellectual developments in England. But his reading also appears to be a link of another kind, a self-imposed task as much as a pastime, a kind of intellectual training, in order to prevent his mind from getting rusty. "I exercised my memory with getting things by heart," he wrote one Sunday in 1711. He hoped by such means to remain intellectually fit. "I read some English which gave me great light into the nature of spirit," he noted on January 27, 1711; but his diary contains nothing about his reflections on the matter. He was moved to tears of repentance on reading one of Dr. Tillotson's sermons, but we are not even apprised of its subject. He might mention that he "read in Collier against the stage," but nothing appears of his own opinion on the controversy. When in April 1721 he went to a play in Williamsburg, he only remarked that the company "acted tolerably well";[7] and he was no more explicit about the performances he saw in London in 1718 or 1719. Unlike Pepys, he never gave any account of the books he read or the plays he saw.

Indeed, one of the most surprising facts in *The London Diary* is that Byrd, so often considered a prototype of the American colonial intellectual, did not say a word about the literary circles of the capital where he was staying. "I rose about five and read a chapter in Hebrew and some Greek"; in London as well as in Virginia, this was the extent of his classical interest as transcribed on paper. He was not really worried about ideas and gave us no insight into whatever literary stimulus the metropolis might have had to offer. His diary might be that of any ordinary man, and in this respect we might go so far as to say that it is as uninteresting, as unliterary. A comparison with Boswell's *London Journal* would show at once how much further a man can go in the revelation of his own sentiments even in a diary that is not intended to remain secret and has been written for some intimate friend. But then Boswell was the kind of man who, perhaps because of his own physical appearance, was willing to make people laugh at his own expense rather than not make them laugh at all. Byrd was too conscious of his dignity to show the same apparent naïveté, and he stuck too much to facts without letting his own feelings display themselves as his pen went on. Few figures of his importance have provided so commonplace a portrait of themselves in a diary. It is so unadorned, so dry that it demonstrates the limitations of the history of everyday life. "A true story," Somerset Maugham said, "is never quite so true as an invented one." Real life sometimes may be too drab, too repetitive to be worth reading, and Byrd's concerns (or what shows of them in his diary) may appear less interesting than his surroundings, about which it is tantalizing to know so little, to be able to glean such scanty information from so many pages.

This might seem a rather negative and disappointing conclusion

---

[7] *Secret Diary*, Jan. 28, 1711; May 7, 1710; Nov. 23, 1709; *London Diary*, April 25, 1721.

about Byrd—that he was a personality without any marked intellectual originality, of whose works only a small part can really be called literary. Was he then only a might-have-been in literature? To judge so would simply be to ask him for what he could not give. The cultural life of the American colonies could not produce the same kind of literature as that of England. It could produce no Shakespeare yet, no Milton or Newton, because people had first to devote themselves not to thought but to action. "In the early days of colonization," Henry Adams wrote, "every new settlement represented an idea and proclaimed a mission. Virginia was founded by a great, liberal movement aiming at the spread of English liberty and empire."[8] This colonization may have reflected an ideal, but the colonists first had to transpose this ideal into action, and build their country. They might enjoy culture, they did not produce it; their intellectual life, as Professor Wertenbaker remarked, was more receptive than creative:

The planter might enjoy fine music, but he was seldom a composer; he might read Shakespeare and Milton, but he did not write plays or poetry; he might purchase fine paintings for his residence, but he was not a painter; he might study the works of Copernicus and Newton and Boyle, but he was not himself a scientist. Virginia in the colonial period produced no poet, . . . no novelist, no playwright, no great theologian, no artist, no sculptor, no outstanding architect. Yet there were hundreds who were interested in literature, art, architecture, music; might themselves be amateur writers, architects, musicians.[9]

As late as 1825, Thomas Jefferson had made a similar observation about his countrymen: "Literature is not yet a distinct profession with us. Now and then a strong mind arises, and at its intervals of leisure from business, emits a flash of light. But the first object of young societies is bread and covering; science is but secondary and subsequent."[10] This describes exactly what literature represented for Byrd and his contemporaries in the colonies. Even if he had decided, against all probability, to devote himself entirely to literature, it could hardly have been in America. He would only have become one among many *English* writers, instead of being the first, and almost the only, writer of any real importance in colonial Virginia.

Thus it is that only a very small part of Byrd's extant works may be judged to have reached any degree of literary excellence. In this

---

[8] *The History of the United States of America during the Administration of Thomas Jefferson* (New York, 1889–90), I, 177.

[9] *The Golden Age of Colonial Literature* (New York, 1949), pp. 109–10.

[10] Jefferson to J. Evelyn Denison, Nov. 9, 1825, *The Writings of Thomas Jefferson,* ed. A. A. Lipscomb and A. L. Bergh (Washington, D.C., 1903) XVI, 129–35.

respect, the publication of his diary has brought him no such fame
as Pepys's *Diary* did to its author. As a writer Byrd will continue to
be appreciated mostly for *The History of the Dividing Line*, a work
of varied interest whose literary affiliations were aptly summed up
by Professor Jay B. Hubbell:

It is a travel book, a history, a nature book with information about animals,
plants and trees, and a collection of character sketches; it is also something
of a satire aimed chiefly at the riffraff along the border. Occasionally it reminds one of William Bartram's *Travels* in Georgia and Florida but more
often it suggests the diary in which Sarah Kemble Knight recorded her impressions of the Connecticut backwoodsmen she encountered on her journey from Boston to New York in 1704.[11]

The last comparison again emphasizes the factual character of Byrd's
writings: Mrs. Knight's *Journal* is a more personal document, a record of emotions and opinions as well as observations colored by a
keen sense of humor.

But if Byrd's *History* is the best literary expression of his urbane
personality, it should be remembered in justice to him that this was
almost the only work he really prepared for publication. The rest
is mostly illustrative material for the history of colonial Virginia and
must be viewed from quite a different angle.

Indeed, for the very reason that most of Byrd's works were written
from day to day, offhand, without thinking twice about what he said
and how he said it, they now stand out as social documents of extraordinary value, helping to recapture the flavor of Southern life
in the early eighteenth century. Even the parts of Byrd's diary that
were rewritten later are so reliable from this standpoint that his works
have become the essential text for the study of social history in colonial Virginia. No other contemporary writer brings us half as much
information on the subject. In fact, all the conditions that prevented
Byrd from being a real man of letters helped him to be a good witness
of his times and his country.

His family, established in the colony before his birth, was already
among the most powerful, financially and politically. This gave him
both a personal interest in colonial matters and a high position which
afforded him a good surveying ground. Then his English education,
his wide reading, and his connection with the Royal Society fitted
him for careful observation and clear expression. They helped him
to keep a fairly open mind; they developed his versatility and his
intellectual curiosity.

His long years in London while his family interests were in Vir-

---

11 *The South in American Literature, 1607–1900* (Durham, N.C., 1954), p. 51.

ginia, his position as agent for the colony, his knowledge of the London side of colonial government, all helped enable him to stand well back and take in the whole picture of his native country, from London as well as from Williamsburg or Westover.

And yet, he was a true Virginian. He was always ready to fight for the interests of the colonists, for their rights as English people and their freedom from despotic control by the Board of Trade or the king's representative. He never questioned the power of the English Crown, only the advisedness of decisions made far from the colony by men who often had no notion of what Virginia was like, men who, in the colonists' view, saw it only as a paying concern for the mother country. After living in the polite circles of Queen Anne's London, he was able to adapt to life on the Carolina border, in the wilderness of the frontier. He knew both sides of Virginia, the great plantation with its stable, aristocratic patterns, and the up-country farm with its approximation of frontier conditions. To their detailed picture of plantation life his works add a full description of colonial Williamsburg with its small English society and its political life, and more than a glimpse of the frontier with its pioneers and Indians. This in itself is no mean achievement. In his own way, Byrd must have been an exceptional character after all to attain to such conspicuous success.

PART THREE

The Painter of Colonial Virginia

Plenty, which in this country is the constant portion of the industrious.

Prose Works, 216

Introduction

BYRD'S reluctance to publish his writings arose from his gentle-manly reserve and a desire for perfection. He believed that too many modern books had no real value to qualify them for publication: "Socrates," he said, "had a modesty which would much better become most of our modern authors, for, being asked why he would not oblige the world with some of his works, [he] replied, ' 'Twould be a pity to spoil so much paper.' "[1] And yet Byrd was led by a real urge to write down the most trivial and intimate facts of his life, and he felt compelled to keep everything that he wrote.

This instinctive writer was no genius, but a versatile mind with a gift (and a training) for observation. He lived in a country with no literature of imagination. At best his contemporaries only felt at times the desire of correcting English misconceptions about their own country: such was the case for Byrd's brother-in-law Robert Beverley. The Virginians of those days were essentially men of action, and whatever they wrote bore the hallmark of their dynamism. Because he possessed these qualities, Byrd represented the kind of man best qualified to give the accurate description of the spirit of an age and a country, particularly such a new country as eighteenth-century Virginia.

In a letter to William Wirt in 1815, Jefferson drew a brief sketch of colonial society in mid-eighteenth century as he remembered it:

To state the differences between the classes of society and the line of de-markation which separated them, would be difficult. The law, you know, admitted none except as to the twelve counsellors. Yet in a country insu-lated from the European world, insulated from its sister colonies, with whom there was scarcely any intercourse, little visited by foreigners, and having little matter to act upon within itself, certain families having risen to splendor by wealth and the preservation of it from generation to gen-eration under the law entails; some had produced a series of men of talents; families in general had remained stationary on the grounds of their fore-fathers, for there was no emigration to the westward in those days. The wild Irish, who had gotten possession of the valley between the Blue Ridge and North Mountain, forming a barrier over which none ventured to leap,

[1] Commonplace Book, p. 40.

and would still less venture to settle among. In such a state of things, scarcely admitting any change of station, society would settle itself down into several strata, separated by no marked lines, but shading off imperceptibly from top to bottom, nothing disturbing the order of their repose. There were then aristocrats, half-breeds, pretenders, a solid independent yeomanry, looking askance at those above, yet not venturing to jostle them, and last and lowest, a seculum of beings called overseers, the most abject, degraded and unprincipled race, always cap in hand to the Dons who employed them, and furnishing materials for the exercise of their pride, insolence and spirit of domination.[2]

These lines, in which Jefferson looks back upon a past era, were written after a sufficient number of years had elapsed for him to see colonial society in its true historical perspective and to define it by contrast with the wider scope of the newly created United States. By mid-eighteenth-century, Virginia society had already taken a more rigid shape than it showed in Byrd's times, but Jefferson emphasizes a few essential characteristics which are borne out by Byrd's diaries and should always be kept in mind. Virginia was then an isolated land, with London and the mother country for its main link—a slender one—with the other colonies. This fact appears strikingly in *The London Diary*. Nothing could be more different than the life of the same man in London and at Westover—a far less obvious and superfluous remark than it may seem. In the latter half of the volume, Byrd feels (and conveys the feeling to the reader) that he is really living in another world, after going through the looking glass. Shut in as it was on all sides, Virginia had fast become a fairly conservative country where classes, however indefinite and overlapping, had formed; and the passage from one to another was very slow and gradual. At the close of the seventeenth century, the golden age of adventurers and fortune makers was definitely over.

Yet Jefferson's sketch is incomplete; he omitted the netherworld of Virginia, people who were as inconsequential in the running of the country as children or animals. He did not look lower than overseers, and thus left out classes which in spite of his liberal opinion on slavery he felt hardly worth mentioning: indentured servants, the already growing group of poor whites on the frontier, and Negro slaves. He also forgot tradespeople, probably because they were a borderline case except in the few towns: they generally belonged to one class of planters or another, unless they were in their service; or they were real woodsmen trading with the Indians. In colonial Virginia the possession of land was almost the only criterion which deter-

2 *Writings*, XIV, 336–37.

mined someone's place in society. But these inconsiderable classes do appear in Byrd's works, even though they remain in the background. What Byrd can show to the reader is precisely the "settling down" of colonial society, to use Jefferson's term, in a cross section which reveals it in everyday life. And this is something none of his contemporaries gave us.

CHAPTER XI

The Plantation World

THE reader of Byrd's diaries should not expect to find there any detailed description of the setting in which he lived. A diary is rarely concerned with the physical aspects of the writer's familiar surroundings, which usually pass unnoticed, until perhaps a long stay away from home restores them to their true importance. The substance of a diary is rather made of events, facts however small, or sometimes personal feelings and moods; it may be something of a novel of action or character, perhaps a period novel or a psychological one, but in any case it lacks those descriptions which often fill the expository chapters of the book. Byrd's diary does not escape this rule, and the reader's imagination must conjure up a vision of Westover, the wide mansion on the bank of James River, about thirty miles from Williamsburg, with a landing-stage for the river sloop plying between Westover and "the plantations above," or between Westover and the Chesapeake; the wooden buildings of the servants' quarters at the back, separated from the master's house by gardens and orchards and lawns; and farther away, the extensive meadows and fields, with cattle, oats, Indian corn, and wheat for the subsistence of the small community, but mostly tobacco, the real source of profit and the main concern of the planter.

Westover itself, the mansion, is said to have remained to this day pretty much as it was in the eighteenth century, in spite of fire and war. For it was partly burned in 1749, and was occupied by troops during the War of Independence and the Civil War. Like most of the James River plantation houses, Westover has two fronts, one commanding the water view to the other bank more than a mile away, the other facing toward carriage road, fields, and back country. It stands on a large level bluff, about 150 yards from the river, with its broad front of red brick, its steep slated roof, its impressive row of tall overshadowing tulip poplars, amidst close-shaven lawns.

The sloping lawn on the river front is defended against the current and periodical freshets by a low wall of massive buttressed masonry. To the right and the left the avenues from the boat landings are cut off to vehicles by small gates among roses, magnolias, and wisteria. The land front is approached through the ornate wrought-iron gates which bear the Byrd coat of arms and the monogram of William Evelyn Byrd, guarded by two lead eagles perched with outstretched wings on the gateposts.

The house itself, without porch, is considered one of the best examples of Georgian architecture in America, with its high, steep roof set with dormer windows and flanked by tall chimneys. The original building of the early 1730's, which is now the center of the mansion, is three stories high and seems perfectly symmetrical from the outside. But the off-center hall divides the rooms into unequal sizes: the reception room and music room on the east side are considerably larger than the dining room and chamber on the west side. The two wings, a story and a half high, are connected with the center building by large passages built later. The passage to the east is entered from the large reception room or the music room and gives access to the library, which was burned during the War between the States and restored later, although with a roof of a slightly different shape.

On the river front, three-sided steps of gray stone lead to the magnificent marble doorway. The door-head is massive, decorated and pedimented, with a broken arch and a pineapple, the symbol of hospitality, in the center. The window frames are painted white, and a white band runs around the center building at second-floor level, enhancing the soft red of the bricks, the dark color of the slates, and the green ivy growing up the walls.

The interior of Westover is as elaborate and beautiful as its exterior, with paneled walls, *rocaille* ceilings, and a fine stairway, five feet wide, with spirally turned balusters made of mahogany. The mantels of the main rooms are remarkable, each in its own way; one in the reception room is of beautiful black marble decorated with elaborately carved white marble, and the set-in oblong mirror above it is surrounded by white carved marble in the pattern of grapes and vine leaves.

Among the outbuildings is a tool house sheltering a dry well, in whose walls, five or six yards down, two doors lead to two small rooms, which in turn lead by underground passages to the river.

The garden is to the west of the main building. There lies buried William Byrd II, later known as "the Black Swan"; his tomb is in the center, with his oft-quoted epitaph on its north and south sides. One half of the garden is planted in shrubs and flowers arranged in formal box-hedged squares, with a pleasant arbor and shaded walk on the east side; in the other half are fruit and vegetables.[1]

---

[1] See *Historic Gardens of Virginia*, ed. Edith T. Sale (rev. ed., Richmond, 1930), pp. 21–26.

To one acquainted with the various periods of colonial Virginia, all this, as it now stands, rather evokes later ages: the time perhaps when in 1782 the widow of William Byrd III entertained the Marquis de Chastellux, one of General Rochambeau's officers.[2] The whole mansion was embellished or restored by several generations, of Byrds and others, before it attained its present aspect. With some toning down, however, with less elegance and elaborate ornamentation, it may give some idea of the setting in which Byrd lived his last ten or twelve years. But one fact remains and should always be borne in mind: most of his life in Virginia, Byrd dwelt in the older frame house, far less opulent, erected by his father in 1690 fifty yards to the west.

Byrd's lands along the James were then among the richest in Virginia, if we are to believe the Swiss traveler who in 1702 described a settlement in the neighborhood:

Conditions here differed in every respect from those of other places. Things that are grown are there in such abundance that many Englishmen come a distance of thirty miles to get fruit, which they mostly exchange for cattle. Gardens are filled there with all kinds of fruit. . . . The cattle are fat because of the abundant pasture. The soil is not sandy, as it is generally in Virginia, but it is a heavy, rich soil. . . . I have seen there the most awful wild grapevines, whose thickness and height are incredible. There are several kinds of grapes, the best are as large as a small nut.

And he added: "It is much healthier there than towards the ocean. The country is full of game and fish."[3]

A large plantation—Westover stretched over 4,700 acres or so— was then a self-sufficient world where, with patriarchal authority, the master led as idyllic a life as any Horace or Virgil ever described. Such at least is the picture Byrd tried to impress upon his friend the Earl of Orrery in a letter written in 1726:

Besides the advantage of a pure air, we abound in all kinds of provisions without expense (I mean we who have plantations). I have a large family of my own, and my doors are open to everybody, yet I have no bills to pay, and half-a-crown will rest undisturbed in my pockets for many moons together. Like one of the patriarchs, I have my flock and my herds, my bondmen and bondwomen, and every sort of trade amongst my own servants, so that I live in a kind of independence on everyone but Providence. However, though this sort of life is without expense, yet it is attended with a great deal of trouble. I must take care to keep all my people to their duty,

---

[2] See Marquis de Chastellux, *Travels in North America in the Years 1780, 1781 and 1782*, ed. Howard C. Rice, Jr. (Chapel Hill, N.C., 1963), II, 430–33 (April 27–30, 1782).

[3] Hinke, "Journey of Michel," *VMHB*, XXIV (1916), 122–23.

William Byrd II. From the Colonial Williamsburg Collection.

Westover: the river front. Courtesy of the Virginia Chamber of Commerce, photo by Flournoy.

to set all the springs in motion, and to make everyone draw his equal share to carry the machine forward. But then 'tis an amusement in this silent country and a continual exercise of our patience and economy. Another thing, My Lord, that recommends this country very much: we sit securely under our vines and our fig trees without any danger to our property. We have neither public robbers nor private, which your Lordship will think very strange when we have often needy governors and pilfering convicts sent amongst us. . . . Thus, My Lord, we are very happy in our Canaans if we could but forget the onions and fleshpots of Egypt.[4]

In another letter written a few months later to Lord Orrery's son, Byrd confided that his daughters liked "everything in the country except the retirement"; they missed the plays, the operas, and the masquerades of London, but they bore the change cheerfully. To another English friend he wrote: "We that are banished from these polite pleasures are forced to take up with rural entertainments. A library, a garden, a grove, and a purling stream are the innocent scenes that divert our leisure."[5] This is the classical ideal of a quiet retreat in the country, free as nature first made man, in a castle of indolence, far from the madding crowd and the monster London—the retreat of the "happy man" described by Maren-Söphie Rostvig in her study of English neoclassicism.[6]

Despite Byrd's proud affirmations, the "trouble" was often greater than the "amusement." Other letters as well as the diary show the reverse of the medal, a less idyllic life. Among foreign visitors who described the planter's way of life in those years, most superficial observers emphasized its independence, luxury, leisure, and loneliness. Only those who lived on a plantation for several months wrote of the hard-working, orderly existence of efficient and responsible masters and mistresses of Virginia households. Like most of his neighbors, even those who owned the largest estates, Byrd did not live a life of leisure. He generally had busy days, although he sometimes confessed that he had been lazy and had not done much during the day.[7] "The successful Virginia planter," as Daniel J. Boorstin observed, "came to live a life far different from that of the indolent West Indian planter; he worked long hours and was close in his supervision."[8]

[4] Byrd to Orrery, July 5, 1726, *Orrery Papers*, I, 60–62. For another letter in the same vein, see Byrd to Mrs. Otway, June 30, 1736, *VMHB*, XXXVI (1928), 216.
[5] Byrd to John Boyle, Feb. 2, 1726/27, *Orrery Papers*, I, 52; Byrd to Mrs. Armiger, June 25, 1729, Byrd Letterbook, 1729, p. 38, V.H.S.
[6] *The Happy Man, Studies in the Metamorphoses of a Classical Ideal*, 2 vols., (Oslo, 1954 and 1958).
[7] *Secret Diary*, June 6, 1712.
[8] *The Americans: The Colonial Experience* (London, 1965), p. 123.

Byrd usually rose about five or six o'clock, sometimes seven in winter, unless in earlier years his first wife coaxed him into staying late in bed. Even in his last years he remained an early riser. On rare occasions he would admit: "We lay in bed till nine o'clock because it rained and we knew not what to do up." When at home, he could always find something to occupy his time in his library. He would first read for a while, not practical information on useful subjects of modern life, not books for mere entertainment, but one or two chapters of Hebrew and a few hundred lines in Greek, whether Homer, Thucydides, Anacreon, Lucian, or another, just to keep in practice. Occasionally the presence of some guest, or the arrival of an overseer from one of his plantations, or the preparations for a journey to Williamsburg interfered with this habit. Once in 1710, when his three-year-old daughter Evelyn was "very ill," he was so concerned for her that he could eat no breakfast; but he "read a chapter in Hebrew and a little Greek in Thucydides," although he acknowledged that he could not keep his mind steady.[9]

After saying his prayers, Byrd had boiled milk for breakfast, or in later life tea or coffee. Then he would "dance his dance," a kind of daily gymnastics, and devote the rest of his time before dinner to various occupations. There were accounts to be settled, orders to be given for the day's work on the plantation, letters to be written to the overseers of "the plantations above," mostly grouped on or near the present site of Richmond, twenty or thirty miles from Westover; or there might be some sick slaves to visit and dose. Public accounts had to be kept. As receiver general, Byrd had to sell the quitrent tobacco, either directly or at public auctions; after which he had to enter the sums he had received or those he paid out to the governor.[10] Sometimes he was fortunate enough to find a spare hour to read some English or Latin, or perhaps some geometry, unless he was interrupted by one of his neighbors or by a business caller. If there were no accounts or letters to write, he took a walk about the plantation or in the garden. He once noted doing so even in early December, "because the weather was very tempting for so late in the year. God continue it for the service of those that have but little corn!"[11]

After dinner, which was served about one, with meat as the staple food,[12] he would spend part of the afternoon in his library, reading

[9] *Secret Diary*, May 16, Aug. 4, 1710.

[10] *Ibid.*, Feb. 4, 1710; July 8–9 and 21–22, 1712. See above, pp. 30–31.

[11] *Ibid.*, Dec. 4, 1709. This was after a bad crop.

[12] A glimpse of meals in a plantation-house may be caught in the journal of William Hugh Grove, an Englishman who traveled in Virginia in 1731–1732:

news from England or books about law, farming, or religion, except when there were some more accounts or letters, or when he took a nap in summer. In such a large library, it once took a whole week to put all the books in good order on the shelves. When a ship arrived from England, it sometimes meant having, among the cargo, new books to unpack and read and show to his friends. Byrd then felt both pleased and proud. Unlike most of the colonists, he had something of a book collector's soul, and it led to little quarrels with his first wife when he was unwilling to let her take a book out of the library. Sometimes he would give up his books to play cards with his wife, although he had to admit once that he had "made her out of humor by cheating her."[13] Or he might play billiards with some friend who had called and stayed for dinner, unless they preferred to converse over a bottle of French wine.

Then came the time when Byrd would walk round the plantation, often accompanied by his wife, and assess the work done during the day. Yet he did not mind letting his attention be distracted from his inspection occasionally: "Then went to see my people plant peach trees and afterwards took a great walk about the plantation and found everything in order, for which I praised God. I was entertained with seeing a hawk which had taken a small bird pursued by another hawk, so that he was forced to let go his prey. My walk lasted till the evening." Sometimes he took his bow and arrows to shoot at partridges or squirrels on the way, "which gave us abundance of diversion, but we lost some of our arrows," he once observed. There were days when this was no mere diversion but a serious expedition against the wild pigeons that ate all the cherries in the orchard; when his fruit was ripe, Byrd liked to eat cherries or apples which he picked from the trees during his inspection rounds. If there was a threat of rain, he walked in the garden, within easy reach of the house, or remained at home and walked in the library. But it was good for the master to keep an eye personally on his people. There was always the chance that a slave was sleeping somewhere in the shade instead of working, or that a servant was riding a horse without leave. There were trees to be planted, fields to be sown, tobacco to be cut or hung; or the car-

---

"The gentry at their tables have commonly five dishes or plates, of which pig's meat and greens is generally one, and tame fowl another; beef, mutton, veal or lamb make another . . ." (William Hugh Grove, Diary, 1698–1732, "Travels in Great Britain and the Netherlands and in America," f. 56, verso, Alderman Library, U. Va.)

[13] *Secret Diary*, Aug. 11–16, 1709; March 15 and 22, 1711, or Aug. 5, 1712; Dec. 30, 1711; Aug. 27, 1709.

penter was at work on the granary because some of its frame was rotten and the roof had to be done again; or the storehouse was found to be "much out of order."[14]

Then there were always a few sick people in need of medical care at the slave quarters. Once a day at least, twice in time of epidemics, Byrd would visit them. A great deal was at stake in maintaining the health of the slaves. The plantation was a complex, self-supporting unit dependent for its successful operation on the skillful and economical employment of manpower. The slave was a valuable piece of property, and his health was of primary concern to his owner. As far as medical and sanitary knowledge went, the planter usually did his best in providing for his dependents. Overseers were instructed to pay particular attention to all matters of health. The airing, cleaning, and whitewashing of the quarters were ordered for the same purpose, as were the slaves' bathing, laundering, diet, and rest periods.[15] The ill-treatment of slaves on a plantation more often came from the unwarranted pride of a poor white overseer intoxicated with his power than from any specific order of severity given by the owner. The health of his own or his neighbors' slaves in time of epidemics is a constant preoccupation in Byrd's diary. Even apart from any consideration of health, in the twenties he made a habit of spending some time "talking to his people" at the end of the day's work.[16] From such current customs may have sprung what was to become a rule on many of the best plantations: the right of any slave to convey a grievance to the master, particularly against the overseer.[17]

In the evening, Byrd would read again, sometimes aloud for his wife and any other possible company, unless they played cards or just talked together. About ten, they retired, he said his prayers and went to bed after a day when he had usually had "good health, good thoughts and good humor, thank God Almighty." Occasionally, when he was worried about his affairs, he confessed: "I neglected to say my prayers and was out of humor extremely, and had indifferent

[14] *Ibid.,* Jan. 18, 1712; Nov. 13, May 21–22, 1711; Sept. 18, 1712 and Feb. 25, 1711; July 14, 1712, and July 28–Aug. 5, 1712.

[15] See William D. Postell, *The Health of Slaves on Southern Plantations* (Baton Rouge, La., 1951).

[16] Robert Carter had formed similar habits. In a letter dated March 3, 1720–1721, he mentions that when too ill with the gout to ride his horse, he went in his coach to visit the sick slaves at the quarters of his plantation (Robert Carter, *Letters of Robert Carter, 1720–1727: The Commercial Interests of a Virginia Gentleman,* ed. Louis B. Wright [San Marino, Calif., 1940], p. 86).

[17] See Ulrich B. Phillips, *Life and Labor in the Old South* (Boston, 1929), p. 324.

health and thoughts, but God send me better if it please His good will."[18]

Such were Byrd's ordinary days at Westover, year in, year out, almost to his death. Sundays were somewhat different. It was not that he rose later or omitted to read Hebrew and Greek, though the latter was chosen rather in the Greek Testament or in "the Christian part of Anacreon" (that is in the "pious anacreontics" of St. Gregory of Nazianus and other church fathers). Sometimes he even "wrote a letter to England, notwithstanding it was Sunday."[19] But at eleven o'clock, he and his family went to church, generally in the coach despite the short distance, for the coach was a token of a planter's position in society. They "heard a sermon," about which he only remarked that it was "good," or "sleepy," or even that "nobody understood."[20] Perhaps he had to acknowledge that he had "slept a little," for which he was sorry. But he always had an eye for "a very handsome woman" and appreciated her beauty enough to mention it in his diary rather than the subject of the sermon. Even as a churchgoer he was not above worldly satisfactions, and he felt very proud when in December 1710 the vestry of Westover Church gave him "the best pew"; it is true that the church was on his own land, only a quarter of a mile from his house. The entry for the next Sunday does not fail to specify that he "took possession" of his pew.[21]

The Church of England was the dominant one in Virginia. In 1705 Robert Beverley said that the colony had "no more than five conventicles amongst them, namely, three small meetings of Quakers, and two of Presbyterians," adding that "as for the Quakers, 'tis observed by letting them alone they decrease daily."[22] The Church of Virginia, which has been very aptly called "an Episcopal Church without bishops,"[23] was loosely connected with the Church of England through the Bishop of London and his representative. As a result of the absence of a bishop in the colony, there was no official leadership in the Church, and slight variations might be found from one parish to the next in some detail of the service. Also, a system of yearly contracts had been evolved by vestries against inefficient ministers, through voluntary omission to ask their induction of the gov-

[18] *Secret Diary*, June 24, 1710.

[19] *Ibid.*, July 3, 1709.

[20] *London Diary*, May 8 and 22, 1720; *Another Secret Diary*, Feb. 17, 1740.

[21] *Secret Diary*, April 17, 1709, and Dec. 9, 1711; Dec. 18 and 24, 1710.

[22] *History*, pp. 261–62. This is confirmed by the 1697 report to the Board of Trade (Hartwell, Blair, and Chilton, *Present State*, p. 65).

[23] Boorstin, *Colonial Experience*, p. 145.

ernor. As a result, some able clergymen refused to serve in Virginia because they were not assured of a stable position, although year-to-year employment, which had progressively become the rule, was by no means a bar to long tenure of incumbencies. Naturally the vestries, composed of the most influential planters in each parish, were not particularly anxious for the appointment of bishops, and the colonial Church was in the eyes of many people a laity-ridden Church.[24] Another consequence of the absence of a bishop was the necessity for native candidates to cross the Atlantic for ordination, a voyage both expensive and dangerous.

The usual description of the Church in the South as "a gentleman's club with a faint interest in religion" certainly contains more than a grain of truth, if we compare it with the harsh rule of the Puritan clergy in the Northern colonies. Byrd's own interest in religion was far from faint, and in 1739 he noted disapprovingly that his neighbor John Carter, of Shirley, although living only four or five miles from the church, attended service infrequently. But the church was not only a place for devotions. It also provided the best opportunity to see people who lived ten or twenty miles away, to meet friends and neighbors, to exchange news. Byrd could thus hear that Dr. William Oastler, "a good-natured man, but too much addicted to drink," had caught a fever and was "very sick and in great danger." During the winter and spring of 1709–10, when there was a very bad epidemic of "the distemper," he learned at church that six people of Colonel Edward Hill's were dangerously ill, that the sickness spread around Williamsburg, and that Colonel Ludwell at Green Spring had lost three or four more Negroes.[25]

After service, there were invitations to dinner. Byrd often brought

[24] Hartwell, Blair, and Chilton, *Present State*, pp. 66–67. Cf. Spotswood to the Bishop of London, Oct. 24, 1710, *Official Letters*, I, 27. Brydon, in *Virginia's Mother Church*, gives a more cheerful view of the condition of the clergy than that of the 1697 report of Hartwell, Blair, and Chilton. His analysis is based on three documents: a report on Virginia by Governor Drysdale in 1726 (*VMHB*, XLVIII [1940], 141–52 and 207–8); a group of parochial reports made by Virginia ministers in 1724 (in William S. Perry, *Historical Collections Relating to the American Colonial Church* [Hartford, Conn., 1870], I), 261–318; and Hugh Jones's *Present State* (1724). In the reign of Charles II, the draft of a charter was prepared for the consecration of a bishop for Virginia (see the English translation, "Draft for the Creation of a Bishoprick in Virginia," *VMHB*, XXXVI [1928], 45–53). This was the first of a number of unsuccessful efforts.

[25] *Another Secret Diary*, Aug. 19, 1739; *Secret Diary*, Dec. 11 and 14, 1709; Jan. 8, Feb. 5, and May 28, 1710.

back to Westover a few of his neighbors, and the parson was generally among them. It was not uncommon for him to have eight or ten guests. Dinner was later than on weekdays and lasted longer. They sat and talked part of the afternoon; most often the company did not leave before five. Some of them might stay overnight, and the evening was a pleasant time. They "drank a bottle of wine and were merry till ten o'clock." At Westover everything remained within the bounds of propriety, but it was not always so elsewhere. Once Byrd was invited to Colonel John Custis's after church. "In the evening," he said, "we drank a bottle of wine pretty freely and were full of mirth and good humor, and particularly Colonel Waters. However we were merry and wise, and went to bed in good time by my means." Drunkenness, with the loss of one's self-control, was quite undignified among gentlemen at any time, but it should be avoided, Byrd felt, on Sundays of all days. Still, there were some slight encroachments on strict Sabbath observance. Once when Byrd was at his friend Colonel Dudley Digges's, he confessed that at night they "played at cards in the belief that there was no hurt in it," adding that they "drank very little and about ten went to bed."[26] People indeed were not always so restrained. There is a story of a dance given by a clergyman's daughter one Saturday night in the last decade of the seventeenth century, when the company caused a scandal by dancing through the night until eleven o'clock on the Sabbath morning. Such an occurrence would hardly have been tolerated at Westover. But one Sunday morning, Byrd did play billiards with his cousin, "because there seemed to be no more harm in it than in talk."[27]

These Sunday invitations were part of the traditional exchange of amenities among Virginia planters. One day among others illustrates their hospitality. On May 13, 1711, Byrd said, "after church it rained extremely, and I sent Mrs. Harrison and Mrs. Armistead and Betty Harrison to my house, and the coach returned and carried us men. I invited the whole congregation to go to our house, but nobody else went; but I sent them a bottle of wine.... The company stayed till the evening, and then because of the rain I sent them home in the coach." There is a tradition that Westover Church was moved in 1731 from its early site a quarter of a mile from Byrd's house to its new site two miles away because the second Mrs. Byrd grew weary of entertaining most of the congregation for dinner on Sundays. In 1710, the diary shows his resolution to refrain from having guests for Sunday dinner

[26] *Secret Diary*, Feb. 19, 1710; Nov. 13, 1709; Nov. 12, 1710.
[27] Bruce, *Social Life*, pp. 187–88. *Secret Diary*, Dec. 18, 1709. For Byrd's opinion on the Sabbath, see p. 62.

because it gave his servants too much work on the Lord's day; but in Virginia it was impossible for him to keep such a resolution for a long time.[28]

There were days when the rain was so heavy that it prevented the congregation from attending service. Then Byrd would stay in and read a sermon in Dr. Tillotson or some other divine.[29] But more often it was the heat that kept him from going, because if he went it meant having to dress. He took care to send his people to prayers while he read a few pages "in a good book."[30] One of those Sundays when he remained at Westover, he noted with self-satisfaction that he had "read some English about the nature of spirit," "thought a great deal about religion," "read some more English about the soul," and said his prayers "devoutly," in spite of a few mundane interruptions, which he did not fail to mention. In his diary he always kept a scrupulous account of the things of the flesh as well as those of the spirit, as he did for instance one Sunday evening in 1720 when "it rained so much [they] had no church": "Read a sermon of Tillotson till nine o'clock, and then went to bed and committed uncleanness with Annie, for which God forgive me, and I was very sorry for it. I slept pretty well, thank God."[31]

When at Westover, Byrd devoted a great part of his time to the management of his plantations. The most important of them stretched over five thousand acres each, like the Falls or Falling Creek.[32] He had one overseer on each of them, and from March 1712 on, a general overseer whose duty it was to inspect them in turn and give directions in the master's stead, for which the latter allowed him 10 per cent of the profit; such at least was the agreement when Byrd appointed a new general overseer in June 1720.[33] In later life, when his lands on the Roanoke were settled and his own activity was reduced by age, Byrd had two general overseers, one for his plantations along the James or north of it and another for those along the Roanoke.

To tobacco, of course, he gave his most constant care. The tobacco

---

[28] See *Secret Diary*, July 9 and 23, Aug. 6 and 20, Sept. 24, Oct. 1, 1710.

[29] See *ibid.*, May 15, 1709; Sept. 17, 1710; Jan. 21, 1711.

[30] *London Diary*, June 12 and July 24, 1720; *Secret Diary*, Aug. 13, 1710.

[31] *Secret Diary*, Jan. 28, 1711; *London Diary*, Dec. 25, 1720. Annie was the maidservant Byrd had brought back from England a year before.

[32] Later in the century, the size of agricultural units was smaller, around a thousand acres, e.g., the plantations of Robert Carter of Nomini Hall, "King" Carter's grandson, in 1775 (Morton, *Robert Carter*, p. 70).

[33] *London Diary*, June 14, 1720. It soon became usual for large planters to have general overseers, though the title might vary. In 1774, Robert Carter of Nomini Hall spoke of his "steward or head overseer" (Morton, *Robert Carter*, p. 95).

that Virginians cultivated for export was the West Indian variety. The native tobacco, as Strachey indicated, was "but poor and weak, and of a biting taste," and was only used by the Indians. In 1612 Strachey referred to the recent planting of "tobacco-seed from Trinidado,"[34] and it was this variety that was cultivated on Virginia plantations. In March or April, the seeds were planted (not sown) in specially prepared seedbeds, on a woody tract cleared by burning the trees. In May or June, the young plants, four or five inches high, were transplanted to the fields and set in little mounds about a yard apart in parallel rows. The transplanting was done only in wet weather. Once Byrd's people planted as many as 26,000 plants in one day, notwithstanding a cold rain and a strong wind, and he granted them all a well-earned dram to warm them after their hard work.[35] When the tobacco had reached the required height and grown the desired number of leaves, the plants were topped, and they were suckered—removing the small shoots—from time to time. Sometimes the plants had to be primed: the bottom leaves, of low quality, were removed.[36] This process produced the broad, full leaves most desired on the market. Late in the summer the ripened plants, periodically weeded and wormed, were cut and hung in tobacco barns to dry, an important operation that Byrd liked to supervise himself, or at least to inspect.[37] When he came back from England after his father's death, he did not know much about the cultivation of tobacco, but he soon set resolutely about studying it, and the entry for May 1, 1709, in his diary shows him endeavoring to learn all that he could from his friend Major Lewis Burwell, "a sensible man skilled in matters relating to tobacco."

When fully cured, a process which took from three to six weeks, the leaves were carefully sorted according to grade and packed in hogsheads for shipment: they were prized as tightly as possible into wooden casks of regulated size made by the carpenter of the planta-

[34] Strachey, *Historie of Travell*, pp. 38, 122–23. See also Jerome E. Brooks, *Tobacco, Its History Illustrated by the Books, Manuscripts, and Engravings in the Library of George Arents, Jr.* (New York, 1937–52), I, 86.

[35] *Secret Diary*, pp. 34, 528, 530, and so on; *Another Secret Diary*, p. 163.

[36] According to a statement of James Blair to the Council of Trade in 1697, not more than five or six leaves were left on a tobacco plant in Virginia (*Calendar of State Papers, Colonial Series, America and West Indies*, vol. for 1696–1697, no. 1253, p. 582).

[37] *Secret Diary*, pp. 42 and 568; *London Diary*, p. 435. Robert Beverley described these barns in 1705: "Their tobacco-houses are all built of wood, as open and airy as is consistent with keeping out the rain; which sort of building is most convenient for the curing of their tobacco." (*History*, p. 290.)

tion. Then the hogsheads were transported by sloop or flat to some warehouse down the river to be shipped to England.[38] All this required constant work the year round and constant supervision of the hands in the fields, in the tobacco barns, and in the warehouses.

Still, it was not enough to have a satisfactory crop. The tobacco trade was a frequent cause of worry for the planters, and Byrd often received letters from England "with a sad account of tobacco."[39] In August 1709 the war with France and Spain made things more difficult: "My letters from England tell me tobacco is sold for nothing there, and skins for very little, that hardly any bills are paid, and very little goods will come by the next fleet. It is time there should be peace to remedy these misfortunes." Two years later, Byrd found the situation a little better and hopefully observed that tobacco was rising at last.[40] But in 1740, a letter to a London merchant shows him wavering between the satisfaction of a good crop and the fear of seeing the market prices fall:

We doubt not but you are told of a mighty crop we are like to make this year. Abundance indeed was to be seen upon the ground, but many favorable accidents have concurred to cut it short. Many of the low grounds have been drowned, and much tobacco on the higher grounds is spotted by too much rain. The want of houses has made many hang too thick, by which a great deal will be house burnt and make work for the inspectors. There has been a mighty hail too up the country, that has done no small execution. By these and other disasters 'tis to be hoped this enormous crop, by that time it comes to be shipped, will prove no excessive burthen to the market.[41]

But there were other worries even after the crop was shipped, for the masters of ships plying between Virginia and England charged high freight; the planters had to drive hard bargains and make concerted decisions in order to keep their costs down. Besides, there were risks on the way to Britain, whether from enemy ships or from pirates. By 1707 the English had adopted a successful system of annual convoy with the ships usually arriving in Chesapeake Bay in October and leaving for England the following May. But a ship might be run down by another or lost in a storm, and then the planter had to bear the loss of his cargo, which was not sold but only consigned to some British merchant.[42]

[38] After 1730 all tobacco had to pass through a public warehouse for inspection.
[39] *Secret Diary*, pp. 48, 98, 135, 195, etc.
[40] *Ibid.*, Aug. 31, 1709, Sept. 17, 1711.
[41] Byrd to Christopher Smith, Sept. 1740, Byrd Letterbook, 1739–1740, pp. 23–24, V.H.S.
[42] See Middleton, *Tobacco Coast*, ch. X, pp. 289–309; *Secret Diary*, pp. 31, 58,

There were also regulations to be reckoned with. The exportation of tobacco to Britain was long prohibited in any form but the whole leaf. Governor Spotswood's tobacco act of 1713, repealed in 1717, contained a clause prohibiting the exportation of cut tobacco; and the British tobacco act of 1723, with a similar provision, was also repealed in 1729 because of the planters' protests. To reduce the cost of carriage of tobacco, the practice of removing the center stem had arisen, and by 1723 most sweet-scented tobacco was dispatched to England in that way. But stemmed tobacco reduced the customs revenue; hence the British act of 1723 ordering that tobacco be shipped in the leaf. Again in 1730 Governor Gooch had a tobacco inspection law passed in Virginia, and the inspectors considered that they were not authorized to pass cut tobacco, a decision which was soon revoked.[43] Byrd himself did not try to export cut tobacco, but in October 1732 he visited Major William Woodford at Windsor near Fredericksburg and took great interest in the equipment of that planter, who had been one of the petitioners against Gooch's decision. The major kept one man employed cutting up sixty hogsheads of stemmed tobacco a year. Yet he was not manufacturing a finished product for local commercial consumption, but a semifinished product for sale to English manufacturers. Byrd reports that his host had his tobacco cut up because it brought more in the English market, eleven pence per pound, while leaf tobacco sold for seven and a half or eight pence. Thus, Byrd said, he "pays himself liberally for his trouble."[44] This practice was uncommon enough in Virginia for Byrd to describe the cutting process at length.

On the whole there was little tobacco manufacturing in early eighteenth-century Virginia beyond the domestic and the experimental. In March 1729 Governor Gooch wrote to his brother at Cambridge, who had asked for some snuff: "We have no snuff in this country; most people here take what is brought from Scotland; I'll see what my friend Randolph can do, if his is not all gone." The ordinary smokers in colonial Virginia must have prepared their own leaf at home to suit their own taste, but the great planters imported their smoking tobacco from London or, like "King" Carter, received it as gifts from English correspondents. The earliest numbers of the

---

333. It was only in the second half of the 18th century that the English merchants generalized the practice of buying crops in the colony itself, even from the great planters. On the consignment system and the economic position of tobacco planters, see Stuart Bruchey, *The Roots of American Economic Growth, 1607–1861*, (New York, 1968), pp. 31–41.

43 *Journals of Burgesses*, vol. for 1727–1740, pp. 123–24 and 131–32.

44 *Prose Works*, pp. 372–73.

Virginia Gazette contain numerous advertisements for "Scotch snuff," "just imported" from Britain. Real tobacco manufacturing only began in Virginia after the Revolution: "Although the evidence is inconclusive and largely negative, it seems probable that as of 1775, Virginia had no commercial manufacture of tobacco or snuff and depended for luxury consumption on imports from Britain and from the other colonies."[45]

Besides tobacco, other crops had to be tended and gathered at the plantation. In late June or early July, there was wheat to be reaped, and Byrd liked to be in the fields, walking among the workers and seeing how good the crop was. Also, within the space of a few days, there were corn—the staple food of the slaves—and oats to be harvested, and hay to be mown.[46] These crops were essential, since they provided most of the food for both men and animals on the plantation. The year 1709 was a bad one, and Byrd was greatly concerned because some of his plantations lacked corn as early as October, reflecting a general shortage that year throughout the colony.

Then there were the gardens and orchards of Westover, already famous in the colony when he inherited the estate. In 1705 Robert Beverley wrote about Byrd's father: "Colonel Byrd, in his garden, which is the finest in that country, has a summer house set round with the Indian honeysuckle, which all the summer is continually full of sweet flowers in which [humming] birds delight exceedingly." Byrd felt very proud of his garden—almost as much as of his library. John Bartram, the Philadelphia naturalist, described Westover in a letter to Peter Collinson after a short stay there in 1738. With its "new gates, gravel walks, hedges and cedars finely twined, and a little greenhouse with two or three orange trees with fruit on them," it was "the finest seat in Virginia." A few months after Byrd's reconciliation with Governor Spotswood, his former adversary presented him with several orange trees which he gratefully accepted. In January 1711 he supervised the planting of many new trees in his garden, and a year later the laying out of a peach orchard.[47] This entailed much work,

<hr>

[45] Gov. Gooch to Thomas Gooch, March 27, 1729, Gooch Correspondence, Colonial Williamsburg ff. 6–8. *Robert Carter Letters*, pp. 29–30. *Va. Gaz.*, June 13–20, 1745, p. 4, and July 31, 1746, p. 6 (examples are more numerous in the 1750's). Jacob M. Price, "The Beginnings of Tobacco Manufacturing in Virginia," *VMHB*, LXIV (1956), 14.

[46] Byrd's were exceptionally well-tended plantations. Durand had observed about most Virginia planters: "They do not know what it is to mow hay; their animals all graze in the woods or on the untilled portions of their plantations, where they seek shelter nightly rather by instinct than from any care given them" (*Huguenot Exile*, p. 122).

[47] Beverley, *History*, p. 299. Bartram to Collinson, July 18, (1740 ?), *Bartram*

which Byrd did himself in large part, at least in the first years. He trusted no one else to prune and trim trees in his orchards and along the walks around the house, preferring to do it himself according to the directions in his own books on gardening.[48] Like his brother-in-law Robert Beverley, he became particularly interested in vines. To his former mentor in Holland, Mr. Tenserf, he specified in 1729: "I have lately planted a small vine[yard] to show my indolent countryfolks that we may employ our industry upon other things besides tobacco. Above twenty sorts of vine have [been] sent to me from other countries, which are all in a flourishing con[dition], and I am endeavoring to get more." To this end he wrote to another correspondent, saying that he wanted "to graft choice vines on stocks of our wild ones, to naturalize them the better to our soil and climate," and asking him for "several kinds of Frontignac, Champaign, and Muscadine vines." The Westover Manuscripts contain copies of two letters by Peter Collinson on the management of a vineyard. But later Byrd confessed to Sir Hans Sloane that success was doubtful because, he said, "our seasons are so uncertain and our insects so numerous."[49]

Running plantations involved making all sorts of bargains besides those concerning the tobacco crop. In his diary Byrd wrote of purchasing slaves, of acquiring a horse after rejecting one that was too high-spirited for his taste, of agreeing to let a woodsman "shoot birds in the marsh provided he brings me the meat and keeps the feathers for himself."[50] He was often buying one piece of land and letting another.

In fact, a large Tidewater planter was not just a farmer with ex-

---

Papers, Pennsylvania Historical Society, copy in Colonial Williamsburg, f. 21. In a letter written some time before, Collinson had mentioned Westover to Bartram: "I am told Colonel Byrd has the best garden in Virginia, and a pretty green-house, well furnished with orange-trees. I knew him well when in England; and he was reckoned a very polite, ingenious man." (*WMCQ*, 2d ser., VI [1926], 311). *Secret Diary*, pp. 286–92 and 471.

[48] *Secret Diary*, pp. 305, 464, 548, etc. About the luxuriance of gardens and orchards in Virginia, see Durand's account in 1686: "The soil is so favorable for fruit-trees that I saw orchards planted, I was told, only ten years before, with larger and better grown trees than our twenty-year-old ones in Europe" (*Huguenot Exile*, p. 115). See also Robert Beverley, *History*, p. 314.

[49] Byrd to Tenserf, June, 1729, Byrd Letterbook, 1728–1729, pp. 34–35, Colonial Williamsburg. Byrd to . . . , June 25, 1729, *VMHB*, XXXVI (1928), 116–17 (Byrd Letterbook, 1729, p. 29, V.H.S.). Westover Manuscripts, pp. 314–19, V.H.S.; printed in Wynne, *History of the Dividing Line*, II, 177–84. Byrd to Sloane, May 31, 1737, *WMCQ*, 2d ser., I (1921), 196. According to a letter to Peter Collinson on July 18, 1736, the frost accounted for the destruction of most of Byrd's grapes in the early spring of that year (*VMHB*, XXXVI [1928], 354).

[50] *Secret Diary*, July 11–17, Sept. 20, 1709.

tensive holdings. He had also to be something of a land speculator and to be "sharp in trade," a quality whose necessity Hugh Jones stressed.[51] Since tobacco quickly exhausted the soil, an important part of the planter's work consisted in acquiring new lands and securing a reserve of fresh land for future years; sometimes he might sell his used tracts to farmers who would plant corn or graze cattle. The planter was given a fifty-acre bounty each time he imported an indentured servant, but these were becoming scarcer in the eighteenth century. He might ask the government for lapsed land or for escheat land, besides buying lots from smaller planters in need of money.[52]

The first two decades of the century saw a shortage of good cheap land: the land of the Tidewater had been taken up, while the Piedmont was not yet open to settlement. Although several governors tried to enforce the forfeiture of grants whenever the owners failed to pay quitrents, in most cases they were not successful, and the planters retained possession of large tracts within the Tidewater area. After 1720, however, Spotswood cooperated with the Council in throwing open the Piedmont with no limitation on the size of grants and no quitrents for ten years, the governor's own share being a private grant of sixty thousand acres in Spotsylvania County.[53] More land was patented in the next twenty years than in the century that had preceded. Grants of ten or twenty thousand acres became frequent, while a few reached a hundred thousand, the largest, of course, going to members of the Council, since the granting was in the hands of the governor and the Council.

This evolution toward larger grants is reflected in the expansion of Byrd's estate as shown by his Title Book. He seized every opportunity that came his way. In the first twenty years, with his main plantations extending over four to seven thousand acres each, he bought small tracts of one or two hundred acres, rarely above five hundred. But after the survey of the Dividing Line in 1728, he bought or patented much larger tracts, from the twenty thousand acres of the Land of Eden in 1728 to the 105,000 acre grant which he obtained in 1735 on the Dan.

A letter of March 1741 in which Byrd gives orders to a Mr. Wood, who had surveyed for him tracts that had just been sold to new settlers at Roanoke, affords good evidence of this activity:

[51] *Present State*, p. 43.

[52] See Hartwell, Blair, and Chilton, *Present State*, p. 20. (Lapsed land: "land which is neither seated nor planted within the three years"; escheat land: "when a man dies seized of land in fee, without will or heirs.")

[53] Hening, *Statutes at Large*, IV, 37–42; *Journals of Burgesses*, 1712–1726, pp. 250–51, 277–79. See also W. Stitt Robinson, Jr., *Mother Earth*.

When any purchasers come, let your first inquiry be into their character and ability to pay for the land according to the terms. If you find them either in cash to pay the money down, or industrious enough to raise it within the time, then survey their quantity and return the survey to me, and I will make out their deeds. Those who bring ready money ought to have the best land to encourage prompt payment. When you have leisure, it will promote the sale of the land to find the nearest way for a road to come from thence both to Warwick and to the Point of Appomattox, the present road being thirty miles about. It may not be convenient to let the purchasers carry the chain for one another, lest they might agree to give too good measure.

Byrd added instructions to attract settlers: "Let them know the advantages that foreign Protestants will have in settling upon that land. . . . Tell them of the fertility of the soil, the many convenient streams that water it, the justice and easiness of the government, the entire security from Indians, French, and Spaniards."[54]

During the last years of his life, Byrd was greatly interested in the sale of lots in the recently laid out town of Richmond. His diary shows him receiving prospective buyers: "After dinner came two Germans to take lots at Richmond, and I was kind to them"; he expressed his pleasure that more settlers were coming soon, dined with one of his buyers, and granted several lots by deeds acknowledged in Henrico Court.[55] In the 1720's there had been several petitions from the inhabitants of the region for a town to be laid out at the falls of the James, a most favorable spot since it was the highest point that small ships could reach. In 1729 Byrd fought hard to defeat the efforts of a "powerful family" to have a town founded there, because he would then have had to sell his land at Shockoe in one piece, probably to the colony itself, for a very low price. He then asked his agent in London, the powerful merchant Micajah Perry, to use his influence with the Board of Trade to forbid the passage of an act by the Virginia Assembly, "a little Assembly, the very shadow . . . of a Parliament," which had no right to force a man's property from him. Later, during his journey to the land of Eden, Byrd decided to lay out the new town himself, on his own plan, at his own time, and for his own price.[56]

[54] Byrd to Mr. Wood, March 10, 1740/41, Byrd Letterbook, 1740–1741, pp. 25–26, V.H.S.

[55] *Another Secret Diary*, April 10 and May 31, 1740; May 28 and June 1, 1741.

[56] Shockoe, or Shacco, was on the north bank of the James, facing the falls; Byrd had a storehouse there. Byrd to Micajah Perry, May 25, 1729, Byrd Letterbook, 1728–1729, p. 9, Colonial Williamsburg; see also *Journals of Burgesses*, 1727–1740, p. 70 (June 3, 1730). Byrd's advertisement in the *Va. Gaz.*, April 15–22, 1737.

This continuous buying and selling of land distinguished the large planters from the English country squires whom they strove to imitate; they retained the spirit of business enterprise of the merchants from whom most of them were but recently descended.

The daily routine of plantation life is generally taken as a matter of course in Byrd's diary. He gave more prominence to incidents, or even accidents, which troubled the course of ordinary life; these were only too frequent and bore heavily on the planter's fortune. Violent storms, short and sudden, were common in May and the following months. Once in 1711, after a thunderstorm followed by a shower of driving rain that stopped all work on the plantation, there came a gust of wind "that blew up several trees by the roots and tore many more and threw down my fence." Fortunately it was soon over and did no damage to the house or to the sloop at the landing stage. But in the evening Byrd's first concern was to take a walk round Westover to see for himself what harm the plantation had suffered. The year before, in the same season, the dam at Falling Creek, one of his plantations on the James above Westover, formed a leak and broke after a violent rainstorm. A few days later the overseer came to report to his master: "He told me of the breaking of the dam, which was like my fortune. It put me very much out of humor."[57] That dam was long a source of worry for the planter: it broke again at the end of 1710 and was not rebuilt until October 1711. It was work of great patience to wipe out the effects of such mishaps.

One day in May 1720, "after dinner there came a violent storm of hail, and broke all the windows, which it might easy do because the hailstones were as big as hens' eggs." But people were used to these episodes of the elemental war, and Byrd, who had a few guests at Westover at the time, added: "When the storm was over, we played at several games and I won about three pounds. We drank good rack punch and were merry till twelve o'clock and then retired." A few days later, in the afternoon, "there came a terrible clap of thunder, and damaged the pigeon-house and killed sixteen sheep that lay under it for shelter." This was a serious loss for the planter, though a real windfall for his servants, who thereby received an unexpected improvement in their daily fare. Yet even this was a minor misfortune in comparison with other storms: wind and rain and hail sometimes ruined the tobacco crop itself, a far greater disaster, particularly if it was repeated on the other plantations.[58] The unexpected wrath of the elements in these climes kept alive in the planters' minds

57 *Secret Diary*, May 24, 1711; May 15 and 28, 1710.
58 *London Diary*, May 30, June 11, 1720; *Another Secret Diary*, Aug. 5, 6 and 22, 1741.

a sense of their wayward and impending power, a strong feeling of subjection to Nature and Providence, which must have helped to keep them more closely bound to their Church than has sometimes been claimed.

Storms were not the only bane of the planter's life. In 1709 the summer was exceedingly hot, and everything at the plantation withered for want of rain. Not a drop fell before late July and a month later Byrd received the visit of a smaller planter of the neighborhood who told him "a sad story of the badness of the crop because of the great drought." The man hoped to get work from Byrd, who had to put him off as courteously as he could, in spite of a letter of recommendation from his friend Colonel William Randolph.[59] Fortunately, excessive droughts were rare, and after a few days of waiting Byrd, with typical pious satisfaction, could generally write an entry such as the following in his diary: "It rained abundantly this afternoon and this evening, thank God, according to my prayers."[60] He had his personal way of foretelling rain, from the way his cellar stank, and was pleased when his prediction came true.[61]

Some troubles were unavoidable on a plantation. A dog who had killed a lamb was penned up with a ram and violently beaten, but the punishment proved ineffective and three days later he killed another. A neighbor's hogs made a habit of coming into Byrd's pasture, and one of his men sprained his ankle chasing them. Some of his own cattle escaped to distant fields and were not found until a fortnight later. In March 1711 Mrs. Harrison's horses broke his fence four times in two days; a few months later the situation was reversed and he received a complaint that one of his steers had twice broken into Mrs. Harrison's cornfield: "I had put a yoke on his neck and put him into the great pasture, but he jumped out notwithstanding, on which I resolved to kill him rather than keep anything injurious to my neighbor."[62] The next day, when the animal had been slaughtered, he "sent her part of it to make her amends." This was common courtesy among planters, and Byrd was on good terms with most of his neighbors. He often gave small farmers extra time to pay their debts, which he sometimes canceled if the debtors were poor.[63]

Other incidents were mere entertainments breaking the monotony

[59] *Secret Diary*, July 23, Aug. 29, 1709.
[60] *London Diary*, July 7, 1720. See an anecdote on the same subject in *Landon Carter Diary*, II, 616–17 (Aug. 19, 1771).
[61] *Secret Diary*, June 15, 1710.
[62] *Ibid.*, Feb. 23–26, 1710; Aug. 17–21, 1709; June 24 and July 8, 1710; March 18 and June 3–4, 1711.
[63] *Ibid.*, Jan. 25, 1710, July 9–10, 1712.

of daily life. Byrd, with a little fever and a headache, was puttering about in his library and halfheartedly putting a thing or two in order when a guest came in suddenly and told him that he had just seen a bear. They all rushed out in great excitement and shot the animal. But, he added, "it was only a cub and he sat on a tree to eat grapes. I was better with this diversion and we were merry in the evening." Such incidents reminded people how near the wilderness still was, only a few miles south of the James and the Appomattox. Other unusual visitors, although eyed suspiciously by the planter, turned out to be profitable: "There were abundant flies like locusts in the wood, which make a shrill noise but do no visible mischief, and the birds eat them, so that we saved our cherries and other fruit from them."[64]

At regular intervals Byrd would visit his other plantations: every two or three months at first, once a year when later he had a general overseer. In his old age he governed his scattered estate from West-over. Byrd's journeys lasted two or three days and enabled him to inspect the six plantations he had up the James, near the present site of Richmond or a little lower. Sometimes he went out of his way to see his land at the falls of the Appomattox, in the neighborhood of what is now Petersburg.

He would set out one morning after breakfast, ride past Westover Church, and call at Shirley where his old friend Colonel Hill lived; then at Bermuda Hundred he would take a small ferry across the James to the south bank, and from there ride two hours to his planta-tion of Falling Creek, where he had a tannery and a sawmill of which he was particularly proud. When Governor Spotswood visited the place in March 1711, on his way to the western part of New Kent County, Byrd was pleased to note his guest's interest. He must have told him of the wager he had won a year before: one John Woodson, who was no particular friend of his, had laid down forty pounds that the mill could not saw 3,000 feet of planks in ten hours: but the work had been completed in nine. "There was abundance of company there," says the diary, "the best of which I treated with wine." One had to draw the line somewhere among neighbors, and some distinc-tion must be made according to their position! Later, when another neighbor wanted to build his own mill, he asked for Byrd's advice, which the latter, with modest satisfaction, wrote that he gave as well as he could. On the same plantation there was also a coal mine, "very good and sufficient to furnish several generations," said Byrd's own coaler in July 1709.[65]

[64] *Ibid.*, Sept. 29, May 19, 1712.
[65] *Ibid.*, March 27, 1711; March 30, 1710 (see Nov. 29, 1709, for a similar wager); Feb. 16, 1712; July 18, 1709. For Falling Creek, see above, p. 50, n. 13.

From Falling Creek, Byrd would go on to Kensington, a smaller plantation seven miles farther on,[66] and from there, stepping from rock to rock, he would wade over the James to another called Burkland, on the north bank. But when the water was so high that the wading place was impassable, Byrd sometimes abandoned all thought of visiting his north-bank plantations, because it meant going a long way round by the great bridge above the falls. The other north-bank plantations were Byrd Park and Shockoe, the largest of the three, where he had a large storehouse built in early 1712 which made a wonderful change: "I had not seen this place since the house was built, and hardly knew it again. It was very pretty."[67]

After crossing the river once more, either by boat or by the bridge above, Byrd reached the Falls, the oldest part of his estate, which his granduncle Thomas Stegge had acquired in 1661. There he had rich and extensive lands in a most favorable position, just below the falls of the James, at the highest point that his sloop could reach. Not only was the soil itself fertile: in 1720 his overseer Henry Anderson (the parson's son) found a very good coal mine in the vicinity.[68] After visiting the last of his six plantations, Byrd would return to Falling Creek. This he did once "the northeast way," and proudly remarked that the trip of seven miles or so between Kensington and Falling Creek was almost all over his own land.[69] When his inspection was over, the planter rode back to Westover, stopping on the way for a brief call at some friend's; if the weather was fair and he was pleased with the management of his estate or wished to set aside all cares, he would slow down and "make some verses on the road."[70]

Every year one inspection was of particular importance; this was in late August or early September when Byrd went round his lands to see how good the various crops were.[71] The plantations along the James and the Appomattox formed a small world, with Westover as its center and two storehouses at Shockoe and Appomattox, the highest points that could be reached by boat, where goods were stored not only for Byrd's own estate but also for his trade with smaller planters. His more outlying plantations he rarely visited and mostly left to the care of his general overseer: because they were on different rivers they really belonged to another world.

[66] The name of this plantation does not appear in the Byrd Title Book.

[67] *Secret Diary*, Feb. 14, 1712. These plantations were approximately on the former site of the Powhatan Town as marked on John Smith's map of Virginia, and on the present site of Richmond.

[68] *London Diary*, Feb. 18, 1720.

[69] *Secret Diary*, Feb. 15, 1712.

[70] *Ibid.*, Dec. 21, 1710.

[71] *Ibid.*, Aug. 18–20, 1709, or Sept. 5–7, 1710.

During these journeys, in addition to inspecting the plantations and listening to his own workmen, Byrd sometimes had to settle differences with his neighbors about boundaries. In March 1709 he found that Captain Giles Webb had built his house on land that was part of Burkland. Two years later another dispute arose about a tract of land on the banks of Falling Creek; fortunately "John Giles could not claim the mill because it was out of his bounds"; but Byrd judged it safer to buy his adversary's claim for a sum of twenty pounds.[72]

As for the overseers themselves, they could not really be trusted. They were generally smaller farmers with a plot of their own in the neighborhood, who hoped to increase their meager income. But they often neglected their charge; or if they were hard-working, conscientious people, they soon extended their land and left the great planter's service. Byrd once arrived at Falling Creek to find his overseer drunk: "I scolded at Mr. G–r–l till he cried and then was peevish." A year later the same man was given leave to go to Carolina for a few days on condition that his brother replace him, but Byrd found both men absent, and no one to run the place.[73] At Burkland, John Blackman "left everything in a sad condition," so that Byrd refused to pay him. The next overseer, Joseph Wilkinson, was little better and had to be replaced after a few months:

About eleven o'clock we went over the river and learned that Joe Wilkinson was not on the plantation but was gone with Mr. Laforce to look after his hogs. He had spoiled all the tobacco by house burn, and carried several things that belong to me home to his house, for all which reasons I wrote to him to forbear coming any more to my service, and appointed Tom Turpin [the overseer of the Falls] to take care of everything till I sent an overseer.

Byrd sued Wilkinson at the next Court session and was awarded "three thousand pounds of tobacco damages."[74]

Labor, more generally, was one of the planter's greatest worries. With the slump in tobacco prices toward the turn of the century, only the great planters with their large estates could continue making substantial profits. But they needed more and more labor, and white workmen could not be procured in sufficiently large numbers. Journeys to England were opportunities to bring back a few white servants. In November 1719 Byrd brought to Virginia a manservant, Tom; a maid, Hannah; and Annie, a girl who was to become his mistress soon after they arrived at Westover.[75]

[72] *Ibid.*, pp. 15, 23, 89, 227, and pp. 340, 363, 384, 419.
[73] *Ibid.*, March 28, 1709; May 15, 1710.
[74] *Ibid.*, Oct. 1, 1709; Dec. 20, 1710; April 21, 1711.
[75] *London Diary*, pp. 345, 352, 353, 377, etc.

There was a hierarchy among the servants of the plantation as there was in colonial society itself. Among them the tutor of the owner's children, who was often secretary and librarian as well, held the highest rank. In the forties at Westover the post was filled by William Proctor, a Scotsman and a Presbyterian who later became a minister of the Established Church in the colony. In July, 1739, he wrote to his brother in Scotland:

I am library keeper and have all genteel conveniences; moreover, to save me a risk [my master] gives me yearly a draught upon his London factor and orders my clothes with his own goods at the English price, which is cheaper than in Scotland. This renders my twenty pounds English money as good as at home, and I have some small addition of one guinea or two per annum for my pupil's companion, besides the kindness of the family in having my linen made or mended, etc. And then for my future advantage I can only see that Colonel Byrd will certainly procure me a parish worth a hundred pounds sterling a year, if I can like it, or help me to commence a husbandman upon land of my own, which last, if rightly understood and managed, is the best employment in the colony. My good master, indeed, frequently is pleasant with me, and says why mayn't I be at once parson and planter, the one assisting the other.[76]

The tutor owed to his rarity as well as to his education a prestige which enabled him to be accepted in the planter's family almost as a social equal and made him as much a guest as a servant at the plantation.

Below him came the overseers and those skilled laborers who worked for wages. These hired servants were jealous of their independence and had to be handled with great care, for labor, especially skilled labor, was scarce. Those who were most punctilious about their social standing were generally those whose station approached the lowest level—a most human reaction. Byrd himself thought nothing of having corn pone for dinner during a visit to the Falls, although it was the usual diet of slaves; but people in humble circumstances were more particular: "The boatwright was affronted that I gave him pone instead of English bread for breakfast, and took his horse and rode away without saying a word."[77]

But the social standing of the servants (and of the slaves too) depended on their degree of skill in some industrial trade even more

---

[76] "Letters of William Proctor," *VMHB*, X (1903), 300–301.

[77] *Secret Diary*, March 3, 1710, and March 2, 1711. On cornpone, "the bread made of Indian meal," see Beverley, *History*, p. 292. Durand said that it made "an excellent but somewhat indigestible soup." With this, he added, "they feed the slaves, and it costs very little to maintain them, particularly the Negroes" (*Huguenot Exile*, p. 117).

than on their independence. The planter employed carpenters to keep
in repair all the buildings, gates, and fences; coopers to make casks
and hogsheads; boatwrights and blacksmiths, tanners and curriers,
spinners and weavers, shoemakers and even sometimes a distiller, besides the house-servants at the mansion. Last came the unskilled field
hands, who were at the bottom of the ladder.

There was a great demand for white labor. Among the "bound
servants" coming from England were convicts who had been transported to "the plantations," but the Virginians often protested against
the policy of sending "jailbirds" to their country because it was
dangerous to the peace and prosperity of the colony.[78] More often
the white laborers were indentured servants who sold themselves for
the price of their passage to America; their average time of servitude
was four or five years. All ages were represented, but there was a
predominance of people in their twenties, who hoped to settle as
farmers. After serving their time, they would be allotted land and
given tools on credit to start an independent life. In 1671, Governor
Berkeley reported to the Board of Trade that of Virginia's total
population of about 40,000, there were "six thousand Christian servants for a short time," who had come over with "the hope of better-
ing their condition in a growing country."[79] In *Moll Flanders* Defoe
dealt with the hopes of such people on leaving England; his heroine
herself is transported to Virginia. In his *Colonel Jack* the hero is kid-
napped in early life and sold as a servant in Virginia.

Good craftsmen were in great demand, but unfortunately they were
scarce. Yet white servitude was at its height in the early eighteenth
century, and offices in London specialized in selling indentured servants gathered by a combination of persuasion, inveigling, and even
downright kidnapping. Once in Virginia, they were protected by
law in some respects, but they could be bought and sold freely during their term of servitude.[80] They worked on the plantations together with convicts and Negroes, and the planter made little distinction among these groups.[81] About fifty servants appear by name in

[78] Hening, *Statutes at Large*, II, 510.
[79] 1671 Report of Sir William Berkeley to the Board of Trade, P.R.O., CO
1/2677 (printed in Hening, *Statutes at Large*, II, 515).
[80] Abbott E. Smith, *Colonists in Bondage: White Servitude and Convict Labor
in America, 1607-1776* (Chapel Hill, N.C., 1947). They were protected against
ill-treatment, and a limit was set to their length of servitude if it had not been
specified by the indentures.
[81] See J. C. Hurd, *The Law of Freedom and Bondage in the United States*
(New York, 1858), I, 220: "The legal condition of indented servants was
essentially different from that of chattel slaves in its origin and duration. . . .
But notwithstanding the difference and the fact that laws were enacted for their

The Secret Diary, but it is usually impossible to tell whether the servants mentioned are blacks or whites; when he does give any such indication, it is to distinguish between two servants bearing the same name. In 1705 Robert Beverley still based the difference between "servant" and "slave" on length of service, not on color, though color certainly became the sign of the slave in public opinion before it was acknowledged as such by law.[82] It is often forgotten that, legally at least, free Negroes could vote in Virginia until 1723. Color emerged "as the token of slave status" not before the end of the seventeenth century as has been often argued[83] but over a quarter century later, when Negroes had become numerous enough to justify before the Board of Trade the passing of "An Act directing the Trial of Slaves committing Capital Crimes; and for the more effectual Punishing Conspiracies and Insurrections of them and for the better Government of Negroes, Mulattoes, and Indians, Bond or Free."[84]

Abbott E. Smith has shown that the main motives behind the servant trade, particularly in the South, were the demand for cheap labor in the undeveloped colonies and the profits to be made by English merchants in selling indentured servants. Moreover, the British government, following the mercantilistic doctrine in the seventeenth century, encouraged the shipping away of the poor and the unemployed, on the theory that England was overpopulated; but in the eighteenth century, this gave way to the theory that a cheap supply of labor in England was necessary, and the activities of merchants in the servant trade were limited accordingly. About 1680 there was a yearly immigration of 1,500 to 2,000 white indentured servants; by 1715 their number had fallen to about one hundred.[85] As a result, the colonists started to turn to Negro slaves,

---

special protection recognizing them as legal persons, yet their general condition and disabilities, during its continuance seem in many respects to have been the same, and much of the colonial legislation . . . in reference to servants applied both to such persons and to Negro and Indian slaves."

[82] *History,* p. 271 ("slaves for life, and servants for a time"). A typical sentence may be found in an act passed in October 1670 about "what time Indians [are] to serve": the word "Negro" is not used, and the distinction is between non-Christians imported "by shipping" or "come by land." (Hening, *Statutes at Large,* II, 283.)

[83] Oscar and Mary F. Handlin, "Origins of the Southern Labor System," *WMQ,* 3d ser., VII (1950), 216.

[84] "A Question of Complexion: Documents Concerning the Negro and the Franchise in Eighteenth Century Virginia," ed. Emory G. Evans, *VMHB,* LXXI (1963), 411–15. On the reasons alleged for the passing of the act, see William Gooch to Alured Popple, May 18, 1736, P.R.O., CO 5/1324.

[85] Abbott E. Smith, *Colonists in Bondage,* pp. 26–42 and 67–86; Wertenbaker, *Planters,* pp. 134–35.

whom they had originally used only as a last resort. Even in Virginia, where the need for labor was acutely felt, there were those who objected to the slave trade on purely economic grounds. Thus the President of the Council, Colonel Edmund Jenings declared in 1708: "The people of Virginia will not now be so fond of purchasing Negroes as of late, being sensibly convinced of their error, which has in a manner ruined the credit of the country." And in 1711, soon after his arrival in the colony, Governor Spotswood explained: "The great number of Negroes imported here and solely employed in making tobacco has produced for some years past an increase in tobacco far disproportionate to the consumption of it . . . and consequently lowered the price of it."[86] These men were not conscious of any wrong in slavery and only saw its economic consequences: overproduction and the cheapness of tobacco on European markets. It was then that a heavy duty was imposed on the importation of slaves. The decline in the slave trade which ensued for a few years was mentioned by Hugh Jones, who also expressed his opinion that "if fewer slaves were imported to Virginia, it would be better for the Virginia planters and merchants," who would replace the slaves advantageously with "all our poor, our beggars, and our notorious rogues."[87]

But in a few years, after the end of the War of the Spanish Succession and the return of prosperity, the situation was so changed that around 1730 planters felt the necessity of cheap labor because, they said, " 'tis well known that the cheapness of Virginia tobacco in European markets is the true cause of the great consumption thereof in Europe." Whoever could lay out all at once the necessary capital to buy slaves costing eighteen or twenty pounds each for an average of twenty or twenty-five years' work (less than a pound a year) gained a decided advantage over those who paid a white servant, when they could find one, from two to three pounds a year. On the subject of indentured servants, Byrd wrote to one of his European correspondents in 1739: "Here they are sold for four years and fetch from six to nine pounds, and perhaps good tradesmen may go for ten," while Negroes "sell for more than double these people will."[88] The price might vary greatly between a "new slave" just arrived from Africa who served as a field hand and a Virginia-born, trained

---

86 P.R.O., CO 5/1362, ff. 369–73; CO 5/1363, ff. 317–24.

87 *Present State*, p. 149.

88 Francis Fane to the Lords of Trade, Dec. 10, 1728, P.R.O., CO 5/1322; Byrd to Mr. Andrews of Rotterdam, Nov. 10, 1739, *American Historical Review*, I (1895), 90. In his *Secret Diary*, on Sept. 18, 1712, Byrd recorded selling two Negroes for sixty pounds.

house-servant or artisan. But the latter rarely came on the market. Buying "new" slaves, on the other hand, yielded results long of fruition: they were cheaper but so inexperienced as to be almost useless for some time after their importation, perhaps for several years. In 1728 Governor Gooch wrote to the Board of Trade about the great planters and their slaves: "Though they may plant more in quantity, yet it frequently proves very mean stuff. . . . Yet the rich man's trash will always damp the market and spoil the poor man's good tobacco which has been carefully managed." Three years later, he insisted that the common people made the best tobacco,[89] but the evolution favoring large estates and cheap labor had made great advances by that time. Small farmers themselves bought one or two slaves as soon as they could afford them.

Some colonists began to feel that the presence of so many Negroes was fast becoming a real danger.[90] Such a considerable slave holder as Byrd was quite conscious of the fact, and in a letter of July 12, 1736, to the Earl of Egmont, he praised Georgia for excluding Negroes. The use of black slaves, he said, was morally bad because, besides its injustice to human creatures, it fostered pride and idleness and robbery among the whites:

I am sensible of many bad consequences of multiplying these Ethiopians amongst us. They blow up the pride and ruin the industry of our white people, who, seeing a rank of poor creatures below them, detest work for fear it should make them look like slaves. Then that poverty, which will ever attend upon idleness, disposes them as much to pilfer as it does the Portuguese, who account it much more like a gentleman to steal than to dirty their hands with labor of any kind.[91]

Besides, the increasing number of slaves made it a necessity for the master to be severe:

[89] Governor Gooch to the Board of Trade, Aug. 9, 1729, P.R.O., CO 5/1321, f. 149, or Gooch Papers, I, 64, V.H.S.; Governor Gooch to the Board of Trade, Feb. 27, 1730/31, P.R.O., CO 5/1322, f. 281, or Gooch Papers, I, 215.

[90] One of the first serious alarms arising from slave conspiracies occurred in 1710, when a large number of slaves in Surry County planned to escape, but failed because the plot was disclosed by another slave (Edmund Jenings to the Board of Trade, April 24, 1710, P.R.O., CO 5/1317, Va. Colonial Records Project microfilm; *Secret Diary*, pp. 167–69; *Journals of Burgesses*, 1702–1712, pp. 270–98, passim). In 1723 again there were fears of an uprising, and this caused the passing of a new black code far more strict and discriminatory than the former laws (see Hening, *Statutes at Large*, IV, 126–34).

[91] John F. D. Smyth, in *A Tour in the United States* (London, 1784) also ascribes the pride of Virginians to their "general intercourse with slaves" (I, 66); and Thomas Jefferson in his *Notes on the State of Virginia* (1787) finds "an unhappy influence on the manners of our people produced by the existence of slavery among us" (ed. William Peden [Chapel Hill, N.C., 1955], p. 162).

Numbers make them insolent, and then foul means must do what fair will not. We have however nothing like the inhumanity here that is practiced in the Islands, and God forbid we ever should.[92] But these base tempers require to be rid with a taut rein, or they will be apt to throw their rider. Yet even this is terrible to a good-natured man, who must submit to be either a fool or a fury. And this will be more our unhappy case, the more the Negroes are increased amongst us.

Byrd could see further ahead than many of his contemporaries, for he added:

But these private mischiefs are nothing, if compared to the public danger. We have already at least ten thousand men of these descendants of Ham fit to bear arms,[93] and their numbers increase every day, as well by birth as importation. And in case there should arise a man of desperate courage amongst us, exasperated by a desperate fortune, he might with more advantage than Catiline kindle a servile war. Such a man might be dreadfully mischievous before any opposition could be formed against him, and tinge our rivers, as wide as they are, with blood. It were therefore worth the consideration of a British Parliament, my Lord, to put an end to this unchristian traffic of making merchandise of our fellow creatures.

But this was in no way the interest of English trade, which had been stated clearly in a letter of Thomas, Lord Culpeper to the Board of Trade in the late seventeenth century: "In regard of the infinite profit that comes to the king by every black (far beyond any other Plantation) at least six pounds per head per ann.; and that the low price of tobacco requires it should be made as cheap as possible, and that blacks can make it cheaper than whites, I conceive it is for his Majesty's interest full as much as the country's or rather much more, to have blacks as cheap as possible in Virginia."[94] The government's

---

[92] In a letter of Dec. 6, 1735, addressed to Peter Beckford of Jamaica (the grandfather of the author of *Vathek*), Byrd had expressed the same opinion, among more optimistic views (for he hoped to have Beckford visit Westover and perhaps to sell him some land): "Our negroes are not so numerous or so enterprising as to give us any apprehension or uneasiness, nor indeed is their labor any other than gardening and less by far than what the poor people undergo in other countries. Nor are any cruelties exercised upon them, unless by great accident they happen to fall into the hands of a brute, who always passes here for a monster." (*VMHB*, IX [1902], 235.)

[93] According to a report of Governor Gooch, the slaves were 30,000 in 1730 and represented a quarter of the population (P.R.O. CO 5/1322, f. 119, or Gooch Papers, I, 189). Governor Berkeley's report of 1671 had estimated that there were 2,000 slaves out of a population of 40,000 (P.R.O., CO 1/2677).

[94] Section 59 of the "Answer of the Lord Culpeper to the several articles of his Lordship's Instructions," dated 20 September 1683, P.R.O., CO 5/1356, f. 138.

economic policy made it evident that Byrd's suggestion would never be considered in spite of the danger that the slaves might represent. "At least," Byrd said to Lord Egmont, "the further importation of them into our colonies should be prohibited lest they prove as troublesome and dangerous everywhere as they have been lately in Jamaica. . . . We have mountains in Virginia too, to which they may retire as safely, and do as much mischief as they do in Jamaica."[95]

Byrd may well have judged that slavery was an "unchristian traffic," but as a planter he could not renounce the use of black labor unless every other colonist did. Slavery might be morally bad; but it was an economic necessity which no man could have any pretensions to change by himself whatever his private ideas on the question might be. "To live in Virginia without slaves," wrote the Reverend Peter Fontaine in 1757, "is morally impossible. Before our troubles you could not hire a servant or slave for love or money, so that unless robust enough to cut wood, to go to mill, to work at the hoe, etc., you must starve, or board in some family where they both fleece and half starve you. . . . This of course draws us all into the original sin and curse of the country of purchasing slaves."[96]

Professor Beatty remarked that Byrd would no more consider setting himself against the majority of his countrymen "than he would consider dressing untidily, or out of accord with the latest available fashion. It was far simpler and pleasanter to be regarded as intellectually advanced, and to content one's self with that."[97] Certainly Byrd did not show the same sensitivity to social injustice, the same sympathy for slaves, as John Woolman, who in *Some Considerations on the Keeping of Negroes* (1754) also called attention to the obnoxious moral effects of slavery on the slaveowners. But it might well be an oversimplification to liken Byrd's attitude to a mere matter of fashion and to the snobbery of affecting to be intellectually advanced. The practical man in Byrd was too conscious of the gulf between ideal and reality, between what was desirable and what

[95] Byrd to Lord Egmont, July 12, 1736, *American Historical Review*, I (1895), 88–90. Byrd had expressed the same anxiety in a letter to Mr. Ochs about 1735. He suggested that the mountains of the back country should be explored and settled, "not only to be beforehand with the French, but also to prevent the Negroes taking refuge there as they do in the mountains of Jamaica to the great annoyance of the King's subjects, and these will be the more dangerous because the French will be always ready to supply them with arms and to make use of them against us upon all occasions." (*VMHB*, IX [1902], 226.)

[96] Fontaine to his brother Moses, March 30, 1757, *Huguenot Family*, p. 352. The "troubles" referred to were those "that came with the French and Indian War."

[97] P. 174.

was possible. As nothing could be done from Virginia itself and nothing would be done from Britain in this respect, the only solution for the individual planter, short of renouncing his estate and fortune, was to be as kind a master as circumstances allowed. Evidence of the planters' sense of their Christian obligations toward their Negro slaves is seen, for example, in Robert Carter's will, in which he provided against the separation of husband and wife in the division of his slaves,[98] and in Ralph Wormeley's ownership of Morgan Godwin's little book *The Negroes' and Indians' Advocate, Suing for their Admission into the Church*, published in 1680.[99]

That most masters treated their slaves kindly is borne out by Governor Gooch, who wrote in 1731: "Some masters . . . use their Negroes no better than their cattle and I can see no help for it, though far the greater number, having kind masters, live much better than our poor laboring men in England." He thus confirmed Robert Beverley's earlier statement in 1705: "I can assure you with a great deal of truth that generally their slaves are not worked near so hard, nor so many hours in a day, as the husbandmen and day-laborers in England."[100]

The fact is that the paternal humanitarianism of Byrd and some of his contemporaries, their concern for the future of their country because of the problem of slavery, is close to Jefferson's attitude at the end of the century. Jefferson's *Notes on the State of Virginia* have often been used as incontrovertible evidence of his antislavery attitude. But his humanitarian advocacy of emancipation should not blind the reader to Jefferson's conviction that the United States must be kept a white man's country, and that all emancipated slaves "should be colonized to such place as the circumstances of the time should render most proper."[101] In 1796 he seconded St. George Tucker's emancipation-exportation plan, in which laws were suggested to encourage the freed Negro to leave America.[102] As a matter of fact, plantation society did not have in itself the power to free its slaves, for this would have entailed checking its own growth; the example of Georgia, which finally had to admit slavery, shows how impossible such an action was economically. With the exception of a few men such as Thomas Jefferson, George Wythe, and St. George Tucker,

[98] *VMHB*, V (1898), 419–20.

[99] *WMCQ*, 1st ser., II (1893), 169–74.

[100] Governor Gooch to Lord . . . , May 28, 1731, British Transcripts, Fulham MSS Virginia, no. 111; Gooch Papers, I, 237; Beverley, *History*, p. 272.

[101] *Notes*, p. 138 (but see pp. 137–43).

[102] St. George Tucker, *A Dissertation on Slavery: With a Proposal for the Gradual Abolition of It, in the State of Virginia* (Philadelphia, 1796), pp. 93–94.

the Virginia planters showed little inclination to abandon the institution; slavery was too much interwoven into the domestic and social order. The opinion of the average planter of Revolutionary Virginia might be summed up in these words of Landon Carter: "Much is said of the slavery of Negroes, but how will servants be provided in these times? Those few servants that we have don't do as much as the poorest slaves we have. If you free the slaves, you must send them out of the country or they must steal for their support."[103] The decision taken in 1791 by his nephew Robert Carter of Nomini Hall to free over 500 slaves not only aroused a wave of protests from his neighbors; it ended in failure even for the slaves themselves. Rejected by their white neighbors, they were unable to sell the produce of their small patch of land; they turned to stealing in order to survive, but were soon caught and sold back into slavery.[104] After the troubles in the nineties following Santo Domingo's liberation of its slaves, after Gabriel's Conspiracy in 1800 and other occasions of slave unrest in the early 1800's, it was felt that general emancipation would result in a bloody war between whites and blacks. This fear was certainly the primary reason for the quiet demise of abolition societies in Virginia around 1800. Later, the hope of some antislavery Southerners that slavery would die out of itself because of economic depression in the South was shattered by the cotton boom between 1790 and 1820.[105] Toward the end of his life, Jefferson saw no acceptable solution to the problem of slavery, and his toleration of it as a necessary evil to be removed only after much time and toil sets him nearer than is often believed to such an adversary of emancipation as John Taylor of Caroline, who objected to St. George Tucker:

Do these hasty, . . . fanatic philosophers, patriots or Christians, suppose that the Negroes could be made free, and yet kept from property and equal civil rights; or that both or either of these avenues to power could be opened to them, and yet that some precept or incantation could prevent their entrance? As rivals for rule with the whites, the collision would be immediate, and the catastrophe speedy.

What could be done? In the light of self-preservation, Taylor's grim answer was this: "The fact is that Negro slavery is an evil which the United States must look in the face. To whine over it, is cowardly; to aggravate it, criminal; and to forbear to alleviate it, because it can-

---

[103] *Landon Carter Diary*, II, 1055 (July 6, 1776).
[104] Morton, *Robert Carter*, pp. 252–69. A typical protest was: "A man has almost as good a right to set fire to his own building though his neighbor's is to be destroyed by it, as to free his slaves" (p. 266).
[105] Avery O. Craven, *Soil Exhaustion as a Factor in the Agricultural History of Virginia and Maryland, 1606–1860* (Urbana, Ill., 1925), pp. 72–121.

not be wholly cured, foolish."[106] To such men as Jefferson, slavery was certainly an evil and steps should be taken quickly to suppress it for it could not last indefinitely; unfortunately most proposals to end it were impracticable, and any effective solution should be gradual and would take a long time. Thus the positions of Byrd and Jefferson, representative of some of their contemporaries in Virginia, hardly differed at the beginning and at the end of the eighteenth century, with due allowance for period and personality. Both felt uneasy and hoped for a change, but did nothing to promote it in their political action. Slavery was imposed by economic conditions toward the end of the seventeenth century and, though already opposed by some, upheld by the British government in the eighteenth. Then, after a short period when abolition and exportation were timidly advocated, the South settled into outright defense of the institution in the ante-bellum period. No evolution away from slavery ever started, for the Virginia slave codes were always primarily concerned with the master and his rights; the slave was a chattel with no legal personality, no right to property, marriage, or parenthood, or even personal security. In the light of history, there was no progress between Byrd and Jefferson in the attitude of the more enlightened planters toward slavery, and more than a century was lost before violence imposed change.[107]

Besides black slaves and white indentured servants from England, Byrd had a few Indians, whose redskin origin he always mentioned. This in itself is a token of their rarity, whether as ordinary servants or as slaves. Not more than two or three appear in the diary: "Indian Peter," "an Indian boy called Harry" who died at Westover about a year after Byrd acquired him, "Indian Ned" . . . . All historians of the colonial era agree that the number of Indian slaves in Virginia was never very large, and always less than in New England or the Carolinas. The Tuscarora War in North Carolina in 1711 prompted the Virginia Assembly to order the transportation and sale of all captured natives belonging to tribes at war with Virginia.[108] "The Indian," as James C. Ballagh stated, "proved an unprofitable and dangerous subject of slavery."[109] Indians might incite other natives to hostility; white indentured servants were more efficient and black slaves were cheaper. Even before the Tuscarora War, the Assembly

---

[106] *Arator, Being a Series of Agricultural Essays, Practical and Political, in Sixty-One Numbers* (2d ed., Georgetown, D.C., 1814), pp. 114–18.

[107] See an interesting comparison in Herbert S. Klein, *Slavery in the Americas: A Comparative Study of Virginia and Cuba* (Chicago, 1967).

[108] *Secret Diary*, pp. 56, 138, 228, 261; Hening, *Statutes at Large*, IV, 10–11.

[109] *A History of Slavery in Virginia* (Baltimore, 1902), p. 36.

specified that non-Christian Indians were to be held as servants only for a specified number of years, twelve for adults and thirty for children.[110]

As the slaves on a large plantation were too numerous to receive proper instruction and supervision at the beginning of their servitude, Byrd sometimes "put them to apprentice" to some neighbor with a small farm, who could train them more easily.[111] On the other hand some of his bond servants were young men from the neighborhood who agreed to work for him and learn the work of the plantation. Among the small farmers, "putting out" children in the family of a greater planter relieved the parents of the burden of feeding and clothing the boy while at the same time enabling him to learn a trade or to be trained in the running of a plantation.[112] But things did not always go as smoothly as Byrd wished, and he had to turn out one boy who "would not follow orders."[113]

Too many servants were badly trained and incompetent. One cut down trees without orders, another let cattle stray away.[114] There were days when Moll, the cook, did everything wrong; she spoiled a good plum pudding, or boiled too little bacon, or forgot to boil some artichokes for dinner, or made a bad sauce.[115] They were slovenly and neglectful. One was entrusted with the key to the store but went away with it on some errand, so that another could not get the paint that he needed for his work. Above all they were lazy and often feigned some illness to evade work. But Byrd was not easily taken in and his medical experience proved useful: "Two of my people pretended to be sick, but only pretended."[116] Or again, "Redskin Peter pretended he fell and hurt himself, but it was dissimulation. . . . [He] was very well again after he had worn the bit 24 hours, and went to work very actively." This Indian was a backslider well known to Byrd, who easily saw through him. Mrs. Byrd's maid Prue, the diarist complained in 1712, "is growing a most notable girl for stealing and laziness and lying and everything that is bad." She had once contrived to get into the cellar by a very small window and steal some strong beer, cider, and wine, which she shared with two

---

[110] This was after 1670; see Hening, *Statutes at Large*, II, 283. About "The Legal Status of the Indian in Colonial Virginia," see W. Stitt Robinson, Jr., in *VMHB*, LXI (1953), 247–59.

[111] *Secret Diary*, June 30, 1711, and March 2, 1712.

[112] Edmund S. Morgan, *Virginians at Home: Family Life in the Eighteenth Century*, 2d ed. (Charlottesville, Va., 1963), pp. 23–24.

[113] *Secret Diary*, April 11, Aug. 14, 1711.

[114] *Ibid.*, April 16, Sept. 7, 1710.

[115] *Ibid.*, pp. 5, 315, 316, 358, 500.

[116] *Ibid.*, July 11, 1709; *London Diary*, April 7, 1720.

other servants. A black servant, Anaka, had a marked partiality for rum and used to fill the bottle up with water after drinking from it.[117]

Drinking, stealing, and quarreling were frequent, the last often caused by intrigues between male and female servants. Johnny was whipped for threatening to strike Jimmy, and so was the girl for whom they quarreled, because she had smugly encouraged the row. Another servant was whipped for beating his wife, and Jenny "whipped for being his whore." Betty "had a Negro husband and was good for nothing."[118] Even among the higher servants, Nurse had an intrigue with Daniel Wilkinson, the secretary, but "she denied with an impudent face, protesting that Daniel only lay on the bed for the sake of the child." A year and a half later, she denied a rumor that she had had a child during a stay in Williamsburg; and she was finally turned away for helping other servants steal from the cellar.[119] Although Byrd often complained of his own servants at Westover, they do not seem so bad compared to others. At Hungars in Northampton County, the home of Colonel John Custis, Byrd was astonished to find "the worst servants in the world."[120]

When scolded, the servants often answered back, particularly to the first Mrs. Byrd, who was moody, high-strung, and easily wrought up. Once she had "a great quarrel" with one of her young maids, said Byrd, "in which my wife got the worst, but at last by the help of the family Jenny was overcome and soundly whipped." The master himself was not always proof against such fits of rebelliousness, and sometimes he forgot his dignity so far as to quarrel with his servants. But when he lost his temper with them he usually expressed regret afterwards: "In the evening I had a severe quarrel with little Jenny and beat her too much, for which I was sorry." He did not like punishments to be too hard, and was angry with his wife when she had Jenny burned with a hot iron. He once intervened to prevent her from beating the girl: "I had a terrible quarrel with my wife concerning Jenny that I took away from her when she was beating her with the tongs. She lifted up her hands to strike me, but forbore to do it. She gave me abundance of bad words and endeavored to strangle herself, but I believe in jest only."[121] Byrd blamed his wife for too often letting her passion get the better of her and for wanting to show her authority before guests. This "spoiled the mirth" of the last evening of 1711, and "for peace sake" Byrd had to make "the first

117 *Secret Diary*, pp. 468, 290–291, 529; 583, 337, 22, 42.
118 *Ibid.*, June 30, 1712; June 17, 1710; June 18, 1712.
119 *Ibid.*, pp. 7, 198, 221, 337.
120 *Ibid.*, Nov. 18, 1709. Colonel Custis was Byrd's brother-in-law's father.
121 *Ibid.*, Feb. 27, 1711; Aug. 22, July 15, 1710; March 2, 1712.

advance towards a reconciliation which I obtained with some difficulty and after abundance of crying."

In fact, the difference between Byrd's attitude to servants and that of his first wife illustrates the range that might exist on eighteenth-century plantations. Byrd inflicted punishments on his servants and slaves which would now seem cruel but were then almost lenient. He never had them branded, as some planters did. He sometimes ordered them to be fastened with a bit in their mouth, or to be tied up by the leg, but it was only reluctantly and as a last resort.[122] Whipping was the most common penalty, inflicted upon children as well as servants,[123] yet at Westover several months might elapse between two whippings, and more often than not the culprits got off with threats.[124] Slaves sometimes tried to escape, and Byrd offered "five pounds for each of [his] negroes run away,"[125] but this does not seem to have been so common an occurrence at Westover as on some plantations. An exception was the Negro woman who ran away three times in a few days, once with a bit in her mouth.[126] Many runaway slaves tried to reach the border of North Carolina. Near the Dismal Swamp, in 1728, Byrd and his companions "came upon a family of mulattoes that called themselves free, though by the shyness of the master of the house, who took care to keep least in sight, their freedom seemed a little doubtful." As he commented,

It is certain many slaves shelter themselves in this obscure part of the world, nor will any of their righteous neighbors discover them. On the contrary, they find their account in settling such fugitives on some out-of-the-way corner of their land to raise stocks for a mean and inconsiderable share, well knowing their condition makes it necessary for them to submit to any terms.[127]

Byrd was not a bad master on the whole. Not only did he give his people warm clothes when the cold season came, "tend them diligently" in time of epidemics, and try to avoid giving them too much work on Sundays; he also inquired of them how everything was, even before he made it a habit to talk to them every evening.[128] From

---

[122] *Ibid.*, pp. 199, 468, 529.

[123] Byrd mentioned whipping his niece Susan Brayne, *ibid.*, Oct. 8, 1710.

[124] *Ibid.*, pp. 56, 65, 75, 306, 338, 355, etc.

[125] *Ibid.*, July 23, 1712. This came as an addition to the two hundred pounds of tobacco that the law promised as a reward for the capture of a runaway slave (Hening, *Statutes at Large*, II, 283–84).

[126] *Secret Diary*, June 24–July 8, 1709.

[127] *Prose Works*, p. 186.

[128] *Another Secret Diary*, Nov. 9, 1740; *Secret Diary*, Jan. 9, 1711 (see the whole winter), Dec. 26, 1711. In the two later diaries, the usual phrase every evening is "I talked to my people."

time to time he ordered cider or rum or "a dram and some cherries" to be distributed as a treat to "the people at the quarters"; although he did not like them to get drunk on such occasions.[129] He was not above drawing twelfth-cake with them at the annual Twelfth-Night celebration. And a few days after scolding his servants for stealing fruit in the orchard, he wrote: "At night I caused cherries to be given to all my people about the house."[130] He thus did his best to avoid the alternative of being "either a fool or a fury." He became more indulgent as years passed, and his paternal management was not far from being a model of humanity by the standards of the time.

Although Westover was no average plantation and Byrd no ordinary planter, all this gives a fairly good illustration of the kind of life the colonists lived from day to day in the little world of a large plantation—on those scattered estates, each more or less economically independent of the others. Negro slavery was already firmly established at the turn of the century in the kind of feudal society that had grown out of the economic conditions imposed by the cultivation and trade of tobacco. The plantation, as much a factory as a farm, was both a large-scale agricultural unit and a commercial center, its servants' quarters a real village. This was perhaps the first modern attempt at commercial agriculture, an agriculture not intended for mere subsistence but for profit—a fact which aroused uneasiness in some colonists and made them plead for a more diversified economy. Byrd himself was well aware of the danger, particularly in the late twenties, when he wrote to one of his correspondents: "We must think of drawing part of our hands from tobacco. I am going vigorously upon hemp and husbandry with part of mine, and hope by my success to encourage others to follow my example." To another he confessed a few months later: "The darling of my projects is the making of hemp in this country. I am so out of humor with tobacco (which is made in too great quantity) that I have turned great part of my force toward hemp. I have met with divers disappointments, especially in the seed that has been sent me, which have stopped my career; nevertheless I have now got the better of them all." Yet hemp, because of the high cost of labor and freight,[131] was unprofitable, and Byrd had to return to tobacco. Virginia, no longer a land of opportunity for new settlers, favored the large tobacco estates and was on

129 *London Diary*, pp. 408, 419, 437, 460, etc.
130 *Another Secret Diary*, Jan. 7, 1740; *London Diary*, May 15 and 20, 1720.
131 Byrd to Mr. Bradley, July 3, 1728, Byrd Letterbook, 1728–1729, p. 18, Colonial Williamsburg; Byrd to Mr. Tenserf, June 1729, *ibid.*, p. 34; Byrd to Sloane, May 31, 1737, *WMCQ*, 2d ser., I (1921), 196.

its way to becoming the conservative country later described by Jefferson.[132]

[132] The process had just started when William Byrd II inherited his father's lands. In the Rent Roll of Virginia for 1704-1705 (copy in P.R.O.), out of 260 planters inscribed for Henrico County, only 33 held more than a thousand acres: 22 between one and two thousand, 7 between two and five thousand, 3 between five and ten thousand (John Pleasants, Colonel Randolph, and Giles Webb, often mentioned in Byrd's diaries). Only Byrd's father held more than ten thousand acres (his lands totalled 19,500). The total land grants for Henrico County being 165,814 acres, the average size of the patent was 637 acres. In most counties there were not more than one or two planters (out of several hundred listed as landholders) owning 5,000 acres or more. So it is certain that the great plantations arose in the first half of the eighteenth century. This rent-roll was established by Governor Nicholson's order. It was published by Professor Wertenbaker as an appendix to *Planters* (pp. 183-247), and serially in *VMHB*, between 1920 and 1926; it has now been made available in a most convenient form in Annie L. W. Smith, *The Quit Rents of Virginia* (Richmond, 1957).

CHAPTER XII

Colonial Society

THE world of the plantation, however closed and economically self-sufficient, still had openings onto the wider world. In spite of distances and the small size of the towns, there was an active social life in the colony, especially among the wealthier planters. Most of the year social activities consisted of visits from one plantation to another, where neighbors and friends gathered for some festivity, instead of meeting in one of the very few towns of the colony. On the Fry and Jefferson map of Virginia, drawn in 1751,[1] the majority of place names indicate large estates or country seats, not real urban settlements.

"One travels very comfortably and cheaply in this country," Durand of Dauphiné observed in 1686. "There are no inns but everywhere I went I was welcome. They cordially gave me to eat and to drink of whatever they had, and if I slept in a house where they owned horses, on the morrow some were lent to me to use for the first half of the next day's journey."[2] Even three or four decades later, the few inns and ordinaries were in Williamsburg and along the road to Fredericksburg, the Northern Neck, and Pennsylvania.

The isolated lives of the planters certainly prompted them to offer openhanded hospitality to any passing traveler, who might bring news from the outer world. Even strangers were always received with courtesy, without any regard to social station.[3] Inevitably that hospitality was sometimes extended to people who did not show much gratitude. On June 19, 1712, Byrd noted that "a Frenchman that had been courteously entertained here took away my boat across the river, but he brought it again and I gave him a severe reprimand."

It was no privilege of the wealthy planters to extend a warm welcome to any unexpected guest. Virginians, high and low, kept open house for the chance traveler: one night he would eat pork and hominy with a rough fellow who was carving a farm out of the forest,

[1] See *The Fry and Jefferson Map of Virginia and Maryland: Facsimiles of the 1754 and 1794 Printings with an Index* (Charlottesville, Va., 1966).

[2] *Huguenot Exile*, pp. 135–36.

[3] See *Secret Diary*, Sept. 4, 1709.

and the next he would sit in a fine-paneled hall, listen to gentlefolk, and dine on roast beef off damask and silver. Once as Byrd was coming back with a few friends from Northampton County across Chesapeake Bay, the wind did not allow the shallop to reach York River, and the party had to come ashore a few miles south, at a Mr. Wallace's, a parson, "who was not at home himself," said Byrd, "but his wife was very kind to us and gave us a good supper. I ate roast beef. In the evening Mr. Wallace came home and gave us some excellent cider." The next morning, the diarist added, "the parson was so kind as to provide us with six horses and would hardly part with us, so that it was noon before we could get away. He lives very neatly and is very kind to all that come to his house."[4]

When Byrd received at Westover a young bride newly come to the neighborhood, he made it a point of honor to give her the most favorable impression of the manners prevailing in her new circle: "I began to read geometry, but was interrupted by the coming of Mr. Will Randolph and his wife and Mrs. Cocke. I was as courteous as possible to them to give Mrs. Randolph a good impression of this part of the country. They dined with us." Byrd sometimes found visitors a burden and complained that he could read nothing because of the company, but he felt that his social position made it his duty to invite people on Sundays or on court days[5] and to keep open table with abundant food and wine.

The return of a local resident from a journey was a godsend, for he generally brought fresh news. The parson, just back from Williamsburg on June 8, 1709, "brought news that there were thirteen men-of-war arrived at New England with design to attempt the taking of Canada." When Colonel Edward Hill came back from England on January 2, 1710, Byrd sent someone immediately to compliment him, and to learn the news: "By him I learned that our governor Colonel Hunter has quit this government for that of New York, and that there is no likelihood of a peace or of the fleet's coming over." These were momentous tidings for the colonists. But groundless rumors were also brought, like that of Louis XIV's death in April 1709.[6]

The sight of a great ship sailing up the river (they came as near as four miles from Westover) always created a commotion, for she might bring letters from England as well as goods. The planters immediately sent on board for the mail, and for any scrap of information. "I heard guns from Swineyard's and sent my boat for my letters. In the meanwhile I walked about the plantation. In the evening the

4 *Ibid.*, Nov. 25–26, 1709.
5 *Ibid.*, Aug. 23, 1709; July 3, 1710.
6 *Ibid.*, April 19–20, 1709.

boat returned and brought some letters for me from England, with an invoice of things sent for by my wife which are enough to make a man mad. It put me out of humor very much." The first Mrs. Byrd often spent money more freely than her husband would have liked. But whether pleasant or unpleasant, the news was always awaited eagerly, and all neighbors were warned of the coming of a ship. "Tom came from Colonel Hill's with a letter by which I learned that a ship was come from England commanded by Captain Harvey, and about an hour after I had several letters from England which came by her which put me out of humor."[7] The news that a ship had just arrived from England at any part of Chesapeake Bay would be an occasion to write to some friends in a neighboring county: "We are told there is a Bristol ship arrived at York River. If she brings any news, be so good as to communicate it to your country friends, and in case you should have nothing foreign we should be glad of a little domestic."[8]

This yearning for news was general, and later Byrd was to learn a good way to make the most of letters when they arrived, which he revealed to his second wife's sister in 1736:

We tear [them] open as eargerly as a greedy heir tears open a rich father's will. But as no pleasure derived from this imperfect world flows clear to us, so every time Mrs. Byrd hears from any of you she sleeps no more the livelong night. Therefore I find it necessary, when any English letters come to hand late in the day, to pocket them up till next morning. Thus when Madam has the whole day before her, perhaps her joy may evaporate so far as to allow her some rest. In this prudent manner female passions require to be managed sometimes, to confine them in bounds and keep them, like a high-mettled horse, from running away with their owner.[9]

Such reactions confirm the paramount importance that England retained in the eyes of most colonists. Of course Byrd, although Virginia-born, still had many relatives in Britain; and as he had lived in London, he had many friends there as well. But the link with the mother country was just as strong for other planters. It takes at least three generations to make a new nation. The members of the most powerful families in Virginia had generally been educated in England, like Byrd. Economically they were dependent upon England and English agents. It was only with the next generations that Virginia-educated colonists became a little less England-conscious, although

[7] *Ibid.*, June 14, 1709; Feb. 26, 1712.
[8] Byrd to Sir John Randolph, Jan. 21, 1735, in *VMHB*, IX (1902), 240.
[9] Byrd to Mrs. Otway, June 30, 1736, *ibid.*, XXXVI (1928), 216.

the economic bond was not to be broken for a long time after Independence.

Mutual visits among the planters brought an atmosphere of elegant informality. "The people spend most of their time visiting each other," said Durand in 1686.[10] The guests would come by the river in shallops or by land in their coaches, and everyone tried to revive the stately festivities of polite society in London, which kept all their glamour in the memories of those who had lived a few years in England. They would walk in the fragrant gardens, play cricket or billiards, ride over the plantation and in the neighboring woods, or join in a hunt. In the evening, they generally made "as merry as they could," a frequent phrase in Byrd's diary on such occasions. Nearly always there were people dancing and playing cards, for these were the two dominant passions among the colonists. In later years, there was even a fixed day called "dance day," when a dancing master came from Williamsburg and taught dancing "in the new French manner."[11] He gave lessons at one of the plantation homes, and other young people came from the neighboring estates to share them.[12] When a planter received guests, the company often danced late into the night. Sometimes they played at proverbs for a change. The older or more serious-minded of them might become engrossed in conversation about the tobacco trade or about world affairs, or even about religion. Byrd himself would sometimes read English verse aloud to the ladies.[13]

Despite the sense of decorum that prevailed among the richer planters, the poorly trained servants and the boorish manners of some of the guests made that effort at refinement largely superficial. Once in 1711 at the dinner table, Byrd said, "my wife endeavored to cut a bone of pork, but Mr. Dunn took the dish and cut it for himself, which put my wife into great disorder and made her void blood so that she seemed to be going to miscarry, and Mr. Dunn had not the manners to ask pardon." When, about the same time, Byrd accompanied Governor Spotswood to New Kent County and they stopped

[10] *Huguenot Exile,* p. 111. See also Beverley, *History,* pp. 308, 312–13.

[11] Cf. *Va. Gaz.,* Nov. 18–25, 1737: "This is to give notice, that this day the subscriber has opened his school at the College, where all gentlemen's sons may be taught dancing, according to the new French manner, on Fridays and Saturdays once in three weeks, by William Dering, dancing-master." This dancing-class, held at the College, was certainly not coeducational; young ladies were taught at their homes.

[12] *Another Secret Diary,* June 16, 1741. Cf. *Landon Carter Diary,* II, 807, (May 7, 1774).

[13] *London Diary,* pp. 478, 501, 511; *Secret Diary,* pp. 29, 109, etc.

at Major Nicholas Merriweather's, "the major sat at the upper end of the table and helped himself first." Cleanliness was often doubtful, in both houses and people. Spending a night at Colonel Digges's, Byrd observed that, "when we went to bed it smelled so bad I could hardly endure it." During a journey up the James to Manakin Town, he shared a bed with the Reverend Mr. Charles Anderson, parson of Westover Parish, who, he discovered, was "no very clean bedfellow."[14]

There were a few occasions for a more formal kind of hospitality, such as when Byrd entertained Governor Spotswood at Westover in March 1711. The governor or lieutenant governor of a colony, the representative of the king, even when he was of middle-class origin, appeared as a gentleman familiar with the refined circles of the English court, far away in London, and he exerted no small influence on the social life of the colony by his gallantry and polish. Colonel Spotswood's visit to Westover was an honor for Byrd, and a real cause for pride.

On the morning of the twenty-fourth, Byrd wrote, "the weather was clear, and about nine o'clock I rode in form to Captain Drury Stith's, where I had appointed several gentlemen to go and meet the governor." But the return to Westover was slow:

It was evening before we got there, and about seven o'clock before we went to supper. We had eight dishes beside the dessert every day. I ate some beef. I gave them several sorts of wine and made them as welcome as I could. After supper, all the gentlemen went home, and the governor and the doctor[15] and I drank two bottles of French wine and talked of many things. The governor seemed satisfied with his entertainment.

The next day was Sunday:

It was twelve o'clock before the governor and the ladies were dressed, and then we went to church and heard Mr. Anderson preach. He and three other gentlemen came and dined with us. I would have no more company for fear of crowding the governor. . . . The governor's cook dressed dinner, and so it was in good order. . . . After dinner the company stayed till five o'clock, and then took leave. The governor and I took a walk about the plantation. He told me that Colonel Bassett agreed to come into the Council again and that he had written to England about it.

How flattering it must have been even for a councillor to take a walk alone with the first man of the land and to be the first to hear about some political piece of news! Two days later, as he was showing

---

14 *Secret Diary*, March 3, March 28, 1711; Nov. 11, 1710; May 29, 1711.
15 Dr. William Cocke, Secretary of State for the Colony, 1712–1720.

Colonel Spotswood round his plantation at Falling Creek, how exalting to note the interest of his guest in the dam and the mill! While the governor spent the next week visiting various parts of New Kent County, he left at Westover Mrs. Katherine Russell, who passed for his niece and kept house for him, although scandalous rumors circulated about the pair. Byrd judged her to be a woman of "good sense and very good breeding"; but, he said, she "can hardly forbear being hysterical, notwithstanding it is with good manners." As a relation of the governor she was treated with the greatest consideration at Westover: "My wife and I paid all possible respect to Mrs. Russell, and I entertained her as well as I could, and her conversation was very agreeable." The next Sunday, they "went to church with two coaches" in spite of the very short distance. There were visits to neighbors, and even when they stayed at home the ladies were never unoccupied: they "spent three hours in dressing, according to custom," while Byrd and one of his friends played billiards and read some news. In the afternoon, when rain kept them indoors, Byrd showed Mrs. Russell some of his prints and read to the ladies. And when Mrs. Russell, accompanied by Byrd's sister-in-law Mrs. Custis, returned to Williamsburg "in the governor's coach and six horses," Byrd "gave the governor's servants some strong beer before they went, and put some meat and wine in the coach for the ladies and their men, and some corn also for the horses."[16] Such was the stately hospitality of the great planters, when for a few days they forgot the plantation and tried to re-create the life of London society.

The social life of the colony was not confined to the large estates scattered along the rivers, in spite of the restricted number of real urban settlements. The English government more than once tried to create towns by artificial means, but only Norfolk really looked like one, according to Byrd's own testimony in 1728.[17] It was essentially a harbor, with twenty ships or more riding at the wharves, engaged chiefly in trade with the West Indies. And like most ports, it was looked upon as a haunt of vices. The ships, Byrd declared, "contribute much toward debauching the country by importing abundance of rum, which, like gin in Great Britain, breaks the constitution, vitiates the morals, and ruins the industry of most of the poor people of this country." As for the town itself, it stood out from all others in Virginia: "The streets are straight and adorned with several good

[16] *Secret Diary*, May 5 and 11, 1711, and Jan. 23, 1712; March 31, March 30, April 3, April 9, 1711.
[17] *Prose Works*, p. 173. About the town in colonial times, see the first chapters of Thomas J. Wertenbaker, *Norfolk, Historic Southern Port* (rev. ed., Durham, N.C., 1962).

houses, which increase every day. It is not a town of ordinaries and public houses, like most others in this country, but the inhabitants consist of merchants, ship carpenters, and other useful artisans, with sailors enough to manage their navigation." Byrd, who had stayed in the Netherlands and had read Sir William Temple's *Observations Upon the United Provinces of the Netherlands*, compared Norfolk to Holland, both for the disadvantages of having neither good air nor good water and for the virtues of industry and frugality, which he attributed to the majority of the inhabitants.

Most so-called towns consisted of little besides a church, a courthouse, and a few taverns and ordinaries. This Byrd felt to be customary in English colonies, as appears from his description of early Jamestown, "where, like true Englishmen, they built a church that cost no more than fifty pounds, and a tavern that cost five hundred." Although this allegation is not borne out by facts, there is no doubt that a century later taverns had become one of the essential features of the towns. On Sabbath days the colonists kept pretty sober, but court days were occasions for excessive drinking: "Some people came to court and got drunk in defiance of the sickness and the bad weather, among whom was Joe Harwood and Mr. Dennis, two great examples of virtue. . . . In the evening I took a walk and saw several drunk people in the churchyard." Elections, which took place in county courts, also favored such excesses: "We went to the courthouse where the freeholders were met to choose burgesses. . . . In the evening . . . I walked to the courthouse, where the people were most of them drunk."[18] In December 1710 the governor signed "an act for the further restraint of tippling houses and other disorderly places," but four months later Byrd observed that it had very little effect, and he saw several men drunk in the churchyard of Westover Parish.[19] These "towns," hardly more than hamlets in fact, were meeting places for Sunday services, elections, petty sessions, and festivities of various kinds. They generally had a building for assemblies and balls, or a banqueting hall, which influential planters had agreed to build for their own entertainment and their neighbors'.[20] They were convenient places for what social gatherings were possible in such a thinly populated country.

Some towns had been created for parties of new emigrants coming from a particular European country. One such case was Manakin Town, a settlement of French Huguenot refugees a few miles above

18 *Prose Works*, p. 160; *Secret Diary*, May 3, Aug. 15, 1710.
19 *Journals of Burgesses*, 1702–1712, p. 298; *Secret Diary*, April 4, 1711.
20 Bruce, *Social Life*, pp. 185–86.

Byrd's plantation at the Falls. Byrd's father proved a kind neighbor for the new settlers; he gave them material assistance when they arrived in 1700.[21] Although Robert Beverley testifies to the richness of the land along the James, where Byrd had his own plantations,[22] the town's beginnings had been difficult, and the French colonists were on the verge of starvation when Byrd's father visited them in May 1701 to report to the governor on their condition.[23] They received assistance from the colony and soon began to prosper, supported at first by the charity of their neighbors and by relief from London. In 1702 Francis Michel, a Swiss traveler, described the rapid progress of the refugees.[24] Manakin Town, which is often mentioned in Byrd's diary, had become a very prosperous place after a decade had passed, despite quarrels between the French minister and a faction opposed to him.[25]

Williamsburg itself was not a very large town. "It has near about one hundred houses, though by the manner of building the offices separately it shows to be three hundred. It is a full mile long and one mile broad," said a traveler about 1730.[26] Years after, in 1759, the Reverend Mr. Andrew Burnaby declared that "it consists of about two hundred houses, does not contain more than one thousand souls, whites and negroes."[27] But Robert Beverley insisted on its evolution in Governor Spotswood's time:

The private buildings are of late very much improved, several gentlemen there having built themselves large brick houses of many rooms on a floor . . . but they don't covet to make them lofty, having extent enough of ground to build upon; and now and then they are visited by high winds,

[21] R. A. Brock, ed., *Documents Relating to the Huguenot Emigration* (Richmond, 1886), pp. 5–7, and "Manakin Town, Va., Account of the Huguenot Settlement," ed. R. A. Brock, *Richmond Standard*, May 17, 1879, p. 4. See also Beverley, *History*, pp. 282–83. On the decision to send the French refugees to Manakin, see "Proposals humbly submitted to the Lords of the Council of Trade and Plantations for sending the French Protestants to Virginia" (1698) by William Byrd II, in the appendix to Louis B. Wright's edition of the anonymous pamphlet, *An Essay upon the Government of the English Plantations on the Continent of America* (1701), (San Marino, Calif., 1945), pp. 64–66. For a detailed history of Manakin Town, see James L. Bugg, Jr., "The French Huguenot Frontier Settlement of Manakin Town," in *VMHB*, LXI (1953), 359–94.

[22] *History*, p. 124.

[23] Brock, *Huguenot Emigration*, pp. 42–44.

[24] Hinke, "The Journey of Michel," pp. 122–23.

[25] *Secret Diary*, Sept. 23, 1710.

[26] Grove, *Diary*, 1698–1732, f. 54 verso, Alderman Library, U. Va.

[27] Andrew Burnaby, *Travels through the Middle Settlements in North America*, ed. Rufus R. Wilson (New York, 1904), p. 33.

which would incommode a towering fabric. They love to have large rooms, that they may be cool in summer. Of late they have made their stories much higher than formerly, and their windows larger, and sashed with crystal glass, adorning their apartments with rich furniture.[28]

Such luxury was only beginning to appear in the first decades of the eighteenth century, as the newly established capital developed quickly. Byrd alludes in his diary to the rising of public buildings such as the Capitol and the governor's new house. On February 8, 1711, he was with Colonel Spotswood: "I walked with him to the house that is building for the governor, where he showed me abundance of faults and found great exception to the proceedings of the workmen."[29] The accounts of the overseer, Henry Cary, were criticized, for he fed his own family as well as the workmen on public funds intended for the Governor's house: "The Governor insisted that he was incapable of the business and should be turned out, and the Council were of his opinion." Despite all these difficulties the house, or Palace as it came to be called, was finished about the end of the year, and Byrd visited the governor there in February 1712.[30]

During the sessions of the Council and the House of Burgesses, at "public times," there was a kind of "season" when political activities were mixed with social life, during the last three weeks of April and October.[31] "At the time of the assemblies and general courts, [the town] is crowded with the gentry of the country: on those occasions there are balls and other amusements; but as soon as the business is finished, they return to their plantations; and the town is in a manner deserted."[32] Every month or so, shorter sessions of the Council required Byrd's presence for two or three days. He would start for Williamsburg in the afternoon, usually in the company of some neighbor who also sat in the Council. They would stop on the way about four miles from town at Green Spring, the home of Philip Ludwell, where they would be hospitably received for supper and for the night. The next morning they would ride together to town to wait on the governor and drink coffee with him before the rest of the Council arrived. When the meetings were over, they were generally invited to the governor's palace: "About three o'clock we dined with the governor where everything was very polite and well served."[33]

28 *History*, p. 289. This passage was added in the 1722 edition.

29 *Secret Diary*, p. 298; see also pp. 250, 259, 311, 429, 440.

30 *Ibid.*, Dec. 7, 1711; Feb. 21, 1712.

31 Rutherford Goodwin, *A Brief and True Report for the Traveller Concerning Williamsburg in Virginia* (Richmond, 1935), pp. 47–50.

32 Burnaby, *Travels*, pp. 34–35.

33 *Secret Diary*, July 5, 1710.

There Byrd would find some of the refinement that he had been used to in London, and "polite" is a word that often recurs in his diary to describe Spotswood's receptions.

The great social event of the year was the ball given by the governor on the queen's birthday. In 1711 Mrs. Byrd was all in a fluster on the eve of the ball: "My wife and I quarreled about her pulling her brows. She threatened she would not go to Williamsburg if she might not pull them; I refused, however, and got the better of her, and maintained my authority."[34] The next day, they were to travel with Byrd's sister and brother-in-law and the latter's father, Colonel Duke. At the last moment Byrd caught a bad cold and was afraid he would be unable to stand the journey. But when his wife resolved to stay with him, he decided to go rather than keep her away from such a treat. Neglecting to say his prayers (which could be pardoned on such a day), he set out in advance to attend a Council meeting:

About ten o'clock I went to Williamsburg without the ladies. As soon as I got there it began to rain, which hindered the company from coming. I went to the president's where I drank tea and went with him to the governor's and found him at home. Several gentlemen were there and about twelve o'clock several ladies came. My wife and her sister came about two. We had a short Council, but more for form than for business. There was no other appointed in the room of Colonel Digges. My cold was a little better, so that I ventured among the ladies, and Colonel Carter's wife and daughter were among them. It was night before we went to supper, which was very fine and in good order. It rained so that several did not come that were expected. About seven o'clock the company went in coaches from the governor's house to the Capitol where the governor opened the ball with a French dance with my wife. Then I danced with Mrs. Russell; and then several others, and among the rest Colonel Smith's son, who made a sad freak. Then we danced country dances for an hour, and the company was carried into another room where was a fine collation of sweet meats. The governor was very gallant to the ladies and very courteous to the gentlemen. About two o'clock, the company returned in the coaches, and because the drive was dirty the governor carried the ladies into their coaches. My wife and I lay at my lodgings. Colonel Carter's family and Mr. Blair were stopped by the unruliness of the horses, and Daniel Wilkinson was so gallant as to lead the horses himself through all the dirt and rain to Mr. Blair's house. My cold continued bad. I neglected to say my prayers and had good thoughts, good humor, but indifferent health, thank God Almighty. It rained all day and all night. The president had the worst clothes of anybody there.[35]

---

[34] *Ibid.*, Feb. 5, 1711.
[35] *Ibid.*, Feb. 6, 1711. The President of the Council was traditionally its oldest

This is the longest entry in Byrd's *Secret Diary*, but the event easily justified it in his eyes. It was a social triumph for himself: his wife had been singled out to open the ball with the governor, while he partnered Spotswood's pretty "niece." Besides, Daniel Wilkinson, one of his own employees, had taken occasion to behave most courteously toward Colonel Carter, the richest planter of the region, and Commissary Blair, the head of the Church in Virginia. Byrd had the agreeable feeling that he had cut a fine figure and been in the limelight. As a contrasting afterthought, there was a not unpleasant tinge of pity for poor Colonel Jenings, the president of the Council, who dressed so badly. This is one of the passages that are most amusingly revealing of Byrd's regard for worldly success. Years later, when old age had made him less susceptible to it, he disposed of a similar circumstance with two lines of his diary. In 1740, Commissary Blair, as president of the Council and acting governor in Gooch's absence, gave a ball for George II's fifty-seventh birthday: "At night ventured to the ball at the Capitol where I stayed till ten and ate three jellies, and then went home and prayed. The president entertained well."[36]

But in 1711 Byrd's diary, in addition to a full account of the queen's ball, also lets the reader behind the scenes for a glimpse of the relations between master and servant. The day after the ball, Byrd went to wait upon the governor and learned the true reason for the perfection of the service: "The governor had made a bargain with his servants that if they would forbear to drink upon the queen's birthday they might be drunk this day. They observed their contract and did their business very well and got very drunk today, in such a manner that Mrs. Russell's maid was forced to lay the cloth; but the cook in that condition made a shift to send in a pretty little dinner."[37]

Sometimes there were less formal dances, arranged on the spur of the moment. After a day's work at the Capitol, Byrd and some of his fellow councillors were invited to dinner at the governor's; there, he said,

we found Mrs. Churchill and several other ladies and my wife among them. The table was so full that the doctor and Mrs. Graeme and I had a little table to ourselves and were more merry than the rest of the company. I ate roast beef for supper. In the meantime the doctor secured two fiddlers, and candles were sent to the Capitol; and then the company followed and we had a ball and danced till about twelve o'clock at night; and then everybody went to their lodgings; but I neglected to say my

---

member, and he served as deputy-governor when the Governor was absent. In 1711 the President was Colonel Jenings.

[36] *Another Secret Diary*, Oct. 30, 1740.
[37] *Secret Diary*, Feb. 7, 1711.

prayers, but had good health, good thoughts and good humor, thank God Almighty. Mrs. Russell was my partner.[38]

Here again, be it said in passing, Byrd's afterthought betrays him more than the rest of the entry.

Ten years later, about 1720, the social gatherings of Williamsburg were already far more frequent. Hugh Jones observed that by then there were enough families of aristocratic pretensions to lead the society of the little capital: "Here dwell several very good families, and more reside here in their own houses at public times. They live in the same neat manner, dress after the same modes, and behave themselves exactly as the gentry in London, most families of any note having a coach, chariot, berlin or chaise." London indeed they felt to be their model and the hub of the universe: "The habits, life, customs, computations, etc., of the Virginians are much the same as about London, which they esteem their home."[39]

Dancing was a necessary accomplishment in the small society of Williamsburg, and a real passion. Balls and assemblies were considered part of a civilized life, and Hugh Jones, in 1724, suggested that the College of William and Mary should provide for dancing lessons, along with music and fencing.[40] During the short season, ladies and gentlemen from the great plantation danced the nights away to the music played by servant-fiddlers. During a two-months' stay in Williamsburg in the fall of 1720, Byrd went to two assemblies at the governor's and one at Commissary Blair's, not to mention balls organized by two dancing masters, Charles Stagg and Christopher Graffenried.

The former, who had been an actor, was in charge of the theater which was run in a dancing school. Plays were a new entertainment in the colony at the time.[41] In April 1720 Byrd mentioned twice going to a play, which he said "they acted tolerably well," though the second time he "stayed not above two acts."[42] Even many years later, the plays were generally performed by amateurs, as appears from the

[38] *Ibid.*, Nov. 2, 1711. Dr. Cocke, a former schoolfellow of Byrd, was soon to become Secretary for the colony. Mrs. Graeme was then visiting Virginia with her husband, an English merchant and a cousin of Spotswood (see Dodson, *Spotswood*, p. 298, and *Prose Works*, p. 358).

[39] *Present State*, pp. 71, 80.

[40] *Ibid.*, p. 111.

[41] See Robert H. Land, "The First Williamsburg Theater," in *WMQ*, 3d ser., V (1948), 359-74, and the chapter entitled "The First Theater in America (Williamsburg, 1716-1745)," in Hugh F. Rankin, *The Theater in Colonial America* (Chapel Hill, N.C., 1965).

[42] *London Diary*, April 25-26, 1721. The playhouse is also mentioned by Hugh Jones in 1724 (*Present State*, p. 70).

following notice in the *Virginia Gazette* for September 3–10, 1736: "Williamsburg, September 10. This evening will be performed at the theater, by the young gentlemen of the College, *The Tragedy of Cato*; and on Monday, Wednesday and Friday next, will be acted the following comedies, by the gentlemen and ladies of this country, viz.: *The Busy-Body*, *The Recruiting Officer*, and *The Beaux' Stratagem*." Byrd himself always showed great interest in this kind of entertainment, not only as a spectator but also as a producer of and actor in amateur theatricals.[43] Yet the theater was still in its infancy in Virginia. It was only a side line for Stagg, whose main activities were the running of his dancing school and, with the help of his wife, the organization of assemblies.[44]

Graffenried, the son of the Swiss founder of New Bern, North Carolina,[45] had settled in Williamsburg and opened an inn; but he and his wife also taught dancing in various planters' homes and gave balls and assemblies for which people had to pay admittance.[46] Byrd himself noted the rivalry prevalent between the dancing masters of the colony. In 1735 he wrote to John Randolph: "Upon the news of Mr. Stagg's death Madame la baronne de Graffenried is in hopes to succeed to part of his business in town, and were it not for making my good Lady jealous (which I would not do for the world), I would recommend her to your favor. She really takes abundance of pains and teaches well."[47] Dancing was one of the main accomplishments among the upper class, and in the last days of 1727, soon after his arrival in Williamsburg, Governor Gooch in a letter to his brother gave the colonists a certificate of good manners: "The gentlemen and ladies are perfectly well-bred, not an ill dancer in my government."[48]

In 1720 Byrd was a widower and spared no opportunity to court a rich and pretty woman. At one time he entertained the idea of proposing to Anne, Colonel Carter's daughter, but she soon discouraged her elderly suitor at one of Williamsburg's assemblies: "I asked Mrs. Anne Carter to dance a minuet, but she pretended she was tired and yet danced soon after with Mr. Armistead, without any

[43] On this subject Carl R. Dolmetsch has made several discoveries which are about to be published.

[44] *London Diary*, Sept. 30, Oct. 3 and 20, 1720. See also Mary N. Stanard, *Colonial Virginia, Its People and Customs* (Philadelphia, 1917), pp. 230–31.

[45] See p. 29.

[46] *London Diary*, Jan. 4, 1721. *Va. Gaz.*, April 15–22, 1737, repeating a notice already published in the issue for Feb. 18–25.

[47] Byrd to Sir John Randolph, Jan. 21, 1735, *VMHB*, IX (1902), 240.

[48] Letter of Dec. 28, 1727, Gooch Correspondence, Colonial Williamsburg.

meaning but only for want of knowing the world."[49] The minuet was then the most formal and fashionable dance. The colonists were always eager to keep up with the fashions, and even at sixty-seven, Byrd was quite willing to let himself be talked into trying the new quadrille.[50] Even upperclass Virginians were not above dancing jigs and reels in addition to the more formal dances, and in the mid-eighteenth century this made them appear somewhat rustic to English visitors.[51]

The effort at refinement among the upper classes of the colony is particularly noticeable in the relations between the sexes. Although manners were sometimes unexpectedly coarse, gentlemen were supposed to show constant deference and courtesy to ladies. In Virginia as in London, it was common belief among men that all women were talkative and noisy and that they could not resist the temptation of a bit of scandal; it was a privilege of their sex to be often without reason cross, to have "tears always ready at command," and to spend three hours dressing.[52] Yet ladies must never be kept waiting and in all circumstances should be treated with the greatest consideration. Byrd often felt proud of his own patience when his first wife was out of humor and a quarrel broke out between them; he "only thanked her" lest he should "say things foolish" in his passion.[53] But his friends did not always behave so well. Once in Williamsburg he went to Colonel Carter's lodgings where he found the master of the house and two guests "almost drunk" and keeping two ladies waiting. He refused to drink with them and at last "persuaded the Colonel not to suffer the ladies to wait on him so long." When he had to hear a court case between two of his own friends, Colonel Hill and Mrs. Benjamin Harrison, he was shocked to see the Colonel and Will Randolph fly into a passion and told them severely that "they ought to be put in the stocks" for their rudeness to Mrs. Harrison.[54]

Virginia gentlemen in general, and Byrd in particular, were certainly no models of morality in their attitude to women belonging to the lower classes, but most historians of the period agree that divorce was extremely rare and that conjugal infidelity among the upper

[49] *London Diary*, Oct. 21 and Nov. 1, 1720. In 1722, Anne Carter married Benjamin Harrison (see *ibid.*, April 30 and May 4, 1721; Byrd himself spoke to Colonel Carter for Harrison). Their son was one of the signers of the Declaration of Independence.

[50] *Another Secret Diary*, April 10, 1741.

[51] Burnaby, *Travels*, p. 57.

[52] Cf. *Secret Diary*, pp. 386, 47, 107, 285, 324, and "The Female Creed."

[53] *Secret Diary*, May 22, 1712. See also pp. 18, 105, 182, 202, 505, etc.

[54] *Ibid.*, Nov. 3, 1711; Sept. 3, 1712.

classes was seldom notorious enough to have been recorded. To be sure, bastardy was by no means uncommon, and a servant woman often bore her master's child. Gentlemen were quite ready to try their luck with a maid or a black girl, at the expense of some short-lived pang of remorse afterwards for their "bad thoughts." But this meant little to them, while the women of their own class were sacred and treated with chivalric deference, at least outwardly. The men rarely ventured beyond a gallant compliment or at most a kiss given jestingly, the height of daring in company, a piece of audacity well worth recording in a secret diary. Once on arriving at Colonel Bray's, Byrd and one of his friends found "abundance of ladies and gentle-men dancing." "We did not dance," he said, "but got some kisses among them." A gentleman like Byrd could be trusted to steal an honest kiss whenever a chance turned up. On the other hand, a lady's modesty did not allow her to remain alone with a gentleman: thus Mrs. Custis, Byrd's sister-in-law, showed proper reluctance to go from Westover to Mrs. Harrison's, only a mile away, alone in the coach with Dr. Cocke, "and so Mrs. Dunn went with them."[55]

As early as the mid-seventeenth century, Virginians had already acquired a solid reputation for heavy drinking, to which John Win-throp testified in his journal: Of one Nathaniel Eaton who was go-ing to Virginia, he remarked that he was "given up of God to extreme pride and sensuality, being usually drunken, as the custom is there."[56] Byrd would have retorted that New Englanders had little right to be so critical since they were largely responsible for drunkenness in the colony, being the main providers of rum to Southerners. The fact remains that on Byrd's own authority it was not uncommon on a Sunday to hear "a great noise of people drunk in the street good part of the night" in Williamsburg. Not that he ever expressed any virtuous indignation when he found "a comic freak of a man that was drunk"; people of the lower classes were not expected to avoid drunkenness altogether, but only to keep out of real mischief. Once at a militia muster he provided strong drink for everybody: "My hogshead of punch entertained all the people and made them drunk and fighting all the evening, but without mischief." On workdays, however, the situation was different, and masters often had to threaten away traders who were only too ready to sell drinks to the servants.[57]

Although Byrd declared himself to be "a great friend to temper-ance," his temperance still allowed him to consume a fair amount of

[55] *Ibid.*, April 26, 1709; Aug. 9, 1711.

[56] *Winthrop's Journal, The History of New England from 1630 to 1649*, ed. James K. Hosmer (New York, 1908), II, 20–21.

[57] *Secret Diary*, Dec. 11, Sept. 21, Sept. 22, Aug. 22, 1710.

liquor. It was not uncommon for him of an evening to be "very merry" in company over a few bottles of French wine, and perhaps to try to get one of the party drunk. Once the victim was the Bishop of London's representative in Virginia, Commissary Blair. On St. George's Day, when all the Council went to dine with the governor, "We were very merry in the evening in drinking the healths and in making the commissary drink them by the help of Colonel Harrison that sat next him." They might then be "merry and almost drunk," but still Byrd was able to add: "However we got well to Major Harrison's and behaved ourselves very discreetly." A gentleman should carry his liquor well in all circumstances. When Byrd reprimanded the Reverend Mr. Arthur Blackamore, the headmaster of William and Mary College, he was probably less angry at his drunkenness than at his being unable to behave himself like the gentleman that a clergyman should be. Yet it was hard to know when to stop, and on the day Byrd was sworn a member of the Council he had to admit that he "drank too much French wine." At a Council meeting, "Colonel Lewis was very drunk with drinking canary," and during the same session, Byrd secretly threw in the Capitol a letter containing a lampoon "which put the House of Burgesses into a ferment." Two days later, while many councillors and burgesses were at the coffeehouse, the whole show was given away by a drunken burgess, George Mason.[58] In fact, excessive drinking was fairly common among the upper classes, even though they flattered themselves that they showed aristocratic moderation. John Fontaine's diary attests to the amount of liquor that was consumed during the Blue Ridge expedition led by Governor Spotswood in 1716; as does Byrd's *Secret History* for the Dividing Line expedition in 1728.[59] The commissary's wife, Mrs. Blair, was not immune to the temptation of liquor. "I was very much surprised," said Byrd, "to find Mrs. Blair drunk, which is growing pretty common with her, and her relations disguise it under the name of consolation."[60]

After a meeting of the Council or a session at court, it was customary for Byrd and his colleagues to adjourn to one of the ordinaries of the small town for drink and dinner. The customers were some-

[58] *Ibid.*, April 23, 1711; March 12, 1712; June 7, 1709; Nov. 10, Nov. 26, 1710. The burgess was the grandfather of the George Mason who drafted the Virginia Declaration of Rights and joined Jefferson in writing the Virginia Constitution of 1776.

[59] *Huguenot Family*, pp. 284, 285, 288–89; *Prose Works*, pp. 52, 55, 58, 67, 69, 96, etc.

[60] *Secret Diary*, March 2, 1709. Mrs. Blair was one of the daughters of Colonel Benjamin Harrison of Wakefield, Surry County, and thus belonged to one of the great planter families of the colony.

times unruly, and in 1712 Byrd noted that several young gentlemen were brought to court for brawling in two of these places one night, but they "came off with paying ten shillings apiece."[61] One of the best ordinaries was Marot's, kept until 1717 by a former secretary to Byrd's father.[62] But even there, one evening, "somebody cast a brick from the street into the room, which narrowly missed Colonel Carter."[63] In the twenties and thirties, these ordinaries acquired, together with a better appearance, the name of inns or taverns, some of which were in particularly good repute. In the last years of his life Byrd often mentioned dining with Henry Wetherburn, who had married Marot's daughter and was the manager of the famous Raleigh Tavern.[64]

When dinner was over, the company often went on to "the coffee-house."[65] There people would play cards or dice, for gaming was among the favorite pastimes of the planters when they stayed in Williamsburg, and large amounts sometimes changed hands. In November 1711 Byrd, who was no real gambling addict but was very fond of a game with friends, returned home after losing more than twelve pounds in one evening, feeling "very much out of humor to think myself such a fool." This, however, did not deter him from playing again the next day and losing another twelve pounds. It was all the harder to resist temptation since gaming was a general habit in the colony, especially among the upper classes. It was difficult for a man like Byrd to refuse a game with one of his own class. All he could do was resolve to stop playing when his losses reached a certain sum, or to forbear dice, which he deemed more dangerous than cards.[66] What a traveler from New York observed in 1777 was already true in Byrd's times: "There is a severe act of Assembly against gaming, but I observe the members of that House are as much addicted to it as other men, and as frequently transgress the law: I have known one of them bet thirty dollars upon an odd trick at whist. Gaming is amazingly prevalent in Williamsburg."[67]

[61] *Ibid.,* April 19, 1712.

[62] See *Secret Diary,* pp. 260, 263, 335, 428, etc., and *WMCQ,* 1st ser., V (1896), 117.

[63] *Secret Diary,* Oct. 30, 1711.

[64] See particularly *Another Secret Diary,* April 15–30.

[65] It is hard to say whether Byrd in his diary entries for 1740 was writing of the same establishment he mentioned in 1710. See *Secret Diary,* pp. 241, 247, 248, 249, etc., and *Another Secret Diary,* pp. 63, 75, 119, etc. Cf. Jane Carson, *Colonial Virginians at Play* (Williamsburg, Va., 1965), pp. 261–65.

[66] *Secret Diary,* Nov. 22, Nov. 24, 1711, April 17, 1712.

[67] Ebenezer Hazard, "MS. Journal of Journeys to the South, 1777–1778," *VMHB,* LXII (1954), 423.

Betting on the most various subjects was also frequent. He once bet two bits (a quarter of a Spanish dollar) that one of his friends would not venture onto the frozen river during a thaw; but the other man did, "and the ice broke with him and took him up to the mid-leg." During one of his stays in Williamsburg in 1711, an acquaintance of his walked "to Jimmy Burwell's and back again in less than three hours for a wager of two guineas, but was almost spent."[68] And well he might be, for King's Creek in York County was about seven or eight miles away. The pleasure and pride of winning, in such circumstances, counted far more than the size of the wager.

Most of the betting was done on horse races. Some were private races, organized by a few planters among themselves. In the afternoon the planters would gather with their families in a field belonging to one of them and hold races in which some of the gentlemen took part. Afterwards, the host would provide dinner for everyone. At Green Spring, Colonel Ludwell's home, "Mr. W–l–s ran two races and beat John Custis and Mr. Hawkins. He likewise jumped over the fence, which was a very great jump."[69] In 1724 Hugh Jones, speaking of the "common planters," observed that they "don't much admire labor, or any manly exercise, except horse-racing." He added ironically, "They are such lovers of riding that almost every ordinary person keeps a horse; and I have known some spend the morning in ranging several miles in the woods to find and catch their horses only to ride two or three miles to church, to the court-house, or to a horse-race, where they generally appoint to meet upon business."[70]

Public races were also frequent. But they were marked by class distinctions. As early as 1674, a tailor of York County was fined one hundred pounds of tobacco for presuming to enter his horse in a race against that of a "gentleman," Dr. Matthew Slader; the court declared that racing was "a sport for gentlemen only."[71] Only the rabble went to some races; these roused the planter's contempt. "I denied my man G–r–l to go to a horse race," Byrd said once, "because there was nothing but swearing and drinking there."[72]

Races at Williamsburg, where there was a mile course, were of another standing. They were held at the time of the fairs or during the sessions of the Assembly and formed part of the fashionable fes-

[68] *Secret Diary*, Dec. 29, 1709; Nov. 8, 1711.
[69] *Ibid.*, Aug. 19, 1710; *London Diary*, May 11, 1721; see also *Va. Gaz.*, Sept. 30–Oct. 7, 1737. *Secret Diary*, April 24, 1709.
[70] *Present State*, p. 84.
[71] "History of York County in the Seventeenth Century," *Tyler's Quarterly Historical and Genealogical Magazine*, I (1919–20), 264.
[72] *Secret Diary*, Aug. 27, 1709.

tivities of the colonial season. After sitting at court, Byrd and his colleagues would adjourn to see the horse race, "and I lost thirty-five shillings," Byrd added once, with his customary precision about money matters. Gentlemen took part in these races, which were a kind of social event to which the planters could take their families.[73] "About twelve," Byrd wrote one day in May 1740, "the company went to the race, and so did my family; and I gave them all money and sent a pistole myself by Mr. Hall who brought back two about four o'clock.[74]

Byrd's Virginia had advanced far beyond the early stages of adventurers and pioneers and quick fortunes. With the slow ebbing away of the Indian tribes and the continuous extension of great estates along the upper reaches of the rivers that flowed into Chesapeake Bay, the former Middle Plantation, a mere gathering of warehouses and ordinaries, assumed a new importance as Williamsburg. Despite the widely scattered settlement of Virginia, the small town, with its growing population and its new public and private buildings, was by degrees becoming a true capital, the hub of the colony. Byrd's diaries bear witness to the emergence of a real urban social life in the capital between 1710 and 1740. The social community was beginning to resemble that of the mother country, divided into unofficial but nonetheless distinct classes, and the line between these was becoming more difficult to cross. In such gatherings as horse races the various strata of society appeared most clearly: people knew their places and kept to them almost instinctively, although real gentlemen were conscious enough of their superiority sometimes to show condescending familiarity to their inferiors.

Perhaps the best insight into the social code of the Virginia planters is provided by *The History of the Dividing Line* and the other works Byrd intended to publish. The judgments he passed on his friends and colleagues, on the people he encountered, and even on himself reveal that Byrd, like most members of his group, despised barbarity, disorder, idleness, intemperance, and selfishness. He valued industry, frugality, moderation, responsibility, justice, and respect for authority. The contrast he drew between Virginia (or rather Tidewater Virginia) and North Carolina reflects the fact that the latter was a newer, poorer, rougher colony, in a less advanced stage of development.

Although the country acquired a social life of its own, cultural life

---

73 *Ibid.*, Oct. 17, 1710. See the victory of Governor Gooch's son, in *Va. Gaz.*, Dec. 7–14, 1739.

74 *Another Secret Diary*, May 8, 1740. On this subject, see W. G. Stanard, "Racing in Colonial Virginia," in *VMHB*, II (1894–1895), 293–305.

was still in its infancy. Byrd himself is not a representative figure, for he had a far greater interest in books and learning than most of his fellow colonists. Not only was his library of thirty-six hundred volumes far wider in size and scope than those of his neighbors, it was also less directed toward utilitarian literature.[75] Even excluding Byrd's personal devotion to Hebrew and Greek and Latin, very few planters took such a broad interest in contemporary literature, whether poetry, drama, or romance. Carl Bridenbaugh doubts that the tobacco planters of Virginia were as well read as the inventories of a few Tidewater libraries suggest, or that they were as interested in cultural matters as their admirers have sometimes claimed. He describes them as practical and public-spirited men who were more concerned with crops and politics than with literature and philosophy.[76] Yet Richard B. Davis and J. A. Leo Lemay have discovered works by dozens of writers in the Chesapeake Bay area in the period of Gooch's governorship, ample evidence that Byrd was not alone in his literary interests and activities. These were mostly by amateurs who, like Byrd, circulated their materials in manuscript only, although some like John Fox or Robert Bolling published their works in England.[77] Scores of unpublished sermons, poems, and letters have been found, some of which are as literary as Byrd's writings, although his remain the best among them.

It should not be assumed that the colonists in general were completely lacking in literary taste. They could hardly afford to order books all the way from London merely for the ostentation of their finely bound covers. When they bought books, it must have been because they felt a real need for them. Even literature was instructive, in those days when none was avowedly without any moral purpose, when people hardly admitted to reading for idle diversion and personal enjoyment. On the whole, the various catalogs of colonial libraries are the best tokens we have of the tastes of Virginia planters.

The scanty libraries of the smaller planters were hardly different in their proportions, literature excepted. They corroborate each

[75] See George K. Smart, "Private Libraries in Colonial Virginia," in *American Literature*, X (1938), 24–52. Many of the libraries dealt with in this article belong to the later eighteenth century. Among the largest libraries after Byrd's were those mentioned by Wright, *First Gentlemen*: Ralph Wormeley's in 1701 had 375 titles; Richard Lee's in 1714 had 300 titles; Robert ("King") Carter's in 1732 had 260 titles (see pp. 197, 217, 249).

[76] *Myths and Realities: Societies of the Colonial South* (Baton Rouge, La., 1952).

[77] Cf. Richard Beale Davis, "The Colonial Virginia Satirist," *Transactions of the American Philosophical Society*, Philadelphia, new ser., LVIII, pt. I (March 1967).

other and bear abundant evidence of the similarity between the colonists' general preferences and those of their English contemporaries. These conclusions receive further confirmation from Byrd's diaries. He often entertained his lady guests with a reading of Garth's mock-heroic poem *The Dispensary*, or Collier's *Short View of the Immorality and Profaneness of the English Stage*, or Gay's *Beggar's Opera*.[78] It goes without saying that this applies only to the upperclass planter families, among whom a taste for reading soon became a status symbol. And it seems that, as in contemporary England, the feminine reading public was fast gaining in importance throughout the first half of the eighteenth century.

First and foremost, there were books of divinity, in a number which might seem surprisingly large in comparison with private libraries in New England. As Professor Wright has stressed, the difference between the Puritans of the North and the Cavaliers of the South was certainly smaller than has often been asserted.[79] If in Virginia the interest in sermon reading (and pious books more generally) was less theological than devotional and practical, it must have been due both to the more liberal tendencies of the Church of England and to the distance that often lay between the plantations and the nearest church. Sermon reading was a frequent substitute for churchgoing, and Byrd's partiality for Tillotson's works is most characteristic. Besides sixteen volumes of Tillotson's sermons, his library also contained many volumes of sermons by William Chillingworth, John Hales, Henry More, Ralph Cudworth, Henry Hammond, Robert South, Jeremy Taylor, Isaac Barrow, Samuel Clarke and others.[80] Shunning theological quarrels and hairsplitting on small points of dogma, these latitudinarian divines mingled exhortations to a good life with advice on everyday living. The sermons of South and Tillotson were also part of Robert Carter's library, as was *A Gentleman's Religion*, by the Irish archbishop Edward Synge. Carter shared many of their views: "The great stress that is laid upon ceremonies, any farther than decency and conformity, is what I cannot come into the reason of. Practical godliness is the substance; these are but the shell."[81] Taylor and Hales were also represented in Ralph Wormeley's library, where John Locke's treatise, *The Reasonableness of Christianity as Delivered in the Scriptures*, was to be found.[82] This world and the

[78] *Secret Diary*, pp. 324 and 110; *Prose Works*, p. 345.

[79] *Cultural Life*, p. 127.

[80] See the catalog of Byrd's library in Bassett, pp. 413–28.

[81] *Robert Carter Letters*, p. 25. For the inventory of Robert Carter's property including his library, see *VMHB*, VI (1898–99), 145–52, 260–68.

[82] *WMCQ*, 1st ser., II (1893), 169–74 (an inventory of Ralph Wormeley's

other could not be separated; spiritual and temporal affairs were woven fine; idleness was sin and industry an essential virtue. Such were the basic beliefs of Byrd and most planters in Virginia, as well as of other English colonists in America, even before Franklin preached the gospel of work which remained the foundation of American economic prosperity.

Besides more than a hundred and fifty works of divinity, the shelves of Byrd's library contained two hundred and fifty historical books, biographies, voyages, and travels, according to the classification of his librarian William Proctor. John Eliot, Richard Brathwaite, Henry Peacham, and other educationists considered such books highly instructive for a young gentleman; they were essential to the education of a great planter's son if he was to become one of the leaders of the colony, and they were as well represented in Robert Carter's library as in Byrd's. A few books on politics and statecraft could not be amiss, and Byrd was well provided, with Thomas More, Thomas Hobbes, Samuel Puffendorf, Lord Halifax, Algernon Sidney, James Harrington, John Locke, and Sir William Temple, who was also among Colonel Carter's favorites. Byrd's three hundred lawbooks were still more useful to the councillor when he sat in court; they ranged from Magna Carta to a most comprehensive collection of reports and statutes, and volumes about English and Virginia laws. Carter, who was particularly interested in law, had about one hundred titles. Even a planter with a very small library had to possess a few lawbooks and be his own lawyer, to draw up his deeds and wills or to defend his interests in some suit over landed property. Byrd himself generally paid a lawyer to do this, but his diary shows him at work in his own library with John Clayton, later attorney general for Virginia, consulting some lawbooks for one of his pending cases.[83] And in August 1712 he read some law and wrote an abridgment of it in his notebook.

Other essential volumes were medical treatises. Byrd, who complained that doctors were too much of a rarity in Virginia, had more than a hundred and fifty medical books on his shelves. Every planter had at least a few, for everyone had to be his own doctor at some time in his life. Byrd also had numbers of books on such various subjects as surveying, farming, gardening, cookery, architecture, and engineering, whereas most colonists were content with an encyclopedia.

In the first decades of the century, all printed matter, whether

library taken from Middlesex County Records). Locke's book was also in Byrd's library (see Bassett, p. 442).
[83] *Secret Diary,* May 6, 1711.

books or newspapers, came from England. Byrd, who always did his best to keep abreast of the times, first mentioned reading "in the *Tatler*" in July 1710, only fifteen months after the first numbers had appeared. In 1736 William Parks started the publication of the *Virginia Gazette*, the first newspaper in the colony.[84] In February 1741 Byrd was glad to receive from him "a letter full of news." But a month later he complained that the *Gazette* he had received was "without news." He must have felt that it could not bear comparison with Steele and Addison's newspaper, in spite of the numerous articles borrowed from English gazettes and newssheets.[85] The real efforts of the colonists at some cultural development were still dependent on English publications. Even at Westover, people felt that they were in another world, far from their old country, not quite at home in their new one.

[84] See chapter I of Douglas C. McMurtrie, *The Beginnings of Printing in Virginia* (Lexington, Va., 1935).

[85] *Another Secret Diary*, Feb. 19, March 22, 1741. For a study of English literary influences upon *The Virginia Gazette*, see Robert M. Myers, "The Old Dominion Looks to London," *VMHB*, LIV (1946), 195–217.

CHAPTER XIII

Public Life

S ERVICE to the state was always considered one of the privileges of the wealthier planters, an honor as well as a duty even when an office brought little financial reward. Philip A. Bruce, in the concluding chapter of his *Institutional History of Virginia*, pointed out that down to the Restoration the basis of the suffrage was more democratic in Virginia than in England: "The right to vote was governed by manhood alone, but after the reaction following the return of the Stuarts had set in, that right was restricted to freeholders and leaseholders, and towards the end of the century was further confined to freeholders. Thus, as time went on, the basis of the suffrage came to resemble more and more closely that of the mother country."[1]

The electorate, wide or narrow, always returned to office members of the upper class, who by education were better fitted for leadership. The yeoman had the vote and could outvote the aristocrat fifty to one; but he voted for the aristocracy to occupy the office which he felt inadequate to fill. By the time Byrd wrote his diaries this tradition was firmly established and the aristocracy of the colony had come to look upon the higher posts as hereditary possessions. Byrd took it as a matter of course when after his father's death he succeeded him as receiver general, and some time later as councillor and colonel of the militia. But when he was sworn a member of the Council in September 1709, he solemnly expressed in his diary the hope that he should be equal to the task and serve the colony well: "God grant I may distinguish myself with honor and good conscience."[2] Indeed, like most of his colleagues, Byrd was very conscientious in the performance of his public duties. However necessary his presence might be at the plantation, he would leave Westover without delay to attend a meeting of the Council in Williamsburg or a general muster of the militia. Of course the variety of offices in the hands of the councillors brought them some financial advantages which had not been intended. The councillors

[1] II, 630. Cf. Hening, *Statutes at Large*, II, 280.
[2] *Secret Diary*, Sept. 12, 1709.

deliberately disregarded the fact that the concentration of these offices in so few hands brought about serious damage to the public interests whenever the Councillor was required by his incumbency of two separate positions to perform two sets of duties really in conflict with each other; a Councillor, for instance, was called upon to pass upon the correctness of his own accounts as collector; as collector, he was obliged, for his own enlightenment as a judge of the General Court, to inform himself of all violations of the Navigation Acts; as a farmer of the quit-rents he practically owed the success of his bid to himself as Councillor.[3]

This abuse had been denounced, as early as 1698, by John Locke in a report to the Board of Trade: "It is a thing of very evil consequence that the Council should sit in so many, and some of them so inconsistent, capacities." Among these Locke mentioned "the places belonging to the Justice and the Revenue."[4] There is no doubt that Byrd's offices helped him to get land grants and to pay fewer duties. But this was not considered dishonest at a time when many offices were sold and their holders were expected to avail themselves of any opportunity that came their way to make money.[5]

This concentration of power makes the accounts of such an insider as Byrd a good source for an all-around knowledge of the public life of Virginia. The impersonal Public Records give a more complete compilation of mere facts, but if the events held nothing of interest to Byrd, he was content to record a vague statement such as "I went to court where I sat almost all day without anything remarkable," or "We went to Council and settled some affairs."[6] He only mentioned facts when he was personally involved or when some particular detail aroused his interest. This personal coloring in the choice of events gives Byrd's account a distinctive flavor and a special value, showing at the same time how differently the planters reacted to facts which the impersonal Public Records set on a par. Moreover, the variety of Byrd's duties helps him to convey the general atmosphere of public affairs almost without any effort.

The most striking characteristic of all public affairs at that time is

[3] Bruce, *Institutional History*, II, 360–61.

[4] John Locke, "Some of the Chief Grievances of the Present Constitution of Virginia, with an Essay Towards the Remedies Thereof," ed. Michael G. Kammen, in *VMHB*, LXXIV (1966), 161. Locke's remark may have originated in the 1697 report to the Board of Trade (see Hartwell, Blair, and Chilton, *Present State*, p. 39).

[5] See for instance the example of Philip Ludwell who added a cipher to turn a grant of two thousand acres of land into one of twenty thousand; his rights went unquestioned though the fraud was notorious (Thomas J. Wertenbaker, *Patrician and Plebian in Virginia* [Charlottesville, Va., 1910], pp. 97–98).

[6] *Secret Diary*, Oct. 20, 1709, April 29, 1710.

their informality, which appears equally on election days, at assembly meetings, or in court. The election of the two burgesses who were to represent a county was quite an unceremonious affair among easy-going people, most of whom knew each other. Very few adult white men were excluded from voting, even with the narrow suffrage, since ownership of twenty-five acres of improved land or one hundred acres of unimproved land was all that was required for an individual to obtain voting rights, and almost every white male of age could and did acquire the necessary property easily.[7] On the appointed day, all the planters owning land in the county would gather at the court-house. After three or four hours' discussion in which the most important among them promoted their favorite candidate, the choice was made, more or less influenced by the "great industry" of a few. Then they would stay on for the afternoon, and perhaps the evening as well, talking to friends and drinking rum, before returning home. Sometimes the election took hardly more than an hour, and the two members were chosen without opposition.[8] But occasionally the electors could not make up their minds until they were swayed by some influential planter. Such was the case, for instance, in Charles City County on August 15, 1710:

About twelve o'clock we went to the courthouse where the freeholders were met to choose burgesses. After a great deal of persuading the choice fell on Colonel Eppes and Sam Harwood, notwithstanding Mr. Parker thought he should have carried it. But Colonel Hill used his endeavors to make the people vote for Colonel Eppes and he had it by one vote. Nothing remarkable happened but that the disappointment gave Mr. Parker a fever.

The unlucky candidate contested the result and was declared elected in place of his rival. But as he died three months later, Colonel Little-bury Eppes succeeded him in the House, and was reelected with Harwood in September 1712.[9]

Contested elections, however, were not always so conveniently solved by fate, and the decisions about their validity were sometimes contradictory. Thus in November 1710, Byrd reported, the committee appointed to inquire into the circumstances of an election in King and Queen County were of opinion that it was void, and the next day the House of Burgesses judged it so.[10] Yet we are informed

---

[7] On the franchise, see the corresponding chapters in Robert E. and B. Katherine Brown, *Virginia 1705–1786: Democracy or Aristocracy?* (East Lansing, Mich., 1964).

[8] *London Diary*, Aug. 30, 1720; *Secret Diary*, Sept. 24, 1712.

[9] *Ibid.*, Aug. 15, 1710; Sept. 26, 1712.

[10] *Ibid.*, Nov. 2–3, 1710.

by the *Journals of the Houses of Burgesses* that the two candidates continued to serve and were later declared duly elected.[11] But on the whole such inconsistencies were rare, and elections may be said to have been far more regular in Virginia than in England at the time. The colonists were proud and jealous of their right as English subjects to have a say in their own public affairs.

Byrd's own opinion about the House of Burgesses (to which he had belonged for a few months in 1696–97) was hardly favorable, and he had a councillor's disdain for that "very shadow of a Parliament," as he wrote to Micajah Perry. In fact, a really popular government in Virginia was quite out of the question at the time and would have been anachronistic. To say that Byrd's family "so far as is known did little to support any popular cause in the history of Virginia"[12] is to forget this. The aim of the colonists was only to be governed by Virginians rather than by distant and uncomprehending Englishmen. The body to do so was still the Council rather than the Burgesses.[13] Besides their greater influence both in the colony and in England, the councillors could more easily leave their plantations whenever their public duties required them to do so. Burgesses might live a long way from Williamsburg, and sometimes their private occupations on a small farm, or the weather, prevented them from going to the sessions. On January 24, 1712, Byrd observed: "There were twenty-five of the Burgesses met today, which was more than could be expected, considering the weather."[14]

The conflict between the colonists' loyalty to the Crown and their insistence on their right to self-government nowhere appears so clearly as in the meetings of the Council and its relations with the governor. One of the most illuminating periods is the first months of Spotswood's government, after the long interregnum during which

---

[11] *Journals of Burgesses, 1702–1712*, pp. 256, 332.

[12] Charles W. H. Warner, *Road to Revolution: Virginia's Rebels from Bacon to Jefferson, 1676–1776* (Richmond, 1961), p. 44n.

[13] Because the small planters wanted cheap government in the seventeenth century, counties often elected only one burgess instead of two or chose people who offered "to undertake the place at low rates"; the practice was so widespread that in 1670 the Assembly had placed a fine of ten thousand pounds of tobacco on any county that did not send two representatives to each session (see Hening, *Statutes at Large*, II, 23, 282). The burdensome cost of Assemblies was then a frequent complaint and some counties would have had them every two or three years (P.R.O., CO 1/39, ff. 194–95, 203, 207–8, 223–27, 236, 243–44, etc.).

[14] *Secret Diary*, Jan. 24, 1712. There were then about 50 burgesses (52, according to Robert Beverley, *History*, p. 241).

no governor or lieutenant governor resided in Virginia and the administration of the colony was left to the Council and its president.[15] The beginnings seemed most promising. Byrd, who had sought the appointment before Spotswood's nomination, did his best to cultivate the new governor's friendship. His first impression was favorable. On arriving in June 1710, "the governor made a courteous speech and told the Council that he was come with a full disposition to do the Queen and Country service, and hoped we should all concur with him in that good design." Appreciative of the consideration he was shown, Byrd added complacently, "He always distinguished me with his courtesy." The next meeting of the Council was no less satisfactory: "The Governor's instructions were read, one of which was to suffer the people have the settlement of the Habeas Corpus Act." Nothing could be designed to please the colonists better than the extension to Virginia of the benefits of the famous act. Besides, the governor was a gentleman just arrived from the English court, and when he invited the councillors to dinner, everything was "extremely polite" and his guests might feel transported to the best circles of London. What a pleasant sensation it was when one of the numerous Randolph clan came to be introduced to the governor, and Byrd recommended him to be clerk of the House of Burgesses: "which I did in the best manner, and the governor promised him."[16] At the opening of the fall session, Byrd admired Spotswood's speech; he "delivered it with the best grace I ever saw anybody speak in my life."[17] Two days later, the governor joined Byrd as a godfather at the christening of Byrd's nephew Daniel Parke.

But as the session went on and more serious matters came up for discussion, Byrd deplored a regrettable tendency: "The governor on several occasions discovered a great inclination to hold the royal prerogative." When the Council drafted a bill for raising a duty on liquor and slaves, "the governor thought fit to find fault" with it and "sent them several messages which they did not like."[18] For one thing, he urged the repeal of a duty on Negro slaves, a trade that the queen was "graciously pleased to countenance," and rebuked the colonists

[15] On the opposition to Governor Spotswood, see Dodson, *Spotswood*; Thomas J. Wertenbaker, *Give me Liberty: The Struggle for Self-Government in Virginia* (Philadelphia, 1958), pp. 160–76; and Richard L. Morton, *Colonial Virginia* (Chapel Hill, N.C., 1960), II, 419–43.

[16] *Secret Diary*, June 23, July 5, July 6, 1710.

[17] *Journals of Burgesses*, 1702–1712, pp. 240–41 (Oct. 26, 1710); *Secret Diary*, Oct. 26, 1710.

[18] *Ibid.*, Nov. 14, Nov. 25–27, 1710.

for making a distinction between Virginian and British owners.[19] At a time when English merchants coveted the monopoly which the treaty of Utrecht was to grant them shortly, the London Government could hardly endorse any proposition of the Council of Virginia tending to restrict the importation of slaves to the colony.[20] Moreover, Spotswood considered the Council to be usurping the royal prerogative when they took it upon themselves to divide counties and parishes.[21] At about the same time, Byrd endeavored to soften him about the passing of a land bill which the governor believed was the prerogative not of the Assembly but of the queen.[22] They were still on very good terms in spite of their differences: "My wife received very great charity from the governor and Mrs. Russell. Spotswood lent them his coach and entertained them "very handsomely." Soon after, the governor prorogued the Assembly till April 1711. Byrd was greatly pleased with the "particular distinction" that Spotswood always paid to him. When Byrd asked for the escheator's place after Colonel Randolph's death, the governor would make no promise but gave him great hope by his compliments; and Byrd did get the office eventually.[23]

The Virginia authorities were then busy improving Williamsburg with new buildings, finishing the governor's new house, and deciding on the creation of a market place. This the Assembly accepted without too much grumbling about the cost. But the main concern in the latter half of 1711 was the affairs of some of the neighboring colonies: confusion reigned in North Carolina where the new governor was prevented from taking over.[24] New York needed help against the Five Nations. And soon again Carolina was urgently asking for assistance against the Tuscaroras. This required new financial resources. The Burgesses wanted to raise twenty thousand pounds by levying extraordinary taxes, particularly on skins, a trade in which Byrd had

19 *Journals of Burgesses,* 1702–1712, p. 281 (Nov. 27, 1710).

20 The fundamental principle of the Board of Trade was clearly stated in one of their rebukes to Byrd: "We are surprised to find that any objection would be made to an instruction of this nature, since it can never be supposed that the Plantations had or could have the power of making any laws which might be prejudicial to the trade and navigation of this Kingdom, for whose benefit and advantage the Plantations were first settled and still are maintained" (P.R.O., CO 5/1365, f. 190).

21 *Journals of Burgesses,* 1702–1712, p. 281.

22 *Secret Diary,* Nov. 28, 1710, and *Legislative Journals of Council,* I, 504–7 (Nov. 29–Dec. 4, 1710).

23 *Secret Diary,* Nov. 30, 1710; April 23, 1711, and Jan. 30, 1712. Cf. *VMHB,* II (1894), 2.

24 *Secret Diary,* June 13, 1711, and Spotswood, *Official Letters,* I, 81 ff.

interests.[25] After heated arguments the Council proposed amendments to the House's money bill. The Burgesses refused, asserting their right to raise money by whatever method they pleased.[26] The governor inclined toward the councillors' opinion but was in favor of having the bill passed even without the amendments, because the money was sorely needed. "However," Byrd said, "I was against it though I was very ready to oblige the governor in anything in which my honor was not concerned." Perhaps his honor was not as concerned as his skins . . . Whatever the case, the Council finally persuaded the governor to adjourn the Assembly for a month.

In the heat of the discussion Byrd had been so undiplomatic as to say that no governor ought to be trusted with twenty thousand pounds, which soon came to Spotswood's ears. Byrd's brother-in-law John Custis warned him that the governor was angry; and on the day when the Assembly reconvened Byrd was rather uneasy as he went to the governor's: "I was a little perplexed what to say to the governor to extenuate what I had said, but I was resolved to say the truth, let the consequence be what it would. . . . He made us wait half an hour before he was pleased to come out to us, and when he came he looked very stiff and cold on me but did not explain himself." Two days later he remarked again: "The governor continued stiff to me, but I took no notice but behaved myself very courteously to him when he came in my way."[27] However, when the House of Burgesses was dissolved without any money bill being passed, Byrd found an occasion for a handsome gesture certainly intended as much to impress Spotswood as to serve the colony:

I went to the Capitol where I found the governor complaining that the House of Burgesses had passed several resolutions which made it plain they intended to spend their time only in dispute; and then he commanded Mr. Robertson[28] to order the Speaker and the House to attend him; and when they came he dissolved them after a short speech and then proposed how he should perform the treaty made with the Indians. Everybody was silent for some time, and then I said notwithstanding there was no money in my hands belonging to the queen, however rather than either Her Majesty's interest or the country's should suffer I would advance five hundred pounds to pay the Indians with, in case they performed their treaty. The Governor took it, and the rather because nobody seconded

[25] *Secret Diary*, July 5, 1711; *Journals of Burgesses, 1702–1712*, pp. 324–25 (Dec. 4, 1711).

[26] *Secret Diary*, Dec. 19, 1711, and *Journals of Burgesses, 1702–1712*, p. 356 (Jan. 30, 1711/12).

[27] *Secret Diary*, Dec. 15, 1711; Jan. 9, Jan. 24, Jan. 26, 1712.

[28] The clerk of the Assembly, William Robertson.

me. Then we rose and I went home with the governor in his coach to dine with him. I ate some boiled goose for dinner.[29]

In fact there were no major difficulties between the two men at first, only slight disagreements about the royal prerogative, which most governors were considered by the colonists to uphold with excessive rigidity, particularly in matters which the Council felt could be judged only by Virginians, not by any outsider, even one empowered by the Crown. Byrd did, however, come into serious conflict with the governor after he returned to London as agent for Virginia.

The colonial agent in London played an important political role, perhaps the more important as it was often unofficial. His duties, as detailed by Ella Lonn, were numerous, varied, and confusing:

> He was a sort of ambassador or minister from the colony to the court of Great Britain, though, as a working rather than a social representative, he came into contact with the many boards far more often than with the sovereign or his ministers. Again, his duty could be defined as looking after the interests of the colony which he represented. . . . He was to defend the laws passed by his colony by preventing their annulment and by following them through all the various boards to which they might be referred. He was to scent far off and prevent legislation by the British Parliament which might prove hostile to the colony. To present petitions to the King, the Parliament and the Board of Trade, and bring them to a successful conclusion was his constant portion.[30]

In brief, the agent for the colony was a kind of lobbyist. When colonial legislation arrived in London, its fate depended on the report of the king's counsel to the Board of Trade. The agent had to present in a favorable light the circumstances under which the act had been passed by the colonial assembly, the effects it was expected to have, the evils it would cure; and perhaps he would have to "fee" the official concerned with the affair. One of the best illustrations of the agent's role is a letter written by Byrd to one of his fellow councillors, probably Robert Beverley, in 1718:

> By every ship I have troubled you with the exact account of my proceedings in the business which the Council did me the honor to commit to my management. I have already informed you what I did with the Council of Trade relating to the Courts of Oyer and Terminer, and that the matter of law had been referred by their Lordships to the attorney general. I thought it expedient to fee the attorney pretty handsomely,

---

[29] *Secret Diary*, Jan. 31, 1712. Cf. *Executive Journals of Council*, III, 299 (same date).

[30] *The Colonial Agents of the Southern Colonies* (Chapel Hill, N.C., 1945), p. 151.

that his report might be as favorable as possible. I stated the case to him in such a manner that he could not choose but give his opinion upon the prudence of trusting American governors with the power of appointing what justices they please in the Courts of Oyer and Terminer, as well as upon the legality of it. I was fearful indeed that he would give the law against us, but was confident he must needs be for us in the prudential part. . . . Without loss of time I drew up an humble petition to the king,[31] setting forth the whole matter and praying His Majesty to restrain the dangerous power of his governor in such a manner as His Majesty by the advice of his Council learned in the law shall think fit. This will according to the prayer be of course referred to the attorney and solicitor general, who have already declared for us. My friend Mr. Southwell, who you know is one of the clerks of the Council, has promised me to get it referred accordingly. Thus I am in hopes I have laid my plot so well that it can hardly fail of success. . . . I make no scruple to disburse all necessary expenses out of my own pocket, relying entirely on the honor of the Council for my reimbursement.[32]

Although in this case Byrd's hopes were to be disappointed, he had done all that was expected of a colonial agent.

His various duties as such required a thorough knowledge of all past legislation in the colony, of financial and military matters, of land grants and Indian affairs, of import and export duties, of convoys and pirates. The agent had to be a versatile, well-informed man. Byrd had an advantage which few other agents possessed to such a high degree. He had many important contacts and was introduced to many of the most consequential persons of the age. The patronage of Sir Robert Southwell, the friendship of the Earl of Orrery, the Duke of Argyle, and many others, together with his own established position in the colony, his culture, and his long experience in England, helped him to fill his duties more efficiently in the course of his five agencies between 1697 and 1721, in spite of the frequent distrust of the various boards and commissions before which he appeared. Indeed the greatest handicap of an agent was the objection of the Board of Trade and other bodies to receiving addresses directly from the Virginia legislature instead of through the governor.[33] He had to be all the more skillful and well introduced as his function was unofficial.

The real quarrel between Spotswood and Byrd, in which personal strife combined with a conflict between governor and assembly, developed during Byrd's stay in England as Virginia agent. Its salient

---

[31] See p. 41, note 25.
[32] Byrd to Robert Beverley (?), Jan. 31, 1717/18 Other Byrd Papers, V.H.S., photostat of a letter at Duke University Library, Durham, N.C.
[33] See pp. 20 and 40.

points have already been expounded in the first part of this study. The existing portions of the diary shed no new light on the quarrel. The reconciliation of the two men, however, is commented upon in much less rosy terms than in Byrd's more or less public letter to Sir John Percival. The event came at a time when Byrd no longer had much hope of it, and the first encounter had hardly been promising:

I went with some of my friends to the Capitol where I presented my orders of Council to the governor and told him I should have waited upon him to his house, but that the message I had received from him at my first coming had discouraged me. Then he railed at me most violently before all the people, but I answered him without any fear or any manner, and came off with credit. However he did not swear me, so I loitered about till the court was up, and then dined with the Council.[34]

But four days later Spotswood must have come to the conclusion that it was impossible for him to go on with most of the colonists against him.

About ten, Mr. Commissary came to my lodgings and we walked to the court and then went into Council where there passed abundance of hard words between the governor and Council about Colonel Ludwell and Mr. Commissary for about two hours, till of a sudden the clouds cleared away and we began to be perfectly good friends and we agreed upon terms of lasting reconciliation, to the great surprise of ourselves and everybody else. The governor invited us to dinner and entertained us very hospitably and the guns were fired and there was illumination all the town over and everybody expressed great joy. The governor kissed us all round and gave me a kiss more than other people. We had also a concert of music at the governor's and drank the necessary healths till eleven o'clock and then we took leave and walked home and said my prayers.[35]

The morning after that memorable day, Byrd was about to go and pay a visit to the governor: "But he prevented me by coming to me first and was exceedingly courteous." And as the next day was Sunday, Byrd "sat in councillors' seat" in Bruton Church, and Commissary Blair gave them "a sermon about peace."

The next session in the fall of 1720 was indeed a rosy period at first. Byrd introduced an address to the governor, which was passed without any amendment. "And then the Commissary, Colonel Digges

---

[34] *London Diary*, April 25, 1720. See p. 43, note 36.

[35] *Ibid.*, April 29, 1720. See the Council Minutes for the same day. For Spotswood's own account, see his letter to Secretary Craggs, May 20, 1720, in *Official Letters*, II, 341: "I embraced with a great deal of satisfaction the occasion that was offered to drop all past contentions, and to unite again for the public service . . . ."

and I were sent to know when the governor would receive it, and he returned for answer that he would come to the Council chamber, which he did about one o'clock and returned a kind answer. The Burgesses also presented their address and were answered very kindly."[36] In the course of that session, the diarist was glad to remark that at one of the meetings the governor and both houses had "agreed in everything."[37] Of course this accord could not last, and there were still some bickerings when the House of Burgesses named Byrd as their agent in London. Spotswood must have felt that Byrd was easier to manage in Virginia than in England, and was not to be trusted too far out of sight without any guarantee. But on the whole, the friendly relations between them in later years testify their mutual esteem. Byrd may have been ambitious of the governorship of Virginia before Spotswood's appointment; he may have had it at the back of his mind sometimes during their struggle; but he cannot be said to have acted out of personal ambition, although there is no doubt that he would have felt greatly flattered to get the post and the title.

When political passions had died out, Spotswood himself must have agreed that Byrd was not far off in the conviction he had expressed to the Duke of Argyle in November 1719: "If he will do me justice, he must own me a fair adversary, and that only in those things wherein I judged him to be in the wrong."[38] Byrd was quite representative of the majority of the great planters, whose interests he consistently upheld, identifying them with the interests of the whole colony. In 1740 again, he was among those who, in his own words, "refused the good king's orders" when the Crown ignored the Council's candidate and appointed another man naval officer for York River.[39] The Council, jealous of their prerogative, resented this action and decided "that an humble representation of the case be made to His Majesty."[40] They eventually won their case. Because of their

[36] *London Diary*, Nov. 5, 1720. Cf. *Journals of Burgesses, 1712–1726*, pp. 254–55.

[37] *London Diary*, Nov. 17, 1720.

[38] Byrd to the Duke of Argyle, Nov. 4, 1719, *Another Secret Diary*, p. 370 (cf. *London Diary*, p. 336). After Spotswood's death, Byrd promised his widow to do all in his power to help her obtain a pension from the King, "not for any want you are in, but to have the consolation of understanding the just esteem the King will have of the General's merit" (Byrd to Mrs. Spotswood, June 1740, Letterbook, 1739–1740, V.H.S., p. 25). He wrote to Sir Charles Wager to ask for his help in this matter in Sept. 1740 (*VMHB*, XXXVII [1929], 105–6).

[39] Cf. Byrd to Major Otway, Feb. 10, 1740/41, *VMHB*, XXXVII (1929), 30–31, in which is mentioned "the apprehension that all our places here are to be filled with people from England," and *Another Secret Diary*, Dec. 10, 1740.

[40] *Executive Journals of Council*, V, 39–43 (April 23, 1741).

social, economic, and political power, the Council looked upon themselves as the champions of the liberties of the colonists (that is, of the
planters) and this sometimes conflicted with their loyalty to the
Crown: it was then that they "refused the good king's orders." Byrd's
antithetic expression of loyalty and liberty is quite typical, though it
is but a dim warning of what was to pass before the end of the century. By degrees, conflicts about appointments to the higher offices
or about taxes grew more and more numerous and bitter, until the
colonists felt that they were wronged and came to the conclusion
that the only solution was to shake off the tyranny of the English
government.

After thirty years' experience in the political affairs of Virginia,
Byrd's conclusion on governors is hardly enthusiastic: "I am sorry to
say it, but most of the worthy gentlemen sent to govern in this part
of the world are more inclined to represent the king's authority than
they are his virtues. They are generally so intent upon making their
fortunes that they have no leisure to study the good of the people and
how to make them useful to their mother country."[41] When he
praised Governor Gooch soon after his arrival, saying that "by great
accident" they had "a very worthy man to represent Lord Orkney,"
he added skeptically: "How long he may hold his integrity I cannot
warrant, because power and flattery corrupt many a hopeful ruler."[42]

In one of his letters to Lord Boyle, hinting at his own readiness to
fill the post, Byrd throws interesting sidelights upon the manner in
which governors and lieutenant governors of distant colonies were
appointed in those days when offices were still sold and bought:

If your fireside should increase upon you too fast, it will be a reasonable
argument to persuade the Earl of Orkney to make over his Government
of Virginia to you in his lifetime: His Lordship is very old and cannot
long enjoy it himself. It would therefore be for the advantage of his
family to get it transferred to one of his sons-in-law, lest if he should die
in possession of it, it might drop into other hands and be lost. If this could
be brought about, Your Lordship might have your choice, whether you
would come over and be monarch of a very fine country, and make a
very good sort of people happy, or whether you would stay in England
and receive a clear remittance of 1,200 pounds a year free from all taxes
and deductions. I should think myself extremely happy if Your Lordship
would honor us with your presence in that station, but if this would be
inconvenient you could by no means comfort me for my great disappointment but by sending me a deputation to represent your person, though at
the same time it would be impossible to represent your perfections; how-

---

[41] Byrd to Sir Charles Wager, July 2, 1736, *VMHB*, IX (1901), 125.
[42] Byrd to the Earl of Orrery, July 5, 1726, *Orrery Papers*, I, 58.

ever I do my best, and believe so well of myself that in such a case you would not have the trouble of any complaints. Thus you see, my Lord, I have contrived very decently for myself either to have the pleasure of your company, or else a good place to recompense me for your absence.[43]

Another political feature, though a negative one, cannot be passed without any mention. The absence of real contacts between the colonies was as true of the governments as of the population. Their independent spirit had already appeared in the North with the failure of the attempt to unify New England in 1684–86, an attempt which was coldly received by the colonists and did not outlive the Revolution of 1688.[44] But it was just as strong in Virginia, whose leaders always condescendingly pitied the neighboring colonies for not being able to defend themselves, and always expressed reluctance to help them more than was necessary for the protection of Virginia. Each colony was inclined to minimize the efforts of its neighbors and to judge its own frontier troubles, whether with Indians, or French, or Spaniards, to be of more vital importance. Such is indeed the general impression to be gathered from Byrd's account of the Indian wars in Carolina in 1711–12[45] or from the beginning of *The History of the Dividing Line*. Little wonder that at the end of the century the colonists were reluctant to accept any narrower bonds than those of a confederation. Apart from the language, their main link was nothing more than their common grievance against the English government, and it may be doubted whether they would have accepted even a confederation if there had not remained an English colony as a possible threat on their northern frontier.

The members of the Council were traditionally members of the General Court, which held two 18-day sessions commencing on April 15 and October 15.[46] Byrd was sworn a judge on October 15, 1709, and sat regularly, although he noted once that he had paid fines for absence, "three bits for every day."[47] The members of the Council received a total of three hundred and sixty pounds annually, and the

[43] Byrd to Lord Boyle, June [15] 1731, *ibid.*, I, 89.

[44] Cf. Wesley F. Craven. *The Colonies in Transition, 1660–1713* (New York, 1968), pp. 212 ff.

[45] *Secret Diary*, pp. 417–526, passim.

[46] Hugh F. Rankin, "The General Court of Colonial Virginia, Its Jurisdiction and Personnel," *VMHB*, LXX (1962), 142–53. "Any cause," said Hartwell, Blair, and Chilton (*Present State*, p. 47), "may commence in the General Court that exceeds the value of 16 pounds sterling or 16 hundred pounds of tobacco, and by appeal, any cause whatsoever may be brought thither . . . . There lies no appeal from this Court at present . . . but to the King in Council, and that only where the value exceeds 300 pounds sterling."

[47] *Secret Diary*, April 26, 1711.

pay of each member was based on his attendance at the General Court. As any five members formed a quorum at Court, they often rotated active duty on the bench so as to receive their proper shares of the annual budget. Once when Byrd had to prepare his quitrent accounts for the next day, he wrote on until he had finished his business. "Then," he said, "I went to Court where I just saved my day, because the Court was just on rising." But another day he "sat diligently all day because two of the judges went home."[48] In 1708 Byrd suggested that Councillors be paid "in proportion to their whole attendance at the Council and General Courts," for some seemed to neglect Council meetings.[49] The proposal was accepted.

On the whole, these men discharged their duties conscientiously, although they were seldom skilled in the law. Byrd, who was one of the most competent among them, wrote to Philip Ludwell to report a conversation with the Lord Chief Justice in London: "Indeed I went upon the absurdity of men's judging of matters of law which they did not understand, which everybody knows is the case of most of us councillors."[50] This opinion, shared by Hartwell, Blair, and Chilton, although not by Robert Beverley, had already led John Locke, inspired by Commissary Blair, to pass a severe judgment in his 1698 report: the councillors were "men utterly ignorant of the law, impatient of contradiction, apt to threaten lawyers and parties with imprisonment if they use freedom of speech, men that cannot be called to account for acts of injustice, men that take no oath to do justice, men that have made an order that they themselves shall not be arrested."[51] The problem lay in the fact that in those days judges were not trained professionally, in England or in the colonies, but other men with less sense of social responsibility might have done worse. In 1742 an English traveler, Edward Kimber, expressed the opinion that in Virginia the courts of justice were conducted "with a dignity and decorum that would become them even in Europe."[52] The councillors were extremely jealous of their prerogatives as

48 *Ibid.*, April 27, Oct. 27, 1711.

49 Byrd to Blathwayt, Sept. 21, 1708, Blathwayt Papers, Colonial Williamsburg, XIII, folder 1.

50 Byrd to Philip Ludwell, Sept. 24, 1717, Lee-Ludwell Papers, V.H.S.

51 Hartwell, Blair, and Chilton, *Present State*, p. 45; Beverley, *History*, pp. 255–60. Locke, "Some of the Chief Grievances of the Present Constitution of Virginia...," ed. Kammen, p. 162.

52 "Observations in Several Voyages and Travels in America in the Year 1736," *WMCQ*, 1st ser., XV (1907), 233. The anonymous author was later identified as Edward Kimber, son of the Rev. Isaac Kimber, editor of *The London Magazine*, 1732–1755 (cf. "Relation of a Late Expedition to St. Augustine," *Papers of the Bibliographical Society of America*, XXVIII [1934], part II).

judges. As we have seen, although Governor Spotswood won the right to appoint noncouncillors to courts of oyer and terminer, he finally agreed to name only members of the Council. These courts were to be held every June and December "whether there were any criminals or not."[53] Through the courts the powers of the Council increased still further.

At the opening of a court session the judges attended a religious service for their spiritual guidance before taking their places on the bench. Byrd often "sat with great patience," in his own estimate, to hear cases which were sometimes of small interest. "About ten o'clock went to court where nothing remarkable happened but that Mr. S–l–n was prosecuted for beating of George Walker. We had no criminals this court."[54] After a few sessions he began to grow accustomed, although not perhaps insensible, to the various cases that came before him, and so gave fewer details about them.

First there were criminal cases.[55] One of his first experiences as a judge was the trial of a man for rape. As a ladies' man, Byrd was somewhat surprised at one fact: the alleged victim was "a very homely woman." Anyway, Byrd said nothing about the verdict but remarked that "there were abundance of women in the gallery," and added, "I recommended myself to God before I went into court." He was fully aware of the importance of his new role, and this kind of unintentional humor often arises from the very concision of the diary. Cases that caused such a stir were rare, however, and the next day was anticlimactic: he "sat almost all day without anything remarkable." Sometimes his sympathy was aroused, as when they "tried an unfortunate man who had against his will killed his nephew, and he was found guilty of manslaughter."[56]

Penalties were heavy, like those inflicted in England. A woman who was "convicted of burglary for breaking the governor's house" was sentenced to death; but in accordance to contemporary law, "she plead her belly" and the next day "a jury of matrons were impanelled to inquire if [she] was with child, and their verdict was that she was quick." When two men were tried for felony and found guilty, "one of the prisoners was burnt in the hand and the other ordered to the whip."[57]

[53] *Secret Diary*, June 10, 1712.

[54] *Ibid.*, Dec. 11, 1711; *Another Secret Diary*, April 17, 1740; *Secret Diary*, April 19, 1711.

[55] See Hugh F. Rankin, *Criminal Trial Proceedings in the General Court of Colonial Virginia* (Williamsburg, Va., 1965).

[56] *Secret Diary*, Oct. 19, 1709; April 27, 1710.

[57] *Ibid.*, Dec. 11–13, June 12–13, 1711.

They also judged other kinds of offenses, such as disrespect for the clergy: "Mr. W–r–t–n was reproved for speaking disrespectfully to Mr. Commissary and telling him that he expressed himself as well as another did in the pulpit." Religion might not be so strict as in New England, but it was not to be trifled with, and its representatives had to be treated with proper deference. On the other hand, in 1720 Parson James Robertson, who was then the minister of Westover Church, was accused of uttering false speeches against the Crown. First the Council had to judge of the complaints in one of its meetings, and then a few months later the case came before the court: "I went to court where Parson Robertson was tried and found guilty, though some pains was taken by the Church to soften matters."[58]

Sometimes the members of the Council sat as a Court of Admiralty for judgments about ships that had tried to evade the Navigation Laws or about prizes in wartime.[59] Also, the seacoast was still menaced by pirates who found convenient hiding places among the numerous islets. Governor Spotswood had waged a vigorous campaign to sweep the Virginia seaboard clear of them, during which the notorious "Blackbeard," Edward Teach, was killed in 1718.[60] But in 1720 Byrd still recorded that a man had been condemned for piracy.[61]

After his voyage back to Virginia in 1720, Byrd wrote to Lord Orrery:

Two days before we sailed by [Bermudas], we understood there had been a pirate of good force, that had plundered several ships, and among the rest a Portuguese admiral who was returning home from Brazil richly laden, out of which the pirate took a prodigious booty in gold. However we had the good fortune to miss him.[62] These rogues swarm in this part of the world, and we are told of seventy sail at least that haunt the several parts of America.

58 *Ibid.,* Nov. 1, 1710; *London Diary,* July 20, 1720, and April 21, 1721.

59 *Secret Diary,* June 12–13, 1711, June 1, 1712. Cf. Spotswood to the Board of Trade, May 15, 1712, *Official Letters,* I, 163.

60 See the account of the affair in a letter written by the man in charge of the expedition against Teach, Lieutenant Maynard, in *The Weekly Journal; or, British Gazetteer,* April 25, 1719.

61 *London Diary,* Dec. 20, 1720. Four had already been hanged in the same year as a warning to others (cf. Spotswood to the Board of Trade, May 20, 1720, *Official Letters,* II, 337–38, and *Executive Journals of Council,* III, 521–22, [Feb. 22, 1719/20]).

62 There is no mention of this in *The London Diary.* But Robert Carter, in a letter to Micajah and Richard Perry dated July 13, 1720, wrote: "The privateers have been very bold and roguish upon our coast this year." (*Robert Carter Letters,* p. 7.)

The traveler added his poor opinion of the captains of the British Navy who were supposed to protect the colonies:

Our Captains of men-of-war are so intent on trade that they neglect their stations, and contrive to be blown away to the country whither their traffic calls them. This is so great an abuse that the nation is at the expense of building and maintaining ships of war for the enabling the commanders of them to ruin the fair traders in every country where they come. For these gentlemen pay neither freight nor custom, nor run any risk, by which iniquity they are in condition to undersell all those that do.[63]

Whether from the voluntary or involuntary failure of the British Navy, or from the attraction of the "prodigious booty," the pirates were not completely driven away from the coasts of Virginia, although a few were captured and punished as examples.

The judicial functions of the councillors were most varied. Justice was sometimes administered in an amateurish manner, and colonial law was very harsh. Nearly every felony carried the death penalty. But on the whole Governor Spotswood, contrasting Virginia with England (perhaps optimistically) early in his administration, could write to the Bishop of London:

I have observed here less swearing and profaneness, less drunkenness and debauchery, less uncharitable feuds and animosities, and less knaveries and villainies than in any part of the world where my lot has been, and whether the natural cause of this blessing be the people's living under less worldly temptations, or being more obedient to their spiritual pastors, or that they are more dexterous in concealing from me their vices, I will not as yet pretend to decide.[64]

Besides his duties as a judge, Byrd was one of the governors of the College of William and Mary, which had been founded in 1693, mainly through the unswerving efforts of Commissary Blair.[65] Byrd regularly attended the meetings, which were usually held in April and October, like most public activities in the colony. They elected new members when necessary, chose the rector of the college, appointed masters, and decided how the funds should be used. In April

---

[63] Byrd to Orrery, March 6, 1719/20, *Orrery Papers*, I, 31–32 (date corrected from MS). Twenty years later, Byrd wrote to Lord Egmont a letter venting similar feelings towards "His Majesty's commanders," whose actions were "not only a shameful breach of duty as to the King, but a certain ruin to all the lawful trade of his subjects" (Oct. 27, 1740, Byrd Letterbook, 1740–1741, p. 13, V.H.S.).

[64] Spotswood to the Bishop of London, Oct. 24, 1710, *Official Letters*, I, 28.

[65] See Knight, *History of Education*, I, 371 ff.

1709, the new rector they elected was Byrd's old friend and neighbor, Colonel William Randolph. When Randolph died two years later, Governor Spotswood himself was chosen to replace him, but the board did not always accept the governor's suggestions as readily as he would have liked.[66] The next year he was succeeded by Commissary Blair, who remained at the head of the college board until his death in 1743.

In June 1709, Byrd learned by his letters from England "that the College was like to be rebuilt by the Queen's bounty" after the fire that had partly destroyed it in 1705. It was soon confirmed that she had granted five hundred pounds to the college for its new building. At their next meeting the governors "determined to build the college on the old walls and appointed workmen to view them and compute the charge." When this was done, "after some debate the majority were for building on the old wall", but, Byrd adds, "I was against this and was for a new one for several reasons." At the end of October 1709, "the committee met to receive proposals for the building the College, and Mr. Tullitt undertook it for two thousand pounds provided he might wood off the College land, and all assistants from England to come at the College's risk." This agreement was confirmed five weeks later, and the construction started. The next we hear in Byrd's diary is that he paid John Tullitt five hundred pounds two years later.[67] The main building must have been finished when, on January 28, 1712, the governors "agreed to give Mr. Tullitt four hundred pounds to build up the College hall."

Despite these new buildings and all the efforts of the governors, the college was still but a very small school. In March 1712 it was John Randolph's ambition to be usher, and Byrd advised him on the best way to obtain the appointment, "but it was rejected because there were but twenty-two boys, which was not a number that required an usher."[68] In 1724 Hugh Jones, who had taught mathematics at the college between 1717 and 1721, could still write: "It is now a college without a chapel, without a scholarship, and without a statute. There is a library without books, comparatively speaking, and a president without a fixed salary till of late."[69] Yet gradually more planters found it more convenient to send their children to Williams-

---

[66] *Secret Diary*, April 20, 1709; April 25, 1711.

[67] *Ibid.*, June 16, Aug. 4, Sept. 13, Oct. 31, 1709; Nov. 7, 1711.

[68] *Ibid.*, pp. 503 and 508. The charter of the college (1693) had provided for six masters and one hundred scholars (Hartwell, Blair, and Chilton, *Present State*, p. 75).

[69] Jones, *Present State*, p. 108.

burg rather than to England; Byrd himself sent his nephew William Brayne to the college in September 1712.[70]

The masters were hardly model teachers. It was difficult to attract good ones from England. In 1709 Byrd reprimanded the Reverend Arthur Blackamore, the headmaster, for being drunk, and in October "it was agreed to turn [him] out for being so great a sot." The next day, however, Blackamore "presented a petition in which he set forth that if the governors of the College would forgive him what was past, he would for the time to come mend his conduct. On which the governors at last agreed to keep him on, on trial, some time longer." When Spotswood became rector of the College, he was displeased that the governors "did not turn Mr. Blackamore out of the school and Mr. Le Fevre in." Mr. Le Fevre, whom Byrd had met a few days before and judged "a Frenchman of great learning," was appointed "professor of philosophy and mathematics with a salary of eighty pounds a year."[71] But he did not even stay a year and was turned out in January 1712 because of his loose life, whereas Mr. Blackamore, with all his faults, stayed on until 1716. Even Hugh Jones, who in *The Present State of Virginia* set forth fairly high standards for the students and expected them to act as gentlemen whether they were to be clergymen or planters, was not immune to criticism.[72] In 1720, Byrd "went to Colonel Jenings to sit upon the [administration?] between the Colonel and Parson Jones about a Negro of the College that came by his death by Mr. Jones's means."[73] But in spite of such shortcomings in the faculty, the college in the next decades was able to offer the elements of a higher education intended to fit boys for plantation life and leadership in the colony. After several generations of students—including Jefferson—had received their education in Williamsburg, the gap widened between Virginia and England, and few went abroad for an education.

Another important public activity of Byrd's was military service. He was a colonel of the militia and in April 1710 was appointed commander-in-chief of two counties, Henrico and Charles City.[74]

[70] *Secret Diary*, Sept. 1, 1712.

[71] *Ibid.*, Oct. 28–29, 1709; April 17–25, 1711. Byrd later referred to LeFevre as Tanaquil Faber (*ibid.*, Jan. 28, 1712).

[72] *Present State*, p. 111.

[73] *London Diary*, Nov. 30, 1720.

[74] *Secret Diary*, April 27, 1710. On the organization of the militia, see Robert Beverley, *History*, pp. 268–70 ("Every freeman . . . from sixteen to sixty years of age is listed in the militia; which by a law is to be mustered in a General Muster for each county once a year," p. 269), and Hartwell, Blair, and Chilton, *Present State*, pp. 63–64 ("Under the Governor the chief command of every

In September of the same year, the governor visited the region and there was a general muster of the militia of the two counties. Such musters usually took place about once a year. The whole neighborhood was in a fever for two or three days beforehand. Byrd wrote letters warning his officers to be ready for the governor's arrival. He sent a servant with orders to Colonel Randolph and Colonel Littlebury Eppes to summon their men for the governor to review. He fired pistols to teach his own horse to stand fire. A frenzy of cleaning came over the plantation; the house and the grounds around it were thoroughly gone over, as was the pasture where the men were to muster. This was no time to read Hebrew and Greek in the morning, or to say prayers at night, for there was too much to do. But then Byrd enjoyed the governor's compliments and the sense of his own importance.

The review was held in spite of a driving rain. "Just as we got on our horses it began to rain hard; however, this did not discourage the governor, but away we rode to the men. It rained half an hour and the governor mustered them all the while and he presented me to the people to be their colonel and commander-in-chief."[75] After the militia of Charles City County, the men of Henrico County gathered the next day:

About ten o'clock we got on our horses and rode toward Henrico to see the militia. Colonel Randolph with a troop met us at Pleasant's mill and conducted us to his plantation, where all the men were drawn up in good order. The governor was pleased with them and exercised them for two or three hours together. He presented me likewise to them to be their commander-in-chief, who received me with an huzzah.[76]

A year later, on the occasion of another muster, Byrd observed: "Everybody showed me abundance of respect"; and he was so pleased that after a few lines he repeated complacently in the same entry: "Everybody respected me like a king."[77]

Byrd felt greatly flattered by the deference he was shown, but he was no mere dress-parade soldier. When the Tuscaroras were a cause of worry for Carolina and the militia in Virginia had to be kept ready for action, he organized games and offered arms as prizes.[78] The men

---

county is by him committed to the gentlemen of the Council, with the title of Colonel," p. 63).

[75] *Secret Diary*, Sept. 21, 1710.

[76] *Ibid.*, Sept. 22, 1710.

[77] *Ibid.*, Sept. 23, 1711.

[78] *Ibid.*, Sept. 14 and 29, 1711.

were set to running and wrestling, and the great day came a fort-night later, in the afternoon of October 3, 1711:

Then I ordered the men to be drawn in single file along the path where the men were to run for the prize, and John Hatcher, one of Captain Randolph's men, won the pistol. Then I caused the men to be drawn into a square to see the men play at cudgels and Dick O–l–n won the sword, and of the wrestling Will Kennon won the gun. Just as the sun went down our games ended and then I took leave.

Other prizes were awarded in the next days. Besides exercising the men and keeping them physically fit, this was a useful way to occupy their minds, and prevent them from complaining about their crops and grumbling about lost time. There was to be a body of rangers in the upper county, but it was difficult to recruit them, "because the pay was too little" and people were reluctant "to range by turns as they had promised." Yet on the whole most men filled their militia duties conscientiously, with no regard to hardships and lost time, and the planters felt it their duty to set the example.[79]

Byrd served most efficiently in such an emergency as occurred in August 1711. "In the afternoon," he wrote on the fifteenth, "I received a letter from the governor with orders to exercise all the militia under my command because we were threatened with an invasion, there being fourteen French men-of-war designed for these parts." He immediately transmitted the orders to his two colonels, Littlebury Eppes and his brother, Frank Eppes, who had succeeded Colonel Randolph a few months before. In a short time everyone was ready. August 23 was a very busy day:

I had a letter from Captain Drury Stith that he had a fever, but all the other officers came except John Eppes who was sick likewise. We dis-coursed of several matters relating to the militia and about the beacons, and we agreed on the places where they were to be put. They dined with me and I ate some pigeon. In the afternoon came Colonel Frank Eppes and several gentlemen with him. We settled several matters and named several officers, and then they all went away. Soon after they were gone I received a letter from the governor dated yesterday that two French men-of-war and several privateers were arrived, and ordering me to send away to Jamestown twenty-five gunners out of each county to work on the battery there. I sent away orders after my two colonels this night. My wife was frightened and would hardly go to bed, but was persuaded at last; but I could not sleep for thinking of our condition and what I was to do.

---

[79] *Ibid.*, Aug. 29, 1711; Jan. 8 and March 5, 1712. See Charles S. Sydnor, *Gentlemen Freeholders: Political Practices in Washington's Virginia* (Chapel Hill, N.C., 1952).

Before the letter from the governor arrived, Byrd had only half
believed in the reality of the danger, but now things had become
serious. The next morning he dispatched his boat for all the guns
and ammunition in his storehouse above at Appomattox and sent his
plate and other valuables to Captain Drury Stith's, whose place was
more secure than Westover. He got his arms in order and made cart-
ridges. In the morning of August 25, Byrd's sloop arrived from down
river, and the crew told him "there were news that our fleet was
taken." On the twenty-sixth, letters came from Williamsburg con-
firming the dark news: "They told me that Colonel Milner of Nansemond[80] had sent an express yesterday about noon which said that
fifteen French men-of-war were come within the Cape and with
several other ships and had landed several thousand men on the Eastern shore." This was more than Byrd could believe. Half way
through the next morning, however, he gathered all his officers for
further orders, gave the command of several new troops to some of
them, and was very glad to observe that "they all seemed to be very
vigorous and polished." Still, on parting with his officers he "recommended to them to inspire the men with vigor." In the afternoon
came a letter with fresh news. Matters seemed to be moving swiftly
toward a decision: "The governor had sent an express to Colonel
Ludwell that seven ships were come up James River and so the
militia of James City were ordered to Williamsburg. Upon this I
sent orders to Colonel Eppes to march all the militia to the lower part
of the county, which was done accordingly and an alarm given."

There was no more news that night. All Virginia was on the alert.
In the morning came Major Joshua Wynne, who told them that
Prince George County was all in arms: "He said John Bolling set
such a heap of straw on fire in the night that it caused two beacons
of Prince George to be set on fire. The Major had his holsters at his
girdle and an armor bearer that carried his pistols, which made a
good figure." Some were fumblers, but the warlike major was a com-
forting sight.

And then came the anticlimax in the evening: "The seven ships
supposed to be French that entered into James River were English."[81]
This false alarm shows how the militia was used. It illustrates the
contemporary obsession about a French menace to the American
colonies, an obsession which endured until the fall of French Canada
and the Treaty of Paris. In fact, the Indian threat was then far more

[80] Nansemond County, northwest of the Dismal Swamp, is about 30 miles
from the mouth of Chesapeake Bay, between Cape Charles and Cape Henry.
[81] *Secret Diary*, Aug. 28, 1711.

serious, and in his diary Byrd gives an account of the expedition to the Nottoway town in October 1711. The show of strength was enough to frighten the Tuscaroras into a treaty less than two months later: "There were about 700 horse beside volunteers and about 900 foot, and there were about 30 volunteers among whom were three parsons." And yet that demonstration hid some difficulties that Spotswood encountered when putting the infantry in order: "He divided the companies and made them about fifty men each, and made captains over them, though when he came to Surry he found it difficult to get captains because everybody refused the governor and made him so angry that he swore at several, which was a thing he seldom did."[82]

After the Tuscaroras had made peace, the militia was hardly used for military purposes. Although it remained in existence, there was little in it to evoke the minutemen of the Revolutionary period. Indeed, Spotswood had found it so difficult to order out the militia and use it efficiently that in a long report to the Board of Trade in 1716 he proposed the abandonment of the militia system in favor of a military force comprising only one third of the freemen, paid by a tax levied on the other two thirds.[83] By degrees the militia companies tended to become more social than military organizations. In 1740 Virginia sent a contingent of troops to fight against Spain at Cartagena in Admiral Vernon's expedition. On June 10, after dinner, Byrd "went to the camp where were about three hundred men, such as they were." They must have compared most unfavorably with Byrd's own troops thirty years before. But most of the soldiers were ex-convicts, according to a very convenient plan designed both to fill four companies and to drain off undesirable people.[84] Among the four captains named by the Council for the expedition was Lawrence Washington, George's elder half-brother.[85] Not until people felt that the breach with Great Britain was fast becoming unavoidable did the militia regain some of its former shape and activity, and the spirit that such men as Byrd had infused into it, in the days when Tidewater Virginia could still fear French invasions or Indian attacks.

---

[82] *Ibid.*, Oct. 18–19, 1711. Cf. an account of the expedition to the Nottoway town written for the Board of Trade, Spotswood, *Official Letters*, I, 121–22 (Nov. 17, 1711). Surry county is south of the James, a little to the east of Westover.

[83] Spotswood, *Official Letters*, II, 194–212.

[84] *Journals of Burgesses, 1727–1740*, pp. xxxi, 424–34. Cf. Byrd to Major Otway, Feb. 10, 1740/41, *VMHB*, XXXVII (1929), 29.

[85] *Another Secret Diary*, Aug. 6, 1740, and *Executive Journals of Council*, V, 22 (same date).

CHAPTER XIV

The Frontier

FEW American writers of the eighteenth century really knew frontier life, which at that time was hardly considered worthy subject matter for genuine literary efforts (if we except travel literature, in which the accounts of the frontier remained superficial).

Byrd was one of the few who knew it well from personal experience. Although the wilderness no longer began, as in the times of his granduncle Stegge and his own father, on the very outskirts of the plantation at the falls of the James, it was still near enough for him to judge it prudent to install an underground passage to the river in case of Indian raids when Westover was rebuilt in the early thirties. When the Dividing Line was run in 1728, the frontier began a few miles south of Norfolk, and the expedition was unable to find guides to lead them to Currituck Inlet; they "might for the same price," said Byrd, "have hired them to make a trip to the other world." At last they were glad to meet a borderer from North Carolina who made them a rough sketch of that part of the country. In the region of Westover, the frontier began a few miles south of the falls of the Appomattox; and on the way back from the Dividing Line, Byrd and his companions felt the change when they arrived at Colonel Robert Bolling's, on the present site of Petersburg, "where first," he said, "from a primitive course of life we began to relapse into luxury."[1] Thirty miles south of Colonel Bolling's plantation, Sapony Chapel was "the first house of prayer" they had seen for more than two months.

The region from a few miles south of the James and the Appomattox to the Dividing Line was hardly settled before the thirties, and the few plantations scattered there could not compare with those along the main rivers. At Captain Embry's on the Nottoway, Byrd "found the housekeeping much better than the house."[2] Still farther south, on the Meherrin River, in 1733 he visited the plantation of a Mr. Nicholson, where a tenant farmed for halves:

[1] *Prose Works*, pp. 52, 174, 319.
[2] *Ibid.*, p. 317.

There was a poor dirty house, with hardly anything in it but children that wallowed about like so many pigs. It is a common case in this part of the country that people live worst upon good land, and the more they are befriended by the soil and the climate the less they will do for themselves. This man was an instance of it, for though his plantation would make plentiful returns for a little industry, yet he, wanting that, wanted everything. The woman did all that was done in the family, and the few garments they had to cover their dirty hides were owing to her industry. We could have no supplies from such neighbors as these but depended on our own knapsacks, in which we had some remnants of cold fowls that we brought from Bluestone Castle. When my house was in order, the whole family came and admired it, as much as if it had been the Grand Vizier's tent in the Turkish army.[3]

On the Carolina border, at Moniseep Ford on the Roanoke, Byrd saw another plantation where he "beheld the wretchedest scene of poverty" he had ever met with "in this happy part of the world." "The man, his wife, and six small children lived in a pen like so many cattle, without any roof over their heads but that of Heaven. And this was their airy residence in the daytime; but then there was a fodder stack not far from this enclosure in which the whole family sheltered themselves anights and in bad weather." But, the writer insisted, "all his wants proceeded from indolence and not from misfortune." Besides his good land and good health, he had a trade very useful to the people living in the neighborhood, for he could make quernstones. "If the man would have worked at his trade, he might have lived very comfortably." Such laziness, dirt, and misery were only too common on the southern frontier of Virginia. When, on their way back to the settled parts of the colony, the Dividing Line expedition reached the first house they had seen for two months, they preferred "to lie in the tent, as being much the cleanlier and sweeter lodging."[4]

The great planters were always in the vanguard of the westward movement in Virginia. Although they did not intend to establish immediate residence on the frontier, they were usually among the first to survey and claim the best land in the new territory before it was invaded by immigrants. The general practice was to send a gang of slaves under an overseer to develop a new quarter and later to sell patches of the land to settlers. On the other hand, the small planter whose soil was exhausted after years of growing tobacco had to sell his farm before starting afresh. He had to be prudent, for he hazarded

[3] *Ibid.*, p. 409.
[4] *Ibid.*, pp. 311–312, 307.

all his possessions; so he was seldom among the first to settle in newly opened territories. Byrd always insisted that the valleys in the back country were "exceedingly rich and the air perfectly wholesome." It would be very easy to plant vineyards, to make silk ("no place being more kindly for mulberry trees"), to raise flax, hemp, and silk grass ("which is stronger much than hemp") to make nut oil, to produce "exceeding good sugar from a tree we call a sugar tree." Farmers could satisfy all their needs with a little industry: "It is a fine place for cattle and hogs, for sheep and goats, and particularly there is a large creature of the beef kind, but much larger, called a buffalo, which may be bred up tame and is good both for food and labor."[5] Although these words were obviously intended to attract new settlers, Byrd was none the less sincere in his admiration of those fertile lands.[6] He had the true pioneer's love for a well-tended farm in a beautiful landscape, and his judgment is confirmed by other testimonies. In 1686 a French traveler noted in his diary that there was "not a house so poor that they do not salt an ox, a cow and five or six large hogs," and added that it was possible for even a small farmer and his wife, when they had cattle in the woods, to live a life of ease and plenty. At the turn of the century, another observer, Francis Louis Michel, was also impressed by the prosperity of the small farmer and the ease with which he made a living.[7]

It was a pity, Byrd felt, that the people of the border (and of North Carolina as well) should be so "intolerably lazy" in a land of such plenty:

I am sorry to say it, but idleness is the general character of the men in the southern parts of this colony as well as in North Carolina. The air is so mild and the soil so fruitful that very little labor is required to fill their bellies, especially where the woods afford such plenty of game. These advantages discharge the men from the necessity of killing themselves with work, and then for the other article, of raiment, a very little of that will suffice in so temperate a climate. But so much as is absolutely necessary falls to the good women's share to provide.[8]

Robert Beverley had reached the same conclusion as Byrd: the laziness of so many pioneers comes from the "exceeding plenty of good

[5] Byrd to Mr. Ochs, circa 1735, *VMHB*, IX (1902), 227. Byrd's brother-in-law Beverley was particularly interested in wine-making and was very proud of his vineyards (see *Huguenot Family*, pp. 264–66, and Beverley, *History*, pp. 133–36). On mulberry trees and silk, see Beatty and Mulloy, *William Byrd's Natural History*, pp. 34–35.

[6] *Prose Works*, pp. 289–90, 384, quoted above, pp. 49 and 51.

[7] *Huguenot Exile*, pp. 122–23; Hinke, "The Journey of Michel," p. 36.

[8] *Prose Works*, p. 312.

things with which nature has blessed them; for where God Almighty is so merciful as to work for people, they never work for themselves."[9]

Byrd's picturesque description of "Lubberland" is one of the most famous passages in *The History of the Dividing Line* and presents the first emergence in literature of a type which was to develop later, the Southern poor white. Few Carolinians have appreciated the humor of Byrd's account, although he was ridiculing a certain turn of mind among many settlers of southern Virginia as well as of North Carolina, reproaching them for living like primitive Indians instead of civilized Christians:

The men, for their parts, just like the Indians, impose all the work upon the poor women. They make their wives rise out of their beds early in the morning, at the same time that they lie and snore till the sun has risen one third of his course and dispersed all the unwholesome damps. Then, after stretching and yawning for half an hour, they light their pipes, and, under the protection of a cloud of smoke, venture out into the open air; though if it happen to be never so little cold they quickly return shivering into the chimney corner. When the weather is mild, they stand leaning with both their arms upon the cornfield fence and gravely consider whether they had best go and take a small heat at the hoe, but generally find reasons to put it off till another time. Thus they loiter away their lives, like Solomon's sluggard, with their arms across, and at the winding up of the year scarcely have bread to eat.[10]

On the other hand, Byrd admired their ingenious way of building log-houses, "finished without nails or other ironwork," from their roofs "covered with pine or cypress shingles" to their doors with wooden hinges and wooden locks.[11] Still, these people represent the ancestry of the poor whites of later ages; they had little in common with the sturdy Scotch-Irish settlers of the Shenandoah, whose ingenuity and industry compare better with those of the pioneers who settled the West in the next century.

Another kind of frontiersmen that Byrd came to know fairly well was the woodsmen who accompanied him on the Dividing Line expedition or on his journey to his Land of Eden. He criticized Virginia woodsmen for usually traveling on horseback. Their passion for riding put them at a disadvantage, for "horses are very improper animals to use in a long ramble into the woods, and the better they

---

[9] *History*, pp. 296–97.
[10] *Prose Works*, p. 204. See Alexander Quarles Holladay, *Social Conditions in Colonial North Carolina* (Raleigh, N.C., 1904), written in refutation of Byrd's criticisms.
[11] *Prose Works*, p. 206.

have been used to be fed, they are still the worse. Such will fall away a great deal faster and fail much sooner than those which are wont to be at their own keeping."[12] Mules or asses would have been better in the woods of the Virginia back country, because they are more sure-footed, hardy, and frugal than horses, which require great care and take up too much time:

Overnight we are now at the trouble of hobbling them out and often of leading them a mile or two to a convenient place for forage, and then in the morning we are some hours in finding them again, because they are apt to stray a great way from the place where they were turned out. Now and then, too, they are lost for a whole day together and are frequently so weak and jaded that the company must lie still several days near some meadow or highland pond to recruit them.[13]

In Byrd's opinion, this partly explains why the Virginia colonists have such a bad knowledge of the back country: "And one may foretell without the spirit of divination that so long as woodsmen continue to range on horseback we shall be strangers to our own country, and few or no valuable discoveries will ever be made." On that score they might gain much from the example of the French:

The French *coureurs de bois* [sic], who have run from one end of the continent to the other, have performed it all on foot or else, in all probability, must have continued full as ignorant as we are. Our country has now been inhabited more than 130 years by the English, and still we hardly know anything of the Appalachian Mountains, that are nowhere above 250 miles fom the sea. Whereas the French, who are later-comers, have ranged from Quebec southward as far as the mouth of Mississippi in the Bay of Mexico and to the west almost as far as California, which is either way above two thousand miles.[14]

But then Virginia woodsmen were far too improvident. They did not even bother to carry part of the game they had killed in case they found none the next day: they "are certainly good Christians in one respect at least, that they always leave the morrow to care for itself; though for that very reason they ought to pray more fervently for their daily bread than most of them remember to do." When their hunting provided them with plenty of meat and they had nothing better to do, for instance when they were detained in their camp by the rain, they whiled the time away cooking and eating. "In such a glut of provisions, a true woodsman when he has nothing else to do,

12 *Ibid.*, p. 282.
13 *Ibid.*, p. 282.
14 *Ibid.*, p. 283.

like our honest countrymen the Indians, keeps eating on, to avoid the imputation of idleness; though in a scarcity the Indian will fast with a much better grace than they." Indeed, it was useless to ask them to do anything before they had swallowed their breakfast: "Till that is duly performed, a woodsman makes a conscience of exposing himself to any fatigue."[15]

The problem of food is certainly one of the most serious for all those who have to live in the wilderness; and yet such explorations would undoubtedly be very useful.

The chief discouragement at present from penetrating far into the woods is the trouble of carrying a load of provisions. I must own famine is a frightful monster and for that reason to be guarded against as well as we can. But the common precautions against it are so burdensome that people cannot tarry long out and go far enough from home to make any effectual discovery. The portable provisions I would furnish our foresters withal are glue broth and rockahominy: one contains the essence of bread, the other of meat.[16]

After giving the recipe of glue broth made from a leg of beef, veal, or venison, he added:

When the pieces are perfectly dry, put them into a canister, and they will be good, if kept dry, a whole East India voyage. This glue is so strong that two or three drams, dissolved in boiling water with a little salt, will make half a pint of good broth; and if you should be faint with fasting or fatigue, let a small piece of this glue melt in your mouth, and you will find yourself surprisingly refreshed.

This broth, comparable with the pemmican of the Indians, similar in origin but different in preparation, was still more nourishing if thickened with half a spoonful of rockahominy, "which is nothing but Indian corn parched without burning and reduced to powder."[17] Thus half a dozen pounds of that food could sustain a man for as many months whenever he was unable to find any game. And Byrd's conclusion on the subject was as follows:

By what I have said, a man needs not encumber himself with more than eight or ten pounds of provisions, though he continue half a year in the woods. These and his gun will support him very well during that time, without the least danger of keeping one single fast. And though some of his days may be what the French call *jours maigres*, yet there will happen

[15] *Ibid.*, pp. 264, 249, 273, 400.
[16] *Ibid.*, p. 279.
[17] *Ibid.*, p. 280. Cf. William Strachey: "Rokohamin: parched corn ground small," *Historie of Travell*, p. 199.

no more of those than will be necessary for his health and to carry off the excesses of the days of plenty, when our travelers will be apt to indulge their lawless appetites too much.[18]

Byrd himself did not dislike that life in the woods, and he learned how to sleep comfortably in the open:

A true woodsman, if he have no more than a single blanket, constantly pulls all off and, lying on one part of it, draws the other over him, believing it much more refreshing to lie so than in his clothes; and if he find himself not warm enough, shifts his lodging to leeward of the fire, in which situation the smoke will drive over him and effectually correct the cold dews that would otherwise descend upon his person, perhaps to his great damage.[19]

Woodsmen had to be very cautious of fluxes or diarrhea, to which they were particularly liable, "by lying too near the moist ground and guzzling too much cold water"; but glue broth, he added, was very good against that kind of ailment. When there were signs of rain, they stretched their blankets upon poles slantwise against the weather and waited for the end of the storm.[20]

The woodsmen's main occupation was naturally the shooting of game for their food. When they were in sufficient number, they often hunted in a ring: "From the circumference of a large circle they all marched inward and drove the game toward the center."[21] Once when they were really short of food, the members of the Dividing Line expedition resorted to fire-hunting, an Indian practice which had been described long before by Captain Smith in his *Map of Virginia* and by William Strachey in his *Historie of Travell into Virginia Britania.*[22] Here is Byrd's account:

They fired the dry leaves in a ring of five miles' circumference, which, burning inward, drove all the game to the center, where they were easily killed. 'Tis really a pitiful sight to see the extreme distress the poor deer are in when they find themselves surrounded with this circle of fire; they weep and groan like a human creature, yet can't move the compassion of those hardhearted people who are about to murder them. This unmerciful sport is called fire-hunting and is much practiced by the Indians and fron-

[18] *Prose Works,* p. 280.
[19] *Ibid.,* p. 266.
[20] *Ibid.,* pp. 280, 248.
[21] *Ibid.,* p. 273.
[22] *Travels and Works of Captain John Smith,* ed. Edward Arber (Birmingham, Eng., 1884), pp. 70, 365–66, and Strachey, *Historie of Travell,* p. 83. Though Strachey often adapted, paraphrased, or condensed material from John Smith, some quotations in the following pages have been made to him for the sake of style.

tier inhabitants, who sometimes, in the eagerness of their diversion, are punished for their cruelty and are hurt by one another when they shoot across at the deer which are in the middle.[23]

Among those who had the best knowledge of the woods of the back country were the Indian traders who went south along the trading path that crossed the Roanoke River at Moniseep Ford near the Dividing Line. Byrd could remember his childhood days, when his father's Indian traders carried goods on their packhorses as far as the land of the Catawbas and the Cherokees, more than four hundred miles through the wilderness to the southwest.[24] Some were killed by Indians; but those who came back brought loads of furs and skins, a rich reward for the dangers and hardships they had braved. From his childhood Byrd had heard terrible and wonderful stories about that trade, and among the members of the Dividing Line expedition were several experienced Indian traders whom he had known for many years. Robert Hix and John Evans are both mentioned in his diary almost twenty years earlier. With the exception of Indian traders themselves, Byrd was certainly one of the men who knew most about the trading path, which he described at length in *The History of the Dividing Line.*

The trading path above mentioned receives its name from being the route the traders take with their caravans when they go to traffic with the Catawbas and other southern Indians. The Catawbas live about 250 miles beyond Roanoke River, and yet our traders find their account in transporting goods from Virginia to trade with them at their own town. The common method of carrying on this Indian commerce is as follows: gentlemen send for goods proper for such a trade from England, and then either venture them out at their own risk to the Indian towns or else credit some traders with them of substance or reputation, to be paid in skins at a certain price agreed betwixt them. The goods for the Indian trade consist chiefly in guns, powder, shot, hatchets (which the Indians call tomahawks),

[23] *Prose Works*, p. 299.
[24] William Byrd I to Lane and Perry, May 10, 1686, *VMHB*, XXV (1917), 51–52. In a "Letter of Mr. Clayton to the Royal Society" in 1688, the writer stated that Colonel Byrd (the father) "is one of the intelligentest men of all Virginia, and knows more of Indian affairs than any man in the country" (*Clayton*, p. 78). On Indian traders, see William E. Myer, "Indian Trails of the Southeast," U.S. Bureau of American Ethnology, *42nd Annual Report* (Washington, 1928), pp. 727–857. On the Catawbas, see Douglas S. Brown, *The Catawba Indians: The People of the River* (Columbia, S.C., 1966). The Catawbas were known in colonial times as fierce and aggressive warriors, but they generally maintained friendly relations with the English. Their number was an estimated 6,000 at the time of their first contact with Europeans.

kettles, red and blue planes, Duffields, Stroudwater blankets, and some cutlery wares, brass rings, and other trinkets.[25]

These goods were gathered as cheaply as possible by several traders for a common expedition:

These wares are made up into packs and carried upon horses, each load being from 150 to 200 pounds, with which they are able to travel about twenty miles a day if forage happen to be plentiful. Formerly a hundred horses have been employed in one of these Indian caravans under the conduct of fifteen or sixteen persons only, but now the trade is much impaired, insomuch that they seldom go with half that number.[26]

Byrd ascribed the decline to the competition of Carolinian traders, but another cause might be found in the dwindling of Indian tribes east of the Appalachians.

Byrd then explained the route the Virginian traders followed in the wilderness:

The course from Roanoke to the Catawbas is laid down nearest southwest and lies through a fine country that is watered by several beautiful rivers. Those of the greatest note are: first, Tar River, which is the upper part of Pamptico, Flat River, Little River and Eno River, all three branches of Neuse. Between Eno and Saxapahaw rivers are the Haw old fields, which have the reputation of containing the most fertile high land in this part of the world, lying in a body of about fifty thousand acres. This Saxapahaw is the upper part of Cape Fear River, the falls of which lie many miles below the trading-path. Some mountains overlook this rich spot of land, from whence all the soil washes down into the plain and is the cause of its exceeding fertility. Not far from thence the path crosses Aramanchy River, a branch of Saxapahaw, and about forty miles beyond that, Deep River, which is the north branch of Pee Dee. Then, forty miles beyond that, the path intersects the Yadkin, which is there half a mile over and is supposed to be the south branch of the same Pee Dee.[27]

In this description there are a few minor errors, perhaps due to the traders who furnished Byrd with his information. For instance it is hardly possible that the path could have been forty miles from Deep River to the Yadkin, even allowing for possible windings or portions where the caravans had to slow down; but this error may have come from a mistaken repetition of the same expression in two successive lines; for maps, whether eighteenth century or modern,

[25] *Prose Works*, p. 308. See "Letters of William Byrd I," *VMHB*, XXIV (1916), 354 (order for goods to be used in Indian trade, April 1, 1686).

[26] *Prose Works*, p. 308.

[27] *Ibid.*, pp. 308–9. Pamptico = Pamlico River; Aramanchy River = Alamance River.

suggest that forty miles is an approximate evaluation for the distance from Alamance Creek to the Yadkin.

The upper valley of the Yadkin is described as a land of plenty: "The soil is exceedingly rich on both sides of the Yadkin, abounding in rank grass and prodigious large trees, and for plenty of fish, fowl, and venison, is inferior to no part of the northern continent. There the traders commonly lie still for some days, to recruit their horses' flesh as well as to recover their own spirits." At last, sixty miles farther, the traders reached Nauvasa, the first town of the Catawbas, on the banks of the Santee River which flows to South Carolina and into the Atlantic fifty miles north of Charleston. "Besides this town, there are five others belonging to the same nation, lying all on the same stream within the distance of twenty miles. . . . It is a charming place where they live, the air very wholesome, the soil fertile, and the winters are mild and serene."[28] The traders' tales, told with many embellishments, could well incite new settlers to go west and grab such fertile, wonderful, enchanting lands.

Virginia traders, said Byrd, generally received a sincere welcome from the natives, for they were more honest than the Carolinians; and no wonder, since North Carolina attracted the scum of Virginia's population.

So soon as the Catawba Indians are informed of the approach of the Virginia caravans, they send a detachment of their warriors to bid them welcome and escort them safe to their town, where they are received with great marks of distinction. And their courtesies to the Virginia traders, I dare say, are very sincere, because they sell them better goods and better pennyworths than the traders of Carolina. They commonly reside among the Indians till they have bartered their goods away for skins, with which they load their horses and come back by the same path they went.[29]

On the other hand, some Carolina traders who lived among the Catawbas exercised a kind of tyranny over them: "These petty rulers don't only teach the honester savages all sorts of debauchery but are unfair in their dealings and use them with all kinds of oppression." In the opinion of Byrd and many other Virginians, such people were to be blamed for most Indian wars.[30]

[28] *Ibid.*, p. 309.

[29] *Ibid.*, pp. 310–11.

[30] Governor Spotswood himself observed that in Virginia the Indians rarely broke with the English except when they had received some "notorious" treatment from them, chiefly from frontiersmen (mostly former indentured servants) who "made no scruple of first making them drunk and then cheating them of their skins, and even of beating them in the bargain" (*Official Letters*, II, 145, 148, 149, 227, 231, ff).

Sometimes, when they still had some goods left, the Virginia traders would take a northwest course from the Catawbas and carry them "for some hundred miles together" to the Cherokees, particularly after the Charleston traders had absorbed so much of the Indian trade.[31] The Carolina government had tried to hamper the activity of Virginia traders, and in his diary for 1710 Byrd noted receiving a letter from England which stated that "the Queen's letter was sent to Carolina to forbid them from meddling with our traders."[32] The roundabout route through Carolina to the land of the Cherokees was a loss of time and money for the traders, as well as a cause of fatigue. Byrd thought it a pity that the season was too far advanced for the Dividing Line expedition (already reduced to its Virginian members) to explore the mountains and find a short cut from Virginia.

The great service such an excursion might have been to the country would certainly have made the attempt not only pardonable, but much to be commended. Our traders are now at the vast charge and fatigue of traveling above five hundred miles for the benefit of that traffic which hardly quits cost. Would it not then be worth the Assembly's while to be at some charge to find a shorter cut to carry on so profitable a trade with more advantage and less hazard and trouble than they do at present? For I am persuaded it will not then be half the distance that our traders make it now nor half so far as Georgia lies from the northern clans of that nation.[33]

Byrd's suggestion was not followed until Daniel Boone ventured into Kentucky in 1769–70 and the first pioneers settled there after using the Boone Wilderness Road.[34] Byrd's evaluation of distances was undoubtedly optimistic, but he was quite right when he observed:

Such a discovery would certainly prove an unspeakable advantage to this colony by facilitating a trade with so considerable a nation of Indians, which have sixty-two towns and more than four thousand fighting men. Our traders at that rate would be able to undersell those sent from the other colonies so much that the Indians must have reason to deal with them preferably to all others. Of late the new colony of Georgia has made an act obliging us to go four hundred miles to take out a license to traffic

31 *Prose Works*, p. 274.

32 *Secret Diary*, Jan. 19, 1710.

33 *Prose Works*, p. 274. Governor Spotswood had expressed similar views as early as 1710 (To the Board of Trade, Dec. 15, 1710, *Official Letters*, I, 40–41).

34 "The Adventures of Col. Daniel Boon . . . ," an appendix to John Filson, *The Discovery, Settlement, and Present State of Kentucke* (Wilmington, 1784), pp. 50–58. See also Joseph Doddridge, *Notes on the Settlement and Indian Wars of the Western Parts of Virginia and Pennsylvania from 1763 to 1783* (Albany, N.Y., 1876), pp. 129–60.

with these Cherokees, though many of their towns lie out of their bounds and we had carried on this trade eighty years before that colony was thought of.[35]

Still more interesting than Byrd's comments on white frontiersmen are his judgments of the Indians, because his attitude was fairly common in colonial Virginia, at least among the educated. Byrd's general sympathy for the Indians goes deeper than a desire for peace based on mere financial interest in the Indian trade. In 1720–21, when the colonists were at peace with the Indians, he often noted in his diary that a group of natives had come to Westover "and I gave them victuals and put them over the river." Or again: "After dinner there came six Sapony Indians and I entertained them with rum and victuals."[36] Byrd made a point of giving them the same hospitality that he accorded to any white traveler. Sometimes in return for this hospitality they would entertain the planter and his family with some Indian songs and dances.[37]

One of the most significant passages in *The History of the Dividing Line* is the account of the religion of the Indians, given to Byrd by their Saponi guide.

In the evening we examined our friend Bearskin concerning the religion of his country, and he explained it to us without any of that reserve to which his nation is subject. He told us he believed there was one supreme god, who had several subaltern deities under him. And that his master god made the world a long time ago. That he told the sun, the moon, and stars their business in the beginning, which they, with good looking-after, have faithfully performed ever since. That the same power that made all things at first has taken care to keep them in the same method and motion ever

---

[35] *Prose Works*, pp. 274–75.

[36] *London Diary*, pp. 390, 410: see also p. 510. In 1712, Governor Spotswood listed approximately 700 tributary Indians, including an estimated 250 fighting men. Their nine nations were of three linguistic stocks: the Algonquian, including the Pamunkey, Chickahomini, and Nansemond tribes, survivors of the Powhatan Confederacy; the Iroquoian, including the Nottoway and Meherrin tribes; and the Siouan, including the Sapony, Stegaraki, Occaneechi, and Totero tribes. See Spotswood to the Board of Trade, July 26, 1712, *Official Letters*, I, 167. In the 1722 ed. of his work, Robert Beverley gives a list of Indian "towns" in Virginia (*History*, pp. 232–33). On the Indians still living on reservations in King William County see John R. Swanton, *The Indians of the Southeastern United States* (Washington, D.C., 1946), pp. 148–49, 152, 164, 175–76.

[37] *London Diary*, March 6–7, 1721. In the seventeenth century a reservation was set aside for the Pamunkey Indians in King William County, about thirty miles north of Westover; their descendants still live there. See Hugh Jones, *Present State*, pp. 172–73, and James Mooney, "The Powhatan Confederacy, Past and Present," *American Anthropologist*, n.s., IX (1907), 129–52.

since. He believed that God had formed many worlds before he formed this, but that those worlds either grew old and ruinous or were destroyed for the dishonesty of the inhabitants. That God is very just and very good, ever well pleased with those men who possess those godlike qualities. That he takes good people into his safe protection, makes them very rich, fills their bellies plentifully, preserves them from sickness and from being surprised or overcome by their enemies. But all such as tell lies and cheat those they have dealings with he never fails to punish with sickness, poverty, and hunger, and, after all that, suffers them to be knocked on the head and scalped by those that fight against them.[38]

Real retribution, however, comes after death:

He believed that after death both good and bad people are conducted by a strong guard into a great road, in which departed souls travel together for some time till at a certain distance this road forks into two paths, the one extremely level and the other stony and mountainous. Here the good are parted from the bad by a flash of lightning, the first being hurried away to the right, the other to the left. The right-hand road leads to a charming, warm country, where the spring is everlasting and every month is May; and as the year is always in its youth, so are the people, and particularly the women are bright as stars and never scold. That in this happy climate there are deer, turkeys, elks, and buffaloes innumerable, perpetually fat and gentle, while the trees are loaded with delicious fruit quite throughout the four seasons. That the soil brings forth corn spontaneously, without the curse of labor, and so very wholesome that none who have the happiness to eat of it are ever sick, grow old, or die. Near the entrance into this blessed land sits a venerable old man on a mat richly woven, who examines strictly all that are brought before him, and if they have behaved well, the guards are ordered to open the crystal gates and let them enter into the land of delight. The left-hand path is very rugged and uneven, leading to a dark and barren country where it is always winter. The ground is the whole year round covered with snow, and nothing is to be seen upon the trees but icicles. All the people are hungry yet have not a morsel of anything to eat except a bitter kind of potato that gives them the dry gripes and fills their whole body with loathsome ulcers that stink and are insupportably painful. Here all the women are old and ugly, having claws like a panther with which they fly upon the men that slight their passion. For it seems these haggard old furies are intolerably fond and expect a vast deal of cherishing. They talk much and exceedingly shrill, giving exquisite pain to the drum of the ear, which in that place of the torment is so tender that every sharp note wounds it to the quick. At the end of this path sits a dreadful old woman on a monstrous toadstool, whose head is covered with rattlesnakes instead of tresses, with glaring white eyes that strike a terror unspeakable into all that behold her. This hag pro-

---

[38] *Prose Works*, pp. 246–47. Cf. Strachey, *Historie of Travell*, p. 89.

nounces sentence of woe upon all the miserable wretches that hold up their hands at her tribunal. After this they are delivered over to huge turkey buzzards, like harpies, that fly away with them to the place above-mentioned. Here, after they have been tormented a certain number of years according to their several degrees of guilt, they are again driven back into this world to try if they will mend their manners and merit a place the next time in the regions of bliss.[39]

In 1612 William Strachey had already given a relation of the beliefs of the Powhatan tribes which shows great resemblance to Bearskin's account of an afterlife.[40] Yet Byrd's page is far more detailed and so deserves this long quotation.

Typical of Byrd is his indulgent judgment of Bearskin's religion, in contrast to Cotton Mather's stern and uncompromising criticism of those worshipers of the Devil, as he described them in "The Life and Death of the Renowned Mr. John Eliot."[41] Byrd's opinion is similar to those expressed by many English Latitudinarians toward the end of the seventeenth century about the natural religion of non-Christian peoples living in various parts of the world. It brings to mind the dispute that arose in Europe around 1700 about the religion of the Chinese, after favorable accounts of it were published by Jesuit missionaries. Byrd was then living in London. Moreover, being a friend of the Orrery family, he certainly heard of the Boyle lectures of 1704–5, in which Samuel Clarke, who had previously defended the thesis that "no article of the Christian faith is opposed to right reason," attempted to prove the existence of God and to derive morality from reason alone, carrying on the spirit of the Cambridge Platonists. It is not surprising that three decades later Byrd should express views which during his formative years in England had been current in the circles he frequented. His library contained John Wilkins's book on natural religion,[42] Robert Jenkin's *Reasonableness and Certainty of the Christian Religion*, Sir William Temple's works, and the Baron de Lahontan's *Voyages*.[43] His acceptance of natural religion did not

[39] *Prose Works*, pp. 247–48. This might be compared with Michel's briefer description: "They . . . believe that if they are disobedient to one of their superiors or kill one of their people or live badly otherwise, that after their death they will come into a land in the north, cold and evil, but those who live honorably, according to their opinion, will come into a land in the east, good and warm." (Hinke, "The Journey of Michel," pp. 131–32.)

[40] *Historie of Travell*, pp. 102–3. See also Beverley, *History*, pp. 195–216.

[41] *Magnalia Christi Americana* (New York, 1967), I, 560.

[42] *Of the Principles and Duties of Natural Religion* (London, 1675); the 8th ed., 1722–1723 has a preface by Tillotson.

[43] See Bassett, pp. 427, 425, 414, 416. Clarke's lectures were also in Byrd's library (*ibid.*, p. 427).

lead him away from the Church of England; it had none of the critical and even hostile deism that slowly came to prevail in the eighteenth century.[44] As a result, Byrd tolerantly concluded:

This was the substance of Bearskin's religion and was as much to the purpose as could be expected from a mere state of nature, without one glimpse of revelation or philosophy. It contained, however, the three great articles of natural religion: the belief of a god, the moral distinction betwixt good and evil, and the expectation of rewards and punishments in another world. Indeed, the Indian notion of a future happiness is a little gross and sensual, like Mahomet's Paradise.[45] But how can it be otherwise in a people that are contented with Nature as they find her, and have no other lights but what they receive from purblind tradition?[46]

Strachey had shown the same pity, but less understanding: "Such is the misery and thralldom under which Satan hath bound these wretched miscreants. . . . Well may these poor heathen be pitied and pardoned until they shall be taught better."[47]

One might expect that it would be easy to convert people who had such reasonable beliefs. But Byrd regretfully acknowledged the total failure of all efforts to this end. As a result of Commissary Blair's success in obtaining for the College of William and Mary a large part of a bequest made by Robert Boyle to be used for the propagation of Christianity among the heathens,

many children of our neighboring Indians have been brought up in the College of William and Mary. They have been taught to read and write and been carefully instructed in the principles of the Christian religion till they came to be men. Yet after they returned home, instead of civilizing and converting the rest, they have immediately relapsed into infidelity and barbarism themselves. And some of them, too, have made the worst use of the knowledge they acquired among the English by employing it against their benefactors. Besides, as they unhappily forget all the good they learn and remember the ill, they are apt to be more vicious and disorderly than the rest of their countrymen.[48]

44 See the analysis of William Wollaston's book mentioned, p. 63, note 24.

45 This may well be a reminiscence of Sir William Temple's essay "Of Heroic Virtue" which was also in Byrd's library (see Bassett, p. 436); cf. *The Works of Sir William Temple*, (London, 1814), III, 381.

46 *Prose Works*, p. 248.

47 *Historie of Travell*, pp. 89, 100 cf. John Smith, *A Map of Virginia, Works*, pp. 79, 374.)

48 *Prose Works*, p. 220. This observation is borne out by William Hugh Grove: at the College, he said, seven or eight of them "learn to read, write, and gabble their prayers twice a day and may be bound to trades, but must return to the old way of life and carry more vices away with them than they [their ?] fellows ever know" (Diary, f. 55). On Boyle's bequest, see Jones, *Present State*, p. 67.

Byrd also mentions the efforts of Governor Spotswood, who placed a schoolmaster among the Saponi Indians, at the salary of fifty pounds a year, to instruct their children. The teacher, Charles Griffin, was particularly qualified for his charitable work: besides "the innocence of his life and the sweetness of his temper," "he had so much the secret of mixing pleasure with instruction that he had not a scholar who did not love him affectionately." Unfortunately for that pious undertaking, he was removed to the College of William and Mary, and the good work he had begun was left unfinished. "I am sorry," Byrd concluded, "I can't give a better account of the state of the poor Indians with respect to Christianity, although a great deal of pains has been and still continues to be taken with them."[49]

After the negative results of these efforts to win the Indians over to civilization and Christianity, Byrd came to the conclusion that it would be impossible to convert them permanently, even the younger ones, if they were to live among their countrymen.

For my part, I must be of opinion, as I hinted before, that there is but one way of converting these poor infidels and reclaiming them from barbarity, and that is charitably to intermarry with them, according to the modern policy of the Most Christian King in Canada and Louisiana. Had the English done this at the first settlement of the colony, the infidelity of the Indians had been worn out at this day with their dark complexions, and the country had swarmed with people more than it does with insects. It was certainly an unreasonable nicety that prevented their entering into so good-natured an alliance. All nations of men have the same natural dignity, and we all know that very bright talents may be lodged under a very dark skin. The principal difference between one people and another proceeds only from the different opportunities of improvement.[50] The Indians by no means want understanding and are in their figure tall and well proportioned. Even their copper-colored complexion would admit of blanching, if not in the first, at the farthest in the second, generation. I may safely venture to say, the Indian women would have made altogether as honest wives for the first planters as the damsels they used to purchase from aboard the ships. 'Tis strange, therefore, that any good Christian should have refused a wholesome, straight bedfellow, when he might have had so fair a portion with her as the merit of saving her soul.[51]

Robert Beverley had expressed the same conviction; and he probably had a still better knowledge of the Indians than Byrd, for he

---

[49] *Prose Works*, pp. 220–21; see P.R.O., CO 5/1316, ff. 162–64. In his own library, Byrd had a copy of John Eliot's Indian Bible in the Algonquian language (see Bassett, p. 442).

[50] These two sentences read very much like Jefferson's remarks on black slaves in *Notes*, pp. 138–43.

[51] *Prose Works*, pp. 221–22; see also p. 160.

had visited their towns and won their friendship.[52] Byrd's views on the question were far more liberal than those of New Englanders, but they were not uncommon among the more enlightened planters of Virginia. He had remarked before that

morals and all considered, I cannot think the Indians were much greater heathens than the first adventurers, who, had they been good Christians, would have had the charity to take this only method of converting the natives to Christianity. For, after all that can be said, a sprightly lover is the most prevailing missionary that can be sent amongst these or any other infidels.[53]

This might have seemed a most unorthodox notion to Northern Puritans. Yet Byrd felt that intermarriage would have had political and social, as well as religious, advantages. It would have prevented much bloodshed, making the country more populous and consequently more powerful, for "the poor Indians would have had less reason to complain that the English took away their land if they had received it by way of a portion with their daughters." The policy of Louis XIV in Canada was far better and greatly strengthened the French interest among the Indians. In fact, said Byrd, "I heartily wish this well-concerted scheme don't hereafter give the French an advantage over His Majesty's good subjects on the northern continent of America."[54]

A good example of such bloodshed, in which the colonists had a share of responsibility, was the Indian revolt of 1711–13. Byrd never made a secret of his opinion that these wars must be laid to the charge of the Carolina traders, an opinion which he set forth before the Board of Trade in London and repeated later in *The History of the Dividing Line*, when he described the regions where the Tuscaroras had lived so long.

These Indians were heretofore very numerous and powerful, making, within time of memory, at least a thousand fighting men. Their habitation before the war with Carolina was on the north branch of Neuse River, . . . in a pleasant and fruitful country. But now the few that are left of that

[52] *History*, p. 195.

[53] John Lawson had expressed the same opinion in 1708: "By the Indians marrying with the Christians, and coming into plantations with their English husbands or wives, they would become Christians and their idolatry would be quite forgotten" (*New Voyage*, p. 245). So did the Reverend Peter Fontaine, probably airing views acquired through Byrd, in a letter to his brother Moses dated March 30, 1757 (Maury, *Huguenot Family*, pp. 349–50). But except for a few white Indian traders who lived among the Indians, the English never married Indian girls. See Spotswood's statement that in seven years he had never seen one such case (to the Board of Trade, April 5, 1717 *Official Letters*, II, 227).

[54] *Prose Works*, pp. 160, 161.

nation live on the north side of Moratuck, which is all that part of Roanoke below the great falls toward Albemarle Sound. Formerly there were seven towns of these savages, lying not far from each other, but now their number is greatly reduced.[55] The trade they have had the misfortune to drive with the English has furnished them constantly with rum, which they have used so immoderately that, what with the distempers and what with the quarrels it begat amongst them, it has proved a double destruction. But the greatest consumption of these savages happened by the war about twenty-five years ago, on account of some injustice the inhabitants of that province had done them about their lands. It was on that provocation they resented their wrongs a little too severely upon Mr. Lawson, who, under color of being surveyor general, had encroached too much upon their territories, at which they were so enraged that they waylaid him and cut his throat from ear to ear, but at the same time released the Baron de Graffenried, whom they had seized for company, because it appeared plainly he had done them no wrong.[56]

This was in September 1711, and a few weeks later Byrd had reported the facts in his diary, from the testimony of an Indian trader who had been sent to the Tuscaroras to demand that the prisoners be released.[57] In the following months, Byrd's diary often mentioned the negotiations of the Virginia Council with the Indians who, however great and real their grievances against the whites were at the start, gravely impaired their case in the eyes of the best-disposed among the colonists by subsequent bloodshed.[58] Lawson's death "was followed by other bloody actions on the part of the Indians which brought on the war, wherein many of 'em were cut off and many were obliged to flee for refuge to the Senecas; so that now there remain so few that they are in danger of being quite exterminated by the Catawbas, their mortal enemies." Yet Byrd is very careful to remark that the Tuscaroras had "grown so dishonest that no man could keep any of his goods or so much as his loving wife to himself"; and he relates an Indian legend which explained their calamities as a visitation of their own god for their sins: "Nor will he leave off

[55] When Governor Spotswood succeeded in getting an accord with the Tuscaroras, their number was estimated at 1,500. (See Spotswood to the Board of Trade, Nov. 16, 1713, *Official Letters*, II, 42.) A few months before, he had reported that they were "said to be about 2,000 fighting men," which would mean upwards of 5,000 persons including women and children (to the Board of Trade, July 26, 1712, *ibid.*, I, 167).

[56] *Prose Works*, pp. 302–3. Cf. p. 29 above for another version of Lawson's death.

[57] *Secret Diary*, Oct. 8 and 20, 1711, and Spotswood to the Board of Trade, Nov. 17, 1711, *Official Letters*, I, 121–22.

[58] *Secret Diary*, Oct. 7, 1711.

punishing and wasting their people till he shall have blotted every living soul of them out of the world."[59] Thus this bloodshed could be seen as a deserved punishment for both Carolinians and Tuscaroras, a visitation of God upon them, while Virginia had practically no share in the war.

The reduction of the number of Indians is a general fact in the colonies. James Mooney, in *The Aboriginal Population of America North of Mexico*,[60] gave 15,000 or 16,000 as a fair estimate for the number of Indians living within the bounds of present-day Virginia in 1607; and in 1666 the English population of the Old Dominion was approximately 40,000 while the natives had declined to about 6,000.[61] Byrd attributed this decline to several causes. He remarked that the Catawbas were once a numerous and powerful people: "But the frequent slaughters made upon them by the northern Indians and, what has been still more destructive by far, the intemperance and foul distempers introduced amongst them by the Carolina traders have now reduced their numbers to little more than four hundred fighting men, besides women and children."[62] The Nottoways too had dwindled to a very inconsiderable number "either by destroying one another, or else by the smallpox and other diseases."[63] Although the higher standards of living of many planters and the sparsely settled countryside made smallpox less a menace than in Europe, its outbreaks were bad enough, particularly in the seaports. When it struck an Indian village, it was not unusual for half or all of the village to be wiped out.[64] But, Byrd noted, "nothing has been so fatal to them as their ungovernable passion for rum, with which, I am sorry to say, they have been but too liberally supplied by the English that live near them."[65]

Diseases and rum were generally brought by the whites; but wars between enemy tribes were hardly less instrumental in thinning down their population, particularly those resulting from the implacable hatred between northern and southern Indians. "Their wars are ever-

---

[59] *Prose Works*, pp. 303–4.

[60] Smithsonian Miscellaneous Collections, LXXX, no. 7 (Washington, 1928), p. 6.

[61] Wesley F. Craven, *The Southern Colonies in the Seventeenth Century, 1607–1689,* (Baton Rouge, La., 1949), p. 269.

[62] *Prose Works*, p. 309. In 1764, Bouquet's estimate was 150 (see Jefferson, *Notes*, p. 106). The same remarks recur in later writers, e.g. William and Edmund Burke, *An Account of the European Settlements in America*, (London, 1757), or Jefferson, *Notes*.

[63] *Prose Works*, p. 219.

[64] See John Duffy, *Epidemics in Colonial America*, (Baton Rouge, La., 1953).

[65] *Prose Works*, p. 219.

lasting, without any peace, enmity being the only inheritance among them that descends from father to son, and either party will march a thousand miles to take their revenge upon such hereditary enemies."[66] And Byrd explained how these expeditions were carried on among the northern tribes:

Some Indian remarkable for his prowess, that has raised himself to the reputation of a war captain, declares his intention of paying a visit to some southern nation; hereupon as many of the young fellows as have either a strong thirst of blood or glory list themselves under his command. With these volunteers he goes from one confederate town to another, listing all the rabble he can till he has gathered together a competent number for mischief. Their arms are a gun and tomahawk, and all the provisions they carry from home is a pouch of rockahominy.[67]

Then they started toward the enemy's country, straggling in small numbers by various routes in order to pass unnoticed.

So soon as they approach the grounds on which the enemy is used to hunt, they never kindle any fire themselves for fear of being found out by the smoke, nor will they shoot at any kind of game, though they should be half famished, lest they might alarm their foes and put them upon their guard. Sometimes indeed, while they are still at some distance, they roast either venison or bear till it is very dry and then, having strung it on their belts, wear it round their middle, eating very sparingly of it because they know not when they shall meet with a fresh supply.

As they drew nearer the enemy, they watched for any smoke or the report of a gun. And Byrd admired their skill as much as their endurance: " 'Tis amazing to see their sagacity in discerning the track of a human foot, even amongst dry leaves, which to our shorter sight is quite undiscoverable."[68] Such details were to become commonplace in American fiction after Fenimore Cooper. Byrd's account derives its interest mainly from the fact that it was one of the first to be at once accurate and detailed.

When the Indian warriors have discovered the enemy,

they squat down in some thicket and keep themselves hush and snug till it is dark; then, creeping up softly, they approach near enough to

---

[66] *Prose Works*, p. 258. Cf. Strachey's similar remark in 1612: "They seldom make wars for lands or goods, but for women and children, and principally for revenge, so vindicative and jealous they be" (*Historie of Travell*, p. 104).

[67] *Prose Works*, p. 258. The "northern Indians" were chiefly the Five Nations of the Iroquois, whose raids were a constant threat to the colony and to its tributary Indians (cf. Spotswood to the Board of Trade, Aug. 29, 1717, *Official Letters*, II, 257; and *Prose Works*, p. 123).

[68] *Prose Works*, p. 258.

observe all the motions of the enemy. And about two o'clock in the morning, when they conceive them to be in a profound sleep, for they never keep watch and ward, pour in a volley upon them, each singling out his man. The moment they have discharged their pieces they rush in with their tomahawks and make sure work of all that are disabled. Sometimes, when they find the enemy asleep round their little fire, they first pelt them with little stones to wake them, and when they get up, fire in upon them, being in that posture a better mark than when prostrate on the ground.[69]

William Strachey had already observed that in war "their chief attempts are by stratagems, surprises and treacheries."[70]

Byrd then came to the most barbarous trait of the Indian character, shown in their practice of scalping their dead or wounded enemies, a practice which he took to be a proof of the Asian origin of the redskins. "They cut the skin all round the head just below the hair, and then, clapping their feet to the poor mortal's shoulders, pull the scalp off clean and carry it home in triumph, being as proud of those trophies as the Jews used to be of the foreskins of the Philistines."[71] As for the prisoners that were so unfortunate as to be taken alive, "they put them to all the tortures that ingenious malice and cruelty can invent. And (what shows the baseness of the Indian temper in perfection) they never fail to treat those with greatest inhumanity that have distinguished themselves most by their bravery." But after all, Byrd added as an afterthought, how are we to reproach the "poor Indians" with doing little more than Alexander the Great or Homer's heroes did? Their usual method was to torture their captives by fire:

Sometimes they barbecue them over live coals, taking them off every now and then to prolong their misery; at other times they will stick sharp pieces of lightwood all over their bodies and, setting them on fire, let them burn down into the flesh to the very bone. . . . While these and such-like barbarities are practicing, the victors are so far from being touched with tenderness and compassion that they dance and sing round these wretched mortals, showing all the marks of pleasure and jollity.[72]

If this happened to take place in their own towns, they used the children to torment the prisoners in order to teach them the same inhumanity.

---

[69] *Ibid.*, p. 259.
[70] *Historie of Travell*, p. 109.
[71] *Prose Works*, p. 259.
[72] *Ibid.*, p. 260.

On the other hand, Indian warriors, when taken prisoners and tortured, remained ostentatiously impassive; they

disdain so much as to groan, sigh or show the least sign of dismay or concern, so much as in their looks; on the contrary, they make it a point of honor all the time to soften their features and look pleased as if they were in the actual enjoyment of some delight; and if they never sang before in their lives, they will be sure to be melodious on this sad and dismal occasion.

Even Indian women showed contempt for pain and death under torture. "So prodigious a degree of valor in the Indians," Byrd concluded, "is the more to be wondered at, because in all articles of danger they are apt to behave like cowards."[73]

Byrd acquired all this information about Indian warriors second hand, mostly through conversation with Indian traders. But other passages are the testimony of an eyewitness. At the end of the spring expedition along the Dividing Line, Byrd and his fellow travelers paid a visit to the Nottoway tribe and he described them at length.[74] Later, when he went to survey the Land of Eden, which had once been the country of the Sauro Indians, he observed that "Indian towns, like religious houses, are remarkable for a fruitful situation; for, being by nature not very industrious, they choose a situation as will subsist them with the least labor."[75] But when he went to the Nottoway town, he was more interested in the people and their way of life. He first described the place: "This fort was a square piece of ground, enclosed with substantial puncheons or strong palisades about ten feet high and leaning a little outward to make a scalade more difficult. Each side of the square might be about a hundred yards long, with loopholes at proper distances through which they may fire upon the enemy." Within these precincts, fortified like a medieval castle against a possible enemy, there were "bark cabins sufficient to lodge all their people in case they should be obliged to retire thither." There lived about two hundred people, including women and children, "the only Indians of any consequence now remaining within the limits of Virginia." Then he briefly sketched the houses, the traditional wigwams of the region: "These cabins are no other but close arbors made of saplings, arched

[73] *Ibid.*, p. 260.

[74] *Ibid.*, pp. 217–19. According to John Lawson, who traveled in the back country in 1700–1701, the Nottoway tribe numbered about 30 fighting men, or 75 persons in all (*New Voyage*, p. 242).

[75] *Prose Works*, p. 251. John Smith had already noted how carefully the site of an Indian town was selected (*Works*, pp. 67, 362). On the Sauras, see Swanton, *Indians* pp. 109–10.

at the top and covered so well with bark as to be proof against all weather." The description is in much the same terms as William Strachey's.[76]

The fire is made in the middle, according to the Hibernian fashion, the smoke whereof finds no other vent but at the door and so keeps the whole family warm, at the expense both of their eyes and complexion. The Indians have no standing furniture in their cabins but hurdles to repose their persons upon, which they cover with mats or deerskins.[77]

The visitors were received in the best "apartment," which was adorned with new mats, very sweet and clean; then they were entertained with war dances.

The young men had painted themselves in a hideous manner, not so much for ornament as terror. In that frightful equipage they entertained us with sundry war dances, wherein they endeavored to look as formidable as possible. The instrument they danced to was an Indian drum, that is, a large gourd with a skin braced taut over the mouth of it. The dancers all sang to this music, keeping exact time with their feet while their head and arms were screwed into a thousand menacing postures.[78]

Naturally Byrd took a great interest in the ladies arrayed in all their finery: "They were wrapped in their red and blue matchcoats, thrown so negligently about them that their mahogany skins appeared in several parts, like the Lacedaemonian damsels of old. Their hair was braided with white and blue peak and hung gracefully in a large roll upon their shoulders." They wore necklaces and bracelets of shells strung like beads. Their usual dress was a kind of apron made of silk grass twisted into a thread. These aprons, Byrd added, "are long enough to wrap quite round them and reach down to their knees, with a fringe on the under part by way of ornament. They put on this modest covering with so much art that the most impertinent curiosity can't, in the negligentest of their motions or postures, make the least discovery."[79] Byrd did not fail to appreciate their charms:

---

[76] "They are like garden arbors ... made ... of such young plants as they can pluck up, bow, and make the green tops meet together in fashion of a round roof. ... The walls are made with barks of trees" (Strachey, *Historie of Travell*, p. 78; cf. John Smith, *Works*, pp. 67, 362).

[77] *Prose Works*, p. 217; John Smith, Works, pp. 67 and 362, describes the beds as "hurdles" a foot above the ground and covered with mats or skins.

[78] *Prose Works*, pp. 217–18. Cf. Strachey's more general description of Indian dancing and singing (*Historie of Travell*, pp. 85–87), or John Smith, *Works*, pp. 73, 368–69.

[79] *Prose Works*, p. 300.

Though their complexions be a little sad-colored, yet their shapes are very straight and well-proportioned. Their faces are seldom handsome, yet they have an air of innocence and bashfulness that with a little less dirt would not fail to make them desirable. . . . The bear's oil with which they anoint their persons all over makes their skins soft and at the same time protects them from every species of vermin that use to be troublesome to other uncleanly people.[80]

Had not the visitors been too many, they would have been offered unmarried girls for bedfellows according to the Indian rules of hospitality, "though," said Byrd, "a grave matron whispered one of the commissioners very civilly in the ear that if her daughter had been but one year older she should have been at his devotion." *The Secret History* reveals a detail that the final version leaves out: the unnamed commissioner was Byrd himself, and the grave matron "the Queen of Weyanoke," that is, the chief's wife.[81] And Byrd went on to explain that among Indian girls the number of gallants is not accounted by any means a loss of reputation, but rather a proof of superior merit. "However," he added, "they are a little mercenary in their amours and seldom bestow their favors out of stark love and kindness." But elsewhere Byrd expressed his opinion that the price they set upon their charms was "not at all exorbitant": "A princess for a pair of red stockings can't, surely, be thought buying repentance much too dear."[82] William Strachey had made similar comments upon Indian girls: "They are people most voluptuous, yet the women very careful not to be suspected of dishonesty without the leave of their husbands; but he giving his consent, they . . . may embrace the acquaintance of any stranger for nothing, and it is accounted no offence."[83] The least that can be said, however, is that customs varied from tribe to tribe and perhaps from one period to another. Robert Beverley, although he also described this "kind ceremony" which, he said, "is used only to men of great distinction," defended Indian girls against the charge of unchastity before marriage: "I believe this story to be an aspersion cast on those innocent creatures by reason of the freedom they take in conversation, which uncharitable Christians interpret as criminal upon no other ground than the guilt of their own consciences."[84]

Yet marriage, Byrd observed, brings a complete change in their attitude to men: "After these women have once appropriated their

[80] *Ibid.*, p. 218. On the use of bear's oil to keep off vermin, see *ibid.*, p. 294.
[81] *Ibid.*, p. 82. For the identification of Weyanoke Creek with Nottoway River, see *ibid.*, pp. 323, 325, 109 and 169–70.
[82] *Prose Works*, pp. 218–19, 314.
[83] *Historie of Travell* pp. 112–13; see also p. 85.
[84] *History*, pp. 171, 189.

charms by marriage, they are from thenceforth faithful to their vows and will hardly ever be tempted by an agreeable gallant or be provoked by a brutal or even by a fumbling husband to go astray."[85] After marriage they have to do what little work is done in an Indian town, while the men remain idle, except for "the gentlemanly diversions of hunting and fishing," or waging war upon some enemy tribe.[86] They

> make every day a Sabbath, except when they go out to war or a-hunting, and then they will undergo incredible fatigues. Of other work the men do none, thinking it below the dignity of their sex, but make the poor women do all the drudgery. They have a blind tradition amongst them that work was first laid upon mankind by the fault of a female, and therefore 'tis but just that sex should do the greatest part of it.[87]

But the true reason, in Byrd's opinion, was that the strongest imposed slavery on the weakest, as is usual in primitive societies.

To him it seemed incredible that, in spite of the example of the English, these Indians should choose to live in "stupid idleness," with all the inconvenience of dirt, cold, and want, whereas a little industry would bring them plenty. For what these men did they did very well indeed. Byrd admired their endurance when traveling on foot: they

> make nothing of going twenty-five miles a day and carrying their little necessaries at their backs, and sometimes a stout pack of skins into the bargain. And very often they laugh at the English, who can't stir to a next neighbor without a horse, and say that two legs are too much for such lazy people, who can't visit their next neighbor with six. For their part, they were utter strangers to all our beasts of burden or carriage before the slothful Europeans came amongst them.[88]

Thus did Indians and Europeans return the compliment to each other, showing how relative are the judgments passed by nations on their neighbors.

Scorn is a sterile attitude, whereas an effort at better understanding is never lost. There is always something to be learned from others, and this knowledge, however unimportant it might be, was the object of Byrd's quest. He recorded the Indian way of lighting a fire by

---

[85] *Prose Works*, p. 219. Cf. Beverley, *History*, p. 170, and Jones, *Present State*, p. 60.

[86] See Strachey, *Historie of Travell*, p. 81: "The men bestow their times in fishing, hunting, wars, and such manlike exercises without the doors, scorning to be seen in any effeminate labor, which is the cause that the women be very painful, and the men often idle." See also p. 114, and cf. Smith, *Works*, pp. 67, 363.

[87] *Prose Works*, p. 397.

[88] *Ibid.*, p. 288.

rubbing together two dry sticks of papaw tree, and their method of dressing deerskins with the brains of those animals, an example followed by English hunters in Virginia. One Sunday one of the guides taught him the Indian way of swimming: "They strike not out both hands together but alternately one after another, whereby they are able to swim both farther and faster than we do."[89] This enables them to catch fish in a most spectacular manner:

In the summertime 'tis no unusual thing for sturgeons to sleep on the surface of the water, and one of them, having wandered up into this creek in the spring, was floating in that drowsy condition. The Indian . . . ran up to the neck into the creek a little below the place where he discovered the fish, expecting the stream would soon bring his game down to him. He judged the matter right, and as soon as it came within his reach, he whipped a running noose over his jowl. This waked the sturgeon, which, being strong in its own element, darted immediately under water and dragged the Indian after him. The man made it a point of honor to keep his hold, which he did to the apparent danger of being drowned. Sometimes both the Indian and the fish disappeared for a quarter of a minute and then rose at some distance from where they dived. At this rate they continued flouncing about, sometimes above and sometimes under water, for a considerable time, till at last the hero suffocated his adversary and haled his body ashore in triumph.[90]

For their other main occupation, hunting, as well as for war, Byrd observed that Virginia Indians had come to use nothing but firearms, which they purchased from the English for skins. Bows and arrows had fallen into disuse. Perhaps because of his own family's interests in Indian trade, Byrd entirely approved of selling them weapons, on grounds both of political economy and of safety:

Nor is it ill policy, but on the contrary very prudent, thus to furnish the Indians with firearms, because it makes them depend entirely upon the English, not only for their trade but even for their subsistence. Besides, they were really able to do more mischief while they made use of arrows, of which they would let silently fly several in a minute with wonderful dexterity, whereas now they hardly ever discharge their firelocks more than once, which they insidiously do from behind a tree and then retire as nimbly as the Dutch horse used to do now and then formerly in Flanders.[91]

---

[89] *Ibid.*, pp. 292, 397.

[90] *Ibid.*, pp. 316–17. Beverley also described, though less dramatically, this "Indian way of catching sturgeon . . . by a man's clapping a noose over their tail, and by keeping fast his hold" (*History*, pp. 148–49).

[91] *Prose Works*, p. 219.

Whatever influence Byrd's personal interests may have had on his own opinion, it must be admitted that he presented a good summary of the arguments which were often put forward by his contemporaries.[92]

When all is said, Byrd gave a fairly objective account of Indians and Indian life in colonial Virginia. Unlike many others, he tried to understand and appreciate the natives. In New England the general opinion was that Indians were devils incarnate, heathens who richly deserved complete destruction. Such was the belief of Increase Mather and his son Cotton Mather.[93] Daniel Gookin, a Puritan who lived in Virginia before migrating to Boston in 1644, was reviled by his contemporaries for expressing compassion for the Indians, but he was an exception, and so was Samuel Sewall, who, in his own words, "essayed to prevent Indians and Negroes being rated with horses and hogs, but could not prevail."[94] In the Southern colonies public opinion was hardly more favorable. Paradoxically enough, John Lawson, the surveyor general of Carolina who was killed by the Tuscaroras in 1711, left in his *New Voyage to Carolina* an account of his travels in the back country, in which he said that he had seen the Indians before they had been corrupted by their contact with the whites; in his dedication he claimed to have presented the country "in her natural dress, and therefore less vitiated with fraud and luxury." Although he took a more kindly view of the Indians than most English settlers, it is hard to say whether this signified something more than the current belief in the value of primitive natural life and the theory of the noble savage.

Robert Beverly, who had been a member of the 1716 expedition across the Blue Ridge Mountains into the Shenandoah Valley, and who had many Indian friends, went much further in the appreciation and defense of the Indians. He believed in their innocence and doubted whether the English settlers had brought any great improvement to

92 Selling firearms to Indians had been prohibited at various times in the seventeenth century, for instance in 1637 (*VMHB*, XIV [1906], 189), in 1642 (Hening, *Statutes at Large*, I, 255), in 1664 (*ibid.*, II, 215). Bacon's proclamation in 1676 insisted on this prohibition (*VMHB*, I [1893], 57). But there is a letter of William Byrd I ordering 18 guns for Indian trade in 1689 (*ibid.*, XXVI [1918], 30).

93 Increase Mather, *A Brief History of the Warr with the Indians in New England* (1676) and *A Relation of the Troubles Which Have Hapned in New England by Reason of the Indians There* (1677); Cotton Mather, *Decennium Luctuosum, An History of Remarkable Occurrences in the Long War Which New England Hath Had with the Indian Savages, from the Year 1688 to the Year 1698*; all quoted in C. H. Lincoln, ed., *Narratives of the Indian Wars, 1675–1699* (New York, 1913).

94 *Diary* (Boston, 1878–82), June 22, 1716.

the country. He felt inclined to prefer the idyllic life of the natives, "without the curse of industry, their diversion alone and not their labor supplying their necessities." Indeed, he added, "all that the English have done since their going thither has been only to make some of the native pleasures more scarce by an inordinate and unseasonable use of them, making improvements equivalent to damage."[95] But then Beverley, protesting against material progress and refusing to introduce it in his own household, was sometimes prejudiced against his countrymen and naturally emphasized the virtues of the Indians by contrast. Byrd's judgment, based on an equally sound knowledge of the natives, is more sober and more objective, if perhaps more conventional.

The outstanding fact remains that in Byrd's day the frontier and the Indians still had in the minds of the Virginia colonists an importance which is not always realized by the twentieth-century reader, who knows that there was no Indian revolt in the colony after 1713. In 1730 Byrd still considered the danger sufficient to warrant providing his house with an escape tunnel. His observations in *The History of the Dividing Line* on the possibility of a Franco-Indian alliance amount to a shrewd prediction of the events of the French and Indian War twenty years later, although the threat to Virginia itself was not so great as he had feared. For Byrd's contemporaries, the frontier was the source of present danger and future wealth. For later generations of Virginians, the danger had vanished; inherited wealth was declining in the nineteenth century, and the great families escaped from present and future into their glorious past.

[95] *History*, p. 156.

CHAPTER XV

Legend and Reality

Uncle Gabe's White Folks

"Fine ole place?" Yes, suh, 'tis so;
    An' mighty fine people my white folks war—
But you ought ter 'a' seen it years ago,
    When de Marster an' de Mistis lived up dyah;
When de niggers 'd stan' all roun' de do',
Like grains o' corn on the cornhouse flo'.

"Live' mons'ous high," Yes, Marster, yes;
    D' cut n' onroyal 'n' gordy dash;
Eat an' drink till you could n' res'
    My folks war n' none o' yo' po'-white trash;
Nor, suh, dey was of high degree—
Dis heah nigger am quality!"

Thomas Nelson Page

Thomas Nelson Page's poem of 1877 suggests the late nineteenth-century picture of early nineteenth-century Virginia, after the Civil War had made it a thing of the past, never to return.[1] It is the legendary, idealized picture of a period of wealth and grandeur, of luxury and leisure, when kind master and faithful slave lived in harmony, each in his place in the stately mansion. It can be readily seen that this has little to do with Byrd's Virginia. Rarely has the relative position of a region changed so much in a century or two through mere stagnation. In the early eighteenth century, it looked as if Virginia might become the stronghold of liberalism among the American colonies. But after the War of Independence it sank gradually into conservatism, refusing to evolve, intent only on keeping things unchanged.

The plantation probably changed little in the century after Byrd's death. Indeed, there was not much difference at first sight, apart from some progress in comfort, an increase in the distance from the frontier, slowly drifting west, and the partial replacement of tobacco by cotton. Plantation life as a whole, for overseers and servants and slaves, remained much the same, although the change toward more luxury and idleness was considerable for the master of the estate.

---

1 "Uncle Gabe's White Folks," *Scribner's Monthly*, April 1877, p. 882.

In his diaries Byrd recorded a truer version than Page's of earlier plantation life, a life of activity more than leisure, often humdrum, with little of romance in it, although the planters' letters to their English friends might imply the contrary.

The diaries also offer Byrd's detailed account of Virginia's social life, which began to coalesce in the early eighteenth century. The brief social season in Williamsburg, a new capital, hardly more than a village, had its beginning with Governor Spotswood at the time of Byrd's first *Secret Diary*; and the change was already quite noticeable by 1740. This season, however, bore little resemblance to the idle circles of London society, first because of its brevity, and then because entertainment merely accompanied the main activities, which were political and commercial.

The public life of Virginia had evolved a style based on English institutions, but adapted to a large country where people scattered over wide spaces were nevertheless determined to avail themselves of their rights as Englishmen. It was practically concentrated in the two fairly short sessions in April and October, and the colonists spent the rest of their time on their plantations. But they were already defending their rights to self-government against what they considered to be the encroachments of the Crown, as they were later to defend them against federal power. Except for the autocratic tendencies of the Council, public life in early eighteenth-century Virginia more than in any other colony foreshadowed the institutions of the new nation at the end of the century. There was the same continuity here that Alexis de Tocqueville pointed out between the old regime and post-revolutionary France. Although the Burgesses and the middle class were to become the primary political power in revolutionary Virginia, the continuity between colonial times and the new independent nation is far greater than has been realized.

Byrd's times were no longer those of the early adventurers, and the difference between life in Tidewater Virginia and life on the frontier was quite marked already. But the frontier was then quite close to the civilized regions, and a man of importance living in the Tidewater would be well aware of the difference, whereas later colonists living in the neighborhood of Williamsburg had little idea of the frontier. Spotswood and his companions in the 1716 expedition to the Blue Ridge, or Byrd in 1728, were able to go far beyond the outposts of the colony and gain some experience of backwoods life, a life of explorers rather than pioneers. There may have been an air of romance about it, but a kind of romance different from what the general reader usually imagines about colonial Virginia. Byrd's picture of the Old Dominion particularly is useful to correct the many misconceptions that arose at various times, and especially the two legends about Virginia that were current in England in colonial times.

The first legend pictured Virginia as a land of plenty. Like the Spanish conquistadores in quest of Eldorado, the first adventurers sailing to Virginia had cherished the hope of finding gold and precious stones. As early as 1606 Michael Drayton gave vent to such romantic views in his ode "To the Virginian Voyage" in praise of Captain John Smith and "the brave heroic minds" going overseas "to get the pearl and gold" in

> Virginia,
> Earth's only paradise.
> Where Nature has in store
> Fowl, venison, and fish,
>   And the fruitfull'st soil
>   Without your toil,
> Three harvests more,
> All greater than your wish.[2]

In London toward the end of the seventeenth century, such images of paradise and wealth were used (when more drastic methods were not) to persuade emigrants to enter into indentures. Defoe set the happiest years of Moll Flanders's life in Virginia and emphasized the fact that many people who had come there "in very indifferent circumstances" had managed to build large estates for themselves, thanks to their industry and thrift. Although such cases did occur, their number was much smaller than Defoe made out. The planters, who wanted white labor badly, encouraged the legend of a paradisiacal country. When Byrd named his Carolinian estate for Governor Eden it was no mere pun; the name was also intended to attract settlers.

The second long-lived legend in England made Virginia the last resort of rascals and criminals. In her play *The Widow Ranter*, which deals with Bacon's Rebellion in 1676, Mrs. Aphra Behn described the Council of Virginia as a pack of illiterate scoundrels, former indentured servants quite incapable of taking part in the government of the colony. In both *Colonel Jack* and *Moll Flanders* Defoe portrayed Virginia as a place where criminals and paupers could begin life all over again with some chance of success and prosperity: "Many a Newgate bird becomes a great man, and we have . . . several justices of the peace, officers of the trained bands, and magistrates of the town they live in, that have been burnt in the hand."[3] When in 1769

---

[2] See also Captain Seagull's stories in Jonson, Marston, and Chapman's *Eastward Ho*, III, iii.

[3] *Moll Flanders* (London: Everyman's Library, 1955), p. 74. In fact, according

Dr. Johnson said of the American colonists that they were "a race of convicts,"[4] he was not merely being his usual prejudiced self; he was voicing an opinion widespread in England, the result of two indisputable facts: the transportation of many convicts (which did not necessarily mean criminals) to the West Indies and to the Southern colonies of America, and the swift ascent up the social scale of a few poor, lucky, hard-working colonists during the seventeenth century. The fact that many were called and few chosen was often overlooked, and the striking exceptions were given more prominence than they really deserved. Actually, the majority of the great planters were sons of merchants or younger sons of the gentry. Few were real members of the English aristocracy like Lord Fairfax; few were indentured servants risen to wealth. As for the criminals who formed a small part of the transported convicts, more often than not their fate was to end either as servants or as fugitives over the Carolinian border.

Besides these misrepresentations of Colonial Virginia in contemporary England, others developed in America itself. First came the Cavalier myth, which grew all through the eighteenth century. Although only a few of the newly established colonists approximated gentlemanly status in England, all coveted it in the New World. Their love of the soil and need for large plantations, their idealization and love of the past, combined to give them the social status of the English rural squire which they did not possess at the start. To this must be added a distortion of the political value of the term. "Like many legends," says Marshall W. Fishwick, "that of the high-stepping Virginia Cavalier is built on a thin stratum of truth. The term originally signified political affiliation, not social status. . . . Time embroidered the truth and made the rough places smooth; more and more Virginians became Cavaliers. It is simple to explain why. They wanted to be Cavaliers."[5]

Later, other legends arose because of the distance between the various colonies and gained strength in the nineteenth century with the antagonism between North and South, fanned by the passionate controversies over slavery. This antagonism was born of a difference in economic and moral perspective which was excellently sum-

---

to modern specialists, few indentured servants succeeded in reaching their goal. Only one in ten became a property owner, "decently prosperous." Another one perhaps became an artisan in a town or overseer on a plantation. The other eight died, returned to England, or joined the body of poor whites (Abbott E. Smith, *Colonists in Bondage*, pp. 299–300).

[4] James Boswell. *Life of Samuel Johnson* (London: Everyman's Library, 1946), I, 526.

[5] *The Virginian Tradition* (Washington, 1956), p. 33.

marized by John Bernard: "The lordly South turned with disdain
from the plodding North, while the moral New Englander looked
with angry disdain upon the idle dissolute Virginian."[6] And this attitude went back a long way, for hardly fifteen years after Byrd's
death the Reverend Mr. Andrew Burnaby had remarked: "Fire and
water are not more heterogeneous than the different colonies in North
America."[7]

The Northern misconceptions of Southern life were acknowledged by James Kirke Paulding, one of the few open-minded Northern writers who traveled south before the Civil War. In his *Letters
from the South* in 1817, he admitted that most Northerners went to
Virginia loaded with a pack of prejudices. He had found the people
there very much like others, only a little more hospitable, and felt that
his countrymen had been much misled by the idle tales of Yankee
traders or by the biased accounts of party politicians.

Yet those prejudices became particularly marked when after 1830
the problem of slavery came to the fore. Writers who had visited the
South before and found nothing to arouse their indignation became
passionate one or two decades later. When Emerson went South for
his health in 1826–27, he felt no deep aversion for slavery and was
impressed by Southern manners, although he looked upon himself as
an exile and held a poor opinion of the state of religion there. Repul-
sion came later, and in the fifties he seemed unreservedly to accept
the Abolitionist legend of a barbarous South. As Howard R. Floan
has shown, many writers, such as Emerson, Whittier, or Longfellow,
began by hating chattel slavery and were soon led into a hatred of
the South as a whole, not just of an institution within the South.[8]
The printing conditions in the United States delayed their influence
for some time: although most printers were in the North, the South
was a good market which they did not want to lose, and for a number
of years they thought it safer to avoid antislavery books, particularly
novels. On the whole the attacks of the Abolitionists had been confined to political writings, until the sweeping and unexpected success
of *Uncle Tom's Cabin* in 1851–52. Before this the bitterest ravings of
the Abolitionists had always remained abstract, almost unreal; they
dealt with principles rather than facts. Harriet Beecher Stowe's picture of the South might be biased and distorted in some of its details,
but readers felt its vividness. In a short time the world saw the problem through her eyes and condemned the South as barbarous and

---

[6] *Retrospections of America, 1797–1811* (New York, 1887), p. 6.
[7] *Travels*, pp. 152–53.
[8] *The South in Northern Eyes, 1831–1861* (Austin, Texas, 1958).

cruel. This was the start of a new type of plantation novel, which came to influence even Southern writers. In William Faulkner's South, degenerate planters have to expiate the sins of their land-grabbing, slave-holding ancestors.

Facing the dark legend of a land of violence told by the North stands the rosy legend told by the South. The Southern idealization of the good old days came years after *Uncle Tom's Cabin*, when the War between the States had ended in the suppression of slavery and the South was no longer felt to be a danger to the Union. Emerson and Lowell and many of the staunchest Abolitionist writers had held out the hand of reconciliation to the South, and the problem seemed solved. Thomas Nelson Page's novel *Red Rock* (1898) was a belated answer to *Uncle Tom's Cabin*, with a picture of plantation life which was idealized but based on a deeper knowledge of the South. It found a sympathetic audience in both South and North. Southerners read it with nostalgia, and Northerners saw it as a historical romance, with strong local flavor, about an era past and dead. The Southern reaction was a belated one because the effects of the defeat had to wear off first: people could raise their heads only when the Northern errors after the Civil War had made it evident to them that their adversaries had not really solved anything. Their antipathy to Northern industry, which seemed to them to establish a far more oppressive, though unavowed, slavery, inclined them to magnify their few Cavalier ancestors and lay claim to real aristocracy in contrast to the all-powerful upstart capitalists of the North. Thus arose the Southern legend of a Golden Age before the Civil War.

Favored by the South and accepted by the North, the legend developed fast. Heroes and heroines were gentlemen and ladies living among faithful slaves, in mansions with wide, beautiful porches and white columns, surrounded by magnolia gardens. These Cavaliers led idyllic lives and followed the code of Southern chivalry. The only villains were the ambitious and unscrupulous overseers and the poor white trash, or when the scene was set in later times, the Northern carpetbaggers and the Southern scalawags. The masters of the wide estates were not active middle-class businessmen but dashing, generous, improvident colonels, or indolent gentlemen dominated by single-minded women who were bent on keeping up the old prosperity of the plantation. That closed world, in which time has stopped and made the past eternal, thus becomes a matriarchy.[9] In treating

---

[9] These characteristics still appear in many modern novels of the South. On this subject, see William R. Taylor, *Cavalier and Yankee, The Old South and American National Character* (New York, 1961), pp. 162–65. The book contains

"Ole Virginia," the writer, clinging to tradition, idealized plantation life in order to justify the slave plantation. Too many Virginians consoled themselves with the picture of an unreal past, even intellectuals whose ancestors, as eighteenth-century revolutionaries, had hoped to rid themselves of slavery, but had come gradually to realize that they were not going to do so. For nearly a century their descendants escaped into romance and sentimentality.

Without quite running to such extremes, Marion Harland's novel *His Great Self*, with the Byrd family as its subject, is a good illustration of what the Southern mind could hardly help doing in the last decade of the nineteenth century, even with the firmest intention of drawing a true picture of plantation life in the 1730's. The book is based on the family tradition that before leaving England in 1725 Evelyn Byrd was violently in love with Mr. Charles Mordaunt, the grandson of the third Earl of Peterborough, but was refused her father's consent to the marriage. Mordaunt, having inherited his grandfather's title in 1735, comes to Virginia under an assumed name to marry Evelyn. But a scheme, devised by Byrd's secretary with his master's half-consent, sends Mordaunt on board a schooner which sails to England during a storm while Evelyn is deliberately prevented from joining her lover on board.

This is the main plot, which is not to be questioned, for it is the undoubted right of the novelist to adapt history to the needs of the story. However, turning over the pages, the reader will meet many real characters besides the members of the Byrd family: the Reverend Peter Fontaine, the minister of Westover Parish, who accompanied Byrd along the Dividing Line; former governor Spotswood, whom Byrd visited during his "progress to the mines"; the Carters, and among them a baby of three, little Lady Bess, the "good-humored little fairy" who was later to marry William Byrd III; Lieutenant Maynard, who in 1718 had killed the pirate Blackbeard. And in order to make the story more true to life, parts of Byrd's conversation are borrowed from his works: for instance, his theory of intermarriage with Indians, his doubtful anecdote on William Penn, his description of Germanna, his observations on bear's oil, his method of drawing out a bad tooth, his anecdote about a thunderstorm, his remarks excusing the cruelty of Indians, his reading of *The Beggar's Opera*, and his conversation with Spotswood on American hemp.[10] Everything

---

a careful study of Southern culture, the myth of the Southern Cavalier, and the plantation legend between the Revolution and the Civil War.

[10] *His Great Self*, pp. 135–38, 143–44, 173, 193–94, 199–200, 202, 205, 275–76, and

seemed to have been done to re-create the reality of early-eighteenth-century life.

Unfortunately the authoress made still greater use of all the family traditions, progressively embellished, and recounted to her by her Westover friends. There is the account of a ball in London in 1716, when the first Mrs. Byrd, a few weeks before her death, danced with the King, who asked "if there were many other birds in America as beautiful as she"—a very neat compliment indeed from George I, who could speak no English. There is the picture of Evelyn Byrd, holding the fan that can still be seen among the relics at Battle Abbey in Richmond. Surrounded by "a bevy of beaux" at a ball, she is the cynosure of a brillant assembly, adored by all, even to the Reverend Peter Fontaine and the obscure secretary of her father.[11] Lieutenant Maynard, the rough Navy officer who had "killed the monster in a hand-to-hand fight," is shown suing for the honor of Mrs. Byrd's hand in a stately dance; and the pirate-killer appears as a former suitor of Evelyn's best friend. This is not a true picture of Byrd's era, but rather of the more refined atmosphere described by Anne Blair in her caustic letters three decades later.[12] Elsewhere, a dinner scene, with innumerable courses served by well-trained black servants, again emphasizes an elegance and a refinement which belonged to later generations.

Byrd himself, "the Black Swan," has become the Virginia colonel of the plantation legend: he is shown riding recklessly to overtake Caliban, a young half-Indian slave (faithfully attached to Evelyn, of course) who has run away: "Even the Dismal would not deter him, for he had headed the party that had laid the dividing-line through it, when Caliban was a little boy."[13] It was out of the question to ride across the Dismal Swamp in those days; and as a matter of fact, in 1728 Byrd had only gone round it while the surveyors crossed it.

Besides, the master of Westover appears as a writer far more than a planter, and his secretary's work is only to copy out his patron's literary work after transcribing the notes "jotted down in cipher" or "scribbled in wayside hostelry," to quote only two details which are quite unbelievable.[14] Byrd would hardly have been reduced to the necessity of putting up at inns even if there had been any; and he

---

296. Cf. respectively *Prose Works*, pp. 160–61, 221–22, 167, 355, 294, 405–06, 281, 259–60, 345–46, and 363.

[11] *His Great Self*, pp. 46–47, 112.

[12] Morgan, *Virginians at Home*, pp. 37–38.

[13] *His Great Self*, p. 184.

[14] *Ibid.*, p. 17.

had certainly not taught his secretary the secret writing he used in his diary.

To crown all, there is the romantic legend of Evelyn: "She was beloved by and betrothed to Lord Peterborough, a Roman Catholic nobleman, but her father prevented the marriage on account of the noble suitor's religion. Refusing all offers from other gentlemen, she died of a broken heart." And now "the pale shade of *the Fair Evelyn* —as she is named in family tradition—walks by night in the corridors of Westover and along the rose-alleys, wan and woful, forever plucking at the ring placed upon her finger by her titled lover."[15]

Thomas Nelson Page had not really founded the plantation's literary legend. It was only a resurgence of something that had appeared in the 1820's as a result of the decline of plantations in late-Jeffersonian Virginia. In that age of dynamic national expansion, the Old Dominion declined rapidly in wealth and influence as well as in population. New tobacco-growing regions of the West superseded a country afflicted with soil exhaustion.[16] Between 1810 and 1840, 28 of the 62 counties east of the Blue Ridge showed a drop in the number of white inhabitants.[17] The planter aristocracy, conscious of an illustrious past which had given the Americans four of their first six Presidents, felt that its days of glory were over. James Mercer Garnett, a planter of Essex County, wrote in 1827 a characteristic expression of their pessimism:

We have made ourselves a tributary to the North and East—every day is augmenting our dependence. . . . Virginia, poor Virginia, furnishes a spectacle at present which is enough to make the heart of her real friends sick to the very core . . . her agriculture nearly gone to ruin from a course of policy which could not well have been worse destructive if destruction had been its sole objective; her general politics degenerated into a scuffle almost universal for office and emolument. . . . Hope is nearly dead, and I can see nothing in the perspective of the times calculated to renew it, or at least nothing which is not too slow in the operation to affect much in our times.[18]

Nor was Garnett alone in his expression of despair. John Randolph of Roanoke felt that with "soil and staples both worn out and a deadly climate in the bargain" Virginia was "in a galloping consumption" which no remedy could cure.[19] Ruin and desolation, the decayed

---

[15] *Ibid.*, pp. 351–52. Cf. "To Erranti," *Another Secret Diary*, pp. 383–85.

[16] Avery O. Craven, *Soil Exhaustion*, p. 124.

[17] U.S. censuses for 1810 and 1840.

[18] Garnett to John Randolph, Oct. 16, 1827, Garnett-Randolph Papers, U.Va.

[19] John Randolph to J. R. Randolph, April 7, 1830, John Randolph Papers, V.H.S.

plantation and the doomed aristocracy of the planters became a common motif in the novel as well. The description of Edward Grayson's return to the family seat in George Tucker's *Valley of Shenandoah* is a typical example:

The sight of this venerable seat of his ancestors reminded him of the fall of his family from their former opulence and consequence to the most absolute poverty; and the tender and not unpleasing melancholy he had formerly experienced, was exchanged for a bitterness of feelings, and soreness of heart, which had nothing in it consolatory or agreeable.[20]

The sight of the drab, shabby, dismal present understandably led to nostalgia for a lost Golden Age, to idealization of the "ancient cavaliers" or the glorious soldiers and statesmen of the Revolution. The novel of George Tucker presented several plantation colonels, the type of the plantation belle, Matilda, and the young beau, brother of the tragic heroine, full of pride, generosity, and nobility of heart, who dies trying to avenge his sister's honor in a fight against the Yankee seducer. On the other side of the social ladder, Primus, the faithful slave-servant, and Granny Mott, with her aristocratic pride in the position of her masters, were not yet the stereotypes of Page's novels. And long before Mrs. Stowe, Tucker drew a realistic picture of the auction in which the Graysons were forced to dispose of their slaves.[21]

But who and what had brought such desolation upon old Virginia? Most of the delegates from the eastern counties at the Virginia State Convention of 1829–30 agreed that all their troubles came from the North, from "Yankee greed." The optimism and liberalism of the Jeffersonian age were discarded in favor of conservatism, of a forlorn fight, alone and unsupported, against the malignant forces from the outside, from the North.[22] This opinion is reflected in such novels as John Pendleton Kennedy's *Swallow Barn* (1832), in which a planter blames federal "misgovernment" in these words: "Things are getting worse and worse. I can see how it's going. What's the use of states if they are all going to be cut up with canals and railroads and tariffs. NO. NO. Gentlemen! You may depend. Old Virginny's not going to let Congress carry on in her day."[23] Disunity was already looming ahead. But in the novel the sadness of the present could be forgotten in an evocation of the splendor of the past.

[20] *The Valley of Shenandoah, or Memoirs of the Graysons*, (New York, 1824), II, 31.

[21] *Ibid.*, p. 203.

[22] *Proceedings and Debates of the Virginia State Convention of 1829–1830*, (Richmond, 1830), pp. 321, 324, 404, 405, 407, etc.

[23] *Swallow Barn* (Philadelphia, 1860), p. 164.

In that splendor, in the embellished memories of many Southerners, novelists of the Romantic era discovered characters and situations which lent themselves to sentimental treatment of historical romance. The background of the War of Independence, to which Virginia had been a prominent party, allowed full play to a young and dynamic patriotism, and furnished a great national theme, which the novelists handled in the liberal and paternal spirit exemplified by Jefferson. But while Jefferson believed and hoped (at least in the first years of the Union) that slavery was on the wane, the novelists, even if they agreed with him, took the institution for granted in their fiction. They preferred to depict Negroes living contented lives with kind masters, aristocrats who were conscious of their responsibility to "their people," in utter contrast to the northern industrial *nouveaux riches*. This optimistic and already nostalgic picture suited a rosy romanticism which was later to find an extension in the genteel tradition.[24]

Thus political, social, economic, and literary factors combined to favor the rise of historical romance and of a Southern legend closely connected with it. To these should be added another factor, a psychological trait, just as important though more restricted in scope: the pride of the old families of Virginia, their sense of tradition, and a cult of the past, rarely equaled anywhere else in the United States, which still finds expression nowadays in the innumerable genealogical studies of Virginia families in books, reviews, and magazines.[25]

The Old South has vanished from the world of reality to reappear in the world of fable; the real South is hidden from view by many legends. A land of plenty and romance, or a land of crime and violence—such are the two extremes between which all shades, all blendings may be found. The dark legend of the Yankees and the rosy legend of the Southern Cavaliers are striking evidence of the inability of authors on either side to judge that divided country dispassionately, without being carried away by their personal positions on slavery.

[24] On the "decadence of romance" in American literature dealing with the Southern frontier, see Hazard, *Frontier*, pp. 70–86. And for a thorough study of the plantation tradition in American literature and thought, see Francis P. Gaines, *The Southern Plantation; A Study in the Development and Accuracy of a Tradition* (New York, 1925), particularly pp. 13–35 for a description of the popular conception and an account of the beginnings of the tradition (1832–1850).

[25] One of the most striking examples, apart from almost any number of the *Virginia Magazine of History and Biography*, is John McGill, *The Beverley Family of Virginia: Descendants of Major Robert Beverley (1640–1687) and Allied Families* (Columbia, S.C., 1956), gathering over a thousand pages of genealogical data about more than 35,000 persons.

And this explains the fact that even today the general view of Virginia in the days of Byrd is too often distorted.

It is distorted by memories of novels and films about pioneers, with their stress upon the adventure and danger of the first decades of the settlement. Such is for instance John Buchan's *Salute to Adventurers* (1915), set in 1685 Virginia.

It is distorted by novels and films based on the plantation legend and generally set in the Revolutionary period, for there is a tendency to ignore the preceding generations as less romantic. Thackeray's novel *The Virginians* is among the most famous and the most typical examples.

It is even distorted by the reconstruction of Colonial Williamsburg, which points to the same period, after 1763 and before the War of Independence. Except for the Capitol, most of its buildings (the Courthouse, the Market Square Tavern, the Wythe House, the Blair House, the Tucker House, or the Peyton Randolph House) evoke the spirits of George Mason, Patrick Henry, George Washington, and Thomas Jefferson rather than of Governor Spotswood, "King" Carter, Robert Beverly, or the first Randolphs—the spirit of William Byrd III rather than William Byrd II. It is revolutionary Williamsburg more than colonial Williamsburg.

Thus, even avoiding the legends, there is still some propensity to imagine Old Virginia either as it was in the period of the adventurers, before 1676, or in the prerevolutionary period, after 1763. Byrd's life and works make it possible to distinguish an intermediary, early-eighteenth-century Virginia, with some fairly marked differences. In his biography of the Harrison family, Clifford Dowdey showed from generation to generation the rise and decline of the Virginia plantation within the framework of Virginia history, and the persistence of the plantation dream long after the planter had lost his political power and economic security.[26] Borrowing his chronological divisions, we might say that William Byrd II, living after "the Age of the Frontier," before "the Golden Age" of the Revolutionary period and "the "Afterglow" of mid-nineteenth century, was one of the best representatives of "the Age of the Aristocrat"—or rather the beginning of it, when Southern aristocracy was still more homespun and hard-working than elegant and leisurely.

Perhaps one of the most striking features of his times was the inner dynamism which marked both land and man. The majority of the

---

[26] *The Great Plantation: A Profile of Berkeley Hundred and Plantation Virginia from Jamestown to Appomatox* (New York, 1957).

great estates were still in process of creation, but their expansion was generally completed by mid-century. Byrd's generation was no longer one of pioneers like his granduncle's or even his father's, but its men were men of action, bent at the same time on building a new country and on making a fortune. That dynamic period contrasts with the next one, which was more inclined to thought and ideas. The prerevolutionary generation, the generation of William Byrd III, saw Virginia at the height of its power and influence. But in spite of appearances many planting families (and the Byrds among them) just managed to hold their positions, and in fact were already on the downgrade. In the first decades of the nineteenth century, the whole of Virginia was apparently in a static period which de Tocqueville, as early as the 1830's, showed to be a real decline.[27]

The pioneer spirit, which infused men like Byrd when the frontier was only a few miles from their plantations, waned as new colonists filled the back country, and later, when others went over the mountains, the Virginia of the great plantations slumbered her years away in sheltered comfort and memories of past splendor, consigning to oblivion the liberalism of previous ages, until the approaching storm of the Civil War opened her eyes to the change of times, to the evolution of opinion, and to darker realities.

But in spite of that youthful energy, early-eighteenth-century Virginia had not yet come of age. The links with Britain were still as strong in individual minds as in the political or economic condition of the colony. Many planters had lived their formative years in England and still had relatives in the mother country, like Byrd. They still felt the need for English protection against the possible menace of the French. After 1763, a new generation, educated in Virginia and relieved of the French threat, would be ready to think of themselves as Americans and be thrown into rebellion by the Intolerable Acts.

Other traits which distinguished Byrd's Virginia from earlier times were to develop as years went by and were to appear more clearly in the Revolutionary period. The Royal Charter of 1624, granting colonists the same liberty "to all intents and purposes as if they had been abiding and born within this our Realm of England," gradually became the foundation of a conception of political liberty and self-government which appears as a kind of idealization of political rights in the mother country.[28] There was also the growing feeling among

[27] *De la démocratie en Amérique*, ed. J.-P. Mayer, (Paris, 1961), I, 397–98, notes 73 and 74.

[28] See the chapter on Richard Bland in Clinton Rossiter, *Seed-time of the Republic: The Origin of the American Tradition of Political Liberty* (New York, 1953), pp. 247–80. Bland, Byrd's neighbor, lived at Jordan's Point, across the river

the planters (later to be followed by disillusionment, as we have seen) that they were living in a real paradise, or at least a country which they could see developing and progressing rapidly, a country blessed by God. Such notions underlie the Declaration of Independence, written by a Virginia planter. But there also loomed the first signs of a certain uneasiness about slavery. Only a few men like Byrd felt it, and it was just a foreboding, lacking the deep philanthropy of an Oglethorpe. Yet it prefigures the difficulties that were later to bear so heavily on the fate of Virginia and the rest of the nation.

---

from Westover, where he had succeeded his father (see *Secret Diary*, Feb. 11, 1709 and *Another Secret Diary*, Sept. 16, 1740). He was a burgess from 1742 to 1775, and his creed had four principal articles of faith: ". . . the eternal validity of the natural-law doctrines most cogently stated by John Locke; the superiority over all forms of government of the English Constitution, of which an uncorrupted model or extension was the peculiar property of the Virginians; the like superiority of those rights and liberties which were the heritage of the free-born Englishmen; and the conviction that the good state rests on the devotion of men of virtue, wisdom, integrity, and justice" (Rossiter, p. 267).

CONCLUSION

Conclusion

BYRD now holds a place apart in American letters. His reputation has varied greatly in a little more than two centuries. On the one hand he had at the start the handicap of being an American and a Southerner; on the other the canon of his writings has been much enlarged in recent times.

For a century after his death, he was read only in manuscript by a few privileged people. He then shared in the general neglect of American literature, which was not felt to have any separate existence. But even when some of his works were published in 1841 and again in 1866, they did not bring him the immediate recognition that might have been expected, for these editions came out in Virginia, in Petersburg and Richmond respectively, and had only a local circulation. Byrd's first publisher, Edmund Ruffin, once explained how the Northern publishing houses had practically acquired a monopoly on the reading public in the South "by combining the credit system and the puffing system."[1] By degrees, however, Byrd gained a reputation, mainly based on *The History of the Dividing Line*, as a "fastidious Virginia gentleman" who drew with "urbane style and mild humor" a "vivid picture of outdoor life."[2]

But to this slender work, which John Spencer Bassett's edition in 1901 made a little more widely known in the North, much has been added by the publication of the secret colonial diaries by Professor Wright in 1941 and Miss Woodfin in 1942. And *The London Diary* (1958) may be taken as a symbol of the fact that no distinction was as yet possible between English and American letters in Byrd's times; the scanty literature of Virginia, or of all America, was in fact, "provincial rather than colonial," as Marcus Cunliffe has observed.[3] Now, after the edition of *The Prose Works of William Byrd of Westover*, which in 1966 superseded Bassett's volume, there remains the need for another publication before Byrd's works can be considered com-

---

[1] *Farmers' Register*, Aug. 1, 1838.

[2] Maurice Le Breton, *The Student's Anthology of American Literature 1600–1865* (Lyon, 1955), p. 19.

[3] Marcus Cunliffe, *The Literature of the United States* (London, 1954), p. 36.

plete in book form (unless new papers should turn up in the future, which seems improbable). A substantial number of his letters, often as interesting as his diary and of greater literary value, are presently scattered in Southern magazines, mostly of the first three decades of this century, and their texts are sometimes incomplete or inaccurate.[4]

The diaries have given Byrd a new reputation as "an American Pepys." But the comparison, though quite apt in many respects, is perhaps unfortunate and even misleading, for it may suggest second-rate achievement and lack of originality or, on the other hand, lead the prospective reader to expect a diary at once more detailed and more literary than is really the case. Byrd resembles Pepys in his frankness and in the weaknesses hidden under a surface of propriety, but his diaries (even *The London Diary*) differ in atmosphere and in style. In London, Byrd unlike Pepys led the idle life of the fashionable society. And his writing, instead of being plain and vigorous, is often dry and slipshod in comparison with Pepys's. Byrd's qualities of style seem to be acquired rather than innate, and they appear only when he writes for someone else.

His style is still more different from that of Boswell, to whom he has also been compared, probably because of the similar substance of the latter's *London Journal*. The freedom of expression in the relation of various love affairs only creates a superficial analogy. Boswell, whose confessions would sometimes recall Rousseau if there were not a twinkle in his eye instead of a soulful gaze, often displays a mild humor similar to that of Byrd's *The History of the Dividing Line*; but however colorful and attractive, however reliable and useful to the social historian who seeks to recapture the flavor of Southern life in the early eighteenth century, Byrd's three diaries lack this humorous turn of mind and remain entirely factual.

With one exception, Byrd's qualities as a writer do not appear equally in all his works. He had a great talent for observation, which most readers will probably agree was his most conspicuous quality—an innate gift developed by an all-embracing curiosity and the training of the Royal Society. In his diaries, his playful temper sometimes led him into ludicrous remarks and involuntary humor. But when he wrote for a public, he could match the pleasant badinage or the graceful wit of the Cavaliers, achieve a sprightly humorous turn, perhaps with a touch of satire, or unfortunately, lapse into the coarseness of the Restoration wits. In the works that he polished for publication, his style is his greatest asset. It is simple and clear, direct and lively,

---

[4] See Bibliography, part II.

it combines ease with elegance. His urbane style is unequaled in the literature of the colonial era.

Here are no provincialisms or solecisms, no lumbering sentences like those of contemporary New England divines. Few early American prose writers had Byrd's lightness of touch. Franklin at his best is a greater writer and Jonathan Edwards plumbs spiritual depths unknown to the master of Westover. Not, however, until we come to Washington Irving do we find an American writer who excels Byrd in those qualities that distinguish him from his contemporaries.[5]

And yet, the odds were against Byrd, in a milieu that could hardly have been more unfavorable. None of the American colonies had such a class of professional men of letters as was then blossoming in England, where Congreve was already an exception when he told Voltaire that he would rather be looked upon as a gentleman than as a writer. Literature was no trade, no means of livelihood (however precarious) as in Europe; it could only be the work of amateurs. The very existence of an American literature was still contested in the United States far into the nineteenth century by some who felt that they should not give up the British cultural heritage.[6]

The South was even less favorable to literary activity than the North, as George Tucker explained in 1816 in an essay "On the Low State of Polite Letters in Virginia."[7] He pointed out the practical turn of mind of the first settlers, the fact that they lived on scattered plantations and in small towns, and the reluctance of gentlemen-planters to consider publication. He felt that in cultural matters Virginia was still a colony since even after Independence people could read only books originally written for foreigners, not for Americans. "Hence it is," he concluded, "that while Virginia can show a long roll of her warriors and statesmen, she can give but a Flemish account of her poets."[8]

Such drawbacks, acknowledged by many writers long after Independence, make Byrd's achievement, a century before, a really outstanding one. At least the straightforward appreciation of these obstacles to great literature may help to set reasonable limits to our

[5] Hubbell, *The South*, p. 51.

[6] See for instance Edward W. Johnston, "American Literature," *Southern Review*, Aug. 1831, in reply to Samuel Knapp's *Lectures on American Literature* (1829) and Samuel Kettell's *Specimens of American Poetry* (1829).

[7] [George Tucker], *Letters from Virginia, Translated from the French*, (Baltimore, 1816).

[8] On the question of a Southern literature, see Jay B. Hubbell, "Literary Nationalism in the Old South," in *American Studies in Honor of William Kenneth Boyd*, ed. David K. Jackson (Durham, N.C., 1940), pp. 175–220.

expectations. When all is said, Byrd remains an author of threefold interest. First in literature he presents a good example of the attractive and elegant style of early-eighteenth-century English prose-writers, though in the minor genres of characters, travels, and chronicles. Then his picture of an era and a country is all the more valuable not only for its uniqueness in colonial Virginia, but also for its freedom from premeditation and contrivance. His raw diaries may be monotonous and too factual in comparison with Pepys's, but his very negligence confirms the trust we can place in his information concerning the whole gamut of colonial society. Finally, his personality, which shows throughout his works, is one of the most attractive of his age. In his diaries as in Pepys's, much of the interest arises from the clash between nature and education, from the contrast between ideal and reality, between morality and temptation, between the seemly behavior of the gentleman in company and the inner self of the man revealed in the solitude of his library. And his protean character makes him appear, as Professor Cunliffe said, "by turns shrewd and ingenuous."[9] In his works, neither the human interest nor the historical one will ever fail.

Byrd, who, as someone said, took equal delight in a well-turned sentence and a well-turned ankle, wrote neither outstanding literature nor purely historical documents. But he was the first Southern writer of real value, in a mixed kind of writing that might be called historical literature. Before Franklin and the Revolutionary period, he stands out from the rest of the colonial writers of the South, a symbol of the best that they could contribute to the cultural history of the country, a mixture of the gentleman-planter and the gentleman-writer, no longer quite English, not yet really American.

[9] *Op. cit.*, p. 34.

APPENDIX

BIBLIOGRAPHY

INDEX

Byrd's Family

A brief record of Byrd's family may be useful for a better understanding of biographical facts. A complete genealogy was given by Bassett, pp. 444 ff., but a few errors were corrected by Miss Woodfin in *Another Secret Diary* (e.g., p. 31, note).

William Byrd I (1652–1704) married in 1673 Mary Horsemanden (1653–1699). They had five children:
1. William Byrd II (see below)
2. Susan, who married John Brayne of London and died in 1710; two children, William and Susan, were sent over to Virginia shortly before her death
3. Ursula (1681–1698), who married Robert Beverley, the historian of Virginia, and had one son, William (c. 1698–1756)
4. Mary (b. 1683), who married James Duke, sheriff of James City County
5. Warham (b. 1685, d. in childhood)

William Byrd II (March 28, 1674–August 26, 1744). Married:
A. In 1796, Lucy Parke (d. 1716 in London), daughter of Colonel Daniel Parke (d. 1710 as Governor of the Leeward Islands), and sister of Frances Parke, who married John Custis. They had four children:
   1. Evelyn (1707–1737)
   2. Parke (1709–1710)
   3. Philips William (b. and d. 1712)
   4. Wilhelmina (b. 1715), who married Thomas Chamberlayne
B. In 1724, Maria Taylor (1698–1771), eldest daughter of Thomas Taylor, of Kensington, England.[1] They had four children:
   1. Anne (1725–1757), who married Charles Carter
   2. Maria (1727–1745), who married Landon Carter
   3. William Byrd III (1728–1777), who married:
      A. In 1748, Elizabeth Hill Carter (d. 1760), four children
      B. In 1760, Mary Willing, ten children
   4. Jane (b. 1729), who married John Page

[1] Her sister married Francis Otway, and part of Byrd's later correspondence is addressed to them.

Bibliography

WILLIAM BYRD'S WORKS

A Discourse Concerning the Plague, with Some Preservatives Against It, by a Lover of Mankind. London, 1721.

Ruffin, Edmund, ed. *The Westover Manuscripts, Containing the History of the Dividing Line Betwixt Virginia and North Carolina; A Journey to the Land of Eden, A.D. 1733; and a Progress to the Mines. Written from 1728 to 1736 and Now First Published.* Petersburg, Va., 1841.

Wynne, Thomas H., ed. *History of the Dividing Line and Other Notes, from the Papers of William Byrd of Westover in Virginia, Esquire.* Richmond, 1866. Vol. I: Introduction, pp. ix–xix; History of the Dividing Line, pp. 1–225. Vol. II: A Journey to the Land of Eden, pp. 1–39; A Progress to the Mines, pp. 41–82; Proceedings to Lay Out the Bounds of the Northern Neck, 1736, pp. 83–139; An Essay on Bulk Tobacco, pp. 140–58, Bassett omitted this from his edition "on the grounds that Byrd did not write it" (p. v);[1] Miscellaneous Papers, pp. 159–265. This edition was based on the Westover Manuscripts now in the Virginia Historical Society. Another text of "The History of the Dividing Line" is in the American Philosophical Society in Philadelphia, together with the only copy of "The Secret History."

Bassett, John Spencer, ed. *The Writings of Colonel William Byrd of*

---

[1] In 1687 there had been an earlier protest against the importation of bulk tobacco into England: "The Merchants, Owners and Planters Adventurers of Virginia, having presented a petition to his Majesty complaining of the exportation of tobacco in bulk from the Plantations, with reasons why the same should be prohibited, and the Lords Commissioners of the Treasury having received the opinion of the Commissioners of the Customs thereupon" (P.R.O., CO 5/1357, f. 147). Whitehall had issued an "order on the foregoing report" on Oct. 28, 1687 (*ibid.,* ff. 159–60). But when Governor Lord Howard of Effingham asked the Burgesses to pass a law prohibiting the export of bulk tobacco from Virginia, the Assembly rejected the bill. Part of the "Essay on Bulk Tobacco" of 1692 repeats the terms of the 1687 petition (P.R.O., CO 5/1357, ff. 148–56), Wynne's edition adding only §6 of p. 155 and §5 of p. 156. Byrd may have come by the text in 1697 or 1698 when he was agent for Virginia in London and the affair was finally settled. The real author of the essay, whoever he was, must have been someone who had access to the archives of the Board of Trade, or who had been one of the 1687 petitioners. It may be noted that among these was Micajah Perry, the London agent of the Byrd family.

Westover in Virginia, Esquire. New York, 1901. Introduction on Byrd's Life, pp. ix–lxxxviii; History of the Dividing Line, pp. 3–255; A Journey to the Land of Eden, pp. 281–329; A Progress to the Mines, pp. 333–86; Miscellaneous Letters, pp. 389–400; A Catalogue of the Books in the Library at Westover, pp. 413–43; Genealogy of the Byrds, pp. 444–51.

Ryan, Thomas F., ed. *William Byrd, Esq., Accounts as Solicitor General of the Colonies and Receiver of the Tobacco Tax 1688–1704 . . . Letters Writ to Facetia by Veramour*. Privately printed, Baltimore, 1913. One of the fifteen copies is in the Virginia Historical Society.

Swem, Earl G., ed. *Description of the Dismal Swamp and a Proposal to Drain the Swamp, by William Byrd of Westover*. Metuchen, N.J., 1922. See *Columbian Magazine* (April 1789), and *Farmers' Register* (Jan. 1, 1837).

Van Doren, Mark, ed. *William Byrd: A Journey to the Land of Eden, and Other Papers by William Byrd*. New York, 1928.

Boyd, William K., ed. *William Byrd's Histories of the Dividing Line Betwixt Virginia and North Carolina*. Raleigh, N.C., 1929. Reprinted with a new introduction by Percy G. Adams, New York, 1967. This is the best edition of the *History*, with an introduction on the story of the manuscript and its publication. The "Secret History" and the final version of it are printed on parallel pages.

Beatty, Richmond C., ed., and William J. Mulloy, trans. *William Byrd's Natural History of Virginia, or the Newly Discovered Eden*. Richmond, 1940. This is a translation from a German version published in Switzerland by Samuel Jenner from Lawson's *New Voyage to Carolina* and notes supplied by Byrd, in order to attract German Swiss colonists.

Wright, Louis B., and Marion Tinling, eds. *The Secret Diary of William Byrd of Westover, 1709–1712*. Richmond, 1941. Introduction by Wright on the diary and on Byrd's daily life, pp. v–xxv; The Secret Diary, pp. 1–591. The original shorthand manuscript belonging to the Huntington Library, San Marino, Calif., was transcribed by Mrs. Tinling and edited with notes by Professor Wright. Selections from this diary were reprinted: *The Great American Gentleman, William Byrd of Westover in Virginia, His Secret Diary for the Years 1709–1712*, New York, 1963.

Woodfin, Maude H., and Marion Tinling, eds. *Another Secret Diary of William Byrd of Westover, 1739–1741*. Richmond, 1942. Introduction by Miss Woodfin on Byrd's life, pp. xiii–xlv; Another Secret Diary, pp. 3–185; Letters, Characters and Literary Pieces, pp. 191–387; Poems from *Tunbrigalia*, pp. 403–9; A Discourse Concerning the Plague, pp. 417–43; The Female Creed, pp. 449–75. These papers were published from two notebooks of William Byrd belonging to the University of North Carolina; the diary, written in code, was, like the preceding one, transcribed by Mrs. Tinling.

Wright, Louis B., and Marion Tinling, eds. *The London Diary (1717–1721) and Other Writings, of William Byrd of Virginia*. New York,

1958. The Life of William Byrd of Virginia, by Wright, pp. 3–46; The
Secret Diary of William Byrd of Westover from Dec. 13, 1717, to
May 19, 1721, pp. 49–530; The History of the Dividing Line (extracts),
pp. 533–97; A Journey to the Land of Eden (extracts), pp. 601–17; A
Progress to the Mines (extracts), pp. 621–31. The *London Diary* was
transcribed by Mrs. Tinling from a shorthand manuscript belonging to
the Virginia Historical Society in Richmond.

Wright, Louis B., ed. *The Prose Works of William Byrd of Westover:
Narratives of a Colonial Virginian.* Cambridge, Mass., 1966. Introduction
on Byrd as a man of letters by Wright, pp. 1–38; The Secret History of
the Line, pp. 41–153; The History of the Dividing Line, pp. 157–336;
A Progress to the Mines, pp. 339–78; A Journey to the Land of Eden,
pp. 381–415; Appendix by Mrs. Leonard on the text and provenance
of the Byrd manuscripts, pp. 417–23; map of the Dividing Line (drawn
during the expedition), p. 177; map of the Land of Eden (drawn during
the survey), p. 413. This volume contains the final edition of Byrd's
main writings apart from the diaries and letters, superseding Bassett and
equaling Boyd.

II

WILLIAM BYRD'S CORRESPONDENCE

Besides those letters of Byrd which were published by Bassett in 1901
(pp. 389–400), by Ryan in 1913 ("Letters Writ to Facetia by Veramour,"
pp. 1–41), and by Miss Woodfin in 1942 (*Another Secret Diary*, pp. 191–
387), many others are scattered in various books and magazines. Dr. Louis
B. Wright is now preparing a collection of Byrd's letters, but he is still
searching for the originals of many of them.

By far the greatest number of Byrd's letters have been printed in the
Virginia Magazine of History and Biography:

"Some Colonial Letters" (Letters addressed to Philip Ludwell, Ludwell
Manuscripts, Virginia Historical Society), *VMHB*, III (1896), 349–53,
contains two letters from Byrd to Ludwell, dated London, July 3, 1717, and
London, Oct. 28, 1717. The Lee-Ludwell Papers in the Virginia Historical
Society now contain a third one, dated Sept. 24, 1717.

"Letters of William Byrd II of Westover, Va.," *VMHB*, IX (1901–2),
113–30 and 225–51. This group of 24 letters includes most of those that
had been published a few months before by Bassett; they were written to
various correspondents between 1733 and 1738.

"Letters of the Byrd Family," *VMHB*, XXXV (1927), 221–45 and
371–89; XXXVI (1928), 36–44, 113–23, 209–22, and 353–62; and XXXVII
(1929), 28–23 and 101–18. These 52 (?) letters or fragments of letters
extending over a period of thirty years (1712–41) were edited from copies

made by Miss Elizabeth Byrd Nicholas in the nineteenth century. A few letters of the preceding group printed in 1901–2 are repeated here, sometimes with variations due to misreadings of the manuscript by the second editor. On one occasion, fragments of letters written to different correspondents have been pieced together and attributed to one of them only: the letter "To Lord Egmont, July, 1736" (XXXVI, 216–17) combines part of a letter to Sir Charles Wager, July 2, 1736 (already published in IX, 124–25), and part of a letter to Mark Catesby, July 1737 (William Byrd II Letterbook, 1736–1737, p. 31). Only the last thirteen lines belong to a letter to Lord Egmont dated July 2, 1737 (Letterbook, p. 32). On the other hand, a letter written to Sir Hans Sloane on April 10, 1741 (Sloane MSS, 4057, f. 20, British Museum) appears partly in "To . . . , June 10, 1740" (XXXVII, 104–5) and in "To Sir Charles Wager, April 12, 1741" (XXXVII, 109), the latter's first four lines being themselves an approximate copy of a passage in a letter to Peter Collinson, July 5, 1737 (Letterbook, pp. 35–37). In this group are four letters to Charmante, which are among the five (numbered 12 to 16) contained in the Commonplace Book discovered in 1964; but two pages of a note concerning Charmante are printed separately, the first in XXXV, 388, and the other in XXXVI, 38.

Because of the poor quality of the text of these letters published in 1927–29, a list of these follows with the corresponding manuscripts or publications giving a more trustworthy text. In a few cases (nos. 25, 26, 36, 40, 41), it was possible to complete the date from the letterbooks.

VMHB, XXXV (1927):

End of introduction articles. Contains a fragment of a letter to John Custis, n.d. (p. 376). See Custis Papers, Virginia Historical Society (a mention of Dr. Oastler's death places the letter in Dec. 1709; cf. *Secret Diary*, Dec. 14–17, 1709).

1. To John Custis, Feb. 4, 1711/12 (pp. 380–81). See Custis Papers, V.H.S.
2. To John Custis, Feb. 7, 1711/12 (pp. 381–82). See Custis Papers, V.H.S.
3. To Charmante, Oct. 23, 1722 (pp. 383–84). See Commonplace Book, pp. 85–86, V.H.S.
4. To Charmante, Oct. 26, 1722 (pp. 384–86). See Commonplace Book, pp. 86–88, V.H.S.
5. To Charmante, Oct. 30, 1722 (p. 386). See Commonplace Book, pp. 88–89, V.H.S.
6. To Charmante, Nov. 9 (printed "Nov. 7"), 1722 (pp. 387–88). See Commonplace Book, 90–91, V.H.S.
7. To John Custis, July 29, 1723 (p. 389). See Custis Papers, V.H.S. (this is a copy of a fragment of the next letter).

VMHB, XXXVI (1928):

8. To John Custis, July 29, 1723 (pp. 36–38). See Custis Papers, V.H.S.
9. To Sir Jacob Acworth, fragment, July 1728 (p. 39). See Letterbook, 1728, V.H.S., p. 21.
10. To Mr. John Warner (printed "Warren"), July 15, 1728 (pp. 39–40). See Letterbook, 1728, V.H.S., p. 21.

11. To Mr. Richard Fitzwilliam, July 16, 1728 (pp. 40–41). See Letterbook, 1728, V.H.S., p. 22.
12. To Edward Randolph, July 27, 1728 (pp. 41–42). See Letterbook, 1728, V.H.S., p. 22.
13. To Mr. Micajah Perry, July 28, 1728 (pp. 42–43). See Letterbook, 1728, V.H.S., p. 23.
14. To Cousin (Mrs.) Taylor, July 28, 1728 (pp. 43–44). See Letterbook, 1728, V.H.S., pp. 23–24.
15. To Colonel Martin Bladen, June 1729 (printed "July 1728") (pp. 113–16). See Letterbook, 1729, V.H.S., pp. 18–21.
16. To . . . , June 25, 1729 (printed "to Mr. Warner" "July 1729") (pp. 116–17). See Letterbook, 1729, V.H.S., p. 29.
17. To Major William Mayo, Aug. 26, 1731 (pp. 117–18). See Other Byrd Correspondence, V.H.S., and *Virginia Historical Register*, IV (1851), 83–84.
18. To Mr. Christopher Smith, Aug. 23, 1735 (pp. 118–19). See *VMHB*, IX (1901), 118–19.
19. To Mrs. Otway, Oct. 2, 1735 (pp. 119–21). See *VMHB*, IX (1901), pp. 121–24.
20. To Mr. Beckford, Dec. 6, 1735 (pp. 121–23). See *VMHB*, IX (1902), 234–35.
21. To Gov. Johnston of N. Carolina, Dec. 2 (printed "Dec. 21"), 1735 (pp. 209–11). See *VMHB*, IX (1902), 232–34.
22. To Colonel Spotswood, Dec. 22 (printed "Dec. 30"), 1735 (pp. 211–12). See *VMHB*, IX (1902), 235–37.
23. To Cousin . . . , (printed "Cousin Taylor") Feb. 25, 1735/36 (p. 212). See Letterbook, 1735–1736, V.H.S., p. 36, and *VMHB*, IX (1902), 246–47.
24. To Francis Otway, fragment, 1736 (pp. 212–13). See *VMHB*, IX (1902), 249–51.
25. To Mr. Christopher Smith, March 20, 1736/37 (pp. 213–14). See Letterbook, 1736–1737, V.H.S., pp. 9–10.
26. To Cousin Taylor, March 20, 1736/37 (p. 214). Only a small part of the letter was published, certainly because of some coarse remarks made by Byrd. See Letterbook, 1736–1737, V.H.S., pp. 10–12.
27. To Mr. John Hanbury, March 20, 1736/37 (pp. 214–15). See Letterbook, 1736–1737, V.H.S., p. 10.
28. To Sister Otway. June 30, 1736 (pp. 215–16). This letter was in missing pages of the 1736–1737 letterbook.
29. "To Lord Egmont, July, 1736" (pp. 216–217). See "To Sir Charles Wager (?)," July 2, 1736, *VMHB*, IX (Oct. 1901), 124–25, and "To Mr. Mark Catesby," July 1737, Letterbook, 1736–1737, V.H.S., p. 31.
30. To Cousin Taylor, July 2, 1736 (pp. 217–19). In missing pages of the 1736–1737 letterbook.
31. To Lord Egmont, July 12, 1736 (pp. 219–22). See *American Historical Review*, I (1895), 88–90.

32. To Mr. Ochs, July 1736 (extract) (p. 353). In missing pages of the 1736–1737 letterbook.

33. To Mr. Peter Collinson, July 18, 1736 (pp. 353–55). In missing pages of the 1736–1737 letterbook.

34. To the Governor of Bermudas (Alured Popple), Jan. 21, 1739/40 (pp. 355–56). See Letterbook, 1739–1740, V.H.S., p. 12.

35. To Sir Robert Walpole, Aug. 20, 1739 (pp. 356–58). See Letterbook, 1739–1740, V.H.S., pp. 1–2.

36. To Sir Charles Wager, May 4, 1737 (pp. 358–59). See Letterbook, 1736–1737, V.H.S., p. 14.

37. To Mr. Campbell of Norfolk, Nov. 3, 1739 (pp. 359–60). See Letterbook, 1739–1740, V.H.S., pp. 9–10.

38. To Mr. Andrews of Rotterdam, Nov. 10, 1739 (pp. 360–61). See Letterbook, 1739–1740, V.H.S., pp. 10–12, and *American Historical Review*, I (1895), 90. In both magazines, only a short passage of the letter was printed (ten to fifteen lines).

39. To Dr. Zwiffler, Dec. 20, 1740 (pp. 361–62). See Letterbook, 1740–1741, V.H.S., pp. 16–18.

VMHB, XXXVII (1929):

40. To Major Otway, Feb. 10, 1740/41 (pp. 28–32). See Letterbook, 1740–1741, V.H.S., pp. 18–21.

41. To Frankie Otway, Feb. 16, 1740/41 (pp. 32–33). See Letterbook, 1740–1741, V.H.S., pp. 21–22.

42. To Major Otway, April 5, 1740 (p. 101). In missing pages of the 1740–1741 letterbook.

43. To the Governor (Sir William Gooch), April 1, 1740 (pp. 101–2). See Letterbook, 1739–1740, V.H.S., pp. 15–16.

44. To Sir Charles Wager, May 26, 1740 (pp. 102–4). See Letterbook, 1739–1740, V.H.S., pp. 21–22.

45. To Mr. Southwell, May 1740 (p. 104). In missing parts of the 1740–1741 letterbook.

46. "To . . . , June 10, 1740" (pp. 104–5). Part of a letter to Sir Hans Sloane, April 10, 1741. See *William and Mary College Quarterly*, 2d ser., I (July 1921), 199–200.

47. To Mrs. Sherrard, Sept. 1 (printed "Sept. 7"), 1740 (p. 105). See Letterbook, 1739–1740, V.H.S., pp. 33–34.

48. To Sir Charles Wager (fragment), Sept. 1740 (pp. 105–6). See Letterbook, 1739–1740, V.H.S., renumbered pp. 25–26.

49. To Mrs. Otway, Sept. 20 (printed "Nov. 18"), 1740 (pp. 106–8). See Letterbook, 1740–1741, V.H.S., pp. 8–10.

50. To Mr. Proctor, Nov. 18, 1740 (pp. 108–9). See Letterbook, 1740–1741, V.H.S., pp. 11–12, and Bassett, pp. 399–400.

51. "To Sir Charles Wager, April 12, 1741" (p. 109). For the first four lines, cf. a letter to Peter Collinson, July 5, 1737 (Letterbook, 1736–1737, V.H.S., pp. 35–37). The rest is part of a letter to Sir Hans Sloane, April 10, 1741 (cf. no. 46 above).

52. "A Scolding Letter to an English Merchant," July 10, 1740 (p. 110). See Letterbook, 1739–1740, V.H.S., pp. 26–28.

"Letters from Old Trunks," contributed by Mrs. Tazewell Ellett, *VMHB*, XLVI (1938), 242–44, contains two letters addressed by Byrd to Governor Gooch, Sept. 1, 1728, and to Mr. Spencer, May 28, 1729. These are in the William Byrd II Letterbook, 1728–1729, in Colonial Williamsburg, the only two in it to have been published.

The Byrd Title Book, which was published in *VMHB*, XLVII–L (1939–42), contains besides the deeds concerning the Byrd plantations many important family papers, among them the wills of Colonel Stegge (XLVIII, 31–34) and of William Byrd I (XLVIII, 331–34), and the agreement between William Byrd II and his brother-in-law John Custis concerning the Parke succession, written on April 25, 1712 (L, 240–41).

Byrd's correspondence with the Orrery family was partly printed in *The Orrery Papers*, ed. Countess of Cork and Orrery (London, 1903). Volume I includes eight letters written by Byrd, but there are six more among the Orrery Manuscripts in Harvard College Library, in Letters upon Various Occasions to and from John Earl of Orrery, His Family and His Friends, I, in 2 parts. The letters published in 1903 were reprinted in *VMHB*, XXXII (1924), 25–36. A complete list may be useful:

To Charles Earl of Orrery, March 6 (printed "March 16"), 1719/20, pt. 1, pp. 3–6 (*Orrery Papers*, I, 30–32).

To Charles Earl of Orrery, July 5, 1726, pt. 1, pp. 23–27 (*Orrery Papers*, I, 59–62).

To Charles Earl of Orrery, Feb. 2, 1726/27, pt. 1, pp. 36–41.

To John Lord Boyle, Feb. 2, 1726/27, pt. 1, pp. 42–45 (*Orrery Papers*, I, 49–52).

To Charles Earl of Orrery, June 29, 1727, pt. 1, 53–58.

To Charles Earl of Orrery, Feb. 5 (printed "Feb. 3"), 1727/28, pt. 1, pp. 70–73 (*Orrery Papers*, I, 57–59).

To John Lord Boyle, Feb. 12, 1727/28, pt. 1, pp. 73–76 (*Orrery Papers*, I, 63–65).

To Charles Earl of Orrery, May 27, 1728, pt. 1, pp. 83–87 (*Orrery Papers*, I, 79–81).

To John Lord Boyle, May 20, 1729, pt. 1, pp. 119–22.

To Charles Earl of Orrery, May 26, 1729, pt. 1, pp. 122–26.

To Charles Earl of Orrery, June 18, 1730, pt. 1, pp. 168–69.

To John Lord Boyle, July 28 (or 20?), 1730, pt. 1, pp. 172–74.

To John Lord Boyle, June 15, 1731, pt. 1, pp. 209–12 (*Orrery Papers*, I, 88–90, only dated June 1731).

To John Earl of Orrery, July 20, 1732, pt. 2, pp. 50–53 (*Orrery Papers*, I, 117–18).

Other letters appeared in the *William and Mary College Quarterly* in the 1920's:

"Letters of William Byrd II and Sir Hans Sloane Relative to Plants and

Minerals in Virginia (Originals in the British Museum among the Sloane Manuscripts)," *WMCQ*, 2d ser., I (1921), 186–200. This contains seven letters written between 1706 and 1741. The sixth, owing to a misprint, is dated 1737 instead of Aug. 20, 1738.

"Letters of John Clayton, John Bartram, Peter Collinson, William Byrd and Isham Randolph (from the library of the Pennsylvania Historical Society)," *WMCQ*, 2d ser., VI (1926), 303–25. This contains two letters of Byrd to Bartram, dated Nov. 30, 1738, and March 23, 1738/39.

Some of Byrd's letters to his brother-in-law John Custis were published in George Washington Parke Custis, *Recollections and Private Memoirs of Washington*, ed. Benson J. Lossing (New York, 1860). Besides five of these, written between 1709 and 1716, it includes an undated letter "to Irene" and another (Veramour to Fidelia, Feb. 4, 1705/6) erroneously attributed to Byrd's brother-in-law.

The Official Letters of Alexander Spotswood, ed. R. A. Brock, 2 vols. (Richmond, 1882–85), includes "A Copy of the Receiver General's Reasons in Writing to the Lieut. Governor against the 6th Article of his New Scheme for the Better Collecting the Quit-Rents" (II, 83–84).

An Essay upon the Government of the English Plantations on the Continent of America (1701), ed. Louis B. Wright (San Marino, Calif., 1945), contains two memoranda by William Byrd II in the appendix: Representation of Mr. Byrd concerning Proprietary Governments (1699), pp. 58–63; Proposals humbly submitted to the Lords of the Council of Trade and Plantations for sending the French Protestants to Virginia (1698), pp. 64–66.

Many letters have not yet been published. There may still be a few tucked away carefully from public view by some descendant or lying forgotten in some old trunk; others are in the letterbooks at the Virginia Historical Society (purchased in March 1964) or at Colonial Williamsburg. These are nineteenth-century transcripts, which in many places were expurgated and modified before a selection of them was published in 1901–2 and in 1927–29. The 1728 and 1729 letterbooks are divided into several portions owned by the Virginia Historical Society and Colonial Williamsburg. In addition, the Virginia Historical Society owns portions of other letterbooks for 1735–36, 1736–37, 1739–40, and 1740–41. And the Commonplace Book they bought in December 1964 also contains copies of the last five letters to "Charmante."

III

BOOKS AND ARTICLES ON WILLIAM BYRD

There is only one full-length biography of William Byrd II, Richmond Croom Beatty, *William Byrd of Westover* (Cambridge, Mass., 1932).

A recent study is Henry A. Robertson, Jr., "A Critical Analysis of

William Byrd II and His Literary Technique in *The History of the Dividing Line* and *The Secret History of the Line*" (doct. diss., University of Delaware, 1966).

Besides the various introductions to editions of Byrd's works by Bassett, Boyd, Wright, and Miss Woodfin, see Thomas J. Wertenbaker's biographical sketch in the *Dictionary of American Biography*; Philip A. Bruce, *The Virginia Plutarch* (Chapel Hill, N.C., 1929); Ella Lonn, *The Colonial Agents of the Southern Colonies* (Chapel Hill, N.C., 1945); and more particularly Louis B. Wright, *The First Gentlemen of Virginia* (San Marino, Calif., 1940), chap. XI, and Jay B. Hubbell, *The South in American Literature, 1607–1900* (Durham, N.C., 1954), pp. 40–51.

Adams, P. G. "The Real Author of William Byrd's *Natural History of Virginia*," *American Literature*, XXVIII (May 1956), 211–20.

Campbell, Charles. "The Westover Library," *Virginia Historical Register*, IV (April 1851), 87–90 (with a communication from Lyman C. Draper).

Cannon, Carl L. "William Byrd II of Westover," *Colophon*, new ser., III, (Spring 1938), 291–302.

Chapin, J. R. "The Westover Estate," *Harper's Magazine*, XLII (May 1871), 801–10.

Fishwick, Marshall. "The Pepys of the Old Dominion," *American Heritage*, XI (Dec. 1959), 5–7 and 117–19.

Gummere, Richard M. "Byrd and Sewall: Two Colonial Classicists," *Transactions of the Colonial Society of Massachusetts*, XLII (1964), 156–73.

Harrison, Constance C. "Colonel William Byrd of Westover, Virginia," *Century Magazine*, XLII (June 1891), 163–78.

Holladay, Alexander Quarles. "Social Conditions in Colonial North Carolina," *North Carolina Booklet*, II (Feb. 1904) (written in refutation of certain criticisms of the people of North Carolina found in Byrd's *History of the Dividing Line*).

Houlette, W. D. "The Byrd Library," *Tyler's Quarterly Historical and Genealogical Magazine*, XVI (Oct. 1934), 100–109.

Houlette, W. D. "William Byrd and Some of His American Descendants," *Tyler's Quarterly Historical and Genealogical Magazine*, XVI (Oct. 1934), 93–100.

Leary, Lewis. "A William Byrd Poem," *William and Mary Quarterly*, 3d ser., IV (July 1947), 356.

Lyle, G. R. "William Byrd, Book Collector," *American Book Collector*, V (May–June 1934), 163–65, and (July 1934), 208–11.

Marambaud, Pierre. "Un grand planteur virginien au XVIIIᵉ siècle: William Byrd de Westover," *Annales de la faculté des lettres d'Aix-en-Provence*, XXXVIII, no. 2 (1964), 367–79.

Masterton, J. R. "William Byrd in Lubberland," *American Literature*, IX (May 1937), 153–70.

Murdock, Kenneth B. "William Byrd and the Virginian Author of *The*

Wanderer," *Harvard Studies and Notes in Philology and Literature*, XVII (1935), 129–36.

Parks, Edd W. "William Byrd as a Man of Letters," *Georgia Review*, XV (Summer 1960), 172–76.

Riback, W. H. "Some Words in Byrd's Histories," *American Speech*, XV (Oct. 1940), 331–32.

Sale, Marian M. "Westover's Colonel Byrd," *Commonwealth*, XXX (Jan. 1963), 17–21 and 47.

Sioussat, St. George Leakin. "The Philosophical Transactions of the Royal Society in the Libraries of William Byrd of Westover, Benjamin Franklin and the American Philosophical Society," *American Philosophical Society Library Bulletin* (1949), 99–113.

Troubetzkoy, Ulrich. "Enough to Keep a Byrd Alive," *Virginia Cavalcade*, XI (Autumn 1961), 36–41.

Weathers, Willie T. "William Byrd, Satirist," *William and Mary Quarterly*, 3d ser., IV (Jan. 1947), 27–41.

Williams, Lloyd Haynes. "The Tragic Shipwreck of the Protestant Switzers," *William and Mary Quarterly*, 3d ser., IX (Oct. 1952), 539–42.

Wilson, J. S. "William Byrd and His Secret Diary," *William and Mary College Quarterly*, 2d ser., XXII (April 1942), 165–74.

Wolf, Edwin. "The Dispersal of the Library of William Byrd of Westover," *Proceedings of the American Antiquarian Society*, LXVIII (April 1958), 19–106.

Woodfin, Maude H. "The Missing Pages of William Byrd's Secret History of the Line," *William and Mary Quarterly*, 3d ser., II (Jan. 1945), 63–70.

———. "Thomas Jefferson and William Byrd's Manuscript Histories of the Dividing Line," *William and Mary Quarterly*, 3d ser., I (Oct. 1944), 363–73.

———. "William Byrd and the Royal Society," *Virginia Magazine of History and Biography*, XL (Jan. 1932), 23–35, and (April 1932), 111–24.

Wright, Louis B. "A Shorthand Diary of William Byrd of Westover," *Huntington Library Quarterly*, II (July 1939), 489–96.

———. "William Byrd, Citizen of the Enlightenment," in Leon Howard and Louis B. Wright, *Anglo-American Cultural Relations in the 17th and 18th centuries: Papers Delivered at the Fourth Clark Library Seminar, 31 May 1958*. Los Angeles, 1959.

———. "William Byrd's Defense of Sir Edmund Andros," *William and Mary Quarterly*, 3d ser., II (Jan. 1945), 47–62.

———. "William Byrd's Opposition to Governor Francis Nicholson," *Journal of Southern History*, XI (1945), 68–79.

Wright, Louis B., and Marion Tinling. "William Byrd of Westover, an American Pepys," *South Atlantic Quarterly*, XXXIX (July 1940), 259–74.

Index

Addison, Joseph, 94, 95, 105, 108, 126, 128, 129, 204
Admiralty, Court of, 220
Agents, Virginia, in London, 212–13
American Philosophical Society, 91
Anderson, Rev. Charles, 165, 183, 186
Andrews, Mr. (of Rotterdam), 170n, 285
Andros, Gov. Sir Edmund, 19
Anne (queen of England), 20, 26, 209
Another Secret Diary, 92, 106, 113, 114, 281
Appomatox River, Byrd's land near the falls of the, 113, 161, 164, 165, 226
Argyle, John Campbell, 2nd Duke of, 42, 47, 94, 213, 215
Ashmole, Elias, 86

Bacon, Nathaniel, 15
Bartram, John, 54, 90, 158, 287
Bassett, John Spencer, 5n, 16, 32, 43, 273, 280, 282, 285
Bassett, Col. William, 186
Bears, 81, 164
Bearskin (Indian guide), 239–42
Beatty, Richmond Croom, 28, 40, 122, 173, 281
Beavers, 80–81
Beckford, Peter, 172n, 284
Berkeley, Gov. Sir William, 31, 172n
Betting, 199
Beverley, Robert, 6, 21, 25, 80, 111, 128, 141, 158, 159, 169, 174, 189, 212, 230, 251, 254–55
Blackamore, Rev. Arthur, 197, 223
Bladen, Col. Martin, 103, 284
Blair, Rev. James (Commissary), 9n, 19, 20, 21, 26, 56, 61, 111, 191, 192, 197, 214, 218, 221, 222, 242
Blair, Sarah Harrison, 197
Blakiston, Col. Nathaniel, 26, 29, 40, 41

Bland, Col. Richard (the elder), 29, 113
Bland, Richard (the younger), 268n
Blathwait, William, 38
Bluestone Castle (Byrd's plantation), 119, 229
Board of Trade, 10–11, 21, 25, 26, 32, 37–41, 120, 137, 169, 212–13, 227, 280n
Bolling, Col. Robert, 228
Boone, Daniel, 238
Boorstin, Daniel J., 147
Boswell, James, 126–27, 134, 274
Boyle, Charles. *See* Orrery
Boyle, Lord John (later 4th Earl of Orrery), 147, 216–17, 286
Boyle, Robert, 79, 242
Brayne, John (Byrd's nephew), 43, 47
Brayne, Susan (Byrd's sister). *See* Byrd, Susan
Brayne, Susan (Byrd's niece), 179n
Brayne, William (Byrd's nephew), 223
Bridges, Charles, 68–69
Burkland (plantation), 165, 166
Burnaby, Rev. Andrew, 189
Burwell, Major Lewis, 155
Burwell, Mrs., 64
Butler, Samuel, 87
Byrd, Anne (Byrd's daughter), 47, 56, 279
Byrd, Evelyn (Byrd's daughter), 28, 34, 36, 45, 47, 56, 65, 262–64, 279
Byrd, Jane (Byrd's daughter), 47, 279
Byrd, Lucy Parke (Byrd's first wife), 26, 27, 28, 34, 178–79, 184, 191, 195, 279
Byrd, Maria Taylor (Byrd's second wife), 45–46, 47, 153, 184, 263, 279
Byrd, Maria (Byrd's daughter), 47, 56, 279
Byrd, Mary Horsemanden (Byrd's mother), 15, 25, 279

Byrd, Mary (Mrs. James Duke, Byrd's sister), 25, 279

Byrd, Parke (Byrd's son), 28, 61–62, 279

Byrd, Susan (Mrs. Brayne, Byrd's sister), 25, 279

Byrd, Ursula (Mrs. Beverley, Byrd's sister), 25, 279

Byrd, Wilhelmina (Byrd's daughter), 28, 34, 36, 47, 56, 279

Byrd, William I (Byrd's father), 15–17, 21, 25, 158, 189, 279

Byrd, William II

Childhood and education, 15–19; first career in Virginia and in England, 19–22; fashionable life in London, 22–24; inherits Westover and his father's offices, 25–26; marries Lucy Parke, 26–28; Colonel Parke's heritage, 28–29; political activity in Virginia in the early days of Spotswood's administration, 29–32; preparations for departure to England, 32–33; the first Mrs. Byrd's death, 34; courtship of Mary Smith ("Sabina"), 34–36; writes a "state of his circumstances," 35; fashionable life in London, 36–37; fight against Spotswood from England, 37–42; reconciliation in Virginia, 42–43; last trip to England and second marriage, with Maria Taylor, 44–46; back in Virginia, 47; the Dividing Line expedition, 47–49; land-hunger, 49–51; the Northern Neck commission, 51–52; rebuilding Westover and trying to get into office, 52–53; efforts to attract settlers, 53–55; the last years, 55–57

"The well-bred gentleman," 58–61; Byrd's religion, 61–63; his belief in the significance of dreams (science and superstition), 64–65; his susceptibility to women, 65–68; solitude and books, 68; the connoisseur, 68–69

Byrd's reluctance to publish his writings, 73–75; correspondence with Sir Hans Sloane, 76–78; Byrd and the Royal Society, 78–80; his interest in natural history, 80–83; and in medicine, 83–87; his pamphlet on the plague, 87–89; the influence of the Royal Society, 90–91; Byrd's fashionable verse, 92–93; character writing and "pictures," 94–97; "The Female Creed," 97–98; the Commonplace Book, 98; Byrd's love letters, 98–100; other letters in the North Carolina notebooks, 100–102; letters unpublished in book form, 102–5; Byrd's secret diaries, 106–8; self-expression in the diaries, 108–11; their historical value, 111–12; evolution in the diaries, 112–14; Byrd and Pepys, 114–16; "A Progress to the Mines," 117–19; *Journey to the Land of Eden*, 119–20; *History of the Dividing Line* and its former drafts, 120; cuts and omissions, 121–22; patriotic additions, 122–24; character sketches and anecdotes, 124–25; hits at the female sex, 126–27; Byrd's style, 127–29; an amateur, more gentleman-planter than writer, 130–33; literary achievement, 133–36; social documents, 136–37

A cross section of colonial society, 141–43; Westover, 143–47; Byrd's ordinary days, 148–51; Sundays at Westover, 151–54; tobacco culture and trade, 154–58; fields, orchards, and gardens, 158–59; land buying and selling, 159–62; daily incidents, 162–64; overseeing the overseers, 164–66; white labor, 166–69; the slave trade, 169–71; Byrd's opinion on slavery, 171–74; a comparison with Jefferson's position, 174–76; Indian slaves, 176–77; conduct and punishment of servants, 177–80; efforts at a more diversified economy, 180–81

Hospitality to travelers and yearning for news, 182–85; mutual visits among planters, 185–86; Spotswood's visit at Westover, 186–89; towns, 187–89; Williamsburg, 189–90; its "season," 190–95; effort at refinement and relations between the sexes, 195–96; drinking, 196–97; taverns and ordinaries, 197–98; gambling, 198; bet-

Byrd, William II (*cont.*)
  ting and horse-racing, 199–200; a new
  society in the making, 200; cultural
  life, 200–202; books, 202–3; printing,
  203–4
    Quasi-hereditary offices, 205–6;
  elections, 207–8; attendance at sessions, 208; conflicts between the
  Council and Governor Spotswood,
  208–12; Byrd as colonial agent for
  Virginia, 212–13; his reconciliation
  with Spotswood, 213–14; further relations between them, 214–15; Byrd's
  opinion on governors, 216–17; independent spirit of the colonies, 217;
  sessions of the General Court, 217–
  20; the Court of Admiralty and pirates, 220–21; the board of William
  and Mary College, 221–23; colonel of
  the militia, 223–25; rumored French
  invasion, 225–26; the role of the
  militia, 226–27
    The frontier, 228; farming on the
  frontier, 228–30; settlers on the Carolina border, 230–31; woodsmen, 231–
  33; food in the back woods, 233–35;
  Indian trade, 235–39; the religion of
  Indians, 239–42; converting Indians,
  242–44; the dwindling of Indian
  tribes, 244–46; Indian wars, 246–49;
  a visit to an Indian town, 249–51;
  Indian women, 250–52; Byrd's judgment on Indians, 252–55
    Byrd's Virginia, 256–57; the Vir-
  ginian legends, 258–62; the legend in
  Marion Harland's novel on the Byrd
  family, 262–64; origins of the plantation legend, 264–66; the value of
  Byrd's picture of Virginia, 266–69
    Conclusion on Byrd and his works,
  273–76
Byrd, William III (Byrd's son), 47,
  262, 268, 279
Byrd Park (plantation), 165

Campbell, Mr. (of Norfolk), 54, 285
Carter, Anne (Col. Carter's daughter),
  194
Carter, Charles (Col. Carter's son), 56,
  89n, 279

Carter, Elizabeth Hill (John Carter's
  daughter), 262, 279
Carter, John (Col. Carter's son), 152
Carter, Landon (Col. Carter's son), 56,
  112, 163n, 175, 279
Carter, Col. Robert ("King"), 5, 56,
  150n, 157, 191, 198, 202, 203
Carter, Robert (Col. Carter's grand-
  son), 112, 175
Cary, Henry, 190
Catawba Indians, 16, 235, 236, 237, 238,
  245, 246
Catesby, Mark, 74n, 78, 283, 284
"Charmante" (Lady Elizabeth Lee),
  44–45, 283, 287
Cherokee Indians, 16, 235, 238, 239
Chesapeake Bay, 4, 156, 178, 183, 184
Cheyne, Dr. George, 79–80
Chiswell, Charles, 50
Chiswell, Mrs., 67
Church of England, 9, 61, 151
Church of Virginia, 151–52
Cibber, Colley, 93
Clarke, Dr. Samuel, 63, 202, 241
Clergy, 151–52
Colden, Gov. Cadwallader, 90–91
Cocke, Dr. William, 78n, 85, 186n,
  193n, 196
Collier, Jeremy, 134, 202
Collinson, Peter, 71, 73, 74, 90, 120, 158,
  159, 285, 287
Colonial Williamsburg, 3, 267
Commissary. *See* Blair, Rev. James
Commonplace Book, Byrd's, 63n, 93n,
  98, 141n, 287
Congreve, William, 18, 275
Cornpone, 167
Council of Virginia, 10–11, 20, 25, 26,
  30, 31, 32, 39–41, 47, 56, 160, 191,
  197, 205–6, 208–16
Court. *See* Admiralty, Court of; Gen-
  eral Court of Virginia
Court of Oyer and Terminer, 32, 39,
  40, 41, 212–13, 219
Cromwell, Lady Elizabeth. *See*
  "Facetia"
Culpeper, Gov. Lord Thomas, 16, 172
Currituck Inlet, 48, 228
Custis, Col. John (father of Byrd's
  brother-in-law), 153, 178

Custis, Col. John (Byrd's brother-in-law), 27, 28, 34, 39, 115, 211, 283, 286, 287
Custis, Frances Parke (Byrd's sister-in-law), 86, 196

Dan River, 49, 51, 55
Dancing, 6, 153, 185, 191, 193–95
Dandridge, William, 48, 121
Defoe, Daniel, 168, 258
Dering, William, 69, 185n
Diet: rules of, 60–61; of slaves, 167
Digges, Col. Cole, 214
Digges, Col. Dudley, 153, 186, 191
Dismal Swamp, 48, 121, 124, 127, 179, 263, 281
Dividing Line, 47–49, 51, 102–3, 228, 229, 231, 234, 235, 249. See also *History of the Dividing Line*
Dreams, 64–65
Drinking, 7, 60, 153, 188, 192, 196–97
Drysdale, Gov. Hugh, 44, 47
Duke, James (Byrd's brother-in-law), 25, 191, 279
Duke, Mrs. Mary. *See* Byrd, Mary
Dunn, Mr. (Parson), 185
Durand of Dauphiné, 5n, 7n, 182, 185, 230n

Eden, Gov. Charles, 49, 258
Edenton, N.C., 126
Education, 7–9, 221–23
Edwards, Jonathan, 109
Egmont, John Percival, Earl of, 42–43, 53–54, 79, 171, 214, 283, 284
Elections, 10, 188, 205, 207–8
Epidemics, 150, 152
Eppes, Col. Frank, 225, 226
Eppes, Col. Littlebury, 207, 224, 225
"Erranti" (Evelyn Byrd's lover), 45, 262–64
Evelyn, John, 62n, 110, 115

"Facetia" (Lady Elizabeth Cromwell), 22–24, 281
Fairfax, Thomas, 6th Lord, 51–52
Falling Creek (plantation), 50n, 162, 164–65, 166, 187
Falls, The (plantation), 165, 166, 167
Felsted Grammar School, 17
"Female Creed," 97–98, 119

"Fidelia." *See* Byrd, Lucy Parke
Fielding, Henry, 97, 105n
Filmer, Mary Horsemanden. *See* Byrd, Mary Horsemanden
Finch, Anne, later Lady Winchelsea, 93
Fire-hunting, 234–35
Fithian, Philip Vickers, 111–12
Fitzwilliam, Col. Richard ("Firebrand"), 48–49, 120–21, 284
Five Nations, 20, 91, 210, 247n
Fontaine, John, 197
Fontaine, Rev. Peter, 173, 262, 263
France: rumored invasion of Virginia by, 225–26; Indian policy of, 243–44. *See also* Manakin Town
Franklin, Benjamin, 91, 275
Fredericksville, Va., 50

Gambling, 6–7, 198
Gardens, 145, 158–59
Garth, Sir Samuel, 79, 202
Gay, John: *The Beggar's Opera*, 68, 202, 262
General Assembly of Virginia, 20, 32, 40, 55, 161, 208. *See also* Council of Virginia; House of Burgesses
General Court of Virginia, 32, 206, 217–21
George I (king of England), 37, 263
George II (king of England), 192
Georgia, 171, 238
Germanna, Va., 50, 262
Ginseng, 84–85, 132
Glasscock, Christopher, 17
Gooch, Gov. William, 56, 68, 157, 172n, 174, 192, 194, 216, 285, 286
Governors, 97, 216–17
Governor's Palace (Williamsburg), 190, 219
Graffenried(t), Christopher, Baron de, 29, 245
Graffenried, Christopher (son of the baron), 193–94
Gray, Thomas, 127
Green Spring, 31n, 152, 190, 199
Gripes, 77, 85, 240
Grove, William Hugh, 148n

Harland, Marion (Mrs. Terhune), 106n, 262–64
Harrison, Benjamin, 106n, 195n

Harrison, Elizabeth Burwell, 195, 196
Harrison, Major Nathaniel, 29, 60
Hemp, 82, 180, 230, 262
Henrico County, 15, 19, 161, 223, 224
Hill, Col. Edward, 152, 164, 183, 184, 195, 207
History of the Dividing Line, 117, 120–29, 136, 280, 281
Holland, 17
Horsemanden, Daniel (Byrd's uncle), 17
Horsemanden, Daniel (Byrd's cousin), 67
Horsemanden, Mary. *See* Byrd, Mary Horsemanden
Horsemanden, Warham (Byrd's grandfather), 15
Horses, 6, 199–200, 231–32, 252
Hospitality, 60, 152–54, 182–83, 185–86
House of Burgesses, 19, 32, 40, 44, 161, 197, 210–11; elections, 10, 188, 205, 207–8; Byrd's judgment on, 208; attendance, 208
Hubbell, Jay B., 136
Huguenots. *See* Manakin Town
Hunter, Gov. Col. Robert, 183
Hunting, 6, 234–35

"Inamorato L'Oiseaux" (*sic*), 22, 24, 45, 58, 61, 65
Indians: wars with, 29–30, 244–46; women, 126; slaves, 176–77; religion, 239–42; conversion of, 242–44; dwindling number of, 246; tribal wars, 246–48; scalping, 248; contempt of pain and death, 249; fort, 249; wigwams, 249–50; dances, 239, 250; dress, 250; men and women, 251–52; swimming, 253; fishing, 253; weapons, 253–54. *See also* names of tribes
Indian trade, 33, 38, 234–39; trading path, 16, 234, 237
Inns of Court, 17–18
Ipecac(uana), 77, 78, 84

Jamaica, 55, 78, 173
Jamestown, 188, 225
Jefferson, Thomas, 11, 135, 141–43, 174–76, 181, 197, 223, 266
Jenings, Col. Edmund, 170, 191n, 192, 223

Jenner, Samuel, 53, 55, 281
Jesuits' bark, 84
Johnson, Samuel, 259
Jones, Rev. Hugh, 111, 122, 128, 130, 193, 199, 222, 223
Journey to the Land of Eden, 117, 119–20, 280, 281

Kennedy, John Pendleton, 265
Kensington (plantation), 165
Knight, Sarah Kemble, 136

Land: buying and selling, 159–62; westward movement, 229–30
Land of Eden, 49, 51, 53, 55, 160, 161, 231, 249. See also *Journey to the Land of Eden*; Roanoke
Law books, 203
Lawson, John, 29, 53n, 245, 254, 281
Lawson, Sir Wilfrid, 78
Lee, Lady Elizabeth. *See* "Charmante"
Le Fevre, Rev. Tanaquil, 223
Library, Byrd's, 79, 87, 94, 107, 128, 131, 148, 149, 201–3, 288, 289
Locke, John, 203, 206, 218
London, Bishop of, 9, 19, 83, 151, 221
London Diary, 67, 106, 109, 113, 114–15, 134, 274, 281–82
"Lubberland" (Carolina), 122. *See also* Carolina
"Lucretia," 100–101, 104
Ludwell, Col. Philip, II, 30–31, 38, 40, 152, 190, 199, 206n, 214, 226, 282
Luttrell, Narcissus, 22
Lynde, Benjamin, 18, 123n

Manakin Town, 188–89
Manners, 185–86, 194–96
Marlborough, Duke of, 26, 29
Marot, Jean, 198
Mason, George, 197
Mather, Cotton, 241, 254
Maynard, Lieutenant, 220n, 262, 263
Mayo, Major William, 51, 284
Meals, 148n, 185, 187
Medicine, 77, 83–89, 132–33, 203
Meherrin River, 48, 49
Michel, Francis Louis, 146n, 189, 230, 241n
"Mignonet," 45, 94

Militia, 10, 223–27
Mill (at Falling Creek), 164, 187, 199
Mitchell, Margaret, 3
Moniseep Ford, 229, 235
Muskrat, dissection of, 78

Navigation Acts, 5
Negroes. *See* Servants; Slavery; Slaves
New England, 123, 196, 202, 217, 254, 260
Newton, Sir Isaac, 76, 78, 79
Nicholson, Gov. Sir Francis, 19, 20, 21, 160
Norfolk, Va., 187–88
North Carolina, 11, 29, 47–49, 122–23, 160, 179, 200, 210, 217, 230–31, 237, 238, 244, 246
Northern Neck, 51, 103
Nottoway Indians, 227, 239n, 246, 249, 251

Ochs, Mr. Johann, 53, 173n, 285
Oldmixon, John, 18, 111
Opera, 68, 95–96
Opossum, 81–82
Orkney, George Hamilton, 1st Earl of, 29, 41–42, 216
Orrery, Charles Boyle, 3rd Earl of, 19, 43n, 47, 58, 79, 146–47, 213, 220, 241, 286
Otway, Col. Francis (Byrd's brother-in-law), 47n, 85, 279, 284, 285
Otway, Mrs. (Byrd's sister-in-law), 103, 184n, 279, 284, 285
Overseers, 119, 150, 154, 166

Page, Thomas Nelson, 3, 256, 261, 264, 265
Pamunkey Indians, 239
Parke, Col. Daniel (Byrd's father-in-law), 26–27, 28, 33
Parke, Lucy. *See* Byrd, Lucy Parke
Parks, William, 83, 204
Paulding, James Kirke, 129, 260
Penn, William, 123, 262
Pepys, Samuel, 65, 70, 107, 108, 110, 111, 114–16, 127, 134, 136, 137, 274, 276
Perry, Micajah, 26, 28, 36, 46, 52, 54, 113, 161, 208, 280n, 284

Perry and Lane, 17
Peterborough. *See* "Erranti"
Pierson, Widow, 37
Pioneers, 228–30
Pirates, 19n, 220–21
Plague, 44, 74, 87–89
Plantations: size of, 5n, 18n; Byrd's, 148, 154, 164–66, 180–81
Pope, Alexander, 22
Prayers, 61, 148, 150
Prerogative, royal, 31–32, 209–10
Printing, in Virginia, 132, 203–4
Proctor, William, 167, 203, 285
Progress to the Mines, 117–19

Quakers, 123
Quitrents, 16–17, 21, 25, 30–31, 37, 148

Races, 6, 199–200
Radcliffe, Dr. John, 79, 132
Randolph, Sir John, 103, 194, 222
Randolph, John (of Roanoke), 264
Randolph, Thomas, 117, 225
Randolph, Col. William, 163, 181n, 210, 222, 224
Randolph, Will, 183, 195
Rattlesnake root, 77, 83, 132
Reading, Byrd's, 131, 133–34, 148, 149, 150, 201–2
Religion, 9, 61–63, 163. *See also* Church; Clergy; Indian; Sermons
Richmond, 52, 74, 148, 161
Roanoke River, Byrd's lands on the, 49–50, 51, 53–54, 74, 160–61
Robertson, Rev. James, 220
Rockahominy, 233, 247
Royal Society, 18–19, 76–79, 83, 85–87, 89–91, 115, 132–33
Rowe, Nicholas, 18
Russell, Mrs. Katharine, 187, 191, 210

Sabbath, 9, 62, 153, 188
"Sabina" (Mary Smith), 34–36, 65, 67, 93, 99–100
Saponi Indians, 239, 243
Sauro (or Saura) Indians, 249
Season, at Williamsburg, 11, 190–95
Secret Diary, 29, 67, 106, 110, 113, 281
Selden, John, 73
Seneca Indians, 245

Sermons, 61, 134, 151, 154
Servants, 63, 149, 154, 166–69, 177–80
Settlers, 160–61; Swiss, 49, 53–54, 55, 74; Scotch-Irish, 54, 231
Sewall, Samuel, 109, 254
Shockoe (or Shacco, plantation), 161, 165
Silk grass, 82, 230
Simms, William Gilmore, 129
Slavery, 171–76
Slaves, 16, 35, 149, 150, 169–77, 179
Sloane, Sir Hans, 76–79, 83, 84, 85, 132, 159, 283, 286
Smallpox, 8, 34, 132, 246
Smith, Captain John, 111, 128, 234, 258
Smith, Mary. *See* "Sabina"
Smollett, Tobias, 97, 105n
Southerne, Thomas, 18
Southwell, Edward, 23, 213, 285
Southwell, Sir Robert, 18, 76, 79, 94–95, 213
Spotswood, Gov. Alexander, 29–33, 37–44, 49, 50, 55, 85, 103, 107, 118, 122, 157, 160, 164, 169, 185–87, 190, 208–15, 219, 220, 221, 223, 224, 227, 243, 257, 262, 284, 287
Sprat, Thomas, 90
Stagg, Mr. (dancing-master), 193–94
Steele, Sir Richard, 94, 128, 204
Stegge, Thomas, 15, 286
Stowe, Harriet Beecher, 260, 265
Strachey, William, 111, 128, 155, 234, 241, 242, 250, 251, 252
Sundays, at the plantation, 151–54. *See also* Sabbath
Swift, Jonathan, 37, 105
Sydenham, Dr. Thomas, 87
Synge, Archbishop Edward, 63n, 202

Tatler, 105, 204
Taylor, John (of Caroline), 175
Taylor, Maria. *See* Byrd, Maria Taylor
Taylor, "Cousin", 104, 125, 284
Teach, Edward ("Blackbeard"), 220, 262
Temple, Sir William, 128, 188, 203, 241, 242n
Tennent, Dr. John, 83
Theater, 103, 134, 193–94

Tillotson, Archbishop John, 61, 63, 111, 134, 154, 202
Tobacco: culture, 3–4, 154–56, 180; cut, 157; trade, 4–5, 156–58, 171; tax, 17, 21, 37; as a remedy, 88–89
Tucker, George, 265, 275
Tucker, St. George, 174
Tunbridge Wells, 22, 37, 78, 92, 115
Tuscarora Indians, 29, 30, 176–77, 210, 227, 244–46

Vernon, Admiral Edward, 55, 56, 227
Vine-growing, 159
Virginia Gazette, 204

Wager, Admiral Sir Charles, 52, 53, 74, 215n, 283, 285
Walpole, Sir Robert, 52, 53, 56, 85n, 285
Washington, George, 11, 112
Washington, Captain Lawrence, 227
Wertenbaker, Thomas, 7, 135
Westover, 17, 26, 33, 47, 52, 56, 57, 144–46, 149–50, 162, 186, 228
Westover parish church, 151, 153, 188, 220
Wetherburn's tavern, 198, 206
Weyanoke, Queen of, 251
Wilkinson, Daniel, 178, 191–92
William and Mary, College of, 8, 9, 19, 29, 194, 221–23, 242, 243
Williamsburg, Va., 11, 42, 189–84, 197–98. *See also* Colonial Williamsburg
Willis, Dr. Thomas, 87
Winthrop, John, 196
Wollaston, William, 63n, 242n
Women, 22–24, 34–37, 65–68, 110, 195–96
Woodfin, Maude, 44, 106, 273, 281, 282, 289
Woodsmen, 231–35
Woolman, John, 109, 173
Wormeley, Ralph, 174
Wright, Louis B., 11, 58, 73, 74, 106, 107, 108, 114, 131, 202, 273, 281, 282, 289
Wycherley, William, 18

Young, Edward, 44